D1569580

FAUSTUS

FAUSTUS

THE LIFE AND TIMES OF
A RENAISSANCE MAGICIAN

LEO RUICKBIE

I will tell thee things to the terror of thy soul, if thou wilt abide the hearing.
– P.F., *The Damnable Life and Deserved Death of Doctor John Faustus*, 1592[1]

To the girl in the graveyard.

First published 2009

The History Press
The Mill, Brimscombe Port
Stroud, Gloucestershire, GL5 2QG
www.thehistorypress.co.uk

British Library Cataloguing in Publication Data.
A catalogue record for this book is available from the British Library.

ISBN 978 0 7509 5090 9

Printed in Great Britain

Contents

Acknowledgements

No book is just a book and this present work is no exception. It is the sum of many years of my life, the result of thousands of kilometres of field trips, the distillation of a million pages of centuries of research and writing, and the cause of my meeting many generous and interesting people. When I began I had no idea of the road ahead, but it has been a journey made significantly easier by the helpfulness of the people I encountered along the way, some of whom it is my pleasure to thank here.

Mechthild Berkemeier, Stadtbibliothek, Bad Kreuznach; Vanessa Dippel, Büdingen; Uschi Flacke, Altweilnau; Rosa Gema, Historisches Dr Faust Haus, Bad Kreuznach; R. Haasenbruch, Halle-Wittenberg University; Heike Hamberger Director of the Faust Museum and Archive, Knittlingen; Susann Henker, SLUB/Deutsche Fotothek; Petra Hesse, Leipzig University; Mr and Mrs Hochwald, 'Fausts Geburtshaus', Knittlingen; Thorsten Hofrath, Verbandsgemeindeverwaltung Simmern-Hunsrück; Alexandra Ilginus, Herzog-August-Bibliothek, Wolfenbüttel; Vladimir Josipovic, Destinacije.com; Gudrun Kauck, Wächtersbach; Harald Kramer, Bürgermeister, Stadtroda; Günter Kroll, Universitätsbibliothek Frankfurt am Main; Tobias Küenzlen, Ephorus, Maulbronn Monastery; Heinrich Laun, Bad Kreuznach; Valeria Maria Leonardi, Sovereign Military Order of Malta; Tim Lörke, Faust Museum and Archive, Knittlingen; Edyta Paruch, Dr Franz Moegle-Hofacker, Hauptstaatsarchiv, Stuttgart, Jagiellonian University, Kraków; Petra Pauly, Stadtbibliothek, Bad Kreuznach; Kristin Pietzner of Wittenberg-Information; Julius Reisek, Heimatwissenschaftliche Zentralbibliothek, Bad Kreuznach; Hans-Rudolf Ruppel, Stadtarchiv Korbach; Dr Klaus Rupprecht, Staatsarchiv Bamberg; Dr Schieck, Helmstadt; Dr Edith Schipper, Bayerische Staatsbibliothek, Munich; Dr Beatrix Schönewald, Stadtmuseum, Ingolstadt; Prof. Dr Wilfried Schöntag, Stuttgart; Dr Steffen Schürle, Boxberg; Sylke Titzmann, Stadtverwaltung Stadtroda; the family Trch, Zum Löwen, Staufen; Dr Michael Vesper, Geschäftsführer, Bad Kreuznach Tourismus und Marketing ; and U. Weck, Touristinformation Trittenheim.

I wish to single out Professor Frank Baron of Kansas University for his generosity in taking the time and trouble to read my manuscript and discuss some of the finer points of interpretation. Especial thanks are also due to my friends Holger Kempkens and Cordula Krause. At the end of that trail, it is also my pleasure to thank my editors at The History Press, Sophie Bradshaw, Simon Hamlet and Jo Howe, who have all worked on the project with great enthusiasm. But most of all my greatest thanks are reserved for my wife, Dr Antje Bosselmann-Ruickbie, who has often and patiently travelled with me on this quest into a dark and disturbing corner of the past.

1

A Renaissance Scandal

Lightning tears the sky asunder. Electric veins of heaven's quicksilver beat a furious, fiery pulse. Thunder, like the demon's drumroll, rumbles in the black, starless sky. The wind howls in the treetops like a chorus of the damned. His candles guttered and snuffed out, his carefully drawn circle spotted and smudged by rain, his nerves in shreds, the magician cries aloud in ancient tongues with names of gods forsaken and words unknown. In a fanfare of shrieks and moans – of the wind in the trees or souls in hell he cannot discern – in the flicker of thunderbolts hurled by a disapproving God, out of flames and grotesque shadows a figure resolves itself. He has delved into every science and mastered all human knowledge to bring himself willingly to this brink of madness and eternal damnation.

A deal is struck between mortal man and infernal power. The parchment pact soaks up the bloody signature like an eager vampire, drawing out the soul to its ruin. In exchange for that insubstantial thing – so hard to find, so easily given – the magician is leased a demon to do his every bidding. Together they travel the world in a riot of adventures. The scholar has shed his study like a chrysalis and revels in the traditional hedonism of wine, women and song. He produces wonders for the entertainment of students, lords and even the Emperor himself. He enjoys fame and fortune, and the favours of a veritable harem, including the most beautiful woman of them all, Helen of Troy. Too late the wastrel laments as the hourglass runs out. He is damned. God has stopped up His ears and barred the gates of heaven. The Devil will redeem his pact.

The seeker after forbidden knowledge is lured into signing a pact with the Devil. He enjoys the fruits of his deal, but cannot escape the clutches of Satan. The story is well known. It is so well known that it has spawned a whole genre, an industry even. The great names of every form of creative endeavour have turned their keen minds to Faustus. From unrivalled dramatists such as Shakespeare's contemporary, Christopher Marlowe, and the giant of German literature Johann Wolfgang von Goethe, to artists such as Rembrandt and Eugène Delacroix, to musical geniuses such as Ludwig van Beethoven and Richard Wagner – all have been inspired by the story of Faustus to produce masterpieces. It was no exaggeration when the former Dean of Princeton Graduate School, Professor Theodore Ziolkowski, argued that the Faustus myth has been central to the formation of Western consciouness.[1]

The number of written works is staggering. Alexander Tille's monumental catalogue of references to Faustus runs to 1,152 closely printed pages, covering only the years up to the eighteenth century, whilst Hans Henning's bibliography of works attributed to or about Faustus runs to two weighty volumes. It has been estimated that three million printed pages have been devoted to Faustus, approximating something like 20,000 books. Goethe's *Faust* alone is believed to be one of the most quoted works of literature, as well as one of the most reprinted, reproduced and re-enacted. It has been claimed that every night around 300 productions of *Faust* are performed on stages across the world. From German, French and British sources, Tille also catalogued a total of 700 artistic representations of Goethe's *Faust*, and that was more than a hundred years ago.

Almost 600 operas and pieces of classical music have been based on the story of Faustus. At least thirty modern recording artists spanning the genres from pop to death metal have released thirty-one songs or albums directly employing the name 'Faust'. The story of Faustus was quite possibly the first to be immortalised on the silver screen in 1896 and in the relatively brief history of cinema 67 directors in 13 different countries have produced a total of 81 films on the theme. Then there is a boardgame and more than ten video and computer games. Beyond reading, hearing, watching or playing things Faustian, one can wear Mephisto shoes, drink Faust beer, or eat 'Faust Brand Choicest Sockeye Salmon' from Washington State. In his influential *Decline of the West* (1918), Oswald Spengler even developed a social theory situating us in a Faustian Age.[2]

Whilst the creative arts have often found paths to enlightenment and redemption in the modern 'Faust', popular usage of the term 'Faustian' is almost wholly negative. The connection between the Devil and the German roots of the story inevitably lead to references to the Nazi regime, exemplified by Klaus Mann's *Mephisto* (1936), while others tap into the Spenglerian characterisation of modernity, which may not be so very different. The idea of the 'Faustian bargain' has even found its way into treatments of US foreign policy and genetics. 'Faust' has become the metaphor for everything modern, from modernity's great achievements to its darkest horrors.

The story of Faustus has, like a Renaissance magician's homunculus, assumed a life of its own. But is it the real story? After following the trail of Faustus through the historical references to him and the places he supposedly visited I have come to believe that the man – the legend we call 'Faust' today – is not the same as the Faustus who lived some five hundred years ago. The image made famous through the works of the great artists and reproduced in myriad forms is false.

From out of the shifting morass of legend emerges a will-o'-the-wisp as illusory as the great spirit he claims as companion and familiar. At the very moment Faustus appears in recorded history he is given the worst sort of reputation, and as with the dog with the bad name he is hung ever after. Look up any dictionary or encyclopedia and what does one read about Faustus? That single word 'charlatan', again and again.

There can be no denying that Faustus was a sixteenth-century scandal. He claimed to be the greatest living master of the forbidden art of necromancy who, with his magic, could rival all of the miracles allegedly performed by Jesus. He caused uproar amongst his contemporaries and was accused of the worst crimes and character flaws they could imagine. Their reaction was also a scandal. Ever since the judgement of history has been against him and it has been wrong. Just what evidence is there for the invocation of Mephistopheles, the pact with the Devil and all the other outrages he is alleged to have committed? To be sure, he was no saint, but the Devil is not always as black as he is painted. Whilst a full biography may be overdue by some five hundred years, so also is a critical, unbiased examination of his life.

Not only is the person of Faustus misunderstood, but any re-evaluation of him is also a re-evaluation of the Renaissance. Since Dame Frances Yates' pioneering study of Giordano Bruno in 1964, placing the occult at the heart of any understanding of the Renaissance, little work has been undertaken to develop this insight, especially as regards the early years of the Northern Renaissance. Although recognised as an 'icon of modern culture' by Professor Osman Durrani in 2004, Faustus is absent from general histories of his own times and poorly represented in even more specialist works.[3] Writing in 1979 Professor Wayne Shumaker of the University of California at Berkeley remarked 'I have come to believe that the traditional understanding of Renaissance thought is, if not wrong, no more than half right'. Faustus is part of that other half. Faustus represents the forgotten and even hidden side of his age. To find the real Faustus is to find the real history of that period.

Although critical to developing a keener understanding of these complex times, it is no easy task. As a biographical subject Faustus presents several challenging problems. We know of him entirely through the words of others, few of whom were even remotely sympathetic and most downright hostile. Everything we know of him is either second-hand and biased, or clearly fabulous. This has given rise to two approaches to Faustus: to take him almost entirely as a literary creation, or to strip him down to only that which can be proven. Both approaches have their drawbacks and ultimately fail to reveal the complex character of both the person called Faustus and the times in which he lived.

Evidence for the life of Faustus is found in a handful of historically authenticated sources. In the last hundred or so years of serious research into the figure of Faustus, only seven contemporary references to him have been discovered. He was first mentioned in 1507 by the Abbot Johannes Trithemius (1462–1516), and by the Abbot's friend Conradus Mutianus Rufus (conventionally just Mutianus, 1471–1526), in 1513. His name then appeared in the account book of Georg III Schenk von Limburg (1470–1522), Bishop of Bamberg, in 1520, but it was eight years before the next references emerged, both coming within days of each other. The first appeared in an entry in the meteorological journal of Prior Kilian Leib (1471–1553) for 5 June 1528, the second in the official records of the city of Ingolstadt for 15 June 1528. Nuremberg made note of him in its records for 1532. Finally, Joachim Camerarius (Joachim Liebhard, 1500–1574) referred to him in a letter dated 1536. When the physician Philipp Begardi came to write of him in his *Index Sanitatis* (published 1539) he stated that Faustus was already dead.

The author of the first reference to Faustus, Abbot Trithemius, is an interesting and complicated case. He was simultaneously a leading magician and a high-ranking churchman, who both condemned and practiced astrology, and who was accused of necromancy and criticised others for it. At a time when aristocratic patronage was paramount, Trithemius was not slow in playing the game, including mounting political attacks against rivals. As much as he condemned those who 'noisily catch the attention of kings and princes' he repeatedly presented his credentials to the great and the good with a boastfulness unbecoming in a monk.[4] He was also a consummate networker who at one time had the ear of Emperor Maximilian I and could count amongst his friends and acquaintances many of those who later expressed ill will towards Faustus, such as Mutianus. He was a mass of contradictions.

Trithemius's letter was a singularity. It was the only time in his voluminous writings that he spoke of Faustus. The initial enquiry and response – if they were made – of his correspondent Johannes Virdung von Haßfurt (*c.* 1463–*c.* 1538) have been lost. But Trithemius did make references that extended beyond the written page. He referred in his letter to a list or document – a sort of business card – that Faustus conveyed to him and had already sent to Virdung. Trithemius could not just invent what he liked about Faustus, since Virdung already had some account of him, significantly from Faustus himself. This does not mean that Trithemius pulled his punches. His invective was strident. However, to convince Virdung, Trithemius would find it difficult to stray from the details about Faustus that they both shared. This is what makes his letter the single most important historical source.

Whilst most of the references to Faustus are hostile, others show different aspects of his reception; together they present a complicated mosaic only imperfectly preserved. A further reference from the matriculation records of the University of Heidelberg of 1509 has been discounted for reasons that will be outlined later. In addition to these there are several more references in the writings of contemporaries – some of whom may have met him – and near-contemporaries published up to the close of the sixteenth century. These are a collection of stories, the *Tischreden* ('Table Talk') of the Reformation leader Martin Luther (1483–1546), the lectures of his disciple Philipp Melanchthon (1497–1560), a letter from the aristocratic adventurer Philipp von Hutten (1511–1546), various semi-historical chronicles, a demonological treatise and a bill of sale for a house in his possible hometown. Even in this small pile of paper there are innumerable clues to the wider sphere of Faustus's life and the trajectory of his career.

The legend began with the first written reference. At the moment he entered recorded history, Faustus entered into legend. It started with Trithemius's poison pen and was shaped through the mounting negative reports of others. However, the lineaments of what we might call the classical legend were not sketched until after the Devil had collected his due.

Luther and his circle were discussing the question of Faustus at least as early as the mid-1530s. Nicolaus Medler noted Luther's reaction when Faustus was mentioned during one of their conversations between 1533 and 1535, but Luther chose to talk about the Devil rather than the magician.[5] Antonius Lauterbach (1502–1569) recorded a conversation of 1537 about magicians and the magic art, and 'how Satan blinded men', in which Faustus was mentioned as being connected with the Devil. Of course Luther immediately saw Faustus as an agent of Satan – there is nothing too surprising in that – and turned the conversation round so as to be able to boast about himself. What is of interest is that Luther was the first person on record to link Faustus with the Devil. Trithemius may have started the legend, but he kept Old Nick out of it. Johannes Aurifaber (1519–1575), who published Luther's comments in 1566, introduced Faustus as a black magician – the first known use of the description. Medler had earlier simply called him a magician. Faustus himself had apparently been styling himself as a necromancer since 1506 – as noted by Trithemius in 1507 – and the term nigromancer ('Nigromantico') was recorded for the first time in the Nuremberg city records of 1532. The widespread confusion between necromancy (divination by the dead) and nigromancy (black magic) makes these terms less straightforward and less damning than 'black magician'. The earliest references in the letters of Trithemius (1507) and Mutianus (1513) employed the Humanist rhetoric of folly against Faustus. It took the Devil-haunted Luther to involve him in the *Teufelspolemik*. It is here in the *Tischreden* of Luther that we can locate the transformation of Faustus from learnéd magician into diabolist.

The new diabolical Faustus would cause an unnamed monastery to be haunted with the Devil's aid and would die savagely at the hands of his master in the work of Johannes Gast (d.1552), Protestant theologian and Deacon of St Martin's in Basel. Writing in 1548, he amplified the diabolical connection, adding an entreaty against becoming 'slaves of the Devil'. Although published after Faustus's lifetime, we must not exclude the likelihood that Gast was telling these stories as part of an oral tradition long before they found their way into print. As a Protestant clergyman, Gast could not help but be influenced by Luther's focus on the active role of the Devil and may have heard from others some account of that 'table talk' about Faustus. His *Sermones Convivales* were immensely popular and played a key role in cementing the image of the diabolical Faustus.

Count Froben Christoph von Zimmern (1519–1566/7) told a similar story of monastic bedevilment caused by the 'black magician' Faustus in his *Zimmerische Chronik*, written around 1565. As a reliable source, the *Chronik* has its supporters and detractors.[6] However, Froben's personal involvement in the black arts suggests that he knew what he was talking about and he supplied a level of detail concerning Faustus's end that we find nowhere else. As to Faustus's worsening reputation, Froben did nothing to ameliorate it.

The Dutch born physician and demonologist Johannes Wierus (Wier or Weyer, 1515–1588) would also contribute much to the growing legend of Faustus. Wierus was a former student of the physician and occultist Heinrich Cornelius Agrippa von Nettesheim (1486–1535), who was himself an erstwhile disciple of Trithemius. Agrippa introduced him to the works of his master and no doubt to some of his opinions on other matters too. It is this connection that one feels strongly in what Wierus had to say about the magician in his *De Praestigiis Daemonum* ('On the Illusions of the Demons' or 'On Witchcraft'). First published in 1563, it was in the fourth edition of 1568 that Wierus raised the topic of Faustus. Arguing against the crime of witchcraft and in particular that old women could be capable of it, Wierus stressed the culpability of the learnéd magicians – another reason why he was not sympathetic towards Faustus. His turn of phrase also implies that he could have said more. He added important information on where Faustus was supposedly born and died, but elected to concentrate on a comical beard-burning incident, probably because it took place near his own hometown of Graves on the River Meuse (Maas), and adds that Faustus called the Devil his brother-in-law.

Around 1570 or 1575 a Nuremberg schoolmaster called Christoff Roshirt (or Rosshirt) the Elder collected his own tales about 'Doctor Georgio Fausto dem Schwartzkünstler und Zauberer' ('Doctor George Faustus the Black Artist and Magician') and added them as an appendix to Luther's *Tischreden* for the years 1535–1542 – a period that encompassed Luther's first recorded mention of Faustus. Roshirt unmistakably identified Faustus as a black magician, although he only mentioned the Devil twice.

The next source is a chronicle begun in the mid to late sixteenth century by Reichmann. His brother-in-law Wolf Wambach was responsible for two sections referring to Faustus, written after 1570, probably around 1580. Unfortunately this so-called *Reichmann-Wambach Chronicle* is now lost and known only through the *Chronicle of Thuringia and the City of Erfurt* written by Zacharias Hogel (1611–1677). Because of this we cannot be certain whether and to what extent Hogel may have interpreted or otherwise changed the original.

Adding shovelfuls of brimstone to his account of Faustus, Hogel/Wambach amplified the diabolical connection more than ever before. Where Roshirt had sprinkled his text with two references to the Devil and Gast with three, Hogel/Wambach saturated his with eleven, adding such other terms as 'black magician' and the piquant 'hellbrand'.

Whilst stories like Gast's and Roshirt's were no doubt told around stove and hearth in taverns and homes across the country, with occasional references creeping into the chronicles of the period, the first full account of Faustus emerged some forty years after his death. It is only in the work of a Nuremberg scribe written around 1580, the *Historia vnd Geschicht Doctor Johannis Faustj des Zauberers* ('History and Story of Doctor Johannes Faust the Magician'), that we have the first surviving Faustbook,[7] the so-called Wolfenbüttel Manuscript, now preserved in the Herzog-August Bibliothek in Wolfenbüttel. However, the relatively good condition of this manuscript suggests that it did not go through many hands.

In 1587 pacts with the Devil were hot news. A widow called Walpurga Hausmännin had been tried in Dillingen that year and 'upon kindly questioning and also torture' confessed to having revelled with the 'Evil One' and committed innumerable blasphemies and forty-three counts of infanticide in his name. She told the judge that events first began in 1556 when, after a night of carnality with the Devil, he commanded her to sign her soul over to him and for ink scratched her below the left shoulder, drawing blood: 'To this end he gave her a quill and, whereas she could not write, the Evil One guided her hand...'[8] The unfortunate Walpurga was torn with red-hot irons before being burnt at the stake. Such was the climate in which the later legends of Faustus were forged. The generosity of the Humanist spirit that had informed the early years of the sixteenth century had given way towards its end to a religiously embattled anxiety that seemed to find release in the persecution of witchcraft.

In 1587 a different kind of 'hot metal' was busy in nearby Frankfurt am Main. The *Zangmeister* ('song master') Ludolphus Lüders, writing from Brunswick on 30 October 1587, recorded that an edition of what he called *doctoris Johannis Fausti historia* was being sold at the Frankfurt Fair for nine Saxon 'gute groschen' and was quickly selling out.[9] This *Historia von D. Johann Fausten, dem weitbeschreyten Zauberer und Schwarzkünstler* – literally, the 'History of Dr Johann Faust' the famous Magician and Black Artist' – was printed by Johann Spies (d.1623) in Frankfurt.[10]

Although published anonymously, Spies himself is often credited with authorship. Spies, however, identified a mysterious 'friend in Speyer' as the source for the book. Spies said that he had written to him enquiring about material on Faustus and that this friend had replied with all or part of the manuscript that Spies printed. Despite the attribution of the 'friend in Speyer' as the source, he intended Faustus to be seen as the author. The subtitle read 'Compiled and Printed, Mostly from His Own Writings'. The *Historia* is highly derivative and clearly more of a compilation than an original creation. There is no 'author' as such. There are obvious borrowings from Sebastian Brant's *Narrenschiff* ('Ship of Fools'), Hartmann Schedel's *Buch der Chroniken* ('Book of the Chronicles'), Martin Luther's *Tischreden* and Augustin Lercheimer's *Christlich bedencken* ('Christian Concern'), and a telling similarity with the Wolfenbüttel Manuscript.[11]

The book is chaotic by today's standards and weakly plotted. There is little regard for any sort of chronology other than following the obvious progression from birth to death. After setting the scene of the scholarly road to ruin, the book sermonises relentlessly on the sin of transgressing the Reformation worldview, but also has didactic interests revealed in the discussion of astronomy and the travel guide loosely appended to Faustus's life. It entertains the reader with a number of anecdotes about duping peasants and Jews, and playing tricks on noblemen.

Now seen as fiction, the book presents itself as the biography and occasionally autobiography of a real person. This was an age when strict divisions between fiction and non-fiction were not applied and the writer or compiler had no qualms about presenting imaginative creations as truths. However, we cannot see it entirely as a work of entertainment as some have done.[12] Spies's express purpose in printing this book – as he revealed in its dedication – was to warn others against the dangers of straying from the path of Christianity as redefined by Luther. To this extent it was an old-fashioned morality play with a new subject, shot-through with didacticism and sharpened by the propagandist into a diatribe against the Church.

The *Historia* ridiculed the Pope in Rome and the Sultan in 'Constantinople'. It named the Holy Roman Emperor Charles V as a patron of the black arts and defamed nobles like Fabian von Dohna and the Prince of Anhalt. However, von Dohna and Anhalt were not Catholics, they were Calvinists. Augustin Lercheimer – the pseudonym of Hermann Witekind (1522–1603) – another Heidelberg Calvinist, immediately picked up on this and interpreted the *Historia* as an attack on Calvinism. In 1597 he called it a libellous book that encouraged curious young men to follow Faustus's example. In 1596 a case involving the student David Lipsius (Leipziger), whom we shall meet again later, brought to light exactly such a misuse. Lercheimer was himself instrumental in transmitting stories about Faustus in his *Christlich bedencken* of 1585 – even before it influenced the *Historia* – and here, in particular, he believed that Luther and Melanchthon had been defamed.[13] The most interesting thing in Lercheimer's reaction is how Spies's warning against diabolical magic was also seen as an incitement to practice it and that, in one sense, has always been the literary appeal of Faustus as a subject.

Spies brought out a second edition of the *Historia* in 1589 with six new chapters derived from the Erfurt legends of Faustus's invocation of the Homeric heroes, the offer to restore the lost comedies of Plautus and Terence, the demonic flying horse, the production of wine from holes in a table, Doctor Klinge, and the Leipzig legend of Auerbach's Cellar. Like a snowball rolling down a hillside, Faustus accrued tales as he passed through subsequent editions. In all, it went through twenty-two editions, spawned a sequel, and was adapted and translated into several languages. Even before he could issue a second edition, the *Historia* was pirated. Carolus Battus (Karl Batten, 1540–1617) produced a Dutch translation in 1592 – with the addition of some helpful dates to the various incidents described. When Victor Palma Cayet (1525–1610), professor of Hebrew at the Collège de Navarre in Paris, brought out a French edition in 1598 (spiced with some of his own anti-Protestant remarks), he was accused of having made a pact with the Devil himself and tried for witchcraft. In 1599 Georg Rudolf Widmann (also Widman, fl. 1560–1600), a councillor in Schwäbisch Hall, published three volumes totalling 671 pages, almost three times the size of Spies's original, adding more stories from Roshirt and Luther.

Whilst Widmann's version – successively condensed into more readable forms, first by Johann Nikolaus Pfitzer (1674) and then anonymously (1725) – would eventually inspire Goethe, it was the English edition of Spies that would lead Marlowe to produce his most famous work. Printed in London in 1592, the translator was simply identified as 'P.F. Gent' (i.e. 'Gentleman') and to this day his identity has not been discovered. P.F., however, was not content to merely translate. With all the swagger and bravado of the stereotypical Elizabethan, he produced a very free translation, or more accurately, adaptation. He threw out some of the dull theological material, elaborated and contracted as he saw fit, interjecting his own anecdotes and descriptions. In particular, P.F. frequently gave us his unflattering opinion of the Germans.

In this welter of different stories, many of them also told about other magicians at different times, there are references to contemporary events and to things Faustus might have done, or was believed to have done. Most significantly many of these stories, so often carelessly dismissed as 'legendary' and hence untrue, are exactly the sorts of things that were not only attributed to magicians, but, more importantly, claimed by them as well. As we will see, many of the legends about magicians, and Faustus in particular, often derive from or are paralleled in their own discourse – the texts on magic written by or for the magicians themselves.

Finally, there is a large body of work bearing the name of 'Faust' as author. The first of these was *Doctor Faustens dreyfacher Höllenzwang* ('Doctor Faust's Threefold Harrowing of Hell') supposedly published in Passau at the unfeasibly early date of 1407. Eighteen examples referred to in this book are included in the bibliography, but more might be counted. The best research has so far revealed forty-five works in manuscript and another forty in print, not all of which are extant.[14] Centres of origination or publication are most commonly Lyon, Passau and Rome, but surprising examples, such as London and Wittenberg, are also found.

An immediately recognisable feature of these Faustian books of magic or grimoires is the dramatic titling. The persistent use and re-use of such phrases as the 'Threefold Harrowing of Hell' and the 'Black Raven' make these names almost as important as that of their reputed author in identifying this particular magical discourse. As exciting as these texts seem in authenticating the existence and career of Faustus, it is beyond doubt that they are the work of later authors cashing in on the legend.

Most of the texts use the later form of 'Johannes' or a variation of it in the title and none use the authentic 'Georgius', which suggests a post-Faustus date of composition – after 1538. Most of the texts use the name 'Faust' as an advert and incentive in a way that is usually alien to authentic works – Agrippa did not call his most famous book *Cornelius Agrippa's Occult Philosophy* – but are symptomatic of what we call 'celebrity tie-ins' today. The earliest printed work is dated 1607, whilst the earliest manuscript is dated to around 1650. Based on their palaeography the majority of the manuscripts have been ascribed to the eighteenth century, while a great many of the printed works appeared in the antiquarian Johannes Scheible's vast compendium *Das Kloster* of 1845–9. We will discuss the more interesting of these texts as they occur in the chronology of Faustus as a way in which to see how a Faustian grimoire genre was developing and being retrospectively fed back into the life of their alleged author.

All of the sources concerning Faustus that have come down to us have to be handled cautiously. What defines an event as either history or legend is the extent to which its occurrence can be verified, but our proof rests entirely on what has been said and written down, and what we can read between the lines. There is little hard truth to be found – there rarely is in any human life – and so this work must also be an evaluation of the possibilities.

The contemporary and near-contemporary sources were, for the most part, all written by scholarly men who enjoyed the respect of their peers. The temptation then is to trust their opinion, but as will become apparent, they were not above ruining the reputations of others as it suited them, especially those writers influenced by Trithemius. Their arguments against Faustus were all *ad hominem*, 'to the man', and in no way objective. Faustus represented something antithetical to their worldview, and if there was no explicit conspiracy against him, then, in sociological terms, the 'in-group' was at the very least closing ranks on an outsider. This was done in a manner reminiscent of the general outrage that attended Philippus Aureolus Theophrastus Bombastus von Hohenheim (1493–1541), the man known more simply by his assumed title of Paracelsus.

Today, through the confusion of later legends about Faustus, it is only too easy to lose sight of the man. Myths grow like weeds in the path of one's career. I should know. I have seen those legends grow in my own path, albeit on a less dramatic scale than Faustus. It began one year at a garden party held to celebrate a neighbour's birthday in the late 1990s. At such events the question always arises of 'And what do you do?' Naturally I told the curious of my PhD work on modern witchcraft. The next year on the same occasion one guest was overheard to say to another that she should be careful about what she said because a 'wizard' lived next door. Within a year a perfectly harmless conversation about academic research had turned me into a practitioner of magic. When an academic in our own 'enlightened' age can so easily become a magician, then how much more so a wandering scholar in the Devil-tormented period five hundred years ago? It is a final caution to sensitise us to the problems of deciphering the life of Faustus.

In writing this biography I have taken a new approach. I have tried to see Faustus and his world from the magician's perspective as much as possible, and not that of the modern literary specialist, as has so frequently been the case in the past. Here especially I think of the Cambridge don E.M. Butler who pioneered research on the subject in English, but who allowed a sceptical perspective as well as an uncritical approach to the sources to colour her interpretation with sarcasm and disparagement.

This does not mean that I do not look for rational explanations, especially as a means of allowing the modern reader to see into the complex world of the times. Much of what Faustus is supposed to have done can be interpreted as trickery, and such techniques were certainly known in Faustus's age. Whereas today we have a far more sophisticated understanding of the magical entertainer's trade, in the sixteenth century only the small elite initiated into the secrets thought such deceptions were anything other than a display of 'real' supernatural magic. Gali-gali men in Egypt still perform the same trick of turning staffs into snakes that Moses and Aaron used to amaze the Pharaoh, and we do not think it a miracle. When Faustus apparently caused people to think that their noses were bunches of grapes we can either dismiss it as 'legendary' as has been the norm so far, or realise that any stage hypnotist today could do the same and that, therefore, Faustus could also have accomplished such an illusion. Both Paracelsus and Michel de Montaigne (1533–1592) were particularly aware of the apparently magical power of the imagination. That said, we should not see Faustus as simply the sixteenth-century version of a Copperfield or a Blaine, because his alleged self-representation was on a higher level than that of a fairground conjurer, putting him at the forefront of the 'science' of his day – Hermeticism, alchemy and astrology – and directly into competition with the Church's interpretation of reality.

It was out of frustration with the fact that there was no biography of Faustus, as such, that this book was born. So much of the existing literature was hard to find, in foreign languages, or written for specialist audiences; the information was scattered and the interpretations of it conflicting. It took years to go through it all and still there were so many questions left unanswered, so many possibilities unexamined, and the entire context of his complex life unexplored. Behind a cage of other peoples' words I sensed an unquiet and discontented spirit move. Bars of prejudice and locks forged in ignorance had too long kept the truth from us. It was time to let the real Faustus out.

2

Born of the Devil
(1466)

He appeared in 1507. Without warning he walked into the pages of history, already infamous and condemned, already a legend. We do not know with absolute certainty where or when he was born, died, or went in between those two dates. Scholarly arguments have even been put forward to prove that he did not exist at all and today many people believe that he was entirely the figment of Goethe's imagination.[1] But they would be wrong. Before there was the legend, there was a man called Faustus.

A miraculous birth is the beginning of every great spiritual career. Whilst virgin-births were common in antiquity, who else but Faustus could be thought to have been born in several places at once and at different times as well? It is no more than the confusion of the past, but out of such things arise great myths.

Sometime in the late fifteenth century, somewhere in the fractured rivalry of the Germany of that time, a man was born who would challenge Merlin, Simon Magus, and perhaps even King Solomon himself to the exalted and accursed crown of magic. We think of him now as Johannes Faust, or just simply Dr Faust, but the first written reference, a letter dated 1507, called him 'Magister Georgius Sabellicus Faustus Junior'. Throughout the sixteenth century the man we tend to think of as Faust was called Faustus by his contemporaries and near-contemporaries.[2]

Is there a difference between Faust and Faustus? Faust is a German surname and there are people to this day who bear it. Although Faustus is also an historically recorded surname, it has generally been assumed that Faustus is simply a Latinised form of Faust. Latinised names were highly fashionable among Humanist scholars and other educated people of the sixteenth century.

If Georgius had really wanted to Latinise the German surname Faust – which means 'fist' in English – he would have added more than just a suffix and translated the whole name into *pugnus*, the Latin for 'fist'. It has also been suggested that the name Faustus is a reference to Knittlingen – a contender for his place of birth. Knittlingen comes from *Knittel* (*Knüttel*, modern *Knüppel*), a club, which, via the Latin *fustis*, is supposed to give 'Faustus', but 'Fustis' itself would be more obvious if this was indeed meant. There is also a persistent and false rumour that Faustus was the printer Johannes Fust (d.1466). Hadrianus Junius (Adrien de Jonghe, 1511–1570) first suggested the connection and it still occasionally resurfaces. Apart from having a different first name, Fust also died long before the magician 'Faustus' appeared in the historical record.

In Latin *faustus* means fortunate or auspicious, which makes it an apt name for a fortune-teller. But there are lots of good epithets to choose from; why should anyone choose this one? The clue lies in the fact that Faustus called himself Faustus Junior. If he wanted to be known as the 'Fortunate' he would hardly have called himself 'Fortunate Junior'. To whom, then, was he acknowledging seniority and why?

We have no reliable evidence that there was an actual relative of Faustus practising magic in Germany before 1507 or after. Of course, just because we cannot find him does not mean that he did not exist, but it does reduce the likelihood. The more plausible explanation is that 'Faustus Junior' was not so much a name as part of a job description, making deference to another sort of predecessor going by the same name.

It is in ancient Rome that we find the earliest recorded usages of the name 'Faustus'. There was a goddess called Faustitas – a name derived from Faustus – who protected the fields and ensured a good harvest, and there were at least three families going by the name of Faustus. One appeared to die out within a generation, the other was high-ranking but unremarkable, only the third, from the time of the Emperor Nero, holds out any promise.

The family comes to light in the fourth century CE writings attributed to Clement of Rome (d. *c.*98 CE).[3] It was popularised in Germany in two medieval retellings of the Simon Magus story that would have still been well-known in Faustus's day.[4] There are conflicting accounts of who Simon Magus was, but he is generally described as a sorcerer of Samaria, converted to Christianity by Philip. He gave the word 'simony'– the buying or selling of ecclesiastical preferment – to the English language by his alleged request to buy the power to impart the Holy Ghost from the Apostles and was reprimanded by Peter (Acts 8:5–24). According to Clement's later story, Simon Magus posed a much greater threat to nascent Christianity during the reign of Nero (54–68 CE) and a magical feud was fought between Simon Magus and Peter, culminating in the sorcerer's death. In this story Clement's father was called either Faustus or Faustinianus and his two brothers Faustinus and Faustinianus or Faustus.[5] The brothers play little part, but the father Faustus/inianus takes on the semblance of Simon Magus to be first used by Simon Magus against his enemies and then by Peter to discredit the real Simon Magus.

Given their relative obscurity, it is unlikely that Faustus Junior thought he descended from either of the first two Roman families or saw them as in some way his spiritual or intellectual ancestors. Clement's father Faustus/inianus is more interesting because he links Faustus Junior with the Simon Magus story. However, Faustus/inianus is both Simon Magus and not Simon Magus; he has his appearance but is not the man himself, he both helps Simon Magus and speaks against him on behalf of Peter. If Faustus wanted to link himself directly with Simon Magus through the use of 'Faustus' this would have been a confusing nomenclature to employ.

There was also a Faustus the Manichæan. We know of him through Augustine of Hippo (354–430), reformed profligate and Christian saint, who mentioned his acquaintance with him in *Confessions* and vigorously denounced him in his *Reply to Faustus the Manichæan* written around 400 CE. During the 470s a certain Faustus, Bishop of Riez, was embroiled in theological controversy. But neither are serious contenders. The young Georgius's imagination was surely uninspired by these dead heresies and captured by something else entirely.

In 1496 one of the most popular pieces of Renaissance pastoral poetry, known widely in Germany and elsewhere, was published. The so-called *Bucoliques* had been written by an Italian Humanist called Publius Faustus Andrelinus (1462–1518). Andrelinus had early made a reputation for himself as professor of rhetoric and poetry since taking up his post in Paris in 1489 where a number of students from Germany had attended his lectures. Andrelinus could also count among his personal friends such influential figures as Desiderius Erasmus of Rotterdam (*c.*1466–1536), the Renaissance Humanist *par excellence*. He also lectured on *astrologia* (i.e. both astronomy and astrology in our uses of the words), publishing a treatise on the influence of the stars in Paris in 1496.

That there was a well-known Humanist using this name at this time makes this a simpler and more obvious derivation. Faustus Junior could draw upon Andrelinus's reputation as a Humanist and as an astrologer, something that would be important to him in his future career. It was all the more necessary to adopt the sobriquet 'Junior' because in 1507 when this form is recorded – the only time it is recorded – Faustus 'Senior', that is, Andrelinus, was still alive.

According to Trithemius's letter, Faustus also called himself Sabellicus. As with the name 'Faustus', people have looked to place names, titles and previous holders of the name to unravel the mystery. The most common explanation is that it is derived from the Sabine Hills in Italy because of its associations with witchcraft for the ancient Romans. The usual interpretation is wrong.

There was another Sabellicus. The Humanist Marcantonio (or Marco Antonio) Coccio (1436–1506), adopted Sabellicus as a *nom de plume* derived from his place or region of birth. Remembered now for his histories, he was in his day also known as an editor of classical works. It is unlikely that he intended to conjure up images of Sabine sorcery. Sabellicus would certainly have been known in German intellectual circles. The influential and much-feted German Humanist Conrad Celtis (also Celtes, 1459–1508) met him in Venice in 1486 and many of his works were in new editions in the sixteenth century – Trithemius even owned one of them.

Digging deeper into Sabellicus's life we discover an interesting association in his past. Together with the Humanists Julius Pomponius Laetus (1425–1498) and Bartolomeo Platina (1421–1481), the future librarian of the Vatican, Sabellicus was involved in the foundation of a semi-pagan academy in Rome around 1457. Laetus had just succeeded the controversial Laurentius Valla – indicted seducer, pederast, and opponent of Christian morality – as professor of eloquence at the Gymnasium Romanum and gathered round him fellow spirits to adopt Greek and Latin names, meet on the Quirinal to discuss classical questions and celebrate the birthday of Romulus and the foundation of Rome. The academy's constitution was similar to that of a priestly college in ancient Rome, and Laetus accordingly styled himself *pontifex maximus*.

Sensing heresy, republicanism and paganism in the activities of the academy, Pope Paul II moved to crush it. Laetus, Platina and the others were imprisoned and tortured in the castle of Sant'Angelo. Sabellicus escaped and went on to become prefect of the Library of San Marco in Venice. Here is a much more attractive figure to an aspiring young magus. If Faustus chose the name of one well-known Humanist as one of his sobriquets, it makes it all the more likely that he chose the other on the same grounds. Interestingly, Andrelinus was also a student of Laetus, making Faustus's choice of both of these names more than just coincidence, since both lead to the very roots of the Humanist movement.

The name Faustus gave himself was a Renaissance code. He used the terms 'Sabellicus' and 'Faustus' because they would arouse certain associations in his audience and that audience was undoubtedly intended to be an educated one – even if that was not always the case. He used a Latin form that immediately connected him with the Humanists and the practice established by the Gymnasium Romanum. His choosing Sabellicus and Faustus specifically associated him with the former's role in a pagan revival and the latter's influential work on astrology – one was a mystic and the other an occultist.

Faustus Junior wished to present himself to the world as a Humanist philosopher with mystico-magical trappings. By associating himself with the distinguished Humanists, Faustus Junior could display his own learning as well as evoke that of the others. He could also lessen some of the stigma attached to his other advertised accomplishments by laying claim to a respectable academic pedigree.

A Mysterious Birth

The man who called himself Georgius Sabellicus Faustus Junior was born in the late fifteenth century, of that almost everyone is agreed. As to when exactly is a more contentious issue. It comes as no surprise that there are a number of wildly differing opinions as to the exact date. Depending on whom one reads, we find the years 1465–1468, 1478, 1480, 1490 and 1491 – covering a span of just over a quarter of a century.[6] As to where he was born, at least six different locations have been forwarded.

The most compelling evidence as to when he was born comes from Faustus's own name and comments attributed to him. Little can be learnt from his various assumed titles, but his first name gives us an important clue. Georgius (Georg or George) is also the name of a saint, which takes on added significance when we realise that it was common practice at the time to name a child after the saint's day on which it was born. In the Christian calendar the feast day of St George is held on 23 April. In the fifteenth century this festival rivalled Christmas in its popularity, and it is therefore probable that Faustus was born on 23 April.

Some years later, Kilian Leib (who shall be discussed in detail later) recorded a statement apparently made by Faustus himself that gave some clue as to the year of his birth. Faustus did not directly refer to his birthdate, but made an astrological remark upon the type of people born at a particular time and the man who recorded it thought that Faustus was also talking about himself. The astrological reference suggests that Faustus was born when the Sun and Jupiter were conjunct in the sign of Taurus. This took place three times on 23 April in the late fifteenth century: in 1466, 1478 and 1490.

He could not have been born in 1490 because of the extent of the claims he is reported to have made in 1506 when he would only have been sixteen. That leaves only 1466 and 1478. The average life expectancy of those who survived childhood was fifty-seven.[7] Therefore, someone born in 1466 would, on average, have been expected to live only until 1524, whilst someone born in 1478 would have been expected to live until 1536. Of course there were exceptions: Erasmus was born in 1466 and lived until 1536, and the Greek scholar Andreas Johannes Lascaris (1445–1535) lived to the age of ninety.

The first report of Faustus's death was published in 1539 and we have documented references that he was still alive after 1524. If he had been born in 1478 he would have been around fifty-eight when he died. If he had been born in 1466 he would have been around seventy. The age of fifty-eight is closer to the average, but, according to the semi-historical *Zimmerische Chronik*, Faustus was reputed to have lived to a great age.

We would also expect that if Faustus had been born in 1466, then there would have been more references to him, especially before 1507. There are earlier references, long overlooked because they do not use the name Faustus, but the real name of the man who would later adopt that title. First, however, to answer the question of when he was born we must first discover where he was born, for, as we shall see, the one explains the other.

The birthplace of Faustus is hotly contested. Civic pride is at stake here as well as tourist revenues. To try and find the answer I looked through the sixteenth-century texts making reference to Faustus.[8] Running my finger across the densely printed black letter script, I found that of these only fifteen made any mention of where Faustus came from. Eight authors mentioned Kundling (or some variation of the name), one said 'helmstet', another said 'Helmitheus Hedelbergensis', one mentioned Heidelberg and a document of 1509 indicated Simmern. We can immediately discount the latter – it is a false identification with an unrelated student of Heidelberg called Johannes Faust from Simmern (Kreisstadt Simmern-Hunsrück since 1966), but we are still left with too many options.

Faced with this confusion the Faustbooks had their own answer. The Wolfenbüttel Manuscript of around 1580 and Spies's *Historia* of 1587 gave 'Rod' and P.F. in his 1592 translation of Spies – and Marlowe after him – said the town was called 'Rhode'. In 1599 Widmann gave the name of a market town called Sondwedel in Anhalt, identified as Salzwedel in today's Saxony-Anhalt,[9] but we can dismiss this because of its late date, Widmann's general unreliability, and not least because he is alone in this opinion. While the references to a place called Kundling outnumber all the others, things are not as simple as they appear – with Faustus they never are.

A certain Roda – renamed Stadtroda in 1925 – lays claim to having once had within its environs the house where Faustus was born. The house was still standing until the late nineteenth century when, according to one unverified story, it was dismantled and sent to Chicago for the World Fair in 1893, and subsequently destroyed by fire.[10] Today there is a small exhibition in the town's museum where a depiction, which may or may not be accurate, of a modest two storey building is shown.

Despite the half-timbered evidence that may have once graced Stadtroda, we can largely discount the birthplace given in the legendary material of Wolfenbüttel, Spies, and P.F.'s English translation. These are not historical documents and differ sharply from the information given in those that are. Furthermore, of all the many Rodas none of them can be proven to have been identified as the birthplace of Faustus prior to the appearance of the Wolfenbüttel Manuscript around 1580. It is not clear why the anonymous author of the Faustbook should have picked Roda, but the proliferation of Rodas may have been the target, since no one could easily check if what was said was true.

Karl Schottenloher, director of the Royal-Bavarian court and state library in Munich, did not believe that Roda was Faustus's birthplace either. In 1913 he reconstructed a new location based on a close analysis of contemporary sources. Reading a journal entry written by Kilian Leib, the prior of Rebdorf Monastery, for July 1528, Schottenloher saw Faustus described as 'helmstet'. However, Christian August Heumann had argued as early as 1742 that we should read the word as 'Wirtebergensis', meaning 'from Württemberg'. At the risk of ruining my eyes, I closely scrutinised this inky sigil, painstakingly comparing each form to other letter shapes in Leib's journal. I can now agree with Schottenloher: Leib wrote 'helmstet'. But Schottenloher went further to interpret this as 'helmstetensis', meaning 'from Helmstet'.

Schottenloher connected this with a letter written by Mutianus to Heinrich Urbanus in 1513 where he called Faustus 'Helmitheus Hedelbergensis'.[11] This connection led him to suggest an entirely different place of birth. Mutianus's letter only survives in the copy made by his correspondent Urbanus and the difficulty is that when he wrote 'Helmitheus Hedelbergensis' he appeared to invent two new words. As it stands the phrase is near unintelligible. In 1742 Heumann argued that 'Helmitheus' was a misspelling for 'Hemitheus', which he thought meant 'half-god'. This view has tended to prevail and in English 'Helmitheus' is routinely translated as 'demi-god'.[12] Although probably unaware of Mutianus's letter, Marlowe accidentally made poetry of the phrase when he had his Faustus exclaim: 'A sound magician is a demi-god' (1.1.63).

Then there is the question of 'Hedelbergensis'. In the nineteenth century the German philologist and historian of literature Johann Düntzer argued for an alternative reading of what he thought was 'Hedebergensis' as 'Hedelbergensis', which was what Mutianus had written in the first place, meaning 'of Heidelberg'.[13] This gives us the bizarre title of the 'demigod of Heidelberg' and based on the poor report of some of his contemporaries, most commentators from Heumann onwards have happily agreed that this indicates that Faustus was a confirmed charlatan.

Schottenloher was rightly dissatisfied with the demigod interpretation. The crucial point is that Mutianus's letter only survives as Urbanus's copy. Thus what we have is Urbanus's interpretation of what Mutianus wrote, leaving much room for speculation.[14] Bringing the two parts of the riddle together Schottenloher suggested that the references to 'helmstet' and 'Helmitheus Hedelbergensis' meant that Faustus actually came from a town called Helmstedt near Heidelberg.[15] The Heidelberg connection is independently supported by reference to 'Haidlberg', i.e. Heidelberg, in the Ingolstadt document of 1528. There is nowhere called Helmstet or Helmstedt today, but the town Helmstadt, which is indeed near Heidelberg, has historically been referred to as Helmstatt and Helmstet. In 1975 it became Helmstadt-Bargen.

All this careful detective work is flatly contradicted by Johannes Manlius. In 1563 he published an account of what he said were the lectures of his teacher Melanchthon in which he is reported to have said that Faustus was born in Kundling. If one looks at a map of modern Germany there is no such place as Kundling to be found. The clue to its whereabouts again comes from Manlius. He said that Faustus came from Kundling near Melanchthon's birthplace. It is well-documented that Melanchthon was born in the town of Bretten in the modern federal state of Baden-Württemberg. This Kundling near Bretten is unmistakably today's Knittlingen. There was a tendency to treat place names casually by today's standards. Many of the other variations of Faustus's birthplace given in the sixteenth-century sources have been used for the modern town of Knittlingen at some time in the past. At least forty-five variations of the name Knittlingen have been recorded, including Kundling.

When Manlius published Melanchthon's words in 1563, Faustus was already long dead. None of the surviving contemporary sources made mention of Kundling (or similar) and all of the many later references to Kundling can be traced back to Manlius's publication. The great weight of independent references to Kundling suddenly becomes one, so just how far can we rely on what Manlius claimed Melanchthon had said?

Melanchthon's reputation as one of the foremost theologians of the Reformation, second only to Luther, has tended to sway opinion from the last half of the sixteenth century to the present day, but his stories concerning Faustus are largely fantastic. Through Manlius he reports in all seriousness feats of flying in Venice and magician-eating in Vienna. Nor was Melanchthon unbiased, calling Faustus 'a wicked beast and sewer of many devils'. Other information he gave on where Faustus supposedly went to university has also proven to be false. The motivation behind his Faustus stories was led by an agenda and told 'for the sake of the young men that they may not readily give ear to such lying men'. Melanchthon is far from reliable, and through Manlius another layer of interpretation and potential manipulation is added.[16]

It could be argued that even if Leib did write 'helmstet' and this did refer to Helmstadt-Bargen, then Knittlingen could still be implicated because in the fifteenth century many inhabitants of Knittlingen were serfs of the Palatinate lords of Helmstadt.[17] Furthermore, Heidelberg, 56 kilometres away, could just as easily encompass Knittlingen as it could Helmstadt, because until 1504 Knittlingen lay within the borders of the Palatinate, which was ruled from Heidelberg. The lords of Helmstadt also owned land around Eichstätt near Leib's monastery of Rebdorf.

Another piece of evidence that has been presented is a bill of sale issued in Knittlingen in 1542 that uses the name *Fausten* (in the German text) to identify a house purchase. The bill of sale notes that the building in question was next to the house where *Fausten* had been born. It was discovered in a crate in the cellar of the town hall and authenticated by the mayor of Knittlingen himself on 3 March 1934. The original document was destroyed in World War II, but thanks to a copyist, a version remains and is now on display in the Faust Museum in Knittlingen.

The bill of sale described the house 'where *Fausten* was born' as that of the late Jörgen Gerlach, which has given rise to the idea that Gerlach was his father. The authoritative *Neue Deutsche Biographie* reports this as fact with the additional details that Faustus's alleged father was the wealthy farmer Johannes Christian Gerlach. However, the generally poor perception of Faustus has led to the rumour in Knittlingen that he was the illegitimate son of a lord and his maid, giving him a below stairs origin and a chip on his shoulder.[18]

Knittlingen today is almost as it might have been then. Square, sturdy half-timbered houses of black-pitched beams and white-washed walls, their roofs raised high against the winter snows, crowd atop the crest of a hill along what used to be an important post and trade route since at least Roman times. In Faustus's day it was on a major route linking the Low Countries and Italy. The size of the old post house still standing by the roadside is a testament to the town's former importance. It now serves a rather good meal and a fine glass of hypocras. Around 1500 the town had 2,000 inhabitants, making it a sizeable community for the period.[19]

A house still stands on the spot where Faustus was said to have been born, although several fires have swept the village since the late fifteenth century and consumed the original building. A plaque proudly proclaims 'Birth-house of Doctor Faust'. Inside the owners showed me curious runes carved on the old oak beams that they believed were connected with the building's reputation. A strange parchment, covered in magical symbols, was found hidden inside a crack in a doorframe and in pride of place a mysterious cabinet inlaid with alchemical signs hangs upon the wall. These unexpected and unique details, although undated, are taken as proofs that this must have been the house of the notorious Dr Faustus.

Next to the building stands the Faust Archive. Across the road is the Faust Museum. Along the street from the old posthouse is the pharmacy, the Faust-Apotheke. The town's old 'Oberschule' has been renamed the Dr Johannes Faust Schule. A dramatic statue of Faustus by Hans Schorp-Pflumm from 1954 stands outside the town hall. We see Faustus frozen in the midst of a conjuration, hands implying the Hermetic mantra 'as above, so below'. There can be no doubt that today's inhabitants of Knittlingen firmly believe that Faustus was born here.

However, all of this speculation hinges upon what Manlius claimed Melanchthon had said, repeated by subsequent authorities until it seemed like unassailable fact. Even if Manlius had accurately reported what Melanchthon had said – and he is known to not always have done so[20] – none of the other information given is provable, and in some cases clearly false. That the lords of Helmstadt owned serfs in Knittlingen proves little, since serfs generally did not go to university. Tax records or muster lists surviving from the first half of the sixteenth century give the names of three people surnamed 'Faust' living in Knittlingen.[21] We have demonstrated that 'Faustus' is an assumed title, so it is much more likely that the word *Fausten* in the bill of sale innocently refers to someone bearing the surname Faust and not to the magician.[22]

The important thing about the journal entry of Prior Kilian Leib is that he was making a private record, it served no polemical purpose for him to falsify his information about Faustus, unlike Melanchthon and his scribe Manlius. To say that Faustus came from Melanchthon's rival village is a way of implying that he was Melanchthon's rival, an interpretation that entirely fits in with the general theme of Manlius's account. Tellingly, Melanchthon or Manlius also got Faustus's first name wrong, calling him Johannes. That Leib's 'helmstet' is closely approximated by Mutianus's 'Helmitheus' adds significant support to the alternative theory. Mutianus's reference to 'hedelbergensis' is further supported by reference in the Ingolstadt record of 1528 to 'Haidlberg', both being variants of Heidelberg.

Finally and conclusively, we have independent verification that someone with the first name of Georgius was connected with Helmstadt, studied at university and subsequently began to develop a career in magic. It was Schottenloher again who found him, tracking down university records of a student variously listed as Georgius Helmstetter, Jorio de Helmstat, Jeorius de Helmstat, Georio de Helmstadt and Jeorius Halmstadt.

Significant new evidence of Helmstetter's existence was published by Professor Frank Baron of Kansas University in 1989. In the Bibliothèque Nationale in Paris he discovered an exchange of letters between Dr Petrus Seuter (also Suter, or Suitter) and Nikolaus Ellenbog. Seuter was a lawyer in Kempten and a graduate of Heidelberg; his friend Ellenbog (c.1480–1543), a monk in the monastery of Ottobeuren with Humanist interests who had also studied at Heidelberg (1497–1502). Although dated 1534, Seuter's letter concerns Heidelberg in the early 1490s and a horoscope made by 'magister Georgius Helmstetten' or 'Helmstetter', astrologer, chiromancer and physiognomist. As we will see, these were all forms of divination practised by Magister Georgius Sabellicus Faustus.[23]

The correspondence between Helmstetter and Faustus not only allows us to confidently state that 'Sabillicus Faustus Junior' was the title assumed by Helmstetter, but also solves the question of when he was born. The university records show that Helmstetter enrolled in 1483 and had to wait until 1487 when he reached the minimum age for graduation as a Master of twenty or twenty-one. He could not, therefore, have been born in 1478, but must have been born in the 1460s, leading us to that fateful conjunction on 23 April 1466.

Thus the evidence leads us forty-six kilometres away from Knittlingen to Helmstadt-Bargen where there are no statues of the magician, no museums, no shops or schools named after him, just a small, unprepossessing village that stakes no claim to be the birthplace of Faustus. Was it out of this obscurity that the young Georgius Helmstetter, one of only a few hundred inhabitants, made his way to university and subsequently embarked on his career as the magician Faustus?

It has been speculated that the student who matriculated in 1483 sought to hide his real surname by providing only his place of origin.[24] However, there is a family that takes its name from Helmstadt, the noble house von Helmstatt. Descended from a knight of King Heinrich I called Rabanus, who flourished around 930, branches of the family were spread across the Kraichgau area that encompassed both Helmstadt and Knittlingen.

Leib wrote 'Georgius Faustus Helmstet', he did not write 'Helmstetensis' as Schottenloher speculated. Leib was writing out Faustus's full name, not that he was someone from somewhere, and he could not use the noble prefix 'von' because he was writing in Latin. Even when Mutianus wrote (according to Urbanus) 'Georgius Faustus Helmitheus Hedelbergensis', it is only the last word that gives the provenance of the man named and Hedelbergensis means of or from Heidelberg, not some other place near Heidelberg.

There was indeed a Georg von Helmstetter of the Oberöwisheimer branch of the Helmstatt family who came into adulthood around 1483–1487; however, his father, also called Georg, died in 1457, either creating an embarrassing problem for his widow or ruling out this particular candidate. There are enough trailing vines on the family tree – unnamed offspring and their progeny – to provide ample scope for a match if the records were not lost in the fog of history.[25]

It would also be tempting to suggest that this resolves the apparent contradiction between Helmstadt and Knittlingen. If Faustus was a von Helmstatt he could still be born in Knittlingen. The fly in the ointment is that Helmstetter was recorded as coming from the diocese of Worms, whilst Knittlingen itself was in the diocese of Speyer.[26]

If Helmstet is part of his name and Knittlingen is in the wrong diocese, where does that leave? Both Mutianus and the Ingolstadt document said that Faustus came from Heidelberg. There are fifteen years between these references and no reason to suppose that the one influenced the other. The von Helmstatt family has historic connections to both Heidelberg town and university, so it is plausible at the very least to say that Faustus came from Heidelberg.

The explanation that most eloquently resolves the contradictions in the material is that Faustus was of the noble family of von Helmstatt. It accounts for the various names and locations found in the contemporary sources and explains another curious piece of information that we learn from Leib: that Faustus held rank in one of the Christian military orders as a knight, a position that was seldom open to commoners. Incidentally, the coat of arms of von Helmstatt sports a black raven, a motif that would re-occur in the otherwise curiously named 'Black Raven' grimoire attributed to Faustus.

The events of Faustus's life suggest a younger son of a younger son, still noble, but far from the wealth and power. He was not so noble that he thought himself above submitting himself to such things as examinations, like the Bishop of Bamberg, as we will see later. There was just enough money for an education, perhaps with a mind to a career in the Church, but there was no high office, land or property to inherit.

Faustus lived within the confines of the Holy Roman Empire that sprawled from the North Sea to the Mediterranean. It was not so dissimilar to the European Union of today, a patchwork of competitive, quarrelsome self-interests stitched together with treaties and fickle loyalties. An impressive enterprise on paper, but a ramshackle thing in operation and just as undemocratic. It was an unstable coalition of princes ruled over by an emperor whose powers were circumspect. In-fighting between the nobles, unrest amongst the commoners and conflict with the papacy added to the political tensions that stretched the empire taught. Its aggressive neighbours France and the Muslim Ottoman Empire would constantly test its political willpower and military might. France was the richest kingdom in Christendom and the Ottomans' power was great. Against Christian vacillation and double-dealing was a strict theocratic regime whose core principles meant war against the infidel.

As Voltaire succinctly put it in 1756, the Holy Roman Empire was 'neither Holy, nor Roman, nor an Empire'. It was instead secular, mostly German, too wild to be under anyone's sole authority and engaged in almost constant warfare that at any moment could spell its destruction. This was the world of Faustus.

3

The Diabolical Faculty
(1472–1489)

Until he is mentioned in 1507 by the hostile Trithemius, we hear nothing of 'Faustus', but what we do hear tells us something of Faustus's early years. Trithemius wrote his letter in Latin and he had evidently seen Faustus's calling card and it seems possible that the Latin was used by Faustus himself. Trithemius also says that Faustus made mention of Plato and Aristotle which hints at a university education and points to some schooling beforehand. The evidence later provided by Mutianus and Leib leads us to the person of Georg Helmstetter and his documented university career, but even if we did not know that Faustus was Helmstetter, the information provided by Trithemius indicates a university background.

Education was theoretically available for everyone. Martin Luther was given a free education at the Franciscan school in Magdeburg, although like the young Johann Butzbach (c.1478–1526) he still had to beg for his bread.[1] In practice only the sons of nobles and merchants could be spared from work and given the monetary investment necessary to pursue even a rudimentary education.

If Faustus was educated, then this hints at his social class. In the Faustbooks he is portrayed as the son of a poor husbandman who is enabled by a wealthy uncle to attend university, but he would still need some grounding in Latin, something that a poor husbandman would have been unlikely to be able to provide. Later claims to nobility made by Faustus himself point to a relatively wealthy background.

Education in the late fifteenth century would most likely have taken place in a day school, in a large class, perhaps of seventy or more pupils, and would have involved learning by rote. Faustus, like Butzbach, probably began his schooling at age six, which would give us the year 1472. Some schools had a Bursa or hostel attached to house students from afar, but that was not the norm and Butzbach travelled far to find one. Such accommodation as the students did find was guaranteed to be lousy, literally. The Swiss Humanist Thomas Platter (1499–1582) slept on the floor rather than risk being eaten alive by the lice in his bed and in Dresden he recalled hearing them rustle through the straw bedding in noisy swarms.

It may have been the Renaissance, but the education was still medieval and school-books were in such short supply as to actively hamper learning. The curriculum taught the essential elements of the *trivium* of rhetoric, dialectic and grammar, but the principal Latin textbook was a grammar written in the fourth century CE. Butzbach was taught with such works as the *Parables* of Alan of Lille (fl. 1200), and the moral distichs of Cato and *Aesop's Fables*. Christianity would be instilled through study of the Lord's Prayer, the Apostle's Creed, the lives of the saints and the Ten Commandments. It was a point on which the Fifth Lateran Council was particularly insistent in 1514, warning that 'every generation inclines to evil from its youth'.[2]

Discipline and obedience would be expected and enforced. One pastor of Nuremberg asked rhetorically 'Is there anything on earth more precious, more dear, or more loveable than a pious, disciplined, obedient child ready to learn?'[3] *Magistrum metue* ('fear your teacher'), as one of Cato's monostichs has it, was the maxim of the day and beatings were frequent and fierce.[4] Luther recalled having been beaten fifteen times in one day.

A schoolboy in Faustus's time was not educated for the sake of it. The son of a merchant would probably leave when he reached the age of between twelve and fifteen to start in his father's business; the son of an artisan would leave just as soon as he had acquired the minimum literacy required for guild membership. Only a few were destined for the church, law or medicine and would progress to the university to complete their education. Faustus's recorded acquaintance with Plato and Aristotle, his use of the title *magister*, and his recorded status as doctor from 1520 onwards, would suggest that he was of that elite minority.

Within the Ivory Tower

Faustus was living through a boom in higher education. The Empire boasted only five universities in 1400, but by 1520 it had nineteen. Across Europe there were more than sixty active universities. The university of the sixteenth century was not the sprawling monster of today with its degrees in everything under the sun, but a rarer, more cloistered place filled with eager minds. Yet it was also situated in the heart of the city and its students, granted special privileges, acquired a reputation for wild living. The universities were also more specialised and more closely associated with the great teachers who lectured in them, giving rise to a reputation for a particular subject or school of thought. Oxford (founded *c.*1208), for example, was identified with theology, and when the new college of Corpus Christi (founded 1517) allowed Humanism to make greater inroads, there was fighting in the streets between the rival factions.

This specialisation of universities gave rise to the wandering scholar, a familiar figure throughout the Middle Ages and into the sixteenth century. Faustus would find himself following in such heel-worn footsteps, roaming across the Empire between the great university towns.

By modern standards they were very young to be leaving home and fending for themselves in foreign cities, but in the sixteenth century, people got on with business just as soon as they could. The remarkable Rudolphus Agricola (1443–1485) was only twelve when he went to Erfurt, and Faustus's fellow occultist, Agrippa, was thirteen when he entered the University of Cologne. Child prodigies aside, students usually entered university when they were fourteen or fifteen years of age. Some, like Luther, were eighteen or older. We know from the record that Georg Helmstetter enrolled on 9 January 1483 at the likely age of sixteen or seventeen.

Many of them may have been mere children, but they worked hard. Faustus's day, like that of Felix Platter (1536–1614) at Montpellier in the 1550s, would start at six in the morning, or even as early as five, as we read in Erasmus's *Colloquies*. His course of study would be determined, not by subject or theme, but according to what books were available. He might be able to choose between lecturers, but courses were usually non-elective. Despite these restrictions, learning was fervently sought and greatly cherished. When Jerome Aleander (1480–1542) lectured in Paris in 1511, 2,000 people turned up to hear him and stayed rapt for the whole two and a half hour oration. The next day all the seats had been taken two hours beforehand and when he arrived the students looked at him as if he had come down from heaven and cried 'Vivat, vivat'.[5]

In the Middle Ages university studies took between four and six years for a bachelor degree. A student would spend his first years in the faculty of arts studying the seven 'liberal arts' established by Alcuin of York in 800 CE. Perhaps already prepared in the basics of the *trivium* – grammar, rhetoric and logic – a young student like Faustus would receive a more thorough grounding in these subjects before progressing to the higher branch of learning, the *quadrivium*. This consisted of arithmetic, geometry, music and astronomy, and completed the liberal arts curriculum. Proficiency in these subjects was tested by the Bachelor of Arts examination before the student could elect to pursue higher degrees in the faculties of law, medicine or theology. It was a rigorous system, built upon solid educational foundations, and produced a class of men who excelled at debate.

Up to twelve additional years were necessary for a master's degree and doctorate. The requirements for doctoral degrees included more specialised training. Those for the doctorate in theology were particularly arduous: by the end of the Middle Ages, the course for the doctorate in theology at the University of Paris was extended to twelve or thirteen years beyond the eight years required for the master's. Their statutes forbade the awarding of the degree to anyone under the age of thirty-five and it was accordingly rare to become a doctor of theology before the age of forty.

By Faustus's time the period of study for the Bachelor's degree, at least, had been reduced dramatically. It took Agrippa three years to be awarded his first degree, whilst after entering the University of Erfurt in 1501, Luther sat his Bachelor's degree just two years later in 1503, and after another two years was awarded the Master's degree. Minimum age requirements were still enforced: twenty or twenty-one – there was some variation between institutions – was the minimum age to be awarded the title of Master.

As he crowded into the lecture room on his first day, who did Faustus find himself rubbing shoulders with? A terrible rabble – according to one account. The theologian and historian Jacques de Vitriaco (or Vitry, *c*.1180–1240) was at his most scathing when writing of the students at the University of Paris. He had been one himself, but had apparently not enjoyed the company. He complained that the other students were enthralled by novelty and denounced their desire to acquire knowledge, fame or gain. The students also constantly bickered about their different opinions and backgrounds, and stirred up ill-feeling with all manner of barbs and insults. Pope Innocent III, who had studied in Paris himself, called it 'the oven that bakes bread for the entire world', even if there were some who thought that bread burnt and stale.

If de Vitriaco had been shocked by the students, he was scandalised by the lecturers. They were such practised obscurantists that 'no one could comprehend their eloquent discourses' and 'not only hated one another, but by their flatteries they enticed away the students of others; each one seeking his own glory, but caring not a whit about the welfare of souls.'[6]

Little seemed to have changed when Paracelsus visited the university in the sixteenth century. With his usual lack of tact he decried the Parisian doctors' vanity and called them ignoramuses. It was one opinion he shared with Luther, who famously dismissed its great theologians as 'the moles and bats of Paris'.[7]

Paris did not hold the monopoly on student rancour. Many another university suffered the criticisms of those who visited or studied in them. Erasmus grumbled that his sojourn at Oxford, for example, was marred by the company of dull and conceited academics, as well as the foul-tasting beer they supplied.

Students lived with a freedom that was extraordinary for the period, but even so they could scarcely ignore economics. Erasmus suffered great poverty whilst in Paris and even with a small allowance from the Bishop of Cambrai had to supplement his income by teaching. Luther, who had experienced their privations, is reported to have said that 'no men are in greater want than the students and scholars'.[8] On 23 July 1507 a concerned John Amorbach, a successful printer in Basel, wrote to his son Bruno, who was studying in Paris, to advise him to throw in his lot with some other students and share the cost of digs and a cook. Amorbach could only spare his son twenty-three or twenty-four crowns per year and at least sixteen to twenty of those would be spent on lodgings.

At the beginning of his studies in the College of Montaigu in Paris, Erasmus stayed in the college's *Domus Pauperum*. The college had revived under the efforts of its principal John Standonck, but he packed in as many students as he could at the expense of their welfare. Erasmus bore the consequences, complaining of being served rotten eggs and foul water.

While Erasmus took private pupils, others supported themselves by working for printers, proof-reading, and composing flattering rhymes and prefaces. They might also turn a penny giving public 'interpretations', as the phrase was, of newly published books as a way of advertising a printer's latest releases. These were uncritical reviews describing the book's contents and best features, and would most likely take place at the printer's office, probably with some frequency as new customers expressed interest. Others with fewer resources or opportunities turned to begging and poaching to support themselves.

Faustus, too, might have found himself toiling over printer's proofs and regaling groups of customers about the merits of the latest tome to roll off the presses. Whether in a *Domus* like Erasmus or in shared lodgings as Bruno Amorbach should have been, Faustus would have experienced a similar sort of life. The proportion of students classified as 'poor' was, however, low: only sixteen per cent at Cologne and nine per cent at Leipzig, for example. We do not know what they meant by 'poor', and we are restricted to what we see through the eyes of the likes of Platter and Erasmus. We might suppose that someone like Innocent III enjoyed an entirely different university life.

For all the hardships, men like Platter and Erasmus pursued learning with a humbling determination and passion. In the universities they found a ladder of books, held as steady as might be by their lecturers, that led upwards out of the dark ignorance that was the lot of most of their contemporaries. With more choice in the sixteenth century than ever before, where did Faustus find his ladder?

The popular tradition beginning with the Wolfenbüttel Manuscript of 1580, Spies 1587 and P.F.'s translation of it in 1592 all place Faustus in Wittenberg studying divinity. During the sixteenth century no fewer than thirteen people called Faust or Faustus are recorded as having studied at Wittenberg.[9] Not one of them matches our magician. If Faustus had studied in Wittenberg then he would only have been able to start in 1502 when the university first opened its doors. By then he was already too old to have taken his first degree there. The historical evidence for Faustus actually having been in Wittenberg at all is slight. Only two late sources – Lercheimer, 1585, and Hogel, seventeenth century – place Faustus in Wittenberg and neither of them mentions his studying there.

The idea that Faustus studied in Wittenberg arose sometime after his death and may represent a confusion between Faustus having stayed there and one of the other individuals called Faust or Faustus who studied there. But the choice of Wittenberg is too loaded with meaning to be dismissed as an accident.

Locating Faustus at Wittenberg is part of the general Christian moralising and especially the specific Protestant polemic of the Faustbooks. Although today few people have heard of Wittenberg outside of Germany, in the sixteenth century it was the epicentre of the Reformation. By placing Faustus there the Faustbooks established him as Luther's shadow, an anti-Luther. The Faustbooks also involved themselves in the Lutheran in-fighting of the late sixteenth century when Wittenberg had become a centre of the Philippists, the followers of the more moderate Melanchthon, and crypto-Calvinists, and was denigrated as a 'hotbed of heterodoxy' by hardliners.[10] Thus the choice of Wittenberg as Faustus's *alma mater* served conservative Lutheran interests.

The first person to actually state where Faustus had been at university was Melanchthon, and he named Kraków. Kraków's Jagiellonian University was one of the oldest and most prestigious. As early as the mid fifteenth century Kraków was the leading academic centre for the study of mathematics, astronomy, astrology, geography and law. Hartmann Schedel vaunted it in his influential *Weltchronik* of 1493. Around 1500 it was at the height of its fame. This reputation was a magnet for scholars: it has been estimated that in the fifteenth century around 45 per cent of students were foreigners. Both Erasmus and Melanchthon were offered chairs here.[11]

More than ninety students called Georgius or Johannes (and their variants) from the southern German regions of Thuringia, Bavaria and Württemberg studied at the university in the late fifteenth century and early sixteenth century.[12] None of them gave a surname or title of Faustus or Sabellicus. There were no Georgiuses, nor even

Johanneses, from any of the places that have been seen as Faustus's birthplace.[13] So just how did Faustus's name become linked to the illustrious Jagiellonian University in Kraków?

The Kraków connection may well be a conflation of Faustus and the legend of a local magus known as Pan ('Master') Twardowski. According to the popular tradition this Master Twardowski also lived in the sixteenth century, also practised alchemy, also made the dead wife of a king appear before him, also visited Wittenberg and also signed a pact with the Devil. Sometimes seen as Faustus's Polish double, Johannes or Jan Twardowski supposedly studied 'natural sciences', alchemy and astrology at the Jagiellonian.[14] In the absence of any evidence for Faustus having been in Kraków at all, this is the most compelling explanation for why Faustus should have become an alumnus of its university.

Was Doctor Faustus even a doctor? Did he go to university at all? No one called 'Faustus' did.[15] He first appeared as a *Magister* (Master) in 1507. By 1520 he was accorded the title of Doctor in the account book of the Bishop of Bamberg and in the official records of Ingolstadt in 1528 and Nuremberg in 1532. Two chronicles – Prasser's *Waldeck Chronicle* (referring to events of 1535/6) and the now lost *Reichmann-Wambach Chronicle* – also called him Doctor. In 1539 Begardi recorded that he signed himself 'The philosopher of philosophers' and Philipp von Hutten, who had consulted Faustus, called him *Philosophus* in 1540.

The first recorded mention of the title of doctor is in 1520. Does this mean that Faustus acquired his title between the years 1507 and 1520? He would have been of age to be granted the title from 1501 onwards. Confusingly, it is also the case that the titles *Magister*, Doctor and *Philosophus* could refer to the same level of academic attainment.

Today one would equate *Magister* with a Master of Arts or Science (MA or MSc), doctor with a Doctor of Philosophy (*Philosophiae doctor* or PhD) or Doctor of Medicine (*Medicinae doctor* or MD) and *Philosophus* with nothing at all. Nowadays, MA (or MSc), MD and PhD are distinct degrees – the PhD is especially distinguished by the requirement to make an original contribution to knowledge – but was that also the case in the sixteenth century?

The conventions in Faustus' day were different. The title of *Magister* would be conferred after a period of further study beyond the bachelor's degree, much as it is now, but it would also specifically imply the study of philosophy, especially Aristotelian philosophy by the scholastic method. Hence von Hutten's use of the title *Philosophus* appears entirely consistent with this. The Master's degree was the highest possible in the study of philosophy, the degree of Doctor was generally reserved for the highest degree in law, medicine or theology. However, it was not uncommon for a Master of Philosophy to be called a Doctor. For example, Trithemius referred to his brother, who only had a Master's degree, as '*artium et philosophiae doctor*'.[16] In his monumental *History of Protestantism*, James Wylie says of Martin Luther after he graduated for his higher degree that he 'became Master of Arts or Doctor of Philosophy'.[17] Thus the apparently different titles given to Faustus need not be contradictory; instead they may confirm that he had received a university education to the highest level and specifically in the field of philosophy, if not also in theology.

The tendency to interpret 'Faustus' as a Latinised German surname led to the magician's misidentification with a student called 'Johannes Faust ex Simmern' who graduated from Heidelberg on 15 January 1509.[18] But this can be easily dismissed. Trithemius's 'Faustus' used the name as a *nom de guerre*, rather than a family name, came from Helmstadt or Heidelberg and in 1507 was reported to hold a Master's degree, whereas this Faust from Simmern had a different first name, came from a different town and only completed his Bachelor's in 1509.

The mention of Heidelberg by Mutianus and in the Ingolstadt document, together with the Helmstet/Helmitheus connection, led Schottenloher to comb the records of Heidelberg with a very particular name in mind – and he found him. From 1483 to 1487 the student Georg Helmstetter was registered at Heidelberg in the study of philosophy. In all likelihood, this was the man who later called himself Faustus.

'Georius Helmstetter' of the Diocese of Worms enrolled at Heidelberg on 1 January 1483 and one and a half years later 'Jorio de Helmstat' applied to sit the bachelor examination. A meeting of the Faculty of Arts was held to consider this. It seemed that Helmstetter did not meet all of the requirements, foremost amongst them, the minimum length of study. He had arrived in the middle of the academic year and it appears that he may not have had the opportunity to attend all of the relevant classes. He was vouched for by Magister Johannes Hasse and a few days later on 12 July 1484 'Jeorius de Helmstat' graduated. He had been awarded his degree in record time, but came near the bottom of his class, sixteenth out of seventeen.[19]

At Heidelberg, students of philosophy had the freedom to choose between two opposing methods of interpreting the ancient Greek philosopher Aristotle: the *via antiqua* and the *via moderna*, the old way and the modern way.[20] Aristotle's metaphysical teachings centred on a criticism of the theory of ideas against which he forwarded his own doctrine of universals, that when a number of individuals shared a predicate it could not be due to a relation to something the same as themselves, but to an ideal. However, differences in interpreting Aristotle amongst the so-called Schoolmen led to the medieval controversy between nominalism and realism.

The *via antiqua* principally looked to the authority of Thomas Aquinas and his espousal of realism, that universal or general ideas have objective existence. On the other hand, the *via moderna* looked to William of Ockham for authority and his espousal of nominalism, that universal or abstract concepts are simply names without any corresponding reality, and made extensive use of the commentaries on Aristotle by the university's first rector, Marsilius von Inghen (1340–1396). His commentaries were influential throughout Europe. It is unsurprising that in Faustus's day it was the *via moderna* that was the more popular approach at Heidelberg. In 1499 its followers even published a volume that included eulogistic epigrams on von Inghen.

What made Heidelberg exciting in the late fifteenth and early sixteenth centuries was its championing of the *studia humanitatis* – what we have come to call Humanism. The Humanists wanted to get away from the Schoolmen, away from the commentators and their endless commentaries, and back to the sources themselves. Introduced to Heidelberg by Peter Luder (1415–1472), Humanism was the latest thing and the best minds of the age gravitated towards it.

Greek and Hebrew studies were pioneered in Heidelberg in the late fifteenth century. Helmstetter's student years were under the chancellorship of Johannes von Dahlberg who had arrived in 1480 fresh from a trip to Italy. Dahlberg's library was noted by Johannes Reuchlin for its many volumes in Latin, Greek and Hebrew. It is thought that Dahlberg may have published *De numerorum arcanis mysteriis* on the mystical value of numbers. Rudolph Agricola arrived in 1484 and was famed for his lectures on Pliny the Younger. Helmstetter's fellow students included the celebrated Conrad Celtis, who graduated Master of Arts on 20 October 1485. Trithemius even studied here, leaving in 1482, shortly before Helmstetter arrived. The Humanist school was much under the influence of the Neoplatonic and hermetic writings of Marsilio Ficino (1433–1499) and Giovanni Pico della Mirandola (1463–1494), which were brimming with spectacular ideas on natural magic. In Faustus's day Heidelberg was getting a reputation for the magic endorsed and practised there.[21]

Helmstetter mastered the philosophical complexities, literally. In 1487 he was awarded the degree of Master. However, there was again a problem. On 1 February 1487 it was recorded that 'Georgio de Helmstadt' had not met all of the requirements. He had only taken part in two out of three obligatory formal disputations and was required to fulfil this. He did so and with flying colours. On 1 March 1487 'Jeorius Helmstadt' graduated second in his class of ten. Some days later, on 20 March, he took the oath that enabled him to use the Faculty of Arts library. Despite his good grades, it had taken him longer than normal to complete his Master's course and this suggests that the delay was caused by failing to meet the minimum age of twenty or twenty-one, which gives us another reason to suppose that he must have been born around 1466.[22]

After graduating, Helmstetter was required by the university statutes to teach for two years in the Faculty of Arts. This would likely detain him up until 1489. In June 1490 plague broke out in Heidelberg and the university granted its staff permission to flee the city.[23] His duties fulfilled, it is unlikely that Helmstetter lingered and when Virdung arrived at the university in late 1492 he was still waiting to meet him by 1507, as we read in Trithemius's letter, so he evidently did not return before then. Even at this early date we know that he had already taken his first tentative steps on a magical career.

When Seuter wrote to his friend Ellenbog on 7 October 1534 he sent him a copy of the speech that Professor Pallas Spangel (d. 1512) had delivered on the occasion of Emperor Maximilian's visit, along with a horoscope drawn up for him by Magister Georgius Helmstetter using judicial astrology, physiognomy and chiromancy. Seuter had himself enrolled at Heidelberg on 28 March 1490, so it seems likely that he came into contact with Helmstetter around this time. Ellenbog enjoyed the speech, but he was critical of Helmstetter's horoscope. Whilst he admitted ignorance in the art of chiromancy, Ellenbog pointed out that Helmstetter had neglected to mark the precise borders of the astrological houses and the planetary positions, and returned the horoscope to Seuter on 12 October. It was not a promising start.[24]

4

The Magus Arrives
(1500–1506)

As the fifteenth century came to a close, millennial fears produced reports of wondrous signs and portents. Prophets sprang up like mushrooms to preach of the Antichrist and the Second Coming, and Arquato (Antonio Torquato) prophesied the destruction of Europe. There were stories of monstrous births, downpours of milk and blood, and stains upon the heavens. A triple moon was seen in the skies over Germany. In 1500 coloured crosses miraculously appeared on people's clothes in two villages near Sponheim and again in Liège the next year; a portent of plague, according to Trithemius. Legions of deformed children were born in Greece. Plague ravaged France. A corona of flaming swords illuminated Italian skies. It was said that a thunderbolt had struck the Vatican and toppled the Pope from his throne.[1]

War touched all corners of Europe. The Ottomans had won two successive battles against the Venetians at Lepanto in 1499 and 1500. Louis XII of France and Ferdinand II of Aragon carved up the Kingdom of Naples between them in 1500. There had been insurrection in the Low Countries (1491, 1492), Alsace (1493) and Swabia (1492). Rebels were swarming across the Empire. Armed and mutinous peasants were demanding better rights and being slaughtered for such temerity. Their discontent would simmer for many more years before coming to a final, bloody reckoning.

Death, pestilence, famine and war – the Horsemen of the Apocalypse – might well have been thought to be gathering. One who saw them more clearly than others was Albrecht Dürer (1471–1528). After a supposed rain of blood he had seen the crucifixion in a stain left on a servant girl's smock. In 1498 he issued his broadsheets on the 'Secret Revelation of St John' amongst which is the famous 'Four Horsemen of the Apocalypse'. Three of the Four Horsemen are depicted in the dress of the ruling classes. They ride rough-shod over the common people. Famine, the only rider not attired in the finery of the elite, tramples a sumptuously be-robed bishop. Above it all an angel hovers in the sky, appearing to bless the scene and mock poor humanity.

Witchcraft and magic were always pressing concerns and millennial tension inevitably heightened the sense of unease surrounding them. The decade to 1500 had seen witches executed in their droves across the Empire. Over the same period numerous works on witches and magic appeared. In 1500 the Inquisitor Bernardo Rategno warned of the spread and increase of witches in his *Tractatus de strigibus*. Europe seemed to be swarming with the agents of the Devil. In time Faustus, too, would be reckoned amongst their unholy ranks.

The Black Magic Pope

Despite the hysterical prophecies and mysterious signs, the world did not end when the arbitrary numbering we give to time changed from one set of figures to another. Things continued largely as they had before and in some ways got better. Leonardo had painted his *La Gioconda* (it was not called the *Mona Lisa* until after his death). Dürer completed his famous self-portrait and began work on the *Lamentation for Christ*. The great Humanist scholar and controversial cabbalist Johannes Reuchlin (1455–1522), whose career would define the intellectual climate of his age, had published his Hebrew grammar – the first of its kind. Some things, of course, became worse.

With the problems of ever increasing numbers of heretics and heathens weighing on his mind, Pope Alexander VI (1431–1503) tried to rally support for a crusade, unsuccessfully, while an estimated 30,000 pilgrims gathered in Rome for the Church's Jubilee year died of plague. Fortunately, Copernicus, also on pilgrimage to Rome in 1500, survived the plague to observe the lunar eclipse of 6 November – an event that could only have looked to the untutored like the shadow of death passing across the moon. Alexander VI had reputedly spared no expense for the Jubilee celebrations, but Rome must have seemed like a city of the dead, heaped with reeking corpses.

As the first printed music appeared in 1501 – mostly intended for use in private homes – Alexander VI issued a Papal Bull demanding that German printers submit their books to ecclesiastical authorities for licensing. Almost in response, a pamphlet against the papacy appeared accusing the Holy See of being a den of iniquity. Alexander himself was denounced as an 'abyss of vice, a subverter of all justice, human or divine'.[2]

While Alexander was celebrating the marriage of his daughter Lucrezia Borgia to Alfonso, son and heir of Duke Ercole of Ferrara, with a party unrivalled for its splendour and extravagance, Faustus, for his part, was supposed to have produced three Latin texts on magic that year graced by the name of His Holiness. It is no wonder that he wanted everything vetted before it got into print. Of the texts, two fall into the Höllenzwang category with prefaces allegedly written by the Pope himself: *D. I. Fausti dreyfacher Hoellen-Zwang* (D[octor] I[?] Fausti Threefold Harrowing of Hell) and *D. Faustus vierfacher Höllen-Zwang* (D[octor] Faustus's Fourfold Harrowing of Hell). The latter is notable for the use of the name Faustus, and the initial I. (J.) could be a contraction of the later and incorrect Johannes or stand for Jörg, an historically recorded version of Georgius. The third text appeared under the title of *Tabellae Rabellinae Geister-Commando*, to be followed the next year by *D. Fausts (Original) Geister Commando*, again printed in Rome under the falsified imprimatur of Alexander VI.

On the cover of the *(Original) Geister Commando* we see the smudged picture of a male head, bearded and wearing a cylindrical fez-like hat. Underneath is the inscription 'The magus Dr Faustus of the city of Kundlingia wrote this'. It claims to be an original work of magic with the place of Rome given, the additional name of Alexander VI and the date of 1502. It further claims to have been through the hands of a certain 'D. Habermanno (Mago)' and privately printed, under penalty of excommunication, in 1510 in the reign of Pope Julius II. This Dr Johann Haberman (1516–1590) was a theologian and Hebraist who also had a reputation as the author of a number of magical texts. The dates of publication and Haberman's own do not match and, given the catalogue of apparently pious Lutheran works in his name, his sideline in grimoire seems to have been someone's idea of a joke.

Alexander VI had the reputation of being a black magician, he was after all a Borgia, and it was said that he had sold his soul to the Devil for the papacy. He would become something of another 'Faust' in Barnabe Barnes's 1607 play *The Devil's Charter*. A connection between the two was thus clearly made at a later date.

There were rumours of grisly black magic in the Castel Sant'Angelo, implicating Alexander VI's son, the infamous Cesare Borgia (1475–1507), and suggesting the presence of an able necromancer. When one of Cesare's enemies – the young Astorre Manfredi – disappeared inside the castle in 1501, never to return, the word was that he had been subjected to the most gruesome rituals.

It has been suggested that Manfredi fell victim to the practice of extispicium (extispicy) or pedomancy, divination by the examination of human entrails. That Manfredi died in the Castel Sant'Angelo, the converted mausoleum of the Roman Emperor Hadrian – also alleged to have practiced extispicium – adds weight to the argument for some.[3] Extispicium was not a skill one could easily pick up, even if Cesare proved he had the stomach for its nauseating techniques. Ambitious and adventurous men were attracted to Cesare, and Faustus was certainly both, but it is too much to say that he was there.

Alas, as with most of the Faustian works of magic, it is most probable that the dates of publication of these grimoires were backdated by unscrupulous printers, with the Pope's preface or imprint added as an extra selling point or opportunistic defamation. The *(Original) Geister Commando* text only has a traceable history to 1846 when it was acquired by the British Museum from a Berlin antiquarian bookseller, and on the basis of textual similarities and typography is thought to have been produced between 1765 and 1780. Likewise, the *dreyfacher Hoellen-Zwang* and *Tabellae Rabellinae* can only be dated to their publication in the nineteenth century.[4] The use of 'Faustus' and the intitial I. (J.) leaves room for doubt in the *vierfacher Höllen-Zwang*, but the text is only traceable to 1680, the date of its supposed second printing. On textual grounds, it is the mention of the spirit Mephistopheles that, as I will argue later, almost certainly seals the fate of these texts as later forgeries.

For all his unsavoury reputation, it is inconceivable that Alexander would have permitted his name to appear on such documents. Faustus could very well have been in Rome, or somewhere in Italy at least, attracted like so many others by the great reputations of that country's venerable universities, but it would be some years later before the first verifiable reference to him would be made.

The Prince of Necromancers

It was 1506 and a weary 44 year-old monk who went by the name of Trithemius was returning from the court of the Prince-Elector, Margrave Joachim I von Brandenburg (1484–1535) in Berlin. He was not in a good mood. Earlier he had been forced to leave the Benedictine monastery of St Martin at Sponheim, near Bad Kreuznach, and his post of abbot and, he said, he feared for his life. He had been painfully laid up in Leipzig for six days with kidney stones before managing to struggle on to Gotha where he visited his friend Mutianus, Canon of St Mary's Church. From there he made his way to Gelnhausen, arriving towards the end of May. Here he would make one of the most fateful encounters in history and provide us with the single most important written reference to Faustus.

Gelnhausen was an old *Freie Reichsstadt* (Imperial Free City) founded by Emperor Friedrich I, Barbarossa, in 1170. It was a prosperous town guarded by its encircling wall, the castle of Barbarossaburg (or Königspfalz) lying on an island in the River Kinzig and the Fratzenstein ('grotesque face stone', later renamed the Hexenturm or 'Witch's Tower'), a reminder of the Hussite Wars in the early fifteenth century. The Knights of St John of Jerusalem had long established themselves here in a building that is now one of the oldest half-timbered houses in Hesse. The town's importance derived from its situation on the old *Via Regia* trade route between Frankfurt and Leipzig.

Beyond Frankfurt lay Sponheim. The exiled abbot's thoughts might well have turned to his old monastery, to the vegetable gardens and orchards now in bud and spring flower, and to the circumstances of his hasty departure. If he kept on the *Via Regia* he could be back once more in the place where he had felt that God had once led him. But now, where would he go? What fresh trials did the future hold? It was then that the legend of Faustus was born.

There are no records to examine, the devastations of war and fire have destroyed anything that might have been buried in the town archives, but there are local theories. According to these, Trithemius stayed in the Arnsburger Hof at 41 Langasse. Founded by Kloster Arnsburg, a Cistercian monastery near Lich in Hesse, in the thirteenth century, the current building was entirely reconstructed in the eighteenth century. Faustus, meanwhile, supposedly stayed across the way in Der Goldene Löwe, nowadays Zum Löwen, but still sporting a golden lion affixed to its half-timbered façade. Trithemius was safely lodged with the ecclesiastics, whilst Faustus shared the fleas with the commercial travellers.[5]

It was a year later when Trithemius told his story. He had received a letter from Johannes Virdung von Haßfurt asking him for information about a certain Faustus. Virdung was eagerly awaiting his arrival and sought out the opinion of Trithemius. In doing so he had inadvertently tossed Faustus's career to the four winds. Trithemius's reply in 1507 was the first recorded reference to Faustus and it was not a flattering one.

> That man about whom you wrote to me, Georgius Sabellicus, who dares to call himself the prince of necromancers, is a wandering vagrant, a driveller and a

cheat, who deserves to be punished with a whip that he may not lightly dare to publicly profess that which is abominable and against the holy church.[6]

Trithemius lost no time in blackening Faustus's name; barely had he mentioned him but he was heaping insult upon insult. For all his hard words, Trithemius's description of Faustus gives us one of the best insights into his career, although we should not, like Trithemius, presume to judge his character on account of that career. Trithemius expanded on his subject, prejudice in every stroke of the quill.

> Indeed, what are the titles assumed by this man, if not the signs of a most foolish and insane mind, who reveals himself to be a fool and not a philosopher? Thus indeed has he formulated an appropriate title: Magister Georgius Sabellicus Faustus Junior, fount of necromancy, astrologer, second magus, cheiromancer, agromancer, pyromancer, second in the art of water. See the foolish rashness of the man, how much madness he displays, how he presumes to declare himself the fount of necromancy, when truly, ignorant of all good education, he should rather call himself a fool than a master.[7]

These titles may well seem ludicrous now, but during the Renaissance it was not thought insane to practice the divinatory arts, although all of these practices had been condemned as unchristian at one time or another. Trithemius was also writing to an astrologer. It was not very politic of him to list the title of 'astrologer' as the product of a 'most foolish and insane mind'. Trithemius was trying to influence Virdung's opinion of Faustus, but he may well have also influenced Virdung's opinion of himself. It is an even stranger remark, since Trithemius dabbled in divination by the stars himself. In 1508 he composed an astrological history of the world for Maximilian I. He also attributed a riding accident to the influence of Saturn. He believed that his form of astrology was entirely in keeping with Christian dogma, but lambasted the astrology of others, particularly judicial or divinatory astrology. It was a highly self-serving position to take. He believed that demons co-operated with its practitioners, and that the astrologer (and the diviner in general) was 'an imitator and disciple of the Devil'.[8]

The Germans had been noted for their use of divination – especially the casting of lots – since Tacitus reported it in his *Germania* as early as the first century CE. It was still widespread enough (or perhaps even more advanced) in the fifteenth century for the Bohemian poet Johannes von Tepl (*c.*1350–*c.*1415) to list eleven different varieties in *Der Ackermann und der Tod* (1401). Writing in 1456 the Bavarian physician, writer and diplomat, Johannes Hartlieb (*c.*1400–1468), reduced the number to seven 'forbidden arts', intended to reflect the seven Liberal Arts. Paracelsus was still using a taxonomy similar to Hartlieb's in 1537–8. The infamous witch-hunters' manual of Kramer and Sprenger, the *Malleus Maleficarum* ('Hammer of the Witches'), listed fifteen types in 1486. Not to be outdone, Trithemius catalogued an astounding 44 varieties of divination in 1508 – a list he would later expand.

Divination was grounded in Aristotelian physics. Isidore of Seville (560–636) established the classic schema of four types of fortune-telling based on the concept of the four elements, i.e. aeromancy, geomancy, hydromancy and pyromancy. The German Hugh of St Victor (1078–1141) added to Isidore's schema with a fifth form: necromancy.

Worse than being an astrological 'imitator and disciple of the Devil', Faustus principally described himself as the *fons necromanticorum*, literally the 'fount of the necromancers'. Necromancy was dangerous magic. The theologians denied that the spirits of the dead were actually raised through necromancy, asserting that their place was taken by demons who assumed the identities of the departed. Hence necromancy was in effect to consort with demons and accordingly defined as black magic, or nigromancy. This caused confusion between the two terms and they were often used interchangeably. This meant that Faustus would be seen as practising more than just foretelling the future by consulting the spirits of the dead. It meant that he would be seen as an exponent of demonic magic.

Hartlieb did not make a sophisticated argument against necromancy, he simply insisted that it must involve the Devil: 'He who wants to practice this art must make various offerings to the Devil ... vow to him and be in league with him.'[9] Such practices as these require the forfeit of one's soul, no light price in an age when life was still scarcely more than nasty, brutish and short for the majority, and the life after death was believed to be everlasting.

In Faustus's own time Agrippa also described this dark art in similar terms, talking of 'infernal invocations' and 'deadly sacrifices'.[10] However, he was more specific than Hartlieb on the mechanisms behind this art. He furnished his description with a plethora of classical and biblical references to Odysseus and Circe, and Saul and the Witch of Endor, amongst others. The dramatic story of Saul, King of Israel, turning to the Witch of Endor to call up the spirit of the Prophet Samuel was an especially popular one amongst occultists and demonologists as both a proof of necromancy and an example of its prohibition. Unlike Hartlieb and the theological view, Agrippa took a classical stance and seems to have believed that the dead could be made to answer a magician's interrogations.

Hartlieb gave us a Christian view of black magic: that it can only be the product of the Devil and that therefore to practise it requires submission to the latter. Hartlieb constantly stressed that the Devil works through deception and that nothing can be truly accomplished with these arts except the eternal damnation of the practitioner. Agrippa, too, was censorious despite his classical leanings and it is unsurprising that his teacher Trithemius had little good to say about necromancers and their art. Necromancers, he wrote, 'are worse than their demons'.[11]

Astrology was the only means of divination that Hartlieb did not castigate as forbidden. He condemned divination by comets and signs in the heavens under the heading of aeromancy, but stopped short of extending this to the stars and planets. We do not have to look far for the answer. Hartlieb was regarded as something of an astrologer himself. Such attitudes persisted into the sixteenth century and beyond. The problem hinged on whether or not astrology contravened scripture by interfering with divinely ordained free will.

However, the rest of Faustus's proficiencies fall foul of Hartlieb's categorisation: chiromancy, pyromancy and hydromancy – all of these, Hartlieb claimed, were snares of the Devil. Of all Hartlieb's forbidden arts, chiromancy (palmistry) is probably the only one that will be familiar to modern readers. For pyromancy sacrifice was made to the 'Angel of Fire' and the practitioner observed the patterns of fire and smoke from burning wood. Hydromancy was performed by gazing into water, usually with the magician employing a child for the purpose, or by pouring molten metals or dropping objects into water.

There was another practice that Trithemius listed that we do not find in Hartlieb: agromancy. Faustus was, said Trithemius, an *agromanticus*, a practitioner of 'agromancy'. However, we do not find agromancy amongst the usual forms of divination. For over a hundred years Faustian scholars have scratched their heads over it, wondering what it could mean and whether Trithemius may have misreported or misspelled what Faustus actually claimed to practice. The problem is not incidental, but crucial to understanding what sort of magician Faustus was or claimed to be.

If the basic categorisation of divinatory practices is based upon the four elements, then, in a list such as Trithemius gives, it would appear obvious to assume that agromancy means either divination by air (aeromancy) or by earth (geomancy), since we have already covered fire and water. It looks closest to aeromancy and *agromanticus* could be a misspelling on Trithemius's part, perhaps due to his over-excitement in so thoroughly condemning Faustus, or simply as a result of the haphazard orthography of the time. However, *agromanticus* literally means 'field diviner', which could indeed be another word for geomancy, 'earth divination', or a branch of it.

Missing from Trithemius's list is physiognomy. Seuter's letter of 1534 provides evidence that Helmstetter was already practising this art in the early 1490s, and from Mutianus in 1513 and Begardi in 1539 we have further confirmation that this formed part of Faustus's repertoire.

Faustus's claims to excellence in all these various forms of divination were just so many more nails in the coffin of his reputation as far as Trithemius was concerned. Describing 'the many vanities dependent upon astrology' in his unfinished *De demonibus*, Trithemius listed 51 types of divination expressly forbidden by the Church. These included necromancy, which he narrowly defined as divination 'from the graves and bones of the dead', pyromancy, hydromancy, geomancy, chiromancy and astromancy, divination 'from the study of the stars'.[12] Faustus, by his own admission, was guilty of practicing all of these.

Zoroaster's Heir

Whilst Faustus may have claimed to be the fount of necromancy, not all of his other assertions appeared so excessive. Where Trithemius severely castigated Faustus for his bombast, a close reading of his self-pronounced titles reveals something that could be mistaken for modesty. He is *in hydra arte secundus*, the second in hydromancy, and *magus secundus*, the second magus. The question is, however, to whom is he second? Who does Faustus acknowledge as first?

It is widely believed that Faustus used the title 'second Magus' in deference to Zoroaster, widely believed on the authority of Isidor and Augustine to have been the first magus, or Simon Magus, whose story is often considered to be a forerunner of the Faustian legend. However, it could also refer to any other predecessor, perhaps a teacher, or one of Faustus's contemporaries, perhaps even Trithemius himself. The problem is that Faustus did not specify who he meant.

We need to look at the writings of his contemporaries to find some clue. In his *Occult Philosophy* Agrippa mentioned both Zoroaster and 'Zamolxis' (Zalmoxis) as the most famous magicians and generally credited as the 'inventors' of magic. Agrippa appended a long roll call of illustrious magi, from which Simon Magus is notably absent. Agrippa discussed 'Simon the Samaritan' – Simon Magus was said to come from Samaria – as the chief of those 'who resist the Apostolical truth' in his hostile *De incertitudine* and decided that he was 'destined to the torments of eternal Fire'.[13] Whilst Agrippa was clearly aware of Simon Magus, he saw Zoroaster and Zalmoxis as the 'first' and between the two it was Zoroaster whom he called the 'father and prince of the Magicians'.[14]

Comparatively little is known about Zalmoxis. He was first mentioned by Herodotus in the 420s BCE as an already legendary figure amongst the Thracian Getae. There was more classical information on Zoroaster. In the first century CE Pliny the Elder credited him with inventing magic some six thousand years before Plato. Amongst the Greek and Roman writers he was everywhere seen as foremost amongst the Magi. If there ever was a first magus, then it was Zoroaster.

Zoroaster was also admired by the influential hermeticists. Ficino viewed Zoroaster as one of the forerunners of his revered Plato, and Pico della Mirandola talked of him repeatedly in his 900 famous theses of 1486 – without mentioning Simon Magus once. Trithemius himself saw the magician as being the originator of the magic arts: 'Witchcraft, and Incantations … were first excogitated by Zoroaster King of the Bactrians.'[15] Also known as Ham or Cham, the son of Noah, Zoroaster is credited as 'the first necromancer' in the *Clementine Recognitions* and later in both the *Malleus Maleficarum* and Scot's *Discoverie of Witchcraft*.

It was Manlius who said that Melanchthon compared Faustus to Simon Magus during his lectures from 1549 to 1560 – long after Faustus's death. In daring to challenge Peter, Simon has gone down in Christian history as 'the father of all heretics' in the words of a father of the early church, Irenaeus.[16] While written in the second century CE, Irenaeus's *Against Heresies* was only published by Erasmus in 1526. To an extent we find parallels in the Faustbook where, like Simon Magus, Faustus also has his Helen, both of them that fabled beauty of Troy. Similarly, where Simon Magus was a former Apostle, so Faustus was a renegade Doctor of Divinity. The Faustbook even makes an explicit connection between the two men, giving the alleged repentance of Simon Magus as an example to Faustus.

However, from the actual life of Faustus there is only a superficial connection to Simon Magus. When Faustus said he could reproduce all of the miracles attributed to Jesus we might also think of Simon Magus and his challenge to the Christian church, but no more. It is only from a hostile Christian point of view that Faustus is seen as second to Simon Magus – and the connection was only made after Faustus's death. Amongst his contemporary magicians – and the witch-hunters – the allusion to Zoroaster would have been immediately recognisable.

Reference to being second in hydromancy also implies a more illustrious predecessor. Neither Zoroaster nor Simon Magus were generally remarked upon for their hydromancy, so we shall have to look elsewhere for the identity of the person Faustus refers to. Augustine had told stories about the legendary Roman king Numa Pompilius that became popular in the Middle Ages. According to Plutarch (*c*.46–127), Numa was descended from the Sabine race and made King of Rome after the death of Romulus in the seventh century BCE. Augustine described him as a compulsive hydromancer, constantly seeking visions in water. The source of this may have been Plutarch's retelling of the legend that Numa had captured two satyrs by mixing honey and wine into the spring from which they drank, and having captured them, forced them to reveal the future.

The story was well known among the magicians; Trithemius knew it and Agrippa was certainly aware of it. In his *De incertitudine*, Agrippa ranked Numa as something like a Roman Zoroaster, attesting to the esteem of this legendary figure. Rather than being a sign of modesty, Faustus's claims to being second can be read as claims to being the true heir of these mighty magical forebears.

Another Ezra

Trithemius's letter continued in the same negative vein.

> However, his worthlessness is not hidden from me. The previous year when I was returning from the Margrave of Brandenburg, I came upon this man in the town of Gelnhausen, and many frivolous things were told to me about him at the inn, promised by him not without great temerity.[17]

One can imagine the gossip round the inn and poor old Trithemius sitting amongst the throng, perhaps feeling slighted that his own great (in his eyes) achievements were not being trumpeted by the commonality. In writing about the incident to Virdung, Trithemius was quick to drop the name of his influential patron, the margrave-elector of Brandenburg.

According to Trithemius's view of events, Faustus 'fled the inn and could not be persuaded to appear in my presence'.[18] Without any other witnesses we should not be quick to accept his interpretation. Trithemius did have a reputation and people, like Agrippa for example, did seek him out. If Faustus saw himself as a pupil, as Agrippa did, or otherwise inferior to Trithemius he may well have tried to meet him and learn from the older man. If, however, he saw himself as superior to Trithemius he may have decided not to condescend to meet him. Apparently Trithemius was trying to persuade Faustus to 'appear in my presence', suggesting both that Trithemius really wanted to meet him and also that he felt he was someone who could command such an audience. Trithemius was known to have boasted that 'great and erudite personages have considered themselves fortunate if I have admitted them into my presence.'[19] Did Faustus really flee from him, or did he just have something better to do? Could it be possible that it was Trithemius who did the fleeing? Alas, we will never know, but if any man dared to forego an audience with the vengeful abbot, one can be sure that he would not forget it.

> His advertisement of foolishness, which he gave to you, as mentioned, he also sent to me through a certain citizen.[20]

Referring here to his earlier quotation of Faustus's long list of titles, Trithemius also revealed the origin of his information. He tells us that Faustus sent this list by way of a messenger. We might conclude, then, that it was something like a letter of introduction, a business or calling card. It also turns out that Faustus had sent one to Virdung and that Virdung had told Trithemius about it. The interesting thing is that where Trithemius is filled to overflowing with bile when he reads Faustus's card, Virdung was impressed or intrigued enough to invite Faustus to visit him. What Trithemius claims as the symptoms of madness, Virdung interprets as the accomplishments of someone he would like to meet. Again we see the slighted Trithemius. After Faustus apparently refuses to come into his presence and submit, it would seem, to Trithemius's authority, Trithemius exhibits the foolishness he attempts to attribute to another. By having already sent his calling card to Virdung, Faustus is shown to have been in communication with at least one high-ranking and influential member of court. Trithemius strikes out at Faustus when he discovers that he has contacted another Humanist and occultist.

> Certain priests in the town told me that he had said, in the presence of many, that he had such an understanding and memory of all wisdom and also knowledge, that if all the books of Plato and Aristotle, with their whole philosophy, were totally lost to the memory of man, he himself, of his own genius, like a second Hebrew Ezra, would be able to restore them all with superior elegance.[21]

Trithemius was clearly curious to learn more about this man, but those 'certain priests' of Gelnhausen would have been unlikely to give an unbiased account of someone like Faustus. According to their report we now see the Humanist bravado of Faustus coming to the fore. This is the sort of claim that someone who recognised Publius Faustus Andrelinus as his intellectual predecessor might make. Faustus boasts, not only of the depth of his learning, but also of the extent of his memory. In a pre-digital age when even printing was still in its infancy, memory was paramount. A scholar would be expected to carry his library with him in his head. According to the father of church history, Eusebius of Caesarea (*c.*275–339 CE), Ezra was famed for his 'restoration' of the sayings of the prophets and the law of Moses after the scriptures had been destroyed during the Jews' Babylonian captivity. Was this Faustus's comparison or that of the priests?

Faustus's claim to be able to restore these philosophical works 'with superior elegance' again shows Humanist interests. Style was as much a preoccupation with the Humanists as was knowledge itself. The claim to be able to rewrite Plato and Aristotle with greater style combines these Humanist concerns with an outrageous boast.

Miracles in Würzburg

> Afterwards, whilst I was at Speyer, he came to Würzburg and, likewise boasting in the presence of many, so it is said, that the miracles of Christ the Saviour were not so wonderful, that he also was able to do all that Christ had done, as often and whenever he wished.[22]

Trithemius had moved on, frustrated in his attempts to meet Faustus, but he was still receiving reports on his activities. It was sometime after 2 June 1506 and Faustus was now in the important town of Würzburg. It was the seat of the Prince-Bishop, who looked down from his residence, the imposing Marienberg fortress, upon a Romanesque cathedral built on the site of a church said to have been consecrated by Charlemagne himself. The austere preacher Johann Geiler von Kaisersberg (1445–1510) had harangued the masses from the cathedral's pulpit for a time before finding a permanent home in Strassburg after 1480. It was the town of sculptor Tilman Riemenschneider (c.1460–1531), sometime mayor and later a leader in the Peasants' War. It was a headstrong town given to demonstrations of radicalism. Riemenschneider was only following in a long tradition that began with the Würzburgers' pilgrimage of protest of 1476 in support of the Piper of Niklasshausen.

It was also an old university town – something that always seems to have attracted Faustus. Here perhaps he could find an audience well-educated enough to appreciate his Humanistic appeal. It had been founded in 1402 on the model of Bologna, but despite the best intentions the university soon acquired a dubious reputation. The students met in the Great Lion Court, a solidly built but modest two-storey building with handsome crow-stepped gables. After the first rector Johann Zantfurt was fatally stabbed in 1423 the university rapidly declined. Writing about the year 1506 Trithemius blamed the students' decadent lifestyle and general riotousness as 'greatly impeding the academic achievement in Würzburg'.[23] The cathedral chapter, made up of members of the nobility, turned up its nose and withdrew its support, and when Faustus arrived it had stopped functioning as a university altogether. This sorry state of affairs led to its being re-founded in 1582.

Trithemius would later follow Faustus to Würzburg, taking up the post of abbot of the old Scottish monastery of St James's. The 1507 letter to Virdung about Faustus was written from there and no doubt the information he had on Faustus was communicated to him when he came to the city. It was in Würzburg that Faustus allegedly chose to make his most dangerous claims. We can imagine him in the market square or perhaps before another audience in an inn, his words silencing the everyday hubbub. We can picture the looks of amazement and shock on the faces of that audience.

There are a number of ways we can view these claims. Faustus was not scandalising Würzburg with the news that he has signed a pact with the Devil – he was never in his lifetime reported to have made that claim – he was instead claiming all the powers attributed to Jesus. Here Trithemius lets the claim stand, evidently confident that it would shock Virdung. However, any stage-magician today could make such claims and apparently demonstrate them without suggesting that he was truly another Jesus.

Was Faustus advertising a magic show? Or again, was he suggesting that he could explain that such apparent miracles could be achieved through natural as opposed to supernatural means? Or was he indeed suggesting that, like another Simon Magus or Appollonius of Tyana (2 BCE–*c*.98 CE), he could rival Jesus with his magic?

We are all familiar with the more well-known miracles like turning water into wine and feeding the 5,000, but there were allegedly many more. The Apostles credited Jesus with performing at least twenty miraculous healings, three resurrections, five exorcisms and many other miscellaneous miracles. Including other sources, such as the apocryphal gospels and even the Koran, there are over eighty miracles attributed to Jesus. Faustus had set himself a challenge.

Later stories of magical banquets suggest that Faustus could perform his own miracles with food and wine. Tricks for walking on water were certainly known. Leonardo da Vinci sketched such a technique and an illustration in Thomas Hill's *Naturall and Artificiall Conclusions* of 1581 shows us a figure balancing precariously on floats tied to his feet and the end of a staff, a small boat bobbing in the distance. Faustus, however, went one better than walking on water and was believed to have flown through the air on more than one occasion. Resurrections would fall more generally under the heading of necromancy and Faustus certainly claimed proficiency in this field. There is a formula for just such an operation in what has been called a 'necromancer's manual', the fifteenth-century manuscript catalogued as *Codex Latinus Monacensis* 849 (hereafter Codex 849) in the Bavarian State Library in Munich. Exorcism, however, was not Faustus's *forté*. Rather than drive demons out of people, he had the reputation of calling them in, reputedly threatening Melanchthon and cursing a monastery with a poltergeist. According to Begardi, Faustus also 'bragged much about his great skill ... in medicine', adding healing – albeit unmiraculous – to the list of his accomplishments. Although Begardi did not report if he had ever been successful in this practice, what he did say suggests that Faustus had acquired an unscrupulous reputation through such claims. Such 'miracles' were within the repertoire of Renaissance magicians and later tales told about Faustus credit him with performing magical feats that support this alleged claim 'to do all that Christ had done'.[24]

5

Sex Crimes in Kreuznach
(1507)

Towards the end of Lent of the present year he came to Kreuznach.[1]

Trithemius had more to say about Faustus. The events he next described took place about a year after his first encounter with the magician in Gelnhausen, in a town 126 kilometres away – by modern roads – now called Bad Kreuznach, but which was then simply Kreuznach. According to Trithemius, Faustus was there around late March or April of 1507.

Kreuznach lies on the River Nahe, a tributary of the Rhine, and its roots stretch back in time. There has been a settlement there since before Roman times. The Celts who lived there called it something like Cruciniac, and the Romans turned this into Crucinacum when they established a camp in the mid-first century CE. After the legionaries came the Franks. In the Middle Ages the town was ruled by the Counts of Sponheim who built Kausenburg castle on a hill overlooking their domain. Their line died out in the early fifteenth century and Kreuznach changed hands several times. The mineral springs that gave it the prefix *Bad* meaning 'bath' or 'spa' were not commercially exploited until the nineteenth century. In the sixteenth century it was the second largest town, after Heidelberg, in the Palatinate.

Across the river from the town centre, but still within the old walls, stands the *Historisches Dr. Faust Haus* on Magister Faustgasse. It is a three-storey half-timbered building with white-washed walls and black beams – the very picture of Germanic quaintness. The façade is decorated with a large portrait of Faustus and gothic lettering proclaiming the building's historical connections. A wrought iron sign, intertwined with devils and showing a scholarly figure holding a book, hangs above the door. Picked out in a white, angularly Teutonic script across the black beams running the length of the building is an inscription warning that Satan befriends the drunkard, whilst making an invitation to come in and enjoy a good drink.

Today one can sit down to enjoy a glass of flaming *Faust-Trunk* with a *Mephisto Salat* or sizzling *Dr. Faust-Schweinshaxe* under wall murals depicting scenes from the legend. On special nights visitors are treated to a dramatic sound and light show – thunder crashes, lightning flashes and the floorboards creak overhead as if Faustus were pacing his study. Upstairs there is a life-size wax figure display of Faustus and Mephistopheles as well as reproductions of many of the historical documents relating to the legend hanging on the walls.

Whilst there is no documentary evidence to prove that Faustus ever stayed here, the building is of the right age (said to have been built in 1492)[2] and the strength of local opinion brooks no dissent. But Faustus, if he were here, was not about to open a restaurant. From having made grand philosophical and Humanist claims in Gelnhausen he had progressed to comparing his own abilities with those of Jesus in Würzburg. How was he going to better that? Trithemius continued, reporting that Faustus,

> with similar foolish pretentiousness made enormous promises, saying that in alchemy he was the most accomplished man ever and that by his skill he could do everything that men could wish.[3]

Having challenged Würzburg with his heresy, Faustus was now out to woo Kreuznach with his alchemy. However, he could expect little in the way of admiration from Trithemius. Trithemius was disparaging of anyone's ability in alchemy, not just Faustus's. In his *Annales Hirsaugiensis* Trithemius called alchemy a 'chaste whore' – a woman who has many lovers but satisfies none of them.[4] The result of practicing alchemy could, according to Trithemius, only be a deleterious one:

> From foolish men it makes insane ones; from rich men paupers; from philosophers, fatuous men; from deceived men, very garrulous deceivers – all who, though they know nothing, profess to know all things, and, although they are very poor, promise to endow their followers with the riches of Croesus.[5]

It is true that alchemy was the ruin of many men and a magnet to legions of the most unscrupulous, but it was also the great adventure of the age. Its promises were many and extravagant, and there was scarcely a cash-strapped princeling in the Empire who was deaf to its siren call. However, not everyone presented the art in such a dismal light. As we might expect, its practitioners, as opposed to its critics, saw alchemy and alchemists in a very different light. Paracelsus was quick to their defence:

> [Alchemists] diligently follow their labours, sweating whole days and nights by their furnaces. They do not spend their time abroad for recreation, but take delight in their laboratories. They put their fingers among coals, into clay and filth, not into gold rings. They are sooty and black, like smiths and miners, and do not pride themselves upon clean and beautiful faces.[6]

Stained and sooty-faced, we might expect to find Faustus seeking some position connected with alchemy, but the story takes an unexpected turn. Kreuznach had a vacancy for a schoolmaster and Faustus found himself with a new job. It was an important appointment, but no official record of it has survived. He only held the post for a short time and even records for the school itself are deficient.

Today there are three gymnasia in Kreuznach – Gymnasium am Römerkastell, Gymnasium an der Stadtmauer and the Lina-Hilger-Gymnasium – and no one is sure which could have been Faustus's school. We can immediately discount the Gymnasium am Römerkastell because it only opened its doors in 1971. The Gymnasium an der Stadtmauer is older, having begun life as the Collège de Creuznach in 1807, but not old enough. The Lina-Hilger-Gymnasium was so named in 1959, having been the state lyceum, but unfortunately only has a history dating to 1926. Faustus could not have taught at any of them.

The phrase Trithemius used in his letter – *munus docendi scholasticum* – means something like the 'post of teaching-scholar' – *scholasticum* by itself would only mean a scholar, or even a schoolboy. The word *scholasticum* is also used in the sense of a rhetorician or grammarian, that is, one who taught rhetoric or grammar as distinct from mathematics. Teaching rhetoric or grammar in the sixteenth century would mean teaching Latin. The usual translation as 'schoolmaster' is not inaccurate, but we should not assume that there was a school, at least in the usual sense of a physical institution set aside for the purpose of education. Faustus could have been employed as a private tutor, but Trithemius's mention of the town suggests that this was a public appointment.

Before state education, cathedral schools were the most common institution providing pre-university training. It was an ancient tradition, even in the sixteenth century, established by the Third Lateran Council in 1179, re-confirmed and extended by the Fourth in 1215, that every cathedral church (and later any that could afford it) should appoint a master to instruct clerics and impoverished scholars. These schools were, of course, run by the religious orders – the Franciscans were active in Kreuznach from their base at St Wolfgang's and the Carmelites from the Nikolauskirche – but it is not inconceivable that Faustus was appointed to teach in a cathedral school or its equivalent. Today the Gymnasium an der Stadtmauer stands on the site of the former Franciscan monastery.

Across the River Nahe in the old medieval town a school opened its doors on a narrow street called the Klappergasse in 1707. It was not, however, a new school but one relocated from the former premises of the Carmelites. Their monastery had been disbanded in 1564 and from 1569 onwards had been used as a Calvinist Gymnasium teaching pupils the basics of theology, Latin, Greek, rhetoric, mathematics and something of the natural sciences in preparation for a career in the Church. Based on the evidence of Trithemius's letter of 1507 it has been supposed that the Carmelites themselves were running a school in the early sixteenth century. This introduces a circularity here that we would want to avoid. That there must have been some sort of schooling available is demonstrated by the number of students from Kreuznach subsequently enrolled at university. It may not have been the Carmelites who were providing that schooling and some have suggested a municipal school, but Kreuznach may not have been affluent enough to afford that expense itself and the established tradition points to a monastic order. The central location of the Carmelite monastery speaks in its favour and this site is also closer to the *Historisches Dr. Faust-Haus*, although we should not read too much into that. The possibility remains that it was here at Poststrasse 6 in the old monastery that Faustus taught his new pupils, however, there is a question mark over the existence of this school and the evidence, such as it is, is wanting.[7]

The monks themselves – used to providing such teaching as was required – could not have been happy to have an outsider foisted upon them and we can only speculate that it was the force of his sponsor's will that carried Faustus's appointment. This introduces a political element: noses were put out of joint, ambitions stymied. Subsequent events would suggest that the monks or others were quick to conspire against him.

A Man Very Fond of Mystical Things

Faustus's declarations of his alchemical ability, and no doubt some recital of his earlier claims, found acceptance with at least one person in the vicinity of Kreuznach. To Trithemius's chagrin this was no clay-brained peasant:

> He was appointed through the influence of Franz von Sickingen, bailiff of your prince and a man very fond of mystical things.[8]

Franz von Sickingen (1481–1523) was one of the great names of the sixteenth century, celebrated by Erasmus and called 'a peerless ornament of German knighthood' by Melanchthon.[9] His was a name that continued to reverberate long after his premature death. In the nineteenth century the Protestant historian James Wylie praised him as a knight who 'united the love of letters to that of arms' and the Marxist historian Ernest Belfort Bax dubbed him 'the last flower of German chivalry'.[10] The dramatist Ferdinand Lassalle immortalised him as a socialist hero in his eponymous play, describing him as 'A distinguished knight – distinguished in wealth, in character, in genius and in arms.'[11]

This eulogistic portrait is not so far off the mark as we might suppose. Von Sickingen would in his day be a king-maker and champion of free-thinkers, but in 1507 his greatest deeds still lay before him, although he was already noted for his love of 'mystical things'. As a 'bailiff of your prince', as Trithemius put it, he was the feudal enforcer for Philipp von Wittelsbach, Elector Palatine. At the time he held this office for Ebernburg, Kreuznach and from 1509 for nearby Böckelheim – clearly his recommendation of Faustus for the position of teacher did not hinder his career.

Contemporary portraits show a frowning visage, brow knit imperiously over a sharp eye and a lavish moustache, or, later in life, clean shaven and somewhat rounder in the face, although still conspiring to give a steely look. His family came from near Knittlingen before moving to the castle Ebernburg near Kreuznach in 1448. In the last few years von Sickingen had taken over the running of the family estate after the death of his father Schweikard. He was technically of the lower nobility, of the *Reichsritterschaft*, or class of free knights, but had been educated at the imperial court of Maximilian I. When Faustus arrived in Kreuznach he had just celebrated his twenty-sixth birthday.

It was no secret that von Sickingen was 'associated with the magical school', as Bax put it. Indeed it was said of him that he had been dedicated to the study of magic since his youth. His fondness for things mystical can in part be traced to his father Schweikard who was also reputed to have had a keen interest in astrology, even practising it himself. Adam Wernher of Heidelberg reported to his brother-in-law, the Reformation leader Georg Spalatin (1484–1545), that von Sickingen undertook nothing of importance without first consulting his astrologer. After von Sickingen's death Wernher discovered an astrological prediction made for him by Virdung for the year 1523 and made a copy of it. His castle doors opened to welcome Humanists, Reformers, occultists and the intelligentsia of his age. These same doors must also have stood open for Faustus.

Von Sickingen did not know Latin, so he could have been looking for a tutor, but it was surely this love of 'mystical things' that endeared Faustus to him. Given such an interest it is nearly inconceivable that von Sickingen and Faustus did not meet. Did Faustus promise to endow him with the riches of Croesus? Did they talk of the ancients, Plato and Aristotle? Did von Sickingen catch some glimpse of his future in Faustus's astrological predictions? Perhaps Faustus reminded him of Aristotle's supposed advice to Alexander the Great in the pseudo-Aristotelian *Secretum secretorum* ('Secret of Secrets'), to never embark on any undertaking without having first taken the advice of an astrologer. The *Secretum secretorum* was a well-known text at the time and may have influenced von Sickingen's view of the importance of astrology.

Their meeting is lost to history. In the halls of Ebernburg there is no more talk of mystical things, only the uninspiring clatter of hotel staff and guests, and in the *Historisches Dr. Faust Haus* there is no bar bill of a Georgius Faustus and company. If there ever was a record of their meeting, not a scrap of it has survived.

The Most Nefarious Fornication

According to the highly biased account of Trithemius, Faustus did not distinguish himself by his knowledge of astrology, 'mystical things' or by his teaching of Latin whilst in Kreuznach:

> Presently, he began to indulge in a kind of nefarious fornication with the boys and when this was at once brought to light, he ran away to avoid the punishment that awaited him.[12]

If von Sickingen had been his patron up until this point, as we suppose he must have been, he surely disowned Faustus now – if Trithemius is to be believed. But what were these nefarious fornications? The Latin *nefandissimo fornicationis genere* was translated rather charmingly in 1936 as 'a dastardly kind of lewdness', which sounds like nothing more devilish than twirling the end of an extravagant moustache, but no one till now has come up with an alternative translation. The language is of its time and the words 'dastardly' and 'lewdness' are not much in vogue these days – and I doubt whether they were trying to replicate a sense of Trithemius's Latin. Some sort of despicable indecency is meant by 'a dastardly kind of lewdness', but the Latin seems to be worded in stronger terms: *nefandissimo*, 'nefarious' or 'wicked', and *fornicationis*, 'fornication', which is voluntary sexual intercourse between a man and an unmarried woman. In a time when the institution of marriage was sacrosanct, fornication was as serious a charge as adultery, but it also raises the possibility that he did not necessarily sexually abuse the boys themselves because in such an instance we would expect a term like sodomy to have been used by Trithemius.

More explicit charges of sodomy would later be made against Faustus. Lercheimer described the Kreuznach incident in just these terms: 'he [Faustus] had to flee from there because he was guilty of sodomy.'[13] Earlier references to unspecified moral misconduct in the source material can also be interpreted as euphemisms for sodomy. When Manlius said that Melanchthon called him a 'wicked beast' whose conduct was shameful, wicked and dissolute, we can read these as indicating sexual deviancy.[14] Hogel, too, denounced his 'evil life', calling him notorious and wicked, and when Faustus was denied entry into Nuremberg in 1532 he was specifically named as 'the great sodomite' in the official report.

The charge of sodomy was a serious one. Sodomy was believed to have provoked God's destruction of cities and whole peoples (Sodom and Gomorrah in Genesis 19). It was expressly forbidden in the first imperial law code, the *Constitutio Criminalis Carolina* of 1532, and punishable by death by burning. The *Constitutio* was only the codification of earlier legal sanctions applied to sodomy. Ulrich Tengler (*c.* 1435–1511) had previously published guidelines for German lawyers in 1509 that stipulated death at the stake for same-sex acts and the 1532 *Constitutio* was based word for word on the 1507 law code for the diocese of Bamberg, but the precedent had been set since at least as early as 1277 when Rudolf I von Habsburg, King of the Romans, sentenced a nobleman to death by burning for *vicim sodomiticum*, the vice of sodomy.[15]

Sodomy was defined as a sin against nature, a generous definition that included such acts as masturbation, same-sex mutual masturbation, as well as same-sex penetrative intercourse, although it has been contended that the Renaissance uses of the term exceed the bounds of strict categorisation. Thus sodomy could be extended to cover usury, treason, lese-majesty or affront to the sovereign, blasphemy, impurity, ethnic difference and much else besides. The connection between sexual taboo and religious transgression was established early on in the prosecution of this 'crime', so that 'heresy' could also mean 'sodomy' and vice versa. Charges of sodomy also became part of the persecution of alleged witches, again showing the link between sexual and spiritual deviance as crimes against Christianity.[16]

It was not just witchcraft, that is, maleficent magic, but all forms of (non-Christian) magic that were associated with sexual transgression. Faustus's claim to be the Second Magus not only associated him with the magical prowess of Zoroaster, but also – and we would presume unintentionally – with the supposed licence of Ham. A child of the sons of Seth, Ham inherited and preserved their demonic magic, according to the early medieval Christian writer John Cassian. Cursed by Noah for uncovering his drunken nakedness, Ham becomes a magnet for unflattering stories of sexual debauchery. In his *Rule* St Benedict prescribed Cassian's *Collations* ensuring that a Benedictine monk like Trithemius would be only too familiar with such salacious tales. It would even seem logical to Trithemius that Faustus must be a sexual deviant.

To someone like Trithemius the mere fact that Faustus was a necromancer, a practitioner of forbidden arts, meant that he was morally debased. In his *Antipalus* Trithemius argued violently that witches were steeped in debauchery, revelling in 'exceedingly defiled sexual relations' with each other, their victims and with demons.[17]

As extreme as they seem to us now, Trithemius's views were not original or exceptional. The Apostle Paul (Romans 1:26–8) had early linked sexual deviance with religious unorthodoxy, a view that Giovanni Francesco Pico (*c.*1469–1533) later took up and specifically directed towards magicians. For Trithemius and many others of his age, necromancy meant trafficking with demons and trafficking with demons meant having sex with them. For a necromancer who was a schoolmaster it follows – according to Trithemius's logic – that his debauchery would have overflowed onto his pupils.

As a self-professed practitioner of the divinatory arts, Faustus would require, by tradition, the assistance of children, especially boys. Hartlieb's descriptions of both hydromancy and pyromancy makes the assistance of a child – a girl or a boy – an absolute necessity. 'When the innocent child sits there' says Hartlieb describing hydromancy, 'the charm master stands behind him and says various secret words to him in the ear', adding, with his usual alarm, 'and the evil Devil arises'.[18]

There is a documented case of a teacher using his pupils for just such an operation. John of Salisbury (1115–1180) recalled an incident from his youth in which a priest, who was teaching him Latin, co-opted him into the magical arts. In one experiment the priest anointed the fingernails of John and an older pupil with consecrated oil in an attempt to see images reflected in the glistening surface. In another, the priest used a polished basin as the reflective surface. The experiments would begin with 'preliminary magical rites' and, after anointing, the priest would call out strange names that, as John recalled, 'by the horror they inspired, seemed to me, child though I was, to belong to demons'. The terrified John saw nothing in either fingernails or basin, but the other pupil reported seeing 'certain misty figures'.[19]

Trithemius began the rumours of unnatural sexual practices that would dog Faustus ever after. Now in the spring of 1507 we must suppose him on the run. Even if the charges against him were the invention of Trithemius, the accusations that he repeats suggest some circulation of scurrilous rumours against Faustus in Kreuznach at this time – and if there were not, then after Trithemius's letter there would have been. Trithemius concluded his report to Virdung in no uncertain terms:

> These are the things that I know through very definite evidence concerning the man whose coming you await with such anticipation. When he comes to you, you will find, not a philosopher, but a fool driven by excessive rashness.[20]

Trithemius's testimony is in reality only hearsay. He never met Faustus and got all of his information about him second-hand, but this does not stop him from thoroughly denouncing him. Trithemius may have trusted his sources, but a court judge or critical historian could never do so, and yet this is the judgement that history has handed down. Most academics – epitomised by E.M. Butler, who wrote so much about Faustus in the middle of the twentieth century – have accepted Trithemius's views unquestioningly and repeated the libels against Faustus. At the very moment Faustus appears in recorded history he is given the worst sort of reputation and, as with the dog with the bad name, is hung ever after.

It is impossible for us to determine whether Trithemius's accusation was true or not. Perhaps that is not even the question we should be asking. When Trithemius's letter is taken on its own – as it so often is – the accusations made in it look exceptional, but they were not. Sexual defamation was (and, sadly, still is) a frequently employed weapon in character assassination and Faustus was not the only target. Just prior to Trithemius's letter, the Alsatian priest and Humanist, Jacob Wimpfeling (1450–1528), was anonymously libelled as lusting after his male students and Johann Geiler von Kaisersberg was preaching against *bübenketzer*, 'those "heretics" who commit sexual acts with boys'.[21]

Accusations of sodomy were particularly effective because they were difficult to disprove and punishable by severe penalties. The connotations of religious deviance also served Trithemius's purpose of ostracising Faustus, especially since the charge of sodomy could have arisen from magical practices in the first place. By repeating or inventing an apparently factual incident of sodomy, Trithemius makes his other denigrations based on the rhetoric of folly – but also straying onto pseudo-medical grounds with accusations of insanity – more persuasive. The purpose of Trithemius's letter was to besmirch Faustus's reputation before he visited Virdung, and Trithemius had career considerations of his own to motivate such an attack. Finally, we should not forget the old adage: 'When Peter talks about Paul, you learn more about Peter than about Paul'.

Harrowing Times
(1507–1512)

What happened to Faustus immediately after his fateful near-encounter with Trithemius? He probably little guessed the abbot's venomous reaction, after all, he had sent him his card and was probably somewhat perplexed that Trithemius had moved on without seeing him. According to Trithemius's report, Faustus had just lost his position in Kreuznach. If Trithemius was right about the situation, then Faustus would have been unlikely to linger long in the town. Trithemius's letter gives the vital clue that Faustus was expected by Johannes Virdung. The question then is, did Faustus visit Virdung?

At the Court of the Elector Palatine

The truth is that no one knows what Faustus did next, but it is likely that he did visit Virdung as intended. It would have been an important step: Virdung was a figure of some standing, a professor at Heidelberg university and court astrologer to Philipp von Wittelsbach (1448–1508), Elector of the Palatinate (1476–1508), and known by the virtuous nickname of 'The Upright'.

Virdung had travelled in France, Italy and Denmark, and studied at the universities of Kraków (BA, 1486) and Leipzig (MA, 1492). Virdung's student days in Kraków brought him into contact with astrology, and manuscripts preserved in the Vatican Library attest to the extent of his occult interests. In 1503 he had even travelled to England with the intention of studying magic there. He produced numerous works on astrology, as well as publishing annual astrological predictions (*practica*). His work was well-known and even admired by the likes of Melanchthon, for whom he had drawn up a nativity. In 1514 Virdung would be hailed as 'the only important astronomer in Germany'.[1] He would also be visited by the mysterious British nigromancer Nicholas of Fairmount in 1520, showing how far his reputation had spread. In 1522 his astrological works would be granted imperial protection against unauthorised reproduction in recognition of his prognostications made for the Emperors Maximilian I and Charles V.[2]

It is the association with von Sickingen that provides the bridge between Virdung and Faustus. We saw earlier how von Sickingen was known to make use of Virdung's astrological expertise. It seems possible that whilst in Kreuznach, Faustus had been directed towards Virdung by von Sickingen, or vice versa. Unlike Trithemius, von Sickingen appears to have taken Faustus seriously and no doubt expected that Virdung would do the same.

When Faustus sought him out, Virdung had been in Philipp's service since about 1493, so his position with one of the most important men of the period was well established. The House of Wittelsbach was a great power within the Empire. The Golden Bull of 1356 had created the Palatinate as one of the secular electorates, turning the Counts Palatine into the Electors Palatine with the hereditary offices of Archsteward of the Empire, Supreme Magistrate and Imperial Vicar. Count of the Palatine since the thirteenth century, Ruprecht III von Wittelsbach rose to become King of the Germans as Ruprecht I von der Pfalz from 1400 to 1410, and their line is anciently connected to the British royal family. But in 1507 Philipp was fifty-nine and only a year from his death. The best part of his greatness as well as his life was behind him.

Trithemius, running the risk of becoming one of those who 'noisily catch the attention of kings and princes' whom he said he so despised and again revealing himself in the insults he cast at others, had already written to Philipp with news of his tremendous schemes.[3] In 1499 Trithemius wrote that the only other person to have been let into the secret of his hidden writing technique or steganography was Philipp, 'whom I have shown the possibility of this craft with a clear demonstration'.[4] Trithemius had evidently tried to win Philipp's favour and indeed Philipp, together with his sons Ludwig and Rupert, had visited Trithemius at Sponheim in 1501. Trithemius had also visited Philipp in Heidelberg in 1506, apparently in connection with his move from Sponheim to St James's in Würzburg. The outcome of this meeting was entirely to Trithemius's advantage. Trithemius wrote that Philipp 'has promised to provide me with as much abundance as is necessary for my life.'[5] In light of this, the letter to Virdung against Faustus takes on ever more mercenary overtones: Trithemius was frightened of a rival.

Heidelberg University was intimately associated with the Wittelsbachers: Ruprecht I had founded it in 1386. As a university man and courtier Virdung moved in the highest circles. He had the ear of the Prince-Elector Palatine and access to the prodigious library of Heidelberg, the Bibliotheca Palatina. When the collection was stolen by the Catholic League during the Thirty Years War it amounted to almost 10,000 volumes, including a copy of Johannes Hartlieb's book on the forbidden arts. It was not just the size of the collection, but also the rarity of many of its holdings that attested to the importance of Heidelberg as one of the foremost centres of learning during the late Middle Ages and Renaissance. In particular, with the encouragement and support of successive Prince-Electors, Heidelberg also became a centre of alchemical study and experimentation by the mid-sixteenth century.[6]

Faustus and Virdung may have sat together in Heidelberg's great library, pouring over rare tomes and searching out the secrets of alchemy. Virdung had, amongst his own manuscripts, prescriptions for such things as imprisoning planetary spirits in finger rings. The method involved using exorcisms, seals, engraved gemstones and a metal appropriate to the character of the spirit to be trapped, as well as animal sacrifice. The manuscript also contained treatises on astrological and magical images. It seems likely that he showed this manuscript to another visitor, Nicholas of Fairmount, so it is again likely that, as one magus to another, he showed it to Faustus.

Some years previously in 1503 Virdung had published a *Practica* dedicated to Philipp in which he especially discussed the effects of the conjunction of Saturn, Jupiter and Mars in the sign of Cancer. It was a topic that Faustus would return to in his discussions with the Prior of Rebdorf some twenty years later. Virdung predicted the appearance of a prophet shortly after the conjunction, but also saw crop failure, pestilence and war in the stars. Virdung also discussed the meanings of comets and in 1506 he published a treatise on the comet of that year, which would have made a rich topic of conversation.

Perhaps Virdung even showed Trithemius's letter to Faustus. They may also have discussed an astrological prediction of Trithemius's ruin apparently made by Virdung or his predecessor around 1487, which was then being widely talked about by Trithemius's supporters such as Beissel, Sicamber, Herbanus and Kymolanus, and of course Trithemius himself. It would have been a subject dear to Faustus's heart. If Faustus made it to Heidelberg and Virdung's opinion of him had not been soured by Trithemius's vilifications, then we can expect that he enjoyed a most productive time here, at least until fate intervened in its usual unexpected and turbulent manner.

The Harrowing of Hell

In 1508, as Michelangelo began work on the Sistine Chapel in Rome, Maximilian I, King of the Romans – as he was until then titled – declared himself Imperator Electus ('Emperor Elect') in contravention of the usual requirement of being consecrated by the Pope. It was the result of military disaster and an act of forced compromise. Using his journey to Rome for the Imperial coronation as a pretext, Maximilian entered Venetian territory at the head of a large army in February 1508. Advancing on Vicenza, he was met by the Venetian army and repulsed. Several weeks later Maximilian tried again. This time he was decisively routed and forced to conclude a truce.

Prevented from reaching Rome, Pope Julius II had to issue a bull permitting Maximilian to confer the title upon himself. The adoption of this grand new title, triumphantly on his native soil, was hubris in the face of humiliation. The obstructiveness of the Venetians would not be overlooked. Calling von Sickingen and others to his banner he marched back into Italy. In addition to the support of his countrymen, Maximilian had persuaded the Pope, Ferdinand of Aragon, Louis XII of France and the Italian states of Ferrara and Mantua to join him in the so-called League of Cambrai, formed on 10 December 1508. There were great spoils to be won from the treasure chest of Italy – Louis XII's support had been secured with the promise of the investiture of Milan. Hell was about to be visited upon Venice: 'destructions and spoils of cities, a liberty of war', in the words of the Florentine historian Francesco Guicciardini (1483–1540).[7]

Italy was the Great Game of the sixteenth century. With more pressing foes on their borders and arguably easier and more strategic territories to conquer, the princes of Europe preferred to sport with each other for the trinkets and trophies of the peninsula. With hindsight it was an expensive and wasteful preoccupation, but there were real fears of growing Venetian power; any state that could say no to the Emperor was not to be taken lightly. As early as 1489 a diplomatic report had warned that Venice was out to subjugate all Europe. In 1499 the French ambassador, Philippe de Commynes, added his voice to the warnings, stating that Venice was 'on the road to future greatness'.[8]

It was not just the big battles that were shaking the foundations of Faustus's world. The Dominican inquisitor known as Bernard of Como (d. *c.*1510) published his comprehensive *Treatise on Witches* that would be reprinted many times in the following years. He described how the followers of this cult met in the presence of the Devil to renounce the Christian faith, specifically arguing against the idea that witchcraft is a delusion. In the cathedral of Strasbourg, Geiler von Kaisersberg was preaching against witches during Lent of 1508.[9] Like Bernard of Como, he too was convinced of the reality of the witches' sabbat. With the Bible as his authority, he demanded that all witches, sorcerers and diviners be put to death. Von Kaisersberg used the vernacular to convey his message – this was not just a Latin epistle for the learnéd, but a war cry for the masses.

Amongst all those calling for violent death, there were natural ones as well. Trithemius's supporter Conrad Celtis died in Vienna on 4 February 1508. As a Humanist himself, Faustus no doubt mourned the loss, but another death closer to home had a potentially more immediate impact on his life. On 28 February 1508, Philipp 'The Upright' died, passing on his titles and possessions to his thirty-year-old son and heir Ludwig V 'The Pacific' (1478–1544). Virdung's situation as court astrologer would immediately have been put into question, just as every courtier feared for their place during the transition from one lord to another. The knock-on effect would have complicated Faustus's own position, assuming he had visited Virdung and was still with him in Heidelberg.

If the immediate impact of Philipp's death had been to throw the court and those at its edges into turmoil, then later clues suggest that Virdung, at least, managed to retain his place. A book subsequently dedicated to Ludwig by Virdung in 1514 implies that he continued in his role and mention is made in his posthumously published work of 1542 that he served the Electors into the year 1538. Whether Faustus was still welcome, assuming that he ever was, we cannot say.

Great and Powerful Magic

According to the spurious tradition that grew up after Faustus, he was supposed to have just published a book at Paris entitled 'Doctor Faust's Great and Powerful Harrowing of Hell'. The same text was apparently published at Prague the following year, 1509, reputedly produced by a Jesuit College. The ambitious publisher of the 'Prague' text might also be credited with some remarkable ability in fortune-telling: the Society of Jesus (Jesuits) was not founded until 1534 and only officially recognised in 1540. Furthermore, the use of the name 'Faust' is not consistent with early-sixteenth century references to him as Faustus. This *Harrowing of Hell* probably dates from the seventeenth century.[10]

The principal object of the book is the conjuration of the spirit Aziel – there is no mention of Mephistopheles – to procure the prodigious, yet strangely precise sum of 299,000 ducats of gold. After warning that Aziel will attempt to secure the operator's soul by compact – unprecedented in the Faustian grimoire – the author unveils the procedure.

The conjuration is long and complicated, manifold permutations of holy names are voiced until the air vibrates with the sound of magic. Finally, Lucifer is threatened, especially with greater torments in the Bottomless Pit, unless he releases Aziel unto the magician. The magician is warned to command the spirit to appear in the shape of a boy of twelve, a presumably less threatening aspect than his usual form, but a guise likely to get any magician into trouble with the authorities, especially in Kreuznach. As the echoes of the magician's voice die, the spirit appears.

The magician is instructed to inform the spirit that his desire is the grace and glory of God before giving the command to deliver the required sum in gold with the additional caveat, carefully added by a suspicious mind, that the gold cannot be transformed into anything else. For such a large cash withdrawal from hell's coffers, the magician must expect Aziel to refuse his request unless something is given in return. The magician must stand firm, for it is now that the spirit will try and wrest his soul from him. He must turn to more magical threats and subdue the spirit. As soon as the gold materialises, Aziel must be ordered to return whence he came without any riot, vile stink or violence to the circle or those within it. Now in possession of his riches, the magician is exorted to charitably give away part of his ill-gotten gains to offset any righteous wrath and the implicit curse of conjured gold.

Whether or not Faustus actually wrote this book – and we are generally led to the conclusion that he did not – it was valued as if he had and for some time enjoyed a sulphurous vogue amongst later German magicians and would-be sorcerers. In the eighteenth century there are at least two recorded examples of its use. A diary published in 1708 by a Leipzig tradesman detailed the use of the *Harrowing* by one of his servants, known only as John George E. The other account appeared in 1716 and is an altogether sadder tale of greed and human folly. During a magical operation to find buried treasure near Jena, three people died in suspicious circumstances. Its dangerous reputation enhanced by such desperate tales, the *Harrowing* was still trading at a high value up until the end of the eighteenth century.

It is puzzling that there is no actual 'harrowing' in the *Harrowing* texts – the spirits are simply called and commanded in the usual manner. The idea of a 'harrowing of hell' derives from Christian mythology. Jesus was believed to have battled with and defeated the Devil immediately after his death in what is traditionally known as the Harrowing of Hell. This idea first appeared as *Descensus Christi ad Inferos* in *The Gospel of Nicodemus*, which is often thought to be a product of the third century (but more probably of the fourth) and a text of particular popularity in the Middle Ages. The Harrowing scene became an important part of the medieval mystery plays and so would have been a well-known reference, especially as Agrippa himself mentioned it in his *Occult Philosophy*.

Faustus's 'harrowing of hell' echoes his earlier documented claim to be able to reproduce the miracles of Jesus. There is also an additional concordance between reference in this myth to Jesus's raising of Lazarus and his triumph over death, and Faustus's own claims to be a great necromancer. Whilst this may provide a convincing derivation, there is little reason to suppose that these points of convergence make the document any more authentic, but they do bring it closer to the specific claims made by the historical Faustus. To harrow hell necessitates some familiarity with it. To be a necromancer would require that one should attempt to bring the occasional spirit out of it.

The Harrowing of Venice

After following the leads in Trithemius's letter we find that there are no clues to his whereabouts now. He was neither at Paris nor Prague overseeing the publication of his books because, despite their claims, they would not be published until long after his death. Had he been drawn into the ferment of war with his former patron Franz von Sickingen? Like any wise man, he may have stayed at home and let the mercenary *Landsknechte*[11] and princes swagger off to bloody the field of honour, but war was a source of wealth and fame. An adventurer like Faustus could have been drawn into it and later claims suggest that he was at some point. The interval between the historical references to him certainly coincides with the fighting in Italy at this time. Like Paracelsus he might have found a position as a surgeon, or, like Agrippa, enrolled as a soldier.

Flight of the Necromancer

How could Faustus have avoided the city? One of the precious jewels of Europe, a centre for trade and industry fought over by all the great powers, Venice was a legend even in the sixteenth century and like a magnet drew other legends, even legends about Faustus, into its sphere. In 1592 P.F. took great delight in describing the wonders of that city during Faustus's supposed world tour: the streets of water and the remarkably cheap supplies to be had, the 'fairness' of Saint Mark's Square and the wonders of the Basilica. For Faustus, who had named himself after Marcus Antonius Sabellicus, the man who had once been the prefect of the Library of San Marco in Venice, there were obvious reasons for wanting to visit the city. It was a Humanist pilgrimage. Conrad Celtis, for one, had undertaken it in 1486 when Sabellicus was still alive. Perhaps Faustus had not yet heard of his death, or went to pay his respects nevertheless.

Whilst the Faustbook has Faustus merely gawking at the tourist attractions, others believed that he was there for his own nefarious purposes. Luther's leading disciple, Melanchthon, had something to say about Faustus in Venice. There is no date given for the alleged event, but Melanchthon told the story during his commentaries on the Scriptures delivered between 1549 and 1560:

> There [in the presence of Nero] Simon Magus tried to fly to heaven, but Peter prayed that he might fall. I believe that the Apostles had great struggles although not all are recorded. Faustus also tried this at Venice. But he was sorely dashed to the ground.[12]

Quoting from Melanchthon's lectures in 1563, his former student Johannes Manlius recorded much the same, but significantly brought in the Devil as an explanation:

When he [Faustus] wished to provide a spectacle at Venice he said he would fly to heaven. So the Devil raised him up and then cast him down so that he was dashed to the ground and almost killed. However he did not die.[13]

Melanchthon's story was retold many times in the late sixteenth century. The earliest manuscript version of the Faustbook also took Faustus to Venice as part of his magical world tour, but made no mention of a disastrous flying attempt. When Marlowe visited the theme of Faustus he too made mention of the whirlwind tour that included Venice, but again was silent on the flying incident – showing the influence of his sources. That Melanchthon's story is absent from the Faustbook is remarkable. Either later tellers of the tale felt that Melanchthon was wrong, or, more likely, excised the incident because it did not find a natural place in the story of the pact-maker, nor could it, like some other incidents that stand outside the plot, be made to serve an anti-papist agenda. We cannot disregard the possibility that they were simply unaware of it.

It is not impossible that Faustus could have claimed to have flown in such a manner. There are enough examples to be drawn from the magical texts to show that flying was a commonly sought magical feat. Certainly, flying would be a recurrent theme in the legends of Faustus and we find him using a demonic horse, a cloak and a holly wand for such purposes. Leafing through the grimoires, an operation for flying can be found in the *Key of Solomon* and we read of the demon Gäap in *The Lemegeton*, who 'can carry and re-carry men very speedily from one Kingdom to another'.[14]

It seems that it was quite usual for necromancers to be thought to fly through the air. In their *Malleus Maleficarum* Kramer and Sprenger rhetorically asked 'what of those Magicians whom we generally call Necromancers, who are often carried through the air by devils for long distances?'[15] Kramer and Sprenger even claimed to have known such supernatural aviators.

They told the story of a former scholar turned priest in the diocese of Freising in Bavaria who made the claim that he had been conveyed through the air by a demon 'and taken to the most remote parts'. Another priest living in Oberdorf, near Landshut, also in Bavaria, – 'who was at that time a friend of that one of us, who saw with his own eyes such a transportation' – was transported or described as having seen a man transported through the air with arms outstretched and shouting, apparently out of sheer enjoyment.[16]

That garrulous old monk, Caesarius of Heisterbach (*c.* 1170–*c.* 1250), had his tale of demonic flight and such a story attaches itself to the name of 'Great John', Archbishop of Novgorod, who captured a demon in a bowl of water and compelled it to take the form of a horse and carry him to Jerusalem. Even Faustus's contemporary, the sainted Teresa of Ávila (1515–1582), claimed to have levitated, although no one said it had been a demon who held her up. But when Joseph Desa of Cupertino (1603–1663) – also to be made a saint – made wild claims about flying through the air, he was discretely removed to an isolated monastery.

The vexing question left unanswered by Melanchthon is why should Faustus travel all the way to Venice to conduct an ill-advised demonstration of magical aerobatics?

Melanchthon's information may have come from a meeting with Faustus himself, but we should not rule out the possibility that it was just some flight of fancy or at best a mere device. Melanchthon's purpose seems to have been to link the antique example of Simon Magus with a contemporary incident, something his students could more readily grasp, and also to surreptitiously compare the Reformers with the Apostles. He explains Simon Magus as a kind of 'Faustus' and links Faustus with the 'crimes' of Simon Magus and his 'just' punishment. He makes reference to unrecorded 'struggles' of the Apostles and then goes on to show that even in their own times the Christian mission, and hence the Reform movement, is challenged by magicians. Unlike the comparison with Simon Magus, the singularity of 'Venice' almost adds credence to the story because, quite simply, it cannot be made to serve any other purpose.

Where Simon Magus was engaged in a magical duel with Peter upon which the very future of Christianity rested, Faustus, in this story, was simply cavorting in the air for fun. Where Simon Magus's attempt took place before the Emperor Nero in Rome, Faustus apparently made his attempt for no one in particular in a completely different Italian city. Melanchthon's story is banal and, like the supposed flight of Faustus, it too falls down flat. If Faustus ever was in Venice and in light of some of his later claims to have been involved in the Italian wars, then Faustus may indeed have been marching south with the heavily armed *Landsknechte* to court the 'Queen of the Adriatic'.

As the winter snows retreated from the Alpine passes, the armies of the League of Cambrai – the Papal States, the Holy Roman Empire, France and Spain – began their advance on Venice. Venice had launched desperate diplomatic missions to try and placate the forces assembled against her and play on her enemies' old animosities, but her entreaties and subterfuges fell on deaf ears. The sound of money rattling in Venetian coffers was too loud. Louis XII and a 30,000 strong army marched out of Milan and entered Venetian territory on 15 April 1509. It took Maximilian until August before he could mobilise his army of 35,000 and it was not until mid-September that he reached the walls of Padua and a desperately outnumbered Venetian resistance.

Artillery bombardment opened the siege on 15 September 1509. For the next two weeks the League's combined cannon of some 100 to 200 pieces would pound the city and successfully breech the walls, but each time Maximilian I's soldiers attempted to press the advantage, they were beaten back by the determined defenders. At Padua the guns fired, by contemporary estimates, between 5,500 and 10,000 cannonballs at the city. Cannonballs and powder were expensive and by 30 September Maximilian had run out of funds. Unable to pay his *Landsknechte* he was forced to lift the siege. He left a token detachment in Italy under the Duke of Anhalt and withdrew, with his tail between his legs, to the Tyrol.

Meanwhile diplomatic negotiations with Pope Julius II had borne fruit. Expensive, humiliating fruit for Venice, but such a choice crop for Julius – who was also now beginning to eye the French with suspicion – that before the year was out he recalled his army and left the League. Julius was no stranger to the inducements of filthy lucre; after all, he had acquired his high office through bribery and even for such turbulent times was widely loathed for his reputed lustfulness, drunkenness, violent anger, deceitfulness and nepotism.

Folly and Philosophy

In the inns and taverns, and between strangers on the road that year, the talk must have been of news of the Italian wars. Wherever Faustus was he could not have avoided it. In Humanist circles the talk turned to different wars: the mounting tide of intolerance towards the Jews and those who appeared to support them, the scholars of Hebrew like Reuchlin.

Emperor Maximilian had proven himself a weak general, but his mind had been on other things. A letter had been sent to the court by a former butcher or moneylender called Johannes von Pfefferkorn demanding the confiscation and destruction of all Jewish books. Despite the complaints of the Archbishop of Mainz concerning his lack of learning and inexperience, Maximilian's devout sister, Kunigunde of Austria, took up his cause. Maximilian was swayed and authorised Pfefferkorn to confiscate all Jewish books that abused Christianity or infringed the law of the Old Testament.

Inspired by the stupidity he saw around him, Erasmus wrote his best-known work, *Moriae Encomium* ('The Praise of Folly'), that year.[17] It could have been written just for Maximilian. Kings and princes bear such heavy burdens, Erasmus observed, that if they truly thought about them they would not be able to sleep, but instead, with the goddess Folly's willing help, they sell titles and fritter away their lives on useless pursuits.

Pfefferkorn was not the only agitator on the domestic front. In 1510 the so-called Revolutionary of the Upper Rhine expressed many common grievances concerning current conditions in the widely distributed *Book of a Hundred Chapters*. The Revolutionary predicted that the 'Emperor of the Last Days', Friedrich I Barbarossa (1194–1250), would rise from his grave to reinstate the primitive German religion, transfer the capital of Christendom from Rome to Trier, end private property and remove all distinction between rich and poor. It was a sorry indictment of the times when Thomas Murner preached in Frankfurt in 1512 that if Jesus were to return this day he would be betrayed again and Judas congratulated on his profit.

As well as decrying the folly of princes, Erasmus also extended his considerable wit to tackling a problem that was always troubling the Renaissance mind, that of witchcraft. There can be no denying the popularity of *Moriae Encomium*, but the sophistication of his argument flew over the head of more than one reader whose eyes were more easily drawn to the sensationalist scare-mongering of other writers. Ulrich Tengler (1435/45–1511) was successfully alarming the reading public with graphic illustrations of the supernatural forces of evil ranged against them in *Layen-Spiegel* (1510) and *Der neu Layenspiegel* (1511). He denounced fortune-telling, magic and the black art, linking them, together with witchcraft, to heresy. A full-page wood-cut showed witches engaged in their various heretical pursuits. We see them riding on goats, cooking up a hail-storm out of a cauldron, stealing milk, conjuring demons with a magic circle and grimoire, and amorously entangled with demons.

Meanwhile, the Inquisitor of Cologne, Jacob van Hoogstraten (*c.*1460–1527), pub-lished his own treatment of the perils of sorcery and dedicated it to Philipp, Archbishop of Cologne. Even the likes of van Hoogstraten and all that clerical class were not themselves immune. In Basel the following year, Urs Graf (1485–1529) executed his *Crippled Devil* (1511) engraving showing a cowled monkish figure with rosary and crucifix, perhaps on some pilgrimage, being accosted by a leering demon hobbling on a wooden peg-leg. Many interpretations have been proffered of this slightly comic and entirely disturbing image, including strange initiation rites, but the engraving is most obviously an indictment of the clergy's especial vulnerability to satanism. It was a saying coined in the sixteenth century that wherever God built a church the Devil had a chapel.

It is in 1510 that we find Cornelius Agrippa von Nettesheim writing to Trithemius to thank him for his hospitality of the year before. He recalled with fondness their discussions on 'many things about alchemy, magic, Cabala, and the like.'[18] He dedicated his newly completed *Occult Philosophy* to his mentor – 'a man very industrious after secret things' – and sent him a copy for approval.[19]

Trithemius may have heartily approved of his young disciple's work, but things did not go according to plan. Before it was finished the work was 'intercepted' and 'did fly abroad in Italy, in France, in Germany through many men's hands.'[20] It is possible that a copy passed through Faustus's hands. He would certainly have been very interested in its contents. 'Magick' explained Agrippa, 'is a faculty of wonderful virtue, full of most high mysteries, containing the most profound Contemplation of most secret things.'[21] Agrippa dealt in detail with Faustus's special fields – the divinatory arts of geomancy, hydromancy, pyromancy and necromancy – and more besides.

Manuscript versions may have been circulated widely, but it would take another twenty or more years before Agrippa's *Occult Philosophy* was published. Yet even if Faustus never saw a copy, Agrippa drew upon stories, theories and practices in circulation during Faustus's lifetime and so reflected the state of knowledge of the occult at that time. There was really little new in Agrippa's occult philosophy, his only innovation was synthesis – something he did not deny – but that does not detract from the value of his work. Agrippa knew he had to tread carefully and his warning to all of those who were industrious after secret things is revealing. The ancient magicians were not Christians: 'we must very much take heed,' said Agrippa, 'lest we should permit their errors to war against the grounds of the Catholic Religion.'[22]

Whilst magicians like Agrippa, Trithemius and Faustus saw themselves as philosophers, the arts they performed were clearly seen as dangerous heresy – as witchcraft – by populist writers like Tengler and were attracting the unwelcome attentions of individuals like the Inquisitor van Hoogstraten. Agrippa's warning only serves to underline how the magicians' interest in the wisdom of the pagan past was always suspect to those who knew nothing of it.

In 1510, with war raging in the north, the Roman public were marvelling at Michelangelo's ceiling in the Sistine Chapel. Milan changed hands again and the Medicis were restored to power in Florence. A new anti-French league of Maximilian I and the Swiss, Ferdinand of Aragon, Henry VIII of England and Venice, was joined by the Papal States in 1511. While Henry VIII did little more than entertain his courtiers with an extravagant tournament at Westminster, the other members saw action at the Battle of Ravenna in 1512. The French under Gaston de Foix (1489–1512) won the day, but before the year was out they were forced to retreat from Italian soil.

There is a gap of six years in Faustus's record from 1507 to 1513, roughly the length of the Italian wars from 1508 to 1512. Fighting for the Emperor, in whatever capacity, could account for this lacuna and claims he is later reported to have made in 1525 and rumours that he was favoured by the lords of Anhalt[23] could support this conjecture, but we will never know for sure. Perhaps he acquired a copy of Agrippa's *Occult Philosophy* whilst in Italy, or back home on native soil – certainly he would come to be reminded of its warning.

The Hellbrand of Erfurt
(1513)

There were portents in the skies and such wonders in 1513. The widely famed scholar Girolamo Aleandro (1480–1542), a native of the war-torn Veneto, noted in his diary for September of that year the extraordinary luminosity of Jupiter. In Paris at the invitation of the French King Louis XII, he pointed out the planet to his students at the Collège de la Marche and together they observed that its brilliance was strong enough to cast a shadow. However, it was not just strange lights in the sky that illuminated Erfurt that year, but the fire of riot and the diabolical radiance of the 'Hellbrand' himself.

It was 25 September 1513 and the Canon of the Church of St Mary's at Gotha, Conrad Mutianus Rufus, was in an Erfurt inn when he overheard Faustus regaling the patrons with his stories. He wrote to his friend Heinrich Urbanus about it eight days later, still shaking with rage:

> There came to Erfurt a certain Chiromanticus Ephurdiam called Georgius Faustus Helmitheus Hedelbergensis, a mere braggart and fool. His claims, like those of all diviners, are idle and such physiognomy has no more weight than a water spider. The ignorant marvel at him. Let the theologians rise against him and try not to destroy the philosopher Reuchlin. I heard him babbling at an inn, but I did not reprove his boastfulness. What is the foolishness of other people to me?[1]

Faustus must have been entertaining the inn with a display of palmistry and face-reading, and was evidently enjoying some success in the town, for 'the ignorant marvel at him' – the ignorant being anyone not as clever as Mutianus thought he was. Mutianus sat there and said nothing. He felt guilty about it later, but sought shelter in intellectual arrogance. But just what did Faustus say? His 'babbling' is of much more interest to us now than Mutianus's high opinion of himself. By calling him a *Chiromanticus* Mutianus singled out that species of fortune-telling known as palmistry. But what is a *Chiromanticus Ephurdiam?* The term is usually translated as soothsayer, but we can immediately see that the word *Chiromanticus* is more precise than this. However, there is no trace of the mysterious *Ephurdiam* in the Latin grammars and dictionaries.

Mutianus led a studious life, being an alumnus of Ferrara and Bologna. He was ranked by some of the Humanists alongside Erasmus and Reuchlin despite the fact that he did not publish a single word in his lifetime. In his defence Mutianus bombastically declared that neither Socrates nor Jesus had published either. Urbanus had been his student and later friend, and through him developed an interest in Humanism. The extent of his devotion can be seen in the fact that all of the few poems and many letters of Mutianus survive mainly due to Urbanus. At the time Mutianus wrote to him about Faustus, he was serving as the steward of the Cistercian cloister of Georgenthal near Gotha.

Mutianus was also intimate with Trithemius – Mutianus had visited him in Sponheim in 1500 and Trithemius had twice stayed with Mutianus in Gotha. Mutianus praised Trithemius as 'another Hermes'.[2] This warns us that we cannot take his account of Faustus as anything other than prejudicial. Mutianus uses much the same language as Trithemius had done in 1507, employing that familiar rhetoric of folly in accusing Faustus of being 'a mere braggart and fool'. Trithemius and now Mutianus seem to have been engaged in an orchestrated campaign against Faustus.

The mind of Mutianus ran on narrow trammels. His vision was entirely bounded by the Church. He read widely – poets, philosophers and historians – but restricted himself to taking from them only what was compatible with the teachings of Rome. He believed that it was impious to want to know more than the Church.

However, he was indulgent towards the magical interests of others as long as they submitted themselves to the dogma of Holy Writ. Only a few weeks before he met Faustus, Mutianus had written to Trithemius recommending his friend Peter Eberbach, who was keen to learn the 'more honourable mysteries of the magicians with which Trithemius was very well acquainted'.[3] Faustus was evidently judged to represent the less honourable mysteries of the magicians.

It could be argued that because Mutianus was not trying to advance a magical career, his report is more objective than that of Trithemius and that the similarity of their judgements adds credibility to them. However, lack of ambition and the same righteous pontification cannot be taken as signs of reliability. If the bigoted Trithemius did not like someone, it is unlikely that the even more pious Mutianus should have shown any sympathy, especially given the friendship between the two.

The similarity of the picture drawn by both men, stripped of its venom, shows a wandering occultist, crying his wares in the marketplace, a man forced to seek a precarious living amongst the commonality, an esoteric entrepreneur, a completely opposite type to the well-fed clerics. For both Trithemius and Mutianus, who lived their lives within the cloister, philosophy was for the elite, for the chosen few like themselves, and not to be bandied about in front of *hoi polloi*. Recall his dismissive, patronising words – 'What is the foolishness of other people to me?' – and yet he found it necessary to alert Urbanus to this man. Faustus threatened their cosy world of privilege and preferment, and their hold upon the occult mysteries.

Mutianus was not content to merely disparage Faustus; he called for 'the theologians to rise against him'. We should not underestimate the theologian of the sixteenth century by comparison to the theologian of today. Van Hoogstraten could arraign wayward thinkers before the Inquisition and even an ignoramus like Pfefferkorn could stir up considerable animosity with his pamphlets, provoking the Emperor into unadvised action. Trithemius himself had Maximilian's ear on occasion. The theologians could imperil someone's life and Mutianus clearly had an agenda. He deployed Faustus as a counterpoint to Reuchlin in the wider debate of the period. He was using Faustus as a scapegoat.

There is the strong possibility that Faustus remained in Erfurt for some time, perhaps on and off for the next seven years at least until our next dated reference in 1520. Unperturbed by the libel of Mutianus – and we might suppose that Urbanus parroted his invective – Faustus may have found the town congenial, certainly the people seemed to have welcomed him. Paracelsus may have been in Erfurt around the same time, drawn by the reputations of the Humanists Crotus Rubeanus (*c.*1480–*c.*1539) and Helius Eobanus Hessus (1488–1540), known as 'deriders of God and men', and renowned for their hard drinking.[4] Faustus, too, may have been drawn by such reputations.

Both were former pupils of Mutianus, which may have coloured their view of Faustus. However, Rubeanus's friendship with Ulrich von Hutten – comrade-in-arms of von Sickingen – may have tempered any hostility. In 1520 Rubeanus had just been elected rector of Erfurt University and so was in a powerful position to influence Faustus's career in the city.

Hogel's legendary *Chronica* of the seventeenth century stated that Faustus arrived at the University of Erfurt, but introduced him with circumspection:

> It is also probably about this time that those strange things happened which are said to have taken place in Erfurt in the case of the notorious black magician and desperate hellbrand, Dr Faust.[5]

Erfurt was a natural destination for any wandering scholar. Lying midway between Gotha and Weimar, Erfurt is an antique settlement of obscure origins, first recorded in history when St Boniface made it a bishopric in 741. Mainz absorbed its ecclesiastical independence in 755, but Charlemagne thought the town sufficiently important to grant it market rights in 805. Under charters granted by Emperor Otto I, the archbishops of Mainz ruled the town with a burgrave and advocatus. The burgraviate eventually disappeared and the Counts von Gleichen appropriated the post of advocatus as their hereditary right. After further rulers, rights and charters, the town emerged as a virtual free city, joining the Hanseatic League at its height of importance in the fifteenth century. By force of arms or coin it had acquired lands and titles until it controlled a sizeable territory and income. With its growing wealth it produced one of the finest churches in Germany, the Beatae Mariae Virginis. The first university to embrace the four faculties was founded here in 1378. Erfurt was one of the foremost cities of the Empire: 'the city of towers' as Luther called it, or, more poetically, the 'Thuringian Rome' according to the historian Ernst Stida (1585–1632). However, incessant feuding with Mainz and ruinous war in Saxony reduced its fortunes and it became a shadow of its former glory.

When Faustus arrived the university was still a beacon of learning. Luther had been drawn here in 1501, studying for a Bachelor of Arts, as well as Ulrich von Hutten.

Luther lived in the Augustinian monastery and his cell was preserved up until the early nineteenth century when it was destroyed by fire.

According to the chronicler Hogel, Faustus took quarters near the 'large Collegium', which the German folklorist Johann Grässe supposed was on the street known as the *Michelsgasse*. Folk memory of his visit has remained, returned or been reinvented. In the first half of the twentieth century, W. Lorenz took a photograph of a street known as *Doctor Fausts Gässchen* ('Doctor Faust's Alleyway'). It shows a narrow cobbled alley running between two rows of houses, their gutters almost touching along the edges of their roofs. The story goes that Faustus drove along this, the narrowest street in Erfurt, with an impossibly wide load of hay, a feat the townspeople commemorated by naming the alley after him.[6]

Faustus secured for himself 'through his boasting' – had Hogel been reading Mutianus? – permission to give public lectures on Homer. He was apparently very effective, describing the heroes of the Trojan War in lifelike detail. The students who attended these lectures were eager for more: 'for there are always inquisitive fellows and there was no question as to what Faust was.' The story goes that he was consequently called upon to produce a marvel 'through his art' and conjure the heroes to materialise and 'show themselves as he had just described them.'[7]

Faustus agreed and a great throng turned out to witness the spectacle. The necromancer conjured the ancient Greek heroes to appear in the lecture hall where each 'shook his head as though he were still in action on the field before Troy.'[8] Whether he hired actors, made use of something like a magic lantern or indeed called forth those antique shades from Hades – as Hogel seemed to believe – the effect must have been electrifying for the audience.

Faustus had more than heroes up the long sleeves of his magician's robe: 'The last of them all was the giant Polyphemus, who had only a single terrible big eye in the middle of his forehead.' It was the Cyclops who had given Odysseus such trouble on his journey home from the Trojan War who now stood before the students of Erfurt. 'He wore a fiery red beard and was devouring a man, one of whose legs was dangling out of his mouth.' The auditorium must have felt suddenly too small for comfort. The eager students in the first row now looked like becoming the monster's next meal.

> The sight of him scared them so that their hair stood on end and when Dr Faust motioned him to go out, he acted as though he did not understand but wanted to grasp a couple of them, too, with his teeth. And he hammered on the floor with his great iron spear so that the whole Collegium shook, and then he went away.[9]

It was a tremendous show, but there was more to come. According to Hogel, Faustus was invited to attend the banquet given for the commencement of masters at the university. He sat with delegates from the town council and members of the faculty of theology – who presumably did not rise against him as Mutianus would have them do. The subject of the comedies of the ancient poets Plautus and Terence was raised, and heads shook sadly at the thought of those works lost forever. If only they had them once more, what good they would do for the curriculum and the learning of

Latin. Here Faustus astonished the gathering by reciting, not one, but several quotations from those vanished masterpieces:

> And he offered, if it would not be held against him, and if the theologians had no objections, to bring to light again all the lost comedies and to put them at their disposal for several hours, during which time they would have to be copied quickly by a goodly number of students or clerks, if they wanted to have them.[10]

Faustus phrased his offer carefully, adding the caveat 'if it would not be held against him', with full knowledge that the theologians might scotch his proposal. He was right to anticipate their timidity at such a daring offer. It was not just the theologians but the councillors too, who rejected it, fearing that 'the Devil might interpolate all sorts of offensive things into such newly found comedies.'[11] It was the universal suspicion of the age: anything that was not strictly in accordance with dogma might be some stratagem of Satan. Consequently, suspicion must fall on anyone who opened themselves to such potential diabolical pollution. The theologians retraced their steps: one could learn good enough Latin from those works that survived, why tempt Temptation itself?

Entertaining the 'Anchor House'

Hogel tells us that Faustus was in the habit of spending much time at the 'Anchor House' (*Zum Encker*) of the 'Junker N.', entertaining his host and the other guests with tales of his adventures. Why was Hogel suddenly so coy in naming this squire 'N.'? We will never know if he was protecting some local lordling, hiding from his disapproval, or simply mystifying an invented character. Hogel's *Zum Encker* on the *Schlöszergaszen* matches the description for the *Haus zum Enker* on the *Schlösserstrasse* in Erfurt. The *Haus zum Enker* was owned by one Wolf von Denstedt. In 1513 he had just married Catharina von der Sachsen. If the story has any historical basis, then Junker N. must have been this Wolf von Denstedt. The *Haus zum Enker* was also frequented by none other than that Humanist hell raiser Hessus and his cronies.

Hessus was somewhat Faustian himself. He would distinguish himself as a Latin poet, but not before he became known for less commendable behaviour. He had entered the University of Erfurt in 1504 and soon after his graduation was appointed the rector of the school of St Severus. However, like Faustus in Kreuznach, he was unable to keep this post for long. Under the cloud of some unknown impropriety, Hessus left Erfurt to take up a position at the court of the Bishop of Riesenburg from 1509–1513. In 1513 he returned to Erfurt. However, through heavy drinking and consequently irregular habits, Hessus was reducing himself to a state of ruin. He would later secure the post of Professor of Latin at Erfurt University (in 1517) and associated with many of the prominent Humanists of the time such as Reuchlin, Ulrich von Hutten and Joachim Camerarius.

According to the legend, Faustus seems to have treated the *Zum Encker*, or some other property on the 'Schössergasse' – Grässe, who tells the tale, does not specify – somewhat familiarly: 'A house in Schössergasse is still said to have a gap in the roof that can never be closed with tiles because Faust used to fly out of it on his magic cloak.' Either here or at the Michelsgasse house he was credited with having created 'a magnificent garden in mid-winter' from which he 'provided numerous delicious meals for numerous noble guests.'[12] The story of the winter garden found its way into the Faustbook, although transposed to Wittenberg in the nineteenth year of his pact. Other legends place it, or a similar event, in the county of Anhalt and Boxberg castle in modern Baden-Württemberg.[13]

Again there are precedents. Trithemius told the story of a Jew called Zedechias, a physician in the reign of Ludwig the German, who in the year 876 created a beautiful garden complete with grass, flowers, trees and singing birds, and all in the depths of winter. That we find this story being re-told by Trithemius is significant because it shows that the tale was, to a degree, current in the sixteenth century. That the story subsequently became associated with Faustus is therefore not surprising. Yet we should not overlook the possibility, far-fetched though it seems, that this was no mere tale.

What seemed like a miracle in the sixteenth century is commonplace in the twenty-first. However, the science behind such miracles, although not understood, was known. The principle of refrigeration had been known since at least 1000 BCE in China. Alexander the Great served his soldiers snow-chilled drinks in 300 BCE and Khalif Mahdi used ice to refrigerate his supplies *en route* to Mecca in 755 CE. An alchemist like Faustus would also surely have been aware of the fact, known since the fourteenth century, that dissolving sodium nitrate in water lowers the water's temperature. Not quite as ancient, greenhousing was known to the Romans who used the naturally occurring and translucent mineral mica in place of glass to cover heated earth pits at least as early as 30 CE. Alchemy and a classical education could have brought Faustus into contact with the technology to produce the marvels attributed to him.

Hogel relates that sometime during his Erfurt period, Faustus visited Prague. His cronies, Junker N., possibly Hessus and others, gathered at the *Zum Encker* as was their wont, but missed the entertaining company of Faustus. Consequently, 'one of the guests jokingly called Faust by name and begged him not to desert them.' The joke would be short-lived: 'At that instant someone in the street knocks at the door.'[14]

Faustus was standing outside, holding the reins of his horse. 'Don't you know me?' he said to the servant who answered his knock, 'I am he whom they have just called.'[15] The servant ran back to report. Junker N. refused to believe it, restating before the assembly that Faustus was in Prague – it was simply impossible that he could now be at their door. However, disbelief is no safeguard against the unbelievable. Hessus was no doubt looking into the bottom of his beerstein and wondering whether this was some sort of delirium.

Faustus, left standing at the door, knocked again. Junker N. and his servant peered out of the window, still not believing that he was there, before opening the door and giving him a hearty welcome. Junker N.'s son took the reins of the horse in some wonder, promising to feed it well, and led it to the stables. Junker N. himself lost no time in demanding of Faustus how he managed to return with such unearthly speed.

'That's what my horse is for,' says Dr Faust. 'Because the guests desired me so much and called me, I wanted to oblige them and to appear, although I have to be back in Prague before morning.'[16]

Satisfied and flattered by the reply, 'they drink to his health in copious draughts.' Faustus, not content with the local beverage, enquired whether anyone would like to try a foreign wine and it was not just Hessus who said yes. Faustus, ever obliging, asked whether they would prefer Spanish, French, 'Rheinfal' (the Istrian wine highly sought after in Germany in the Middle Ages), or Malmsey wine from Greece. Someone – was it Hessus? – called out 'They are all good.' Faustus sent for an augur and used it to make four holes in the table, which he then closed with plugs. He brought fresh glasses and tapped from the table each of the four different wines and 'continues drinking merrily with them.'[17]

Junker N.'s son came running back into the room in a fluster, crying 'Doctor, your horse eats as though he were mad; he has already devoured several bushels of oats and continually stands and looks for more.' Faustus was nonplussed: 'Have done ... he has had enough; he would eat all the feed in your loft before he was full.' He returned to 'drinking merrily' until midnight. At the witching hour the horse uttered a piercing neigh that stopped the drinkers in mid-quaff. 'I must go' said Faustus, but delayed to finish his glass. The horse neighed again, but Faustus was difficult to drag away from company. The horse neighed a third time and now Faustus took his leave. His friends saw him outside, their bellies full of wine and happily staggering, where he mounted his steed and rode up the Schlössergasse, 'but the horse in plain sight rises quickly into the air and takes him back through the air to Prague.'[18]

Grässe had also heard that 'he once came riding a horse that ate and ate and could never be satisfied.'[19] Writing in 1569, Ludwig Lavater (1527–1586) recalled that

to this very day there are black magicians who boast that they can saddle a horse on which they can in short time make great journeys. The Devil will pay for course and steed, and money for shoeing and saddle. What wonders is the notorious sorcerer Faustus said to have done in our own times?[20]

The story is a classic necromantic wonder. The author of an anonymous manuscript of the fifteenth century now in Oxford's Bodleian Library (Rawlinson MS D 252) tells such a tale of summoning a demon in the form of a horse to transport him at great speed over vast distances. Codex 849 has four operations for 'obtaining a horse' and Hartlieb too had stories of magical horses obtained with bat's blood and pacts with the Devil. In *The Lemegeton* we read of demonic spirits like the horse-fetching Shax and of the horse-shaped Orobas. In the *Malleus Maleficarum* Kramer and Sprenger also mentioned the use of a horse 'which is not really a horse but a devil in that form', adding that 'one of us has very often seen and known such men' who performed such magic.[21] Then there are all those more general operations for flying we encountered earlier in connection with Faustus in Venice.

Kramer and Sprenger's Landshut flying story, examined earlier, and that of Faustus in Erfurt share the same context of beer-drinking scholars, suggesting that the story was a not unknown tale. It conveyed elements of the popular distrust of scholarship and the hint of ridicule implied in connection with drinking itself, as well as disapproval of both as leading to the Devil. Even if the story appears to be another typical yarn, Faustus was not unknown in the town to which he supposedly travelled.

Prague, with its *Zlatá ulička* ('Golden Lane') named after the alchemists who toiled there, was an obvious destination for Faustus. Local tradition names a building on *Karlovo náměstí* in the New Town after our magician. This *Faustův Dům* ('Faust House') is said to have been built in the fourteenth century and lived in by a succession of occultists, such as Prince Václav of Opava, John Dee's collaborator Edward Kelley and Count Ferdinand Mladota in the eighteenth century. According to this same tradition, Faustus had a brother in the Jesuit seminary at the Klementinum in the Old Town, whom he would occasionally visit secretly at night because visitors were forbidden. Faustus was said to have been so impressed by the observatory in the Klementinum that he knocked a hole in his own roof so that he could install a telescope. Rumour has it that this hole was also the one used by the Devil to haul the unfortunate necromancer off to hell. Understandably, the new owners were keen to close the opening. Repair work done in the daylight hours was found undone the next morning with the attic reeking of smoke and sulphur. The story reads like a more embellished version of that related by Grässe of his house in Erfurt. The ghost of Faustus was said to remain in the *Faustův Dům*, haunting the halls and corridors in the midnight hours. Few owners kept the property for long. Rather fittingly the building is today used as a pharmacy.[22]

The Magical Banquet

Faustus returned from Prague some weeks later, loaded down with the expensive gifts he had received for his services – at least according to the legend. To celebrate his return he invited his friends to be his guests at St Michael's – the university's church and apparently also available as a banqueting hall. Von Denstedt, Hessus (one presumes) and the rest of the gang duly turned up, but found the church empty and no signs of preparation in progress. They no doubt shuffled somewhat ill at ease, stomachs rumbling and throats dry, but Faustus was unperturbed. He picked up his knife and knocked on the table with the hilt. A servant entered and enquired what Faustus wished. Before ordering, Faustus asked 'How quick are you?'. The servant replied that he was as quick as an arrow. Faustus shook his head, 'No … you shall not serve me.' He sent him back and knocked again on the table. Another servant appeared. Faustus repeated his question. 'As the wind' replied the servant. 'That is something' mused Faustus, but again sent the servant back. He knocked on the table a third time and a third servant entered. Faustus posed the question to him again and the servant answered that he was as fast as thought. 'Good … you'll do' said Faustus and gave his instructions, bidding his guests to wash their hands and sit down. As soon as they did so the third servant and two assistants entered bearing covered dishes: 'Thirty six courses or dishes were served … with game, fowl, vegetables, meat pies and other meat, not to mention the fruit, confections, cakes, etc.'[23]

Of course, no Faustian gathering would be complete without strong drink, but 'all the beakers, glasses and mugs were put on the table empty', no doubt to the consternation of Hessus. Faustus was not such a poor host as to let his guests go without and so he asked what beer or wine each would like to drink. Going one better than his earlier wine-producing magic, he 'put the cups outside of the window and soon took them back again, full of just that fresh drink that each wanted to have.' There was music, too, played by one of the mysterious servants: 'so charming that his guests had never heard the like.' Thus beguiled the party 'made merry until broad daylight.'[24]

Faustus's miracle of turning a wooden table into a wine bar and feeding a dinner party with enough for (almost) 5,000, recalls to mind those claims he made in Würzburg about bettering Jesus, but these feats also have their precedents in the magical manuscripts. The *Sword of Moses* – believed to date from the third or fourth centuries CE – had its spell for appeasing the appetites of famished wizards. Codex 849 also had a spell for producing a magical banquet and one guaranteed to satisfy the most exquisite of tastes. The author or compiler of Codex 849 added his personal warranty when he reminded his reader 'you have often seen me exercise at your court the art of summoning banquet-bearers'.[25] It is an involved operation requiring the conjuration of no less than sixteen spirits.

In contrast to Codex 849, Faustus reputedly brings forth his wine without any magical flimflam, but only a little simple carpentry, or, as in the last example, no apparent preparation at all. However, as the compiler of Codex 849 explains, once the complex operation has been performed, the spirits are primed and ready to be called forth again and more swiftly at a future date with only a brief invocation recited under one's breath. As Faustus knocked holes in the table, did his drinking companions miss the movement of his lips and the whisper of secret formulae?

Similar stories of magical banquets were already in circulation. Plutarch (*c.*46–*c.*120), who enjoyed a particular vogue during the Renaissance, retold a story connected with the legendary Roman King Numa Pompilius. Numa invited a large number of citizens to a feast, but one can imagine their disappointment when the Roman King served up a peasant's banquet. As the long-faced guests sat down, Numa announced to them that the Goddess Egeria had arrived, whereupon all the mean fair and tableware was transformed into the most luxurious and costly. Michael Scot (*c.*1175–1234) was believed to have feasted his guests with dishes spirited from the royal kitchens of France and Spain. In 1526 Agrippa wrote down the tale of a certain Pasetes who could make sumptuous feasts appear and, just when the audience was salivating, disappear again. It was a popular story, retold by Francesco Guazzo and Robert Burton in the early seventeenth century.

The particular idea of holding the wine cup out of the window and bringing it back in full is of a similar type to stories told about other magicians. Albertus Magnus was once said to have procured a plate of oysters for a prince in 1248 by simply knocking at the window. In the *Zimmerische Chronik* Ludwig von Liechtenberg performed a similar feat, magically pilfering a plate from the French king's table. Rabbi Adam was said to have used similar means to banquet Emperor Maximilian II (1564–1576) in Prague. The similarities here do not necessarily indicate direct borrowings, for as we have seen, the tradition of magic is not just a literary tradition.

Magical assistants are an old idea. Some of the earliest examples are found among the Greek magical papyri of the second to fifth centuries CE. The three-fold testing of magical assistants and the idea of acting as fast as thought later transferred itself to the quintessential Faustian familiar, Mephistopheles, in the Faustbook. The specific testing of familiar spirits to find the fastest also occurs in the *Black Raven* fancifully supposed to have been published in Lyon in 1469.

Faustus royally entertained his friends at the Anchor House in Erfurt, but he was not above playing meaner pranks on them. One story has Faustus bewitching a group of inebriated drinkers so that they 'think that they saw grapes, which they would attempt to cut from the vine, but when he [Faustus] put a stop to their hallucinations, each one had someone else's nose between his fingers instead of grapes.'[26] According to legend, he would later repeat the trick at Boxberg castle.

When Philipp Camerarius (1537–1624) re-told the story in 1591 he embellished it and added a sanctimonious conclusion, but the details were the same. There is an element of 'once upon a time' that alerts us to the fairytale quality of this yarn and a censure against drinking creeps into it. Camerarius was keen, perhaps too keen, to re-interpret what might otherwise be seen as an amusing tale as an instance of a great Satanic stratagem.

The month of December was almost out and Faustus's 'friends' wanted to test his powers by demanding something that they thought impossible: 'a full grown vine with ripe grapes.' Faustus agreed, but commanded them to be silent and sit still until he gives the order to cut the grapes:

> By his tricks he so befuddled the eyes and senses of this drunken crowd that there appeared to them on a beautiful vine as many bunches of grapes of marvellous size and plumpness as there were people present.[27]

His friends pulled out their knives, eager to cut off the juicy fruit, but, obedient to the magician, awaited his command. Faustus held them in suspense:

> Suddenly the vine with its grapes disappeared in smoke and they were seen, each holding, not the grapes which each thought he had seized, but his own nose with his knife suspended over it.[28]

As Camerarius told it, the story was another of those dealing with out of season produce with a macabre twist. The magical feat itself involves no mention of Satanic forces, but Camerarius contrived to make it another example of the Devil's work. Drunkenness comes into the story too, giving the tale another layer of moral condemnation. Camerarius ended on a stern note.

> And it would have served them right and they would have deserved other mutilations, since, with intolerable curiosity, they occupied themselves as spectators and participants in the illusions of the Devil, which no Christian may be interested in without great danger or rather sin.[29]

Camerarius was a hard man, but no different from many another of his time, happily wishing disfigurement on people who transgress the Church's rules. Here it was curiosity that Camerarius singled out for reproach. Despite his repeated characterisation of the story as ridiculous and an illusion of the Devil, Camerarius appeared to have believed it, as well he might. Any stage hypnotist today could produce the same effects and do we understand hypnotism any more than Camerarius did Faustus's magic?

Accursed Child of the Devil

The legends that grew up around Faustus in Erfurt thus find echoes in much older magical material, but, asked Hogel in his *Chronica*, 'what was to be the outcome?' News of his magical banquets, flying horse, wonderful winter garden and the rest – 'the man played so many tricks' – quickly spread, everyone was talking about him, and 'many of the nobility of the country came to Erfurt to him.' It was inevitable that 'people began to worry lest the Devil might lead the tender youth and other simpletons astray', as Hogel put it, by following Faustus's example and dabbling in the black art.[30]

It did not take them long to decide that another monk was required. Hogel's inter-polation of this event shows its late composition. He wrote that because the Junker of the *Zum Encker* – again not actually naming him – was a 'Papist', a monk was sent for, although if Faustus was in Erfurt in 1513 we are still four years away from Luther's nailing of those famous theses to the door of the castle-chapel in Wittenberg that her-alded the Reformation that followed.[31] Everyone in 1513 was nominally still a 'Papist', Anabaptists and the like aside.

This monk, charged with the task of tearing Faustus away from the Devil, was, according to Hogel, 'Dr Klinge', a Franciscan described as 'neighbouring'.[32] Konrad Klinge held a doctorate in theology and is believed to have been Erfurt cathedral's preacher from 1520 to 1556, again suggesting that the events about to unfold happened, if they did happen, some years after Faustus's first documented arrival in Erfurt in 1513. We should not overlook the possibility that Klinge may have been in Erfurt some time before his appointment. Frustratingly we cannot be sure, but the important matter is that we do have evidence that there was a Dr Klinge and that he was in Erfurt. There are also traces in other texts that could support this story. He might have been the unnamed pious old man mentioned by Lercheimer and could have been the origin of the similar figure who turns up in the Faustbook. Against the possibility of this event having taken place we have to consider the use of the name 'Faust' rather than 'Faustus' and the reference to the pact, although Hogel may have changed the original Reichmann–Wambach manuscript to accommodate seventeenth century ideas.

Once summoned, Dr Klinge duly turned up at the *Zum Encker* and spoke to Faustus 'at first kindly, then sternly'. He told him of 'God's wrath and the eternal damnation that must follow on such doings.' Klinge added that as Faustus was well-educated he could support himself by less ungodly and more honourable means. He should 'stop such frivolity, to which he had perhaps been persuaded by the Devil in his youth, and should beg God for forgiveness of his sins.'[33] Faustus must have been less than overjoyed to be doorstepped by this Bible-thumper, but his reply is recorded as being most civil. Faustus politely pointed out that he had signed an irrevocable contract with the Devil.

We will discuss the question of the pact presently; meanwhile Dr Klinge was not to be put off. Was he rubbing his hands together, thinking of the indulgences he might sell Faustus and of masses sold for the safety of his soul? 'We will hold mass for you in our cloister' he promised, 'so that you will without a doubt get rid of the Devil.' Faustus was not impressed. 'Mass here, mass there' he said, adding 'my pledge binds me too absolutely.' He had abandoned God and bound himself by word and blood to the

Devil, adding sincerely 'The Devil has honestly kept the promise that he made to me, therefore I will honestly keep the pledge that I made and contracted with him.'[34]

What little patience Klinge may have had now ran out. 'Well,' said the monk, 'then follow your path, you accursed child of the Devil, if you will not be helped and will not have it otherwise.'[35]

Furious at his defeat, Klinge went stomping off to a higher authority – 'his Magnificence, the Rector' and complained about the obduracy of Faustus. He also told the city council – indeed, he must have gone about telling anyone who would listen – what a fiend incarnate Faustus was and how he should be sorely punished for it. The council was moved to take action. Faustus was driven out of town: 'So Erfurt got rid of the wicked man.'[36] Faustus might be counted lucky. Luther later recalled the story of a black magician of Erfurt who was burned to death for his 'crimes' not long after.

Klinge was not to enjoy his victory for long. According to Hogel 'the Lord God afflicted Dr Klinge, so that he despaired of his life.'[37] Was it God or Faustus? Such a 'child of the Devil', ejected from his home and driven out of the city, could hardly be expected to have only turned the other cheek, would he have not summoned a legion of demons to torment the meddling monk? Klinge may have thought so, but his time had not come. He recovered to write *Catechismus Catholicus* in reply to rumours that he had become a Lutheran, referring to the fact that he had preached in Erfurt for thirty-six years, from 1520 until his death. Klinge's end came just before Easter in 1556. He preached at the church of Our Lady in Erfurt on the fourth Sunday before Easter, called Oculi, and on Tuesday he was dead. He was buried in the church's graveyard, opposite the chancel, and according to Hogel his epitaph could still be seen in the seventeenth century.

Mutianus's first-hand witness statement supports Hogel's *Chronica*, which in conjunction with the strong local tradition gives us several reasons, of differing levels of reliability, to believe that Faustus was in Erfurt. The invocation of Greek heroes is in line with his earlier pronouncements on his superior grasp of Plato and Aristotle, as reported by Trithemius. Hogel's semi-legendary story thus finds a supporting echo in Trithemius's contemporary letter. The attempted intervention of Dr Klinge reveals later accretions to the story – the reference to Papists and the pact – either suggesting a later date of the encounter with Klinge, or indicating a purely spurious addition to the legend. That this Dr Klinge was a real person adds some small weight to the balance of probability in favour of this remarkable encounter having taken place.

Dr Klinge was not alone in his concerns – in December 1513 Pope Leo X warned that the Devil was abroad, spreading 'extremely pernicious errors'.[38] There were blasphemers everywhere, taking every sort of holy name in vain and a whole series of socially stratified punishments was laid down for them. But there was worse than blasphemy, there was 'sorcery, by means of enchantments, divinations, superstitions and the invoking of demons' and 'Judaising'.[39] Harsh penalties were set to deter malefactors. These concerns had earlier taken concrete form in one of the most scandalous cases of the early sixteenth century: the trial of the great Humanist Johannes Reuchlin by the Inquisition.

Reuchlin was one of the foremost scholars of his day. He had studied at the universities of Freiburg, Paris, Basel and Tübingen, and pioneered research into Hebrew and the cabbala. Reuchlin knew that this line of enquiry was a controversial, not to say dangerous one. He would have been aware that Pico della Mirandola's cabbalistic studies had landed him in trouble with the Inquisition.

Despite that, he spoke unguardedly in his report to the Emperor on the confiscation of Jewish books instigated by Pfefferkorn. The theological faculty at Cologne examined the report and condemned it as Judaising and heretical. A protracted legal battle with the Inquisitor General, Jacob van Hoogstraten, ensued. The Humanists rallied round, with Ulrich von Hutten and Crotus Rubeanus anonymously publishing the hugely successful *Letters of Obscure Men*, ridiculing Reuchlin's enemies. Eventually the Pope suspended proceedings. Technically neither side won, but it was widely seen as a moral victory for Reuchlin. It looked like the Church was losing its iron grip, which has led many to see in Reuchlin's case a spearheading of what would become known as the Reformation.

Rome's equivocal judgement and van Hoogstraten's continued aggression led Ulrich von Hutten to bring in von Sickingen to settle the case once and for all. With his usual bravado, von Sickingen threatened the Dominican Order – the organisation that was responsible for running the Inquisition – with violence unless they could force van Hoogstraten to abandon his persecution of Reuchlin. Reluctantly drawn to the negotiating table the Dominicans signed an agreement with von Sickingen. Van Hoogstraten was deprived of his high offices and the case was duly re-opened.

Sensing a growing tide of revolt, the Pope came down hard on Reuchlin in 1520. He overturned a previous court decision in his favour, ordered Reuchlin to pay a fine, condemned his report and reinstated van Hoogstraten. It is not known whether the judgement was ever enforced, but the protracted affair had used up Reuchlin and he died two years later.

European Jews were a pariah caste and association with them brought with it the same dangerous taint, and yet their possession of the cabbala was an irresistible magnet for magical explorers. Through Pico della Mirandola, Reuchlin and Agrippa, the cabbala attained a central place in Christian occult theory. As such we must suppose that Faustus concerned himself with the subject despite the lack of any documentary evidence to this effect. The name of cabbala would certainly become attached to that of Faustus. An eighteenth-century grimoire masquerading as having been published at Passau in 1505 contains a section on his supposed 'black cabbala'.

The key role played by Faustus's old patron von Sickingen forms another link, albeit a tenuous one. Did von Sickingen seek Faustus's astrological advice or ask him to magically influence the outcome of his negotiations with the Dominicans? Mutianus added another connection when he called upon the theologians to abandon their case against Reuchlin and persecute Faustus. Given the controversy stirred up by the whole issue, Faustus could not have been unaware of it and given his sympathies, we can be sure that he was of Reuchlin's party, even if that party was not for him. He would have seen the Humanism that he professed brought before the Inquisition and he would have seen Hebrew studies, including the cabbala, denounced as heretical. All this would have weighed on his mind the next time he pronounced cabbalistic formulae in his magic circle.

Meeting Mephistopheles
(1514)

Now at last the demonic spirit so central to the tale, so bound up with Faustus, appears, but why so late? There are no contemporary or even near-contemporary references to Mephistopheles in the historical sources. If the real Faustus did invoke him, then he did so quietly and without apparent publicity. The name of this spirit is recorded for the first time around 1580 and the only date we have to go by comes from an unreliable source – Carolus Battus's 1592 Dutch edition of Spies's 1587 *Historia* – but as it is the only source let us entertain it, if only as a chronological fancy.

The Klinge story represented in an even later source – that of Hogel in the seventeenth century – suggested that Faustus signed the pact between 1513 and 1520. According to Battus, Faustus signed it in 1514. The legend tells us that when he signs the pact, Mephistopheles appears to him for the first time, therefore, if there ever was a Mephistopheles, then he too would have appeared in 1514. Of course, it will be argued that he never did.

It would have been a good year for such a devilish spirit to make his first visit to the mortal world. Mysterious signs in the skies over Württemberg had been seen: three moons appeared in the night sky with the middle and largest one bearing the sign of the cross. Virdung had noticed them and wrote a tract on their meaning, publishing it quickly that same year, predicting that the commoners would be industriously conspiring against the nobles. Ulrich von Württemberg's (1487–1550) extortionate taxation to support his extravagant court helped fulfil the prophecy. With good cause the commoners did conspire and in 1514 took up arms in the so-called 'Poor Conrad' uprising. Ulrich was caught out, but after some manoeuvring held the rebels to the Treaty of Tübingen, burdening them with almost a million ducats of the profligate Duke's debts in return for some small checks on his power that were never realised. Ulrich's calls to his noble neighbours for reinforcements were heard and he unleashed a vengeful and murderous army upon his disbanded and unsuspecting subjects.

Virdung was particularly mindful that the French king, Louis XII (r. 1498–1515), should be on his guard against the events of 1314 repeating themselves. In 1314 the ill-fated Louis X succeeded to the throne to find the treasury empty and the lesser nobles close to revolt; after a short reign he died of suspected poisoning. Louis XII died on 1 January 1515. His contemporaries attributed the cause not to poison, but to the beauty and vigour of his young bride, Mary of England. One thing Virdung did not expect of the moons was the manifestation of Mephistopheles.

The Invocation

> Being expert in using his Vocabula, Figures, Characters, Conjurations, and other Ceremonial actions, that in all the haste he put in practise to bring the Devil before him.[1]

With wand and grimoire tucked under his arm, the dauntless Faustus of legend sets off into the woodland around Wittenberg. He heads for what the Wolfenbüttel Manuscript named as 'Spesser Wald', which was identified by Adolphus Ward in 1901 as the *Specke*, a patch of grazing land near Wittenberg that was previously much frequented by students, including Luther. When the English traveller Fynes Moryson enrolled at Wittenberg university in 1591 he was taken to a spot in the woods and shown 'a tree all blasted and burnt … where [Faustus] practised his Magick Art.'[2] In the Faustbook the sun is setting as Faustus arrives at a crossroads and here with his wand he draws his magic circle, embroidered with the outlandish sigils of his art. At about nine or ten in the evening he was finished: 'Then began Doctor Faustus to call for Mephostophiles [*sic*] the Spirit, and to charge him in the name of Beelzebub to appear.'[3]

According to the Faustbook the spirits fail to materialise at first. The *Specke* is full of fearsome noise, the wind howls, thunder claps and lightning flashes 'as if the whole world, to his seeming, had been on fire.' Just as Faustus's will begins to falter, the cacophony is replaced by a sweet and charming music. Encouraged, he renews his invocations: 'suddenly over his head hanged hovering in the air a mighty Dragon.'[4]

The writer of the Faustbook, like most novelists, does not give the actual form of the conjuration used. The printer Spies said that he had intentionally omitted the magical formulae lest they be put to wicked use. Marlowe, seeing a missed opportunity, described the scene more carefully, showing a familiarity with magic: 'Within this circle is Jehovah's name, / Forward and backward anagrammatiz'd' (1.3.5–15). He also invented or borrowed a suitably Latin invocation for Faustus to hurl upon the howling wind.

There is a confusion (or intentional convergence) in Marlowe's invocation between the rigorous ritual of high magic that constrains the infernal spirits with the mystical names of God and outright satanism as when Faustus decries the name of Jehovah and calls upon Gehenna. This is a necessary ploy for Marlowe, allowing him to have Faustus congratulate himself when Mephistopheles appears – 'Such is the force of magic and my spells' – but reveal that he has lost control of the situation, as Mephistopheles explains 'the shortest cut for conjuring / Is stoutly to abjure the Trinity, And pray devoutly to the prince of hell' (1.3.46–53).

Marlowe's invocation scene captures the tension between two opposing views of magic. Here Faustus, like any other necromancer, believes that it is his power – his knowledge of the art and his skill in operating it – that invokes and binds the spirits to his service. The view that Marlowe puts in the mouth of Mephistopheles, whether he knew it or not, is that of Arnold of Villanova (c. 1235–1313), who argued that the demons could not be coerced and that if they did indeed appear at the necromancer's summons then they did so by their own volition. Any indication to the contrary was simply a ruse on the part of the demons to entrap the necromancer more surely. The theologians' problem was that they could not accept that God would aid the necromancer in his endeavours. The necromancers had engineered a technological solution that was entirely rational within the theocentric world view of the period: if the invocation of the names of God could be used to drive demons out in the rite of exorcism, then those same names could be employed to raise demons up out of hell to do the magician's bidding. As always, the theologians were in a bind and went through their usual mental contortions to try and extricate themselves from the problem and at the same time pull the rug from under the necromancers.

The later Faustian grimoires could not, of course, avoid their own formulae for invoking Mephistopheles. With such texts we are firmly on the necromancers' home ground. There is no indication that it is anything other than the power of magic itself that calls forth and constrains the infernal spirits. One version of the *Geister Commando* that claimed to have been printed in Rome in 1501 had its 'Citation for Mephistophilis' and his 'Seal or Character for Coercion and Obedience' to be written on virgin parchment with the blood of butterflies on the night of the full moon. Chapter X of the fearsome 'Cabalae Nigrae' contained in the infamous *Dreyfacher Höllenzwang* (supposedly Passau, 1505) gives another formula of invocation with a further 'High Conjuration of Mephistophiles' in three parts requiring lengthy roll-calls of magical words and spirit names to be read out. When at last Mephistopheles appears, if he does, there is a special binding to be performed and, most importantly, instructions are given on how to send him back to the spirit world again.

With a cry 'as if hell had been open', Mephistopheles falls like a lightning bolt onto the *Specke*, resolves into a globe, forms the shape of man out of fire before finally assuming the 'manner of a grey Friar'.[5] From dragon to man of fire to monk, Mephistopheles flickers through his forms until he settles upon the one most pleasing to Faustus and the writer of the Faustbook. That Mephistopheles finally appears as a grey friar, a Franciscan, alerts us to the resurfacing of Protestant prejudices. Nothing could please the Protestant mind more than casting Mephistopheles as a brother of one of the Catholic mendicant orders. Faustus appears nonplussed at this disguise, but a Renaissance magus would surely have been happier with something more classical, a toga, or some other antique dress. Going through the grimoire I have yet to encounter any other spirit appearing in ecclesiastical vestments. They usually manifest as aristocrats, sometimes soldiers, animals, or in grotesque forms. If his garb appears contrived, it is the assumption of various forms and often at the request of the invoker that rings true as a genuine element from the magicians' grimoire.

We find Mephistopheles taking other forms elsewhere. The *Geister Commando* contained in *The Seventh Book of Moses* calls him Mephistophilis and ranks him amongst the Seven Great Princes.

> MEPHISTOPHILIS is ready to serve, and appears in the form of a youth. He is willing to serve in all skilled arts, and gives the *spiritus Servos*, otherwise called 'familiars'. He brings treasures from the earth and from the deep very quickly.[6]

When Marlowe wrote the part for his 'Mephastophilis' it seemed self-evident what sort of spirit he was. He needed no other introduction than to acknowledge his master: 'I am servant to great Lucifer' (1.3.39). When Goethe came to write his 'Mephistopheles' in the eighteenth century he described him as 'the spirit which eternally denies.' There was no mention of 'great Lucifer' for Mephistopheles had become the Devil himself.[7]

This is a purely dramatic development. A demonic underling, even if a 'Great Prince', is much less impressive for the theatre audience or reading public than the Devil in person. Yet it is a mistake. A grimoire like Codex 849 had its operation for invoking Satan and it was not unique. Another fifteenth-century German manuscript now in Prague gives a further example and a relatively short and direct one at that.[8] If Faustus had wanted to summon the Devil there were invocations enough to choose from. Instead, according to the tradition, he chose Mephistopheles and there must have been special reasons for doing so.

Talk of the Devil

'Talk of the Devil and he'll appear', as we read in Erasmus's *Colloquies*, which is a fine way of demonstrating the importance ascribed to the power of names. Names were magical. Names could make things happen. Names could whip all the devils out of hell. To know the true name, the secret name was to know how to command a thing. Yet the magician faced a problem. It was not only Mephistopheles's form that was subject to some changeability, but his name as well.

The demon we have come to know as 'Mephistopheles' first made his entrance in the Faustbook as 'Mephostophiles'. This earlier form of the name was used in the Wolfenbüttel Manuscript of *c.*1580 and first appeared in English in P.F.'s 1592 translation of Spies, and continued to be in use up until 1755. In Marlowe's *Dr Faustus* he is Mephastophilis in the 1604 edition and Mephostophilis in 1616. In the magical texts attributed to Faustus we find Mephistophiel, Mephistophiles, Mephistophilus and Mephistophielis. Other forms include Memostophiles, Megastophiles and Methostophiles – indeed, from the puppet-plays and legends written between the sixteenth and eighteenth centuries, no fewer than nineteen versions of the name have been recorded.[9]

Despite all the variations, none of which seem so very great (especially given the cavalier attitude to spelling of former times), the name was then and continues to be one to conjure with, but who or what is Mephistopheles? Is it possible that the name itself, seemingly so mysterious, can tell us anything? Goethe, irrevocably associated with the story of 'Faust', wrote to Carl Zelter in 1829 and confessed that he did not have a clue what the name Mephistopheles meant or where it came from. However, there are some clues in his distinctive name and it is surely of some importance, even if we do not believe that knowing the true form will call the spirit from his abysmal lair.

There are some curious theories as to whence this piece of linguistic flotsam originated. I have recently read that the name comes to us through Greek from ancient Mesopotamia. The first person to tackle the problem said much the same. Widmann argued in 1599 that the name was of what he called Persian origin. That trail, however, appears to be false.

A feature common to many of the names given to the so-called demons is that they derive from pagan pantheons, especially those in opposition to that of the ancient Hebrews. Thus we find the Philistine god Baal Zebul, 'lord of the house', being derided by the Jews as Beelzebul, 'lord of filth', with the intentional pun of Beelzebub, 'lord of the flies', in reference to the ancient Canaanite god 'Fly'. Berith, whom we met earlier in a conjuration from Codex 849, was another god of the near east: Baal Berith, 'lord of contracts'. Likewise the demon Asmodeus in the Apocryphal book of Tobit is a corruption of the Persian god Aeshma Daeva.

We would look in vain for a god called Mephostophiles or Mephistopheles, but in Roman mythology there was a goddess Mephitis. She had the unpleasant task of preventing 'pestilential exhalations' from the sewers and elsewhere. Her name lives on in our words *mephitis*, meaning 'a poisonous stench', *mephitic*, which describes anything that smells like one, and in the scientific name for the skunk, *Mephitis mephitis*. The suggestion of *mephitis* is interesting since demonic spirits were thought to manifest with noisome stenches, although no particular smell, bad or otherwise, is popularly recorded in connection with Mephistopheles. If we add the Greek *philos*, 'friend/lover', to Mephitis we arrive at something like 'a friend/lover of poisonous stenches', although W. Weber, writing in 1836, thought that the name meant someone who arose from hell and exuded an unpleasant smell. However we interpret it, the derivation is a plausible but inexact fit: Mephitis is not Mephosto-.

There are a thousand or more spirit names to choose from in magical literature, so why should anyone invent yet another one? Magic proceeds through the use of traditional formulae and ancient names. It revels in forgotten languages. Its claims for authenticity rest upon the desire for the original words for things – the language Adam spoke when he named the plants and animals – because that original language is seen as being fused with those things themselves. The word ceases to be a sign and becomes, in effect, the world. Magic does not generally invent exotic names for decorative effect, even if to the untrained eye that appears to be the case.

'Mephostophiles' (and all its variations) is not one of those ancient spirit names. It is especially noticeable by its absence from Wierus's much quoted detailing of the hellish hierarchy, the *Pseudomonarchia Daemonum* of 1577. It first appears in the sixteenth century, only in connection with Faustus and only in the legends and derivative material. The first mention outside the Faustbook literature was made by Jacob Ayrer as late as 1597. We are led to the conclusion that it is not a true spirit name, not one of that ancient host of unborn beings, but simply a novelist's invention. However, it can still have meaning; perhaps because it has been purposely invented it has even more meaning.

Evil Name is Evil Fame

The man who coined the name must have had some reasoning behind it, however obscure, and must have intended to convey something to his audience when he hit upon Mephostophiles. Since we find the word first used in a German language text, a German origin would seem to be the most obvious. However, painstaking research unpicking the name syllable by syllable reveals, disappointingly, that its origin must lie elsewhere. If German is a dead-end, what other language might hold the secret?

The -*philes* ending suggests a Greek origin and Greek was a fashionable language amongst the Humanists of the period. The study of Greek Antiquity and the Greek language had taken off after the fall of Constantinople to the Ottomans in 1453 when Greek-speaking Christians fled to Europe. This did not go unnoticed. In 1676 Johannes Conradus Durrius argued that Mephostophiles was a corruption of Megastophilos, meaning, so he claimed, 'great and superior to everyone'. Not long after, someone called Stunz argued that Magistopheles was the original form of the name, meaning 'highly useful' and referring to the god Hermes, so beloved amongst occultists. However, both of these attempts to solve the mystery try to do so by forcing it into some other shape that no longer bears much resemblance to the original. They are too far-fetched to be convincing.[10]

It would take another three hundred years for anyone to come up with an alternative. In the nineteenth century Karl Kiesewetter pulled out his Greek grammar and suggested that Mephostophiles was formed from *me*, a negative prefix, *phos* (light) and *philos* (love), meaning 'not-light-loving'. However, he still had *to* left over. In order to account for this he argued that it was a 'half-learned' fill-in, or that it could have been part of a misspelling of *phosto* for *photos* (light). Some have dismissed this interpretation as artificial, but it has become the most authoritative.[11] The problem is that we must make assumptions about the inventor of the name that cannot be proven.

Hypothesis follows hypothesis, each relying on either faulty Greek grammar or too much learning. It is bad Greek to those who have some knowledge of it and 'all Greek' to those who have none. The puzzle is why should an author have taken the trouble in the 1580s to invent a name, the meaning of which only becomes clear after reading an explanatory footnote written centuries later by a classical scholar? If the name was not Greek what other language could it be in? It would also have to be a language that the audience would have had some chance of knowing or at least being aware of; indeed, it would have had to be a language that the inventor, presumably a German living in the sixteenth century, would have had some chance of knowing or being aware of. Latin and Greek were the first loves of Renaissance Humanism, but another ancient language was also beginning to receive scholarly attention.

Hebrew was the language of the Bible, it was older than Greek, its script less familiar and written backwards, or so it seemed, and hence promised more direct access to that secret wisdom and magic power that Faustus and every other magician before and since has sought. Hebrew was also in fashion. Leading Humanists like Reuchlin had pioneered its study, but it was Luther's translation of the Bible into the German vernacular (the New Testament in 1521 and the Old Testament in 1534) that made it accessible to a much wider audience than before, placing many Hebrew personal and place names directly in their hands. These factors suggest that the author of the Faustbook had good reason to trust that his allusions to Hebrew and to Scripture would be understood and appreciated by his readers.

Given that the Bible would have been the principal source of reference and entertainment for many, through private readings and public sermons, what can we find out by pouring over the pages? Some have looked to Moses, unsuccessfully, for clues to the meaning, but there are more obvious examples to explore.[12] The Hebrew for Memphis, capital of Lower Egypt, is Moph or Noph. Memphis, as with all things Egyptian, was the place of magic. There is a city called Mephaath, meaning 'appearance, or force of waters', but this suggests nothing remotely diabolical. However, all of these leave a large part of the name wanting explanation.

Looking at Hebrew editions of the Bible other candidates present themselves. We find *mefiz* and *tofel*, which, when fused together, might well be an appropriate etymology for Mephistopheles. The suggestion, when first made in the early twentieth century, was not well received. The debate centred round whether *mefiz* meant 'ruining' or 'spreading', and whether *tofel* was actually *tiflut* refracted through the pronunciation of the Ashkenasi Jews as *tiflus* and meaning 'nonsense' or 'foolishness'. The result is largely the same. The problem is that it is unlikely that the author of the Faustbook would have understood more than a few words in biblical Hebrew, let alone an altogether more obscure one in Mishnaic. Furthermore, this derivation is based on Mephistopheles and not the earlier Mephostophiles.[13]

The dense throng of bizarre names in the Old Testament throws up still more possibilities. In 2 Samuel 15:12 we find a man at King David's court called Achitophel. Achitophel means 'brother of insipidity or impiety', but despite this unfortunate name he was a man greatly renowned for his wisdom among the Jews before an ignominious ending as a Judas figure. In 2 Samuel 15:31 Luther translated a suggestive line as 'Oh Lord, befool Achitophel's advice' and just as Achitophel tried to befool David, it has been argued, so Mephistopheles tried to befool Faustus. There seemed to be some sort of sympathy of action between them. Could Achitophel be the source of the ending to 'Mephistopheles'?[14]

Staying with Samuel we also find Mephibosheth or Mephiboshet, meaning 'exterminator of shame' or 'out of my mouth proceeds reproach'. The crippled grandson of Saul, Mephiboshet was an unfortunate and uninspiring figure who was outwitted by his servant – but he could be the other half of our puzzle. Chop Mephiboshet and Achitophel in half and splice them together, and we get Mephi-tophel.[15]

That we can cut-and-paste the two names together is not justification alone. Despite all these attempts we simply cannot escape the fact that the hybrid name Mephi-tophel is still some way from being Mephistopheles, far less the earlier Mephostophiles. If the author of the Faustbook wanted to conjure up associations with Mephiboshet and Achitophel, then why did he not stick with Mephitophel?

Neither *mefiz-tiflus* nor Mephi-tophel supplies enough of Mephostophiles to be convincing. So far as our demon is concerned, Hebrew is a false trail.

Given the number of different versions of the name 'Mephistopheles' that have been in use at different times, it is also possible that different authors have understood it to mean different things. By itself it seems to mean nothing, but contains a rich variety of nuances that may have been differently stressed as one author preferred Greek and another Hebrew (or indeed as one knew nothing of either). In the end there appears to be no real solution, but out of all those offered so far there is one explanation a little more convincing than the others.

When they were not corruptions of other people's gods, demons since Mesopotamian times have generally been named after whatever pestilence or evil they were thought to especially embody. We must ask, then, what pestilence or evil does Mephistopheles embody? For the writer of the Faustbook, who dressed him as a monk, he must embody everything that the Protestants despised about Catholicism, and that was a long list. The original Mephostophiles is, on this Mesopotamian principle, much more likely to be derived, however badly, from *me photos philos*, meaning a light-hating demon, the light being the 'light of the Gospels' – which could at least mean something that a Protestant might apply to a Catholic.

Everyone who has tried to crack the Mephistopheles enigma has been too clever (and thus implied considerable sophistication on the part of creator and audience) or too arrogant in assuming stupidity or ignorance (or both) on the part of the original inventor. People have strained too hard to find an exact meaning and their efforts have all ended inconclusively, however suggestive and intriguing they may have been. This is perhaps the real secret. The name sounds Greek and so conjures up associated ideas, but remains impenetrable, luring us like a will-o'-the-wisp into trying to decipher it and losing us amongst the fetid swamps of overheated imaginations.

Deal with the Devil
(1514)

If Faustus must have his Mephistopheles, then Mephistopheles must have his pact: 'he will buy my services with his soul' states Marlowe's spirit; 'Give me a line or two, I pray' solicits Goethe's gentlemanly demon.[1] The pact has become a central element in the legend of Faustus. It has entered into our language as a 'Faustian bargain'. After reading Marlowe and Goethe we are convinced that the pact was the source of all Faustus's power as well as the legalese of his destruction. And yet we all know Marlowe and Goethe to be dramatists, spinning tales for our delight and occasional edification. So which is it? Fact or fiction? Where did it come from, this idea of the pact, and what truth is in it?

One version of the legend published by Battus in 1592 tells that Faustus signed his pact in Wittenberg on 23 October 1514. Surprisingly, the date is a plausible one. The legend also tells us that the pact was fixed at the term of twenty-four years, which would mean – if it were true – that Faustus would have had to have signed the document in 1514, if indeed he did, because he died around 1538. Damningly, there is no mention of a pact in the contemporary references to him. The idea is first found in the Wolfenbüttel Manuscript of around 1580 and Augustin Lercheimer's *Christlich bedencken* printed at Heidelberg in 1585, although there is possibly an earlier hint in one of Roshirt's anecdotes (*c.* 1570–1575).

According to the legend, as we read in P.F.'s version, the actual details of the pact were thrashed out in the comfort of Faustus's chamber rather than in the windy and badly lit woods where he invoked Mephistopheles. Faustus began by laying down three articles that Mephistopheles should observe: that he would be obedient; that he should bring anything that Faustus desired; and that he should always tell the truth.

The first is simply the expectation of any master of his servant. The second is a catch-all clause for granting Faustus his every wish, taking him beyond the money-specific invocation of the spirit Aziel in his spurious grimoire the *Harrowing of*

Hell (supposedly Paris, 1508). The third reveals that general fear of duplicity implicit in all transactions with the supernatural and the more specific belief when dealing with infernal powers that they are, after their Father of Lies, all inveterate deceivers. As pacts go it seemed watertight, the only problem was that Mephistopheles refused to sign.

The reason being, explained Mephistopheles, that he did not have executive powers and first had to check with his master down below. Faustus was not satisfied and demanded a more detailed account of why this should be. It might have ended there with an argument, but Faustus made Mephistopheles swear to come back the next evening and true to his word he returned to resume their negotiations. Faustus had expanded his original articles to five.

With an eye on the next life, Faustus had decided that it would be better to be a spirit like Mephistopheles than any other sort of inhabitant of hell. Images of the damned being pitch forked onto gridirons for an eternity of roasting no doubt heavily influenced article one. The other new addition to the list was that Mephistopheles should attend him, invisible to all but himself – he had obviously thought through the consequences of always having such a strange attendant at his side. Mephistopheles relented on condition that Faustus agreed to a number of articles of his own. Faustus not only had to sign over body and soul in his own blood, but must agree to deny the Christian faith and make himself an enemy towards its believers, and should not let anyone talk him out of it.

Faustus had been expecting to hand over body and soul, Mephistopheles had already given away that much. The blood pact adds extra magical weight to his word alone. The remaining conditions ensured that he cut himself off from all aid and influence from the 'opposition'. We are reminded of Dr Klinge in Erfurt and that in a world full of enthusiastic religionists, a magician was sure to be hectored and cajoled into changing his mind. A specific term was also agreed 'to give him certain years to live in health and pleasure, and when such years were expired, that then *Faustus* should be fetched away.' Dreaming of all that he might have and do, 'his mind was so inflamed, that he forgot his soul', and he readily agreed to everything that Mephistopheles demanded in return. The Faustbook puts his rationalisation of this act rather nicely: 'he thought the Devil was not so black as they use to paint him, nor hell so hot as the people say.'[2]

The next day Mephistopheles returned for Faustus's signature. With an easy air Faustus took up his knife and pricked a vein in his left hand. In the blood that pooled in his palm words appeared, *o homo fuge* ('O man, fly'), sending Mephistopheles to flight, reminding the demon, no doubt, of the words from the Bible (1 Timothy 6:11): *Tu autem o homo Dei haec fuge*, 'But thou, O man of God, flee these things.' Marlowe had his Faustus regard the problem and finding himself without a refuge to fly to – 'If unto God, he'll throw me down to hell' (II.1.79-80) – believed himself without any other option.

The Faustus of the Faustbook dipped his pen, unconcerned, and signed over 'body, soul, flesh, blood' for the fulfilment of his every desire, according to his stated articles, for the term of twenty-four years.[3] It was not a long time. The number also has symbolic meanings and should not be taken literally. It reminds us of the twenty-four hours in a day and thus creates an extreme contrast between the brevity of Faustus's time on earth and the eternity of damnation that awaits him – twenty-four hours or even twenty-four years is but a blink of the eye in comparison.

A variation of the story is given in the eighteenth-century *Black Raven* that pretended to have been published in Lyon in 1469. According to this version, a much more innocent Faustus happened upon a grimoire and in a spirit of experimentation decided to give it a go. He began with a casual incredulity, reading out the invocations for fun rather than out of serious expectation. Imagine his surprise, then, when Astaroth appeared before him, demanding to know why he had been summoned. Not quite believing his luck Faustus hurriedly asked the spirit that he should be useful to him in the fulfilment of any desire he should have. Astaroth agreed on condition that Faustus sign a pact. Of course Faustus had no wish to do so, but realising that his protective circle was carelessly drawn, he was forced to concede. The agreement was quickly drawn up with the usual terms: the spirit's service for a fixed period in return for Faustus's soul.

The blood pact was a well-attested practice up to the early Middle Ages in Germany, Scandinavia and Ireland, where such pacts formed family-like ties between unrelated men. The Classical writers Herodotus and Pomponius Mela told stories about the Scythians using blood to conclude agreements. First year students at German universities were said at one time to write messages in blood in each other's albums and elsewhere we find accounts of blood-drinking rites amongst Italian bandits in the 1890s that would have made good material for Bram Stoker.[4] The pact sealed a two-way bond because both gave blood. In the Faustus myth it is only Faustus who gives his blood; it is even debatable whether as a spirit the Devil or any of his officers could have any blood to give.

The magical use of blood is similarly well-known. It is the core of Christianity: 'Drink ye all of it; / For this is my blood of the new testament, which shall be shed for many unto remission of sins' and 'Whoso eateth my flesh, and drinketh my blood, hath eternal life.'[4] Through the words of his Apostles we are given to understand that Jesus's blood had magical properties when consumed by his followers. Even at the symbolic level of the Sacrifice of the Mass it is difficult to put aside thoughts of Transylvanian counts.

In the Germanic myth of the *Nibelungen* blood is seen as having the power to renew strength because it was thought to contain the life-force. In central Europe in the Middle Ages it was used in love magic to bind would-be lovers, elements of which survived up to the modern period. In combination with the consecrated Host it could drive out illness. Painted on doorposts it could keep witches and evil spirits at bay. Fear of its misuse – the so-called 'blood libel' – was an important ingredient in the persecution of the Jews during Faustus's lifetime.[5]

It was a widespread belief that blood attracted spirits. In the literature of Classical Antiquity, Odysseus most famously conjured up the shades of the dead using blood, as per the sorceress Circe's instructions. Michael Scot (*c.*1175–1232), sometime astrologer to Emperor Friedrich II, described the practices of necromancers as always involving some sort of sacrifice: blood, wine that looks like blood, flesh of corpses or a slice of the magician's own hide. A manuscript of the thirteenth century, now at Paris, stipulated that the blood of a bat must be used in the conjuration described and closer to

Faustus's own time we find examples of animal sacrifice in Codex 849. The Faustian grimoires also recommend their share of gore. The *Geister Commando* – purporting to date from 1501 – called for the blood of white doves and butterflies to be used in its rites. The magical value of blood has not diminished down the centuries, as we see from the Toradjas tribe of Celebes who smear blood on new buildings, to Angelina Jolie who used it during her marriage ceremonies.[6]

Blood could bind and repel, depending on at whom it was directed, and re-invigorate. It symbolised life itself and so could influence life. It was the essence of life, of the creature from which it was shed, and thus could magically be that creature. As the essence of life it was sought by that which did not live, attracting the dead and the unborn, the hungry ghosts and greedy demons. It was just the right ink for infernal contracts.

That such contracts with the Devil or his agents were made was so widely and authoritatively reported that it was believed as a fact. As early as the fourth century, Augustine of Hippo wrote censoriously of 'pacts with demons' in his *De Doctrina Christiana*. In the thirteenth century, Thomas Aquinas argued that any work of sorcery implied a pact with the Devil. In the fourteenth century, Pope John XXII (1316–34) ordered the inquisitors at Toulouse and Carcassonne in the south of France to take action against *maleficos* – sorcerers or witches defined as worshipping demons or making pacts with them. The idea of pacts resurfaced in his bull *Super illius specula* of 1326. In 1398 the University of Paris declared that sorcery implied a pact, even if there was no formal agreement made, and that sorcery conducted with a pact was heresy. Johannes Nider used John XXII's bull a century later in his handbook for confessors. In 1437 Pope Eugenius IV used similar language when writing to his army of inquisitors, making reference to written contracts. Nider wrote the same year that

> They are called necromancers, who, through a pact with demons [and] through faith in ceremonies, predict future events, or manifest certain hidden things by the revelation of demons, or who harm those around them by evil sorcery.[7]

Kramer and Sprenger's influential *Malleus Maleficarum* (1486) made frequent reference to pacts, asserting that 'witches are bound to make this pact [with the Devil], which is exacted by that enemy either wholly or in part', and used phraseology identical to John XXII's bull.[8] Nider went further to argue that there was no essential difference between those who were called necromancers and those who were called witches.

Faustus was a self-declared necromancer who claimed to be able to predict the future, among other things, *ergo*, he must have made a pact with demons. That is how his case would have been viewed by Nider and others of a similar persuasion, and even if there was no evidence of a pact, a pact was nevertheless implied by his practice of sorcery. There could be no escaping the logic of the Church. Faustus could not win.

Trithemius, who would have known the texts just cited, could not help but view Faustus as anything but the worst sort of person. Trithemius also turned his mind to the diabolical pact in the *Eight Questions* – written after his discussion with Emperor Maximilian I – and his answer was treated as authoritative for some time.[9]

However, we find Trithemius's erstwhile student Agrippa arguing against the idea of pacts in his *Occult Philosophy*. He confessed that he had once confused the details of

ancient magical rituals with 'certain occult agreements of the devils' and it was only
after more serious study that he perceived them for what they were, which was 'not
the compacts of devils'.[10]

If even Agrippa could see certain magical instructions as agreements and compacts
of devils, how much more so the ordinary man, untutored in magic? The unusual
and unfamiliar suggested magic and where there was magic the Devil would not be
far behind. Such learnéd interpretations as Agrippa offered were to be distrusted, for,
as Johann Geiler von Kaysersberg wrote in 1508, magic was simply a way of com-
municating with the Devil who carried out the operations on the magician's behalf:
'So what the witches do is only a sign, not the deed itself.'[11] Writing in 1529, Martin
de Castagena reinforced the notion that the magician was essentially powerless, at the
mercy of the Devil and bound to do his terrible will.

This discourse was a forcible expression of the belief that magic itself could have no
intrinsic power. It attempted to limit the threat posed by the magician, although as a
consequence increased the Devil's empire. By concentrating all forms of magic in the
Devil's camp it could be dealt with by the established methods of the Church. Being
a good Christian was the best defence. If, however, the magician had power over the
universe through his mastery of magical procedures, then not even being a good
Christian would be protection enough.

The Devil Taketh Him Up

The example of Jesus in the wilderness put temptation by the Devil at the heart of
Christianity and not everyone was so stubborn as to refuse him. Faustus was not
the first person in history reputed to have made a pact with the Devil, nor the last.
Two great examples preceded him – St Basil and Theophilus – and many more
thronged about him in his own time. Many of the great men in history have been
accused of filling the legal department of hell with their writings. The pact was a
mainstay of Christian legend, used to reveal the saintliness of some and revile the
satanism of others – a two-edged weapon in the war of words fought between
sanctioned 'truth' and outlawed knowledge.

Claiming the dubious honour of being the first in the Christian era to enter a pact
with the Devil was a slave of Heradius or, according to another version, of Senator
Proterius of Caesarea, whose soul was saved by the intercession of St Basil (330–379).
According to the fourth-century legend, he was said to have solicited Satan's help to
win his master's beautiful daughter in marriage. He traded his eternal service for possession of the girl and she duly fell madly in love with him, threatening to kill herself
if her father forbade the match.

The man's new bride soon became suspicious when he refused to make the sign
of the cross or enter a church. He assured her that nothing was wrong, but unsatisfied
with this she sought out the advice of Bishop Basil. Basil subjected him to an interrogation during which he confessed that his soul belonged to the Prince of Darkness.
Basil threw the man in a cell and locked the door while he went to pray for him. The
man was apparently now assailed by devils. When these 'demonic attacks' subsided, Basil

hauled him out and dragged him off to church. Here he prayed over the young man, demanding the return of the contract, and lo and behold, from a balcony a scrap of paper 'fluttered down through the air and fell into his hands, in the sight of all'. The saint tore the paper in two, expelled the 'howling demons' and, now freed from the pact, the servant was 'worthy once again to receive the sacraments'.[12] Luther's friend Georg Major published the life of St Basil, including this story, with an introduction by Luther, in Wittenberg in 1544, attesting to the value attached to the tale in Faustus's age.

The most popular and widely known tale of pact-making was that of Theophilus the Penitent. Composed sometime between 600 and 850 CE, the story relates to events dated as 537 CE. Translated into Latin at least as early as the ninth century, it was circulated throughout Europe, although the use of blood to write out the pact only entered the tale as late as the thirteenth century. Before the legend of Faustus, this was the Faustus legend.

Theophilus was a high-ranking clergyman of Adana in Cilicia (now Turkey) before the Persian invasion of the Byzantine Empire. When the old bishop died, his steward Theophilus was seen as the natural successor. Theophilus, however, did not want the job. He claimed that he was unworthy of such high office, going on about sins that no one had noticed. The mitre and crosier could not be forced upon him and another man was promoted in his place.

Theophilus's former supporters turned against him and had him removed from his office of steward. He now realised that he had made a big mistake and turned to 'a certain wicked Jew, a practitioner of all sorts of diabolical arts' described as having 'plunged many into the deep pit of perdition by his unchristian counsels' – clearly this man was a successful practitioner of magic with a healthy client list. The magician invoked the Prince of Hell who appeared with a retinue of white-robed demons, carrying candlesticks and uttering loud cries. The Devil agreed to aid Theophilus, who was only too keen to conclude the deal, boldly denying Christ and the Virgin. He wrote out his renunciation 'with his blood', folded it and sealed it with wax, putting the mark of his ring upon it.

Theophilus's fortunes were immediately reversed. He got his old job back with double salary and extended powers. Once the novelty wore off, Theophilus grew increasingly uneasy and stayed up late, praying and not eating, thinking particularly of 'the gnashing teeth and the worm that dieth not' that awaited him in hell.

Utterly broken by worrying about eternal damnation, Theophilus sought out the nearest church and prostrated himself on its cold floor before a representation of Mary for the next forty days and nights. Starving, sleep-deprived and in an over-excited mental state, Theophilus now began to hear a voice, purportedly that of Mary, reprimanding him for abandoning Christianity. In his defence he made a long-winded argument that can be summarised as follows: Theophilus now believed in everything Christian again; it is Jesus's job to forgive him; and he, Theophilus, was not really responsible for his own actions anyway. Convinced, Mary went off to talk to her son, whilst Theophilus 'prayed and beat his face violently against the floor … remaining without food and flooding the place with tears' for another three days. He heard the voice again telling him that he was acquitted, but Theophilus demanded that the pact be returned to him. Theophilus had to wait another three days before Mary reappeared 'in a vision as it seemed' and handed over the pact. After confessing the whole sordid story to the bishop – who used the occasion as a great marketing exercise – Theophilus died, no doubt on account of his prolonged fasting and violent hysteria.[13]

The implicit message seems to be: make a deal with the Devil, get what you want and back out of it later to avoid the fiery pit – although it is doubtful that that was the intention. Because he is the ultimate evil, the reversal of everything Christian, a pact with the Devil is the ultimate sin and the intentional message is that, however great you think your sins are, the Church will embrace you and you will be saved. The story of Theophilus is a clear-cut Christian morality tale with, in the version cited, a heavy and distasteful dose of anti-Semitism (and anti-Magianism) as well as an agenda to promote the cult of Mary. Jews – whom Luther would later call 'the Devil's children' – and magic are the central threats, conduits to the enemy of Christianity, and are singled out for condemnation.[14] The Jewish magician is later summarily executed and Theophilus regards the matter with an easy conscience. The original author apparently did not notice how self-centred and utterly craven Theophilus appears in the story. Rather than edifying, it is disturbing. The Faustus of legend at least had the strength of character to keep his word, but in doing so demonstrated a theological shift: the sinful Protestant would not be redeemed.

With the success of the Theophilus story, diabolical pacts were a popular subject and great propaganda. Attached to the life of a saint they could be used to amplify his holiness. Attached to the name of an enemy they could be used to discredit him. Two twelfth-century tales exemplify the former type. St Wulfric (d. 1154), the hermit of Haselbury in Dorset, was reputed to have interceded in a case of diabolical pact-making. The Archdeacon of Oxford, Walter Map (c. 1160–1210), told the story of a young French nobleman called Eudo who had reduced himself to poverty through his extravagance and sought a way out by making terms with the Devil. He was absolved by the Bishop of Beauvais on condition that he burn himself to death as penance.

It was not just the poverty-stricken who turned to the Devil. Similar stories attached themselves to anyone who stepped out of line with convention. Socrates, Apollonius of Tyana, Apuleius, Roger Bacon, Raymond Lull, Julius Caesar Scaliger, Cornelius Agrippa, Paracelsus, Nostradamus, Michael Servetus, Giordano Bruno and Galileo Galilei were all thought to have sold their souls to the Devil. Nor were popes above such accusations. Pope Boniface VIII was posthumously tried for a catalogue of crimes that included making a pact, and Alexander VI was also held to be in league with the powers of darkness. Trithemius did not escape such calumny and the religious reformers Luther, Melanchthon and Calvin were similarly tarred with the same brush.

Notwithstanding Luther's own supposed pact with the Devil, he himself claimed that Trithemius's patron (and Luther's political opponent) Prince-Elector Joachim I von Brandenburg had signed a pact with the Devil, as had his religious rival Johannes Eck. He also told the story of an unnamed soothsayer and practitioner of black magic discovered in Erfurt in 1537 to have contracted with Satan and burnt to death.

Only a few months later Luther was himself called in to deal with a case of pact-making at the University of Wittenberg. Struggling in the direst poverty, the student Valerius Glöckner had been approached by Satan when his need was at its greatest. In return for some hard currency the student signed over his immortal soul in the time honoured tradition. Luther laid into him with a torrent of religiously-flavoured verbal abuse before dragging the hapless student off to church where he prayed for him, laid his hands upon him and squeezed a repentant confession out of him.

Another case of a pact-making student came to light on 11 December 1596 when the Senate of Tübingen University called before it the student David Lipsius (Leipziger), whom we met earlier, to examine the charge that he had signed a contract with the Devil. The student confessed his sins and pleaded that it was his first offence – he blamed a fellow student and his reading of Spies's *Historia*. The Senate judged him leniently – at least they thought so – and Lipsius was sentenced to be incarcerated only until Christmas Day and thereafter bound for six months to keep to his lodgings, attending only university and church. Almost immediately Lipsius was out carousing the local inns and pocketing some expensive cutlery and silver goblets on the way. Report of his new transgressions reached the Senate on 8 January 1597 and they threw him out of the city. Lipsius went on to take a degree at Heidelberg and successfully pursued a medical career in Erfurt.[15]

More cases might be named, but the point has been made. Supposed pacts with the Devil were not so very rare and Faustus was not alone in having been thought to have made such a deal. Not all of these pacts were legendary; to be sure, the evidence is often weak, but there are apparently genuine cases of individuals having entered into some sort of agreement with supernatural agents of evil. Every age it seems has had its share of daring souls willing to risk eternal damnation against a deal with the Devil – or who have been ignobly denounced as having done so by their enemies. It is, therefore, all the more strange that Faustus has come to be represented as the pact-maker *par excellence*.

His Damnable Practices

According to the Faustbook, Faustus's pact was discovered in his house after 'his most lamentable end' together with 'all the rest of his damnable practises used in his whole life', which is a neat literary device to explain how the pact could be reprinted in the Faustbook.[16] If someone called Faustus ever made a pact, it has not survived nor has any contemporary reference to it.

The legend here runs against the grain of actual practice. The Renaissance magus would not have condescended to enter into a pact with hell. Such unbecoming behaviour was for students like Glöckner and Lipsius, mere tyros in the art. The magus set out to storm hell and subdue its monstrous spirits, to seat himself like Trithemius's magus-king on Lucifer's throne. With hell at his feet, the magus extracted wealth, power and knowledge as tribute from the conquered demons. In 1597 James VI of Scotland expressed this in his *Demonologie*: 'Witches are servants only, and slave to the Devil; but the Necromancers are his masters and commanders' (Bk I, Ch. III). It was only the interpretation of those like von Kaysersberg, de Castagena and the anonymous author of the 1587 Faustbook, who wanted to explain away and delimit magic, that ascribed magic's sole means of operation to the intercession of Satanic powers. How the theologians saw the necromancer and how the necromancer saw himself are irreconcilable opposites. We are generally only left with the theologians' view because they have destroyed and suppressed the writings of those they disagreed with.

In all the wonderful and incredible claims recorded by his contemporaries and attributed to Faustus, there is no mention of a pact with the Devil. Even the spurious *Harrowing of Hell* is careful to point out that the magician should not enter into a pact with the spirits invoked. It is only the Church that believed a pact with hell must be involved because for complicated theological reasons they had to deny that any person was capable of invoking and controlling supernatural forces.

The pact may have become a central element in the legend of Faustus. It may have entered into our language as a 'Faustian bargain'. But it is false to the tradition of magic, whilst being only true to the Church's idea of what magic must entail. It also presents a logical problem. If a magician has struck a deal with the Devil to provide him with anything and everything he should desire, then that magician has no need to broadcast his skill in necromancy, astrology, alchemy and divination, since all of these magical techniques rest on the interpretation or manipulation of intermediary phenomena to achieve their desired goal. It could be argued that Faustus made his bargain after already practising magic for some time, trading in his magical circles, astrolabes and alchemical retorts for a direct, diabolical line to the satisfaction of every desire. However, it cannot be denied that, given the widespread attribution of pacts with the Devil, they cannot be taken seriously. Has anyone sat down and tried to analyse the evidence concerning Luther's supposed contract with hell? Do we really believe that all those popes said to have had truck with Satan actually set it out in writing? The pact is another typical motif attached to persons who are viewed with suspicion by others. Like Trithemius's sexual slanders, commerce with the powers of evil is a standard calumny intended to insult the victim and damage his reputation. It is only interesting that Trithemius, who could allege so much and so vociferously, should not also have thrown this taunt at Faustus.

We see that, whilst the contemporary references were bereft of pact-making, later stories about Faustus from as early as 1580 were beginning to attribute his supposed magical feats to the power of the Devil and that alleged agreement between them, in line with Christian tradition. Peculiarly Protestant elements inform the legend of Faustus: besides the many points of agreement with Luther's own writing, Faustus, most significantly, is dragged off to hell at the end. Even the craven Theophilus, regarded as the common point of origin for pact stories, manages to escape eternal damnation through his descent into religious hysteria. There is no such reprieve offered Faustus. The message of the Protestant Faustbook is that anyone who practices magic is in league with Satan and utterly doomed, and from the sixteenth-century Protestant viewpoint this encompassed not only necromancers like Faustus, but Jews, Catholics and indeed everyone else they disagreed with.

The legend that grew up around Faustus and in particular the pact and the consequences of his making it, become a retrospective trial and interrogation of him. Having escaped the punishment his enemies would have gladly inflicted upon him – 'let the theologians rise up against him' as Mutianus demanded – the legend becomes the vehicle of retribution. The anonymous authors of the Wolfenbüttel Manuscript and Spies's *Historia* rewrite history in the way in which they would have liked it to happen. Faustus thus meets the same fate as the black magician of Erfurt and the good burghers can rest easy in their beds, the smell of another sinner's burnt flesh in their nostrils and the smoking ashes warming the cockles of their hearts. As such it reflects a high level of anxiety around the apparent fact that Faustus could flagrantly practice necromancy and other magic arts and not be struck down by a thunderbolt hurled from the Christian heaven, nor be apprehended by God's servants on earth.

The power of Faustus also becomes a cause of concern. It is not just his blasphemous existence, but also the fact that he can accomplish so many marvels that are beyond the ability of mere Christians to achieve that exacerbates the deep-seated dread of magic felt by the non-magician. Throw into this mix intellectual curiosity and sexual promiscuity, and all the horrors of the sixteenth-century Christian mind are made flesh in Faustus. Where Trithemius's insults and distortions were so palpably obvious, in the Faustbook they become more subtly woven into the story. The Devil in the Faustbook thus comes to act like Satan in Job: the strong-arm of God sent to punish. The author of the Faustbook and other writers make the Devil into their own instrument and have their revenge upon Faustus. In effect, the legend of Faustus is one long Protestant sermon. But not so the life.

It is a central element of Christianity that if one should abjure all other faiths and follow God exclusively and to the letter of His commandments, then the believer will be rewarded in heaven. The pact with the Devil is an inverted form of the covenant with God that all Christians enter into. The idea of the pact with the Devil is an outpouring of the suppressed fear concerning this pact lying at the heart of Christianity. Something for something, the basis of all economic exchange, except this is what we might call religious exchange: unquestioning belief for everlasting bliss. Indeed, this is not so very different from all religious belief systems. However, it is also a source of guilt and anxiety. What if I cannot (or will not) keep my part of the bargain? What if God does not keep His part of the bargain? It is a central element of the pact with the Devil that both parties seek to defraud the other. In the same way the Christian or other believer attempts to live life the way he or she wants to, whilst at the same time trying to justify this in religious terms.

One thing in all of this appears more and more certain: Faustus's signing of the pact appears only after he is dead. He is conflated with the Wittenberg student and others who confessed under duress to having concluded deals with the Devil, and comes to serve the interests of the late sixteenth-century religious propagandists. Where Lercheimer related the story of Faustus's pact with the Devil, he also told the story of Valerius Glöckner, but in the Faustbook these two become one. The writers of that age used history in a cavalier fashion, concerned more with the moral value of a tale than its accuracy. Spies's false biography of Faustus in 1587 was in fact a fictional subterfuge, enhancing the spectacular to increase its entertainment value as well as its moral purpose. Another thing is also certain: despite refuting the authenticity of Faustus's pact, people will still believe that he signed it. The story has more momentum than historical accuracy alone can stop. If we are to rescue the real Faustus from the clutches of the Protestant myth-makers, we must reject this central theme in their damnation of the magician.

The Philosophers' Stone (1516)

Driven out of Erfurt sometime after 1513 – the only dated reference to him being there – Faustus resurfaced closer to home sometime in 1516. The intervening years were ones of change and warfare – dangerous times to be wandering the highways and byways of the Empire. François I had been crowned King of France in 1515 and resumed the Italian game with a victory at the Battle of Marignano (Melegnano) to regain control of Milan. Social dissent was widespread. The Gypsies were expelled from Burgundy and more than five hundred people were said to have been executed for the crime of witchcraft in the city of Geneva in the course of just three months. On a more personal scale, von Sickingen's wife had died giving birth to what would have been their seventh child. Perhaps Faustus had been sent for to intercede with astrological medicine or seek out her shade with necromancy.

Ferdinand II of Aragon had died and was succeeded by Charles (later Emperor Charles V), although he did not arrive to collect his new crown until 1517. In 1516 Maximilian I was back in Italy, invading the Milanese. He lasted a single day in Milan before he ran out of money and his mercenaries deserted. The Ottomans were more successful in conquering Syria. The Fifth Lateran Council tried to control heresy and prophecy in preaching as Erasmus published his new edition of the New Testament.

Faustus, meanwhile, according to local legends, was given sanctuary in the monastery of Maulbronn by Abbot Johannes Entenfuß of 'Evisheim', now Unteröwisheim (d.1525).[1] Maulbronn is quite unexpected. It is not a ruined monastery lying forlorn amidst the brambles as one comes to expect of such places, but is little short of a walled city, protected by a defensive ditch and entered across a drawbridge. Once through the narrow gate the interior expands into a large central court divided in two by a more recent group of buildings dating from the seventeenth and eighteenth centuries. Around the inside are ranged modern businesses as well as Maulbronn's town hall. Lying across the courtyard directly in front of the visitor is the church and cloister. When Faustus arrived in 1516 he would have had to go through three gates, not the one surviving today, and his view across the courtyard would have been blocked by a large barn, since demolished.

The monastery was begun in 1147 after the monks in nearby Eckenweiher realised that they had chosen a poor site and relocated to the narrow valley of Salzach. The old Roman road had run through the valley and when the monks arrived it was still an important imperial route (*Reichsstraße*). According to the legend, it was Walter von Lomersheim, leading his mule laden with a sack of gold in search of a good place for a monastery, who found the present location. Mules being as they are, this one suddenly and stubbornly stopped, threw its load and stamped on the ground, bringing forth a spring. Von Lomersheim dropped to his knees and praised God for the sign and founded the monastery on the spot. The name Maulbronn comes from, or is humorously associated with, the German for mule, *Maultier*, and *bronn* (*Brunnen*) meaning a spring.

The monks' religious directive to undertake hard manual work soon had them producing a surplus, which, when traded on the market, brought in wealth. Maulbronn expanded through land purchase and building programmes into a sprawling Gothic fortress on a Romanesque foundation. Maulbronn had become a rich prize, and still is. In 1993 the monastery was made a UNESCO World Cultural Heritage site. When Faustus arrived it was in the hands of Duke Ulrich von Württemberg. During an aggressive campaign to expand his duchy at the expense of the Palatinate in 1504, Ulrich had successfully besieged the monastery, as well as capturing nearby Knittlingen.

There is the faint possibility that Entenfuß and Faustus were old school friends – a seventeenth-century source called Entenfuß Faustus's '*Collega*'.[2] Legend has it that Faustus won over the abbot by promising him an abundance of alchemically produced gold.[3] Entenfuß was in need of it; he had an expensive mania for building.

In the six short years of his abbacy he built the *Herrenhaus* (1512–1514) with rooms fit for the best guests, an imposing festival hall to receive them and a delightful oriel window from which to survey his domain. He also added the spiral staircase leading from the *Herrenhaus* to the locutory (a long hall where the monks were allowed to converse), the bathhouse, winter refectory, and completed the jewel of the cloister – the fountain house. In the vault spandrels of the monks' refectory he had delicate red chalk paintings executed, it is thought, by Jörg Ratgeb – one of which is considered to be a portrait of Ulrich von Württemberg.

Entenfuß wanted to make his mark on history, but it would not be for his ambitious building programme that he would be best remembered. Local tradition certainly remembers Faustus: it has named a tower on the monastery's old wall, the *Faustturm*, a *Faustküche* ('Faust's Kitchen'), and, when I visited, Entenfuß's modern successor showed me a secret room known as the *Faustloch* ('Faust's Hole'). Rumour also had it that there was a secret passage leading out of the monastery, much used by Faustus on clandestine drinking binges.[4]

Received into the *Festhalle* of the *Herrenhaus* (today's Ephorat) on the far side of the monastery complex, Faustus would have found himself gazing down two rows of stone pillars holding up a wooden beamed ceiling. The heraldic device of Entenfuß could be seen carved on the first pillar to the right as he entered, but his gaze would have been drawn to the man seated at the end of the hall.

The *Festhalle* is where Entenfuß would have received secular visitors and conducted his business. Here Faustus would have presented his card, the infamous card that caught Virdung's interest and drew Trithemius's bitter scorn. Entenfuß had no doubt heard of these arts, perhaps even had some of those rare and forbidden manuscripts in his library. Faustus surely repeated the claims he had, according to Trithemius, made in Bad Kreuznach: 'that in alchemy he was the most learned man of all times and ... could do whatever anyone might wish.'[5] Here was a man an abbot with an ambitious building programme could use.

Entenfuß must have known that alchemy had a bad reputation and worse still was under the censure of the Church. Pope John XXII had forbidden the practice of alchemy in his bull *Spondent pariter* (1317). The authors of the *Malleus Maleficarum* added their disapproval: 'Writers on Alchemy know that there is no hope of any real transmutation.'[6] Nor was it just the Church that expressed its opprobrium; alchemists despaired of those who dragged their profession into disrepute. In the *Compound of Alchymy*, his treatise on producing the Philosophers' Stone, George Ripley (d. *c.* 1490), included a long satire on charlatans and would-be alchemists, warning the apprentice to beware the ragged 'multipliers' with corroded fingers and red-rimmed eyes. Even Paracelsus bemoaned that the art had 'fallen into contempt'.[7]

Amongst the crowd of threadbare charlatans, real alchemists walked. Two kings of England, Henry VI and Charles II, James IV, King of Scotland, Marie de' Medici, the Queen consort of Henri IV, King of France, and princes of the Empire, such as Wilhelm IV (1493–1550), Duke of Bavaria, and the Elector Palatine Ottheinrich (d. 1559), had all been known to employ alchemists. Entenfuß was in good company and the glitter of gold was enough to blind anyone to the disreputable side of alchemy.

The Laboratory

If Entenfuß expected Faustus to produce gold, he would have to furnish him with a suitable *laboratorium*. Hidden from curious monks, the secret room would have provided an excellent location, but for want of a chimney he would have been forced to use the window to vent his furnace – an obvious giveaway. Did he sequester himself here under the vaulted ceiling with a thin shaft of light to pierce the fug of his experiments? The isolated *Faustturm* was another good location, far enough away from the main buildings in case of fire or explosion and far enough away from the working heart of the monastery not to attract too much suspicion, yet easily accessible from the Abbot's personal quarters in the *Herrenhaus*. The choice of venue was the least of Faustus's worries: just how was he to go about making gold?

Faustus may have been working with the latest theories and practices drawn from such works as the *Pretiosissimum Donum Dei*, 'the most precious gift of God'. There exist today over sixty manuscripts versions of this important alchemical treatise in Latin, German, French, Italian and English, the earliest dating from the fifteenth century.[8] Several of these manuscripts are ascribed to Georgius Aurach de Argentina (also Anrach) and dated 1475. There is in addition a manuscript said to come from the hand of a nobleman of Trier in Germany. Written in 1453, it claims to be *The most excellent and true booke of the ph'ers stone.*[9]

We also find *Alchemical Sayings*, again from the fifteenth century, a single folio sheet that shows in a large coloured design what appears to be a furnace surrounded by the figure of a king on his throne, with the sun and moon, and a lion.[10] In 1433 Johannes von Bayreuth, the eldest son of Friedrich von Brandenburg, commissioned an edition of the *Book of the Holy Trinity*, which is found again in copies from c.1467 and 1492.[11] Alchemical recipes attributed to Arnold of Villa Nova and Andreas de Farlinio were circulating in manuscript form,[12] as well as Raymond Lull's *Animae transmutationis metallorum*[13] and the *Vom silber und vom golde* of Nicolaus of Paris.[14] One could scour the 147 paragraphs of the *Omne bonum a Domino deo est* of the mid-fifteenth century for clues of the secret of the philosophers,[15] or leaf through the so-called alchemy book of Martin Vreter and read the famous *Tabula smaragdina* of Hermes Trismegistus and the *Rosary of the Philosophers.*[16] Faustus would not have been stuck for alchemical texts; sixteenth-century Germany was all but carpeted with them, but which one would lead him to the prize?

Faustus may have followed the same sort of procedure so elaborately detailed in Ripley's *The Compound of Alchymy* (1471).[17] Ripley had studied in Rome and Louvain, travelled through Germany, and reputedly made gold for the Knights of St John on Rhodes. Ripley's process was a lengthy one and if Entenfuß expected a speedy result he would be disappointed. The art of alchemy was not to be rushed. Equipment would need to be bought – could we really expect Faustus to have dragged his own apparatus from Erfurt, even with a demonic supersteed for transport? Chemicals would need to be purchased, and if Entenfuß thought all it took was a lump of lead, he would need to be reminded of the alchemists' maxim: 'to make gold, take gold', or, in this case, gulden and lots of it. Did Entenfuß open his monastery coffers, eyes shining with the thought of super-abundant wealth, or did he pull on the purse-strings of Ulrich von Württemberg?

Although Ripley advised that 'one thing, one glass, one furnace, and no more' was sufficient, the list of apparatus could be a long one and, of course, an expensive one.[18] As an example of what was required, we might consider the archaeological excavations at Oberstockstall/Kirchberg am Wagram in Austria. Here, beneath the sacristy of a church adjoining the town hall, a rubbish dump of alchemical equipment was uncovered containing fragments of some eight hundred artefacts all dating from the sixteenth century. Working at high temperatures with corrosive substances in an environment devoid of health and safety regulations, Faustus, or any other alchemist of his day, was bound to go through a great deal of equipment.

Equipping an alchemist's laboratory was not something that could be done with much secrecy. Everything would have to be made to order. Special glass vessels, high quality ceramics and furnaces were required; glass-blowers and potters would be commissioned to produce the bizarrely shaped instruments. Even if these commissions were carried out in Maulbronn's own workshops, the monks and lay brothers, and the villagers living outside the walls, could hardly be unaware of these preparations. Travellers along the *Reichsstraße* would catch whispers of what was going on and pass them on to the next village and the next, and so rumours would spread. A sudden energy would enthuse the torpid monastery as mysterious deliveries from local artisans arrived and the monks were put to work cleaning out the tower, or the secret room, and carrying all the fabulous gear to and fro.

We might imagine his laboratory arranged after Pieter Bruegel the Elder's *The Alchemist* of 1558. We see a room crowded with instruments, the robed alchemist sitting at a table reading out instructions from his book, whilst his plainly-attired assistant sits before the fireplace, dropping some substance into a beaker. We see tubs of strange substances with spoons sticking out of them. A large still bubbles behind the assistant, whilst in front of him thick black smoke rushes up the chimney. If he decided to distil *aqua vitae* after Hieronymus Braunschweig's description in his *Book of Distillation* of 1512, then he would have had to set up a complicated system of glass pipes woven through a central upright cylinder where they were fed by the vapours of two alembics heated on their own furnaces. In Braunschweig's woodcut the alchemist hangs rather limply on the apparatus, hands seeming to caress the glass, whilst his assistant, as flamboyant as any *Landsknecht*, draws off the magical liquid from a dragon-headed tap at the base of the main pipe.

The historical model of an alchemist's laboratory in the Faust Museum, Knittlingen, shows again the typical scene of long-necked glassware, large and bizarrely shaped stills (one apparently modelled after Braunschweig's description), and no less than three assistants busy about their work. The alchemist himself is in his tented oratory, consulting the books of his art. A stuffed crocodile hangs from the wooden beams – a mainstay of the alchemical scene – and a human skeleton swings from a stand.

Bruegel's purpose was, however, satirical. Between the alchemist and his assistant we see a woman and a fool, clearly up to no good. The woman is emptying a purse into her hand and her sly look seems to say that it is not her own, whilst the fool, hiding behind the alchemist's table, puffs furiously with bellows on some overturned vessels, sending a cloud of smoke up the woman's skirts. Behind them a child with a cauldron on his head helps two others to climb up into a cupboard. The alchemist strikes an authoritative pose and his assistant looks busy, but it is a scene of chaos and an hourglass by the assistant's elbow suggests time wasted.

In contrast, Jan van Straten's *Die Alchemie* of 1570, like Bruegel, shows another busy scene, but this time the impression is one of order. The alchemist in his fur-trimmed doctor's robe and spectacles directs his assistants. In the foreground a boy pounds a mortar. A man with a spoon in some compound stares intently at a glass vessel, whilst another, a sixteenth-century Vulcan in red doublet and hose, is busy at the furnace with a look askance. However, the alchemist is not the centre of attention. Drawing the viewer's gaze is an effete-looking young man clutching a large, bulbous vessel. To the alchemical eye he is the hermaphrodite, the child born of the union of the sun and moon. His white shirt speaks of luna and mercury and his golden hair signals sol and even the elixir itself. From under his elbow a cat stares, wide-eyed with a look somewhere between terror and madness. We see a labour-intensive operation requiring many hands and much apparatus, but the steam, fumes and noise are resolved in the mannered, classical pose of the central figure, the hermaphrodite.

Both the *Faustturm* and the secret chamber at Maulbronn are too small to cater to tented oratories or decorative crocodiles. The available space would have concentrated Faustus's mind upon the essentials: the still and the furnace. The still, called an alembic in the alchemists' jargon, could be as complicated as Braunschweig's or simpler after Geber's designs. The name alembic comes from the Arabic *al-anbiq*, which is in turn from the Greek *ambix*, meaning a cup or beaker, and strictly speaking meant only the head of the still, but was used popularly for the whole apparatus. The furnace, called an athanor, was the other essential piece of equipment. The name comes from the Arabic *al-tannur* and refers to the so-called digesting furnace in which constant heat is supplied by a fire with a self-feeding supply of charcoal housed in a tower.

In addition to these, Faustus would require a number of bolt-heads – globular glass vessels with long necks that led to them being compared with ostriches or giraffes – retorts – another globular glass vessel but whose long neck was bent to curve round, making it look like a stork – and crucibles – pottery vessels made to withstand immense heat, usually with a narrow base widening into a round or triangular body.

Crucibles were traded across Europe in huge quantities at that time: three hundred triangular crucibles were recovered from the Oberstockstall excavations alone. Despite this we know relatively little about their manufacture and the reasons they were so highly valued. Using optical and energy-dispersive scanning electron microscopy (SEM-EDX) of cross-sections of the ceramics found at Oberstockstall, researchers at University College, London, were able to discover that all the crucibles were made from the same type of clay mixture, which was significantly different from other ceramics. The highly refractory clay was mixed with varying amounts of sand, grog and sometimes crushed graphite to improve the heat and chemical resistant properties of the vessels. The graphite in particular gave the crucibles improved conductivity and higher resistance to corrosive substances. The crucibles were then deliberately fired in a smoky potter's kiln that gave them a strikingly black sooty surface.[19]

With the bolt-heads and retorts Faustus would distil his chemicals, and in the crucible he would liquefy metals. He would most probably also have on hand several small glass phials for coagulation and solution, perhaps a circulatory still with two side-arms called a pelican (because of an imagined resemblance to that bird), and a urinal or ursale named after the bear (*ursa*) it was thought to resemble, which was another glass vessel, this time with a figure of eight shape and a projecting narrow glass snout in the upper globe. Shallow ceramic plates known as scorifers would also come in useful for a range of less demanding operations, such as the oxidation of lead bullion, or the initial melting of a metal before further refining.

Whilst the apparatus and techniques of alchemy were sometimes openly depicted and often in some detail – as in Braunschweig or the *Alchemiae Gebri Arabis* – the texts themselves were almost always inscrutable. Even the greatest amongst them like Nicholas Flamel could sympathise when he said 'this operation is indeed a Labyrinth'.[20] With all his equipment set up in the tower or the secret chamber, surrounded by gleaming glass and unburnt charcoal, just how was Faustus going to proceed? It was time to fire-up the athanor.

The Great Work

Armed with his thurible and retort, versed in the arcana of Geber and Arnoldus, begrimed with blackened residues, eyes stinging with acidic vaporisations, and reeking of sulphurous fumigations, what did the alchemist hope to achieve bent over his furnace late into the night? Gold? Immortality? The secrets of the universe? Greed and genius, glory and gain, knowledge and power; such desires drove the alchemist on through the mystical, maddening texts with their allegories of red kings and green lions, and on through endless experiments, part scientific, part spiritual exploration. The Great Work, the *magnum opus*, promised everything and concentrated into the single expression of the *lapis philosophorum*, the Philosophers' Stone. It was thought to produce a substance of universal transformative power. Its application purified base metal into gold, purified man from death, purified the soul from sin, and made perfect all that was imperfect.

What sort of man was the alchemist?[21] Part proto-scientist, the alchemist was also a mystic. Working before the advent of science as we know it (and before the word was used as such) the alchemist was also experimenting with the chemistry of the spirit. Just as he sought to purify his metals, so he also sought to purify his soul. Seen as a spiritual process, alchemy approaches the status of religion. While Roger Bacon (*c*.1214–*c*.1294) distinguished between 'operative' and 'speculative' alchemy, in practice the alchemist could make little separation between the sacred and profane in his operations; there was not spirituality on the one hand and secular science on the other. All of his experiments were concerned with the sacred, the sacred in nature and the sacred in man. A.E. Waite famously called the more exalted forms of alchemy the Yoga of the West in 1908, yet with its strong sexual metaphor I am inclined to think of it as the Tantra of Chemistry.

Did any alchemist achieve such spectacular goals? Some claimed they did. After 'years of unremitting labour', Flamel recorded how he achieved the impossible in 1382 and produced what he called 'pure gold'.[22] Nearer Faustus's own time an unknown German of the fifteenth century wrote *The Book of Alze* in which he confessed, 'I was almost on the point of giving up the whole thing in despair … I communicated my discovery to a friend, who faithfully executed my instructions, and brought the work to a successful issue.'[23] Faustus's contemporary, Paracelsus, also claimed to have made gold. The alchemists' experiments are not readily repeatable in the usual scientific manner. They tantalise us with possibilities whose secrets lie locked in the past, sealed with the twisting conundrums of their jargon.

For all his high talk, Faustus now had to produce something if he was not going to outstay his welcome in Maulbronn Monastery. All the equipment was in place with Entenfuß on the threshold of the laboratory demanding his gold. With Ripley's *Compound of Alchymy*, or something like it, there was an established procedure Faustus could follow. The process was described by Ripley in twelve stages, or as he called them 'gates' leading into an imagined Castle of the Philosophers. It would take over a year to complete. Faustus sets light to his charcoal, the athanor glows into life, the operation of alchemy has begun.

1. Faustus would begin with *calcination* or what Ripley also called 'the purgation of our Stone', a process that alone could take up to a year or more. The alchemist is instructed to turn earth into water, water into air, air into fire, to reverse the process and repeat it twice. If successful Faustus would be rewarded with what was variously called 'the head of the Crow', the crow's bill, the ashes of Hermes's tree, 'Our Toad of the Earth which eateth his fill', or 'the spirit with venom intoxicated'.[24]

At the end of the year, before Faustus could have had time to complete calcination, that great thorn in his side was plucked: Trithemius was dead. He had passed away in his monastery at Würzburg on the feast day of St Lucia (23 December 1516). Johannes Butzbach was at his internment to orate a eulogy to his friend as they lowered the body into the cold clay of the *Schottenkirche*. Carved above his body was a portrait from the workshop of Tilman Riemenschneider with an inscription as pompous as the man they commemorated. Part of it read 'May he be far from suspicion concerning the magical art of the Demon.'[25] Those would not have been Faustus's final words for him.

2. Faustus now subjects the 'hard and dry compaction' to the process of *solution* or *dissolution* where 'we dissolve into water which wets no hand' until it becomes 'intenuate', meaning thin, or liquid. 'Every metal,' explained Ripley, 'was once a Water mineral, therefore with Water they turn to Water all.'

3. Next Faustus turns to *separation* to divide 'the Subtle from the gross, from the thick the thin'. This should give Faustus water, the 'thin', and oil, the 'thick', and be repeated 'oft times' until 'Earth remain beneath in colour blue'. Faustus must now add distilled water seven times. This stage is often pictured as raising the birds from their nest as in the *Viridarium chymicum* published at Frankfurt in 1624. As Ripley rhymes it, 'Raise up the birds out of their nest, And after again bring them to rest.'

4. Faustus must now unite the four elements, earth, water, air and fire, through the process of *conjunction*, which is 'of deserved qualities a Copulation'. The 'Woman' is impregnated by the 'Man', meaning mercury is united with sulphur. The silver-coloured, flowing mercury, called *quicksilver* by the medieval alchemists, meaning literally, 'living silver', was depicted by Ripley as 'in her working … full wild', referring to the metal's volatility. According to the chemical theory of the period, mercury was the mother of metals, sulphur was their father. The *Rosarium philosophorum* (Frankfurt, 1550) depicts their union literally as intercourse between the 'King' and 'Queen'.

The 'Woman' must now be sealed in a vessel and allowed to lie for five months. This offered no respite for the alchemist, he had to lavish great care and attention on the gestating substance: 'Close up your matrix and nourish the seed, With continual and temperate heat if you will speed' advised Ripley.

The winter snows had melted and the worms had had their fill of Trithemius: 1517 must have been well advanced by the time Faustus reached conjunction, if he did. With the Ottoman Turks triumphant in Egypt, Pope Leo X was planning a new crusade. The future Emperor meanwhile was in Spain to collect his latest titles as King of Aragon, Majorca and Valencia, and Count of Barcelona from his deceased grandfather and the crown of Castile and Leon from his mother Joanna 'The Mad', to become Charles I of Spain. Ulrich von Hutten was made poet laureate by Maximilian I, although he surely did not write the latest book of magic then supposed to be on the market, the *Grimorium Verum* – the work was more likely a product of the eighteenth century. It was also at this time that the greatest change of the age was wrought: on the door of the castle chapel in Wittenberg Luther supposedly nailed his theses for all to read. Sequestered in his laboratory and diligent at his furnace, Faustus would have been unaware of any changes taking place outside of his 'matrix'.

5. The work continues with *putrefaction*. Faustus must inspect the 'glass tomb' and apply a 'moist', temperate heat for ninety nights until he sees the substance begin to turn black. Faustus must now turn up the heat and in this 'purgatory' his substance will become 'like liquid Pitch' that will 'swell and burble, settle and Putrefy'. Faustus will see the 'Woman' turn all the colours of the rainbow – the so-called Peacock's Tail – before finally turning white.

6. Faustus must now transform this liquid substance into a solid state through *congela-tion*, which is 'of soft things Induration of Colour White, and confixation of Spirits which fleeing are.'This is probably what Geber called coagulation, which he defined as 'the Reduction of a Thing Liquid to a Solid Substance, by Privation of the Humidity.' The substance should become thick and of form, according to Rulandus, 'like ice on water'. However, Ripley was nonchalant: 'you need not much to care, For Elements will knit together soon.'[26]

7. Faustus now has to start adding material back to his solid substance. Hortulanus in his *Hunting of the Green Lion* compared fermentation to a process of nourishing the alchemical child with drink, which is called *cibation*, or 'feeding the matter', but Ripley made this a separate and prior stage. Ripley also defines this process as 'feeding of our dry matter', adding 'With milk and meat, which moderately you do'. Alternately feeding it and letting it want, Faustus will observe dark 'leprosies' grow and diminish on his substance until it returns to a white waxy form that is 'Most like in figure to leaves of the hawthorn tree', and called 'Magnesia' and 'our White Sulphur without combustibility' by Ripley.

8. Another forty days of temperate heat are required for *sublimation*. Again colour changes are to be expected, this time of black and brown. With care and attention Faustus will see that 'the soul begins to come out, From his own veins, for all that is subtle, Will with the spirit ascend without doubt' and 'in the air our child must thus be born'. Faustus should then bring this soul back into its body and repeat seven times until his substance turns 'whiter than snow'.

9. Ripley warned that 'True Fermentation few workers understand'. Faustus must putrefy his substance, utterly destroying its former qualities, before fermenting proper. Ripley is vague on how this should be done, perhaps suggesting that more sulphur and mercury should be added to again produce a waxy substance. The mass should be 'fermented' according to this procedure three times with the added provision that 'you must ferment your gold with gold'. Faustus will observe the colours green, red and white again until he produces a fragrant smelling oil: 'Which heals all diseases in man'.

10. Faustus must now proceed to another form of sublimation called *exaltation*, which Ripley explains as if Jesus were speaking: 'If I exalted be, then shall I draw all things

unto me'. The Woman and Man are now buried and afterwards 'revived by the Spirits of Life' and 'up to Heaven they must Exalted be, there to be in Body and Soul glorified'. They ascend in 'clouds of clearness uniting together with Angels'. They then 'draw as thou shalt see, all other Bodies to there [*sic*] own dignity'. It seems that vaporisation and condensation are meant, although Ripley talks of 'loosening' and more 'putrefying', 'subliming' and 'calcining'. Faustus's strange substance is now more precious than gold, according to Ripley.

11. The next stage is multiplication where, by repeated fermentation, cibation and the addition of more mercury, Faustus must increase his substance 'in Colour, in Odour, in Virtue, and also in Quantity'. In his glass vessel Faustus, if successful, will see the fabled Tree of Hermes begin to grow. Faustus's fire must never go out and by continual feeding with mercury he shall have 'more than you need to spend'. Ripley adds a moral lesson, calling upon the alchemist to 'dispose you virtuously, helping the poor at need', which suggests that at this stage in the process the transformation into gold has already been achieved, but Faustus is not finished yet.

12. Finally, Faustus is ready for *projection*, the transmutation of base metals by use of the substance he has produced. He is instructed to take his 'medicine' and 'cast' it on metals that have been cleansed to prevent the result from fading and becoming 'brittle, blue and black'. Faustus will now find out if all of his long labours have paid off: 'In Projection it shall be proved if our practice be profitable.'

We can picture Entenfuß rushing across the little garden at the back of the *Herrenhaus* or climbing the stairs within the monastery to enquire 'is it ready yet?', whilst Faustus in his tower or secret chamber, sweating from the heat of the athanor, calls back 'not yet' or 'more charcoal', until the fateful day of projection arrives, if it ever does.

Today the opinion is that it could never have worked and the testimonies of those who swore that it did are dismissed as the ramblings of fools or cheats. If we take this view, then it seems incredible that alchemy was practiced so determinedly for so many hundreds of years. Many people firmly believed that the promises of alchemy were attainable, but if it was a question of faith alone, then we would be more advised to think of alchemy as a religion rather than a proto-science. What of Ripley and all the others? Are we to dismiss them as deluded believers in a false faith? Was Faustus entirely without hope of success?

The Transmutation

The answer is that alchemy worked. It worked in a way that would not stand up to today's higher standards of assaying and greater chemical knowledge, but, to all sixteenth-century intents and purposes, it worked.

Perhaps as early as the age of the Pharaohs – the word 'alchemy' is sometimes thought to derive from the Arabic for Egypt – the ancient Egyptians had discovered a technique for doubling gold called *diplosis*, although the best evidence only survives in Leyden Papyrus X, a Graeco-Egyptian recipe of the third or fourth century CE. To 'double' gold one is instructed to heat a mixture of two parts gold to one part silver and one part copper, and, indeed, a gold alloy is produced that appears to be double the amount of gold one had before. The Egyptians believed that the gold used in the operation acted as a seed that once sown in the silver and copper, grew, consuming them as it did so. Using copper alone gives the result a reddish tint; silver a light greyish one; combined the result was hardly discernable. This process makes sense of Ripley's instructions to 'ferment your gold with gold' and 'mingle gold with gold'.

The result, if it looked like gold, was generally thought to be gold. The problem for alchemy and society generally was that it was unclear what gold actually was. The tests for gold purity were rudimentary at best. In cases where an alloy had been produced it was thus difficult to establish that it was what we would consider an alloy and not pure gold itself. The principal test used was the hard, black stone called a touchstone. Scraping a piece of gold across it left a streak of metal and, depending on the brightness of the streak, an experienced eye could estimate how much gold was in the sample, usually by comparing it to samples of established quality. Pure gold left a bright yellow streak, whilst iron pyrites, so-called 'Fool's Gold', left a green-black streak. However, the touchstone was not a precise test and could not determine whether the gold was only a coating on a metal of lesser value.

The Mesopotamians had discovered a method for purifying gold as early as 1500 BCE. Called 'cuppellation', this involved melting impure gold in a ceramic cup, the 'cuppel'. Impurities were absorbed by the ceramic, leaving a button of pure gold. A misunderstanding of this process led later alchemists to believe that they had produced gold. If one takes a piece of lead and melts it in a cuppel a small amount of gold does appear to be produced. As we know now, most lead ore contains traces of gold or silver and so melting enough of it in the cuppel would eventually leave a residue of precious metal.

Dyeing or tinting is hinted at by Ripley's reference to 'your tincture', a tincture being a colouring or staining liquid thought to possess the power to transmute instantly. In the Middle Ages a process of making 'golden tin' was known that involved applying a yellow lacquer made from saffron called *doratura* to ordinary tin. Paracelsus was aware of such techniques and claimed to have used them.

A story told about Paracelsus relates how he changed a woman's kitchen fork into 'solid gold' by smearing a 'yellow ointment' on it. This miraculous transformation was obviously a tinting, but it is recounted as if gold was really produced. Change in colour alone could be seen as an actual transformation, although most alchemists, such as Paracelsus and before him Albertus Magnus, did distinguish a difference in quality between 'chemical gold' or 'our gold' and its natural cousin 'vulgar gold', but all of them still considered the result to be gold and goldsmiths were prepared to pay a high price for the manufactured metal.[27]

The probability is that by using diplosis, cuppellation or dyeing Faustus could have produced something that looked like gold and, to the sixteenth-century eye, was gold. He would have needed it. By the end of the process, Faustus would have spent almost two years on the operation and a good deal of Entenfuß's (or Ulrich's) money. The athanor and still would not have been cheap and a store of crucibles and glass vessels, easily broken, was required. A good deal of expensive sulphur and mercury, sometimes antimony as recommended by Basilius Valentinus, even gold, were required.

We have not even begun to think of the cost of keeping the athanor burning all that time. Writing in 1557, Thomas Charnock noted that he spent over £3 a week on keeping his fire going and that in the nine months of his experiment this cost him over £100. Working on the basis of a sixteen-to-one depreciation,[28] £100 in 1557 would be equal to about £7,000 today. Using the same calculations we would expect Faustus to have needed almost £20,000 to keep his athanor burning for up to 24 months. For most of its working life the monastery at Maulbronn only had one heated room, the calefactory – for all the sweat of his brow, Faustus would have been envied his athanor in the cold months.

Then there were the assistants' wages, after all the alchemist must sleep and someone would be needed to tend the athanor. The Bristol alchemist Thomas Norton wrote in his *The Ordinall of Alchimy* of 1477 that eight assistants were desirable, but at a pinch one could make do with four. The number was necessary, as he explains, because 'one halfe of them must werke/ While the other Sleepeth or goeth to Kerke.'[29] Add to this his board and lodging (and probably that of any assistants, although he might have made use of the free labour of the monks), and we begin to see that having one's own alchemist was a pastime for the wealthy. Yet many monasteries produced a surplus and what was another shovel full of charcoal to a self-sufficient and no doubt profitable concern like Maulbronn?

It was too much. Whether it was the cost alone or the nature of the operation, or something else entirely – we can never exclude that – by 1518 the course of events was about to take a drastic swerve. Entenfuß was dismissed from his post. We have yet to find a satisfactory reason why this was so. A register of past abbots drawn up in the eighteenth century has the words '*sancta simplicitas*' ('holy fool') against Entenfuß's name, opening up a wide vista of error, but Entenfuß's modern successor at Maulbronn was inclined to believe that financial profligacy was the chief cause. Entenfuß was not the only one to leave. In 1440 130 monks and lay brothers were counted in the monastery, but by 1530 they had dwindled to only 24. The work on the *Herrenhaus*, completed in 1517, was the last ecclesiastical building project in the monastery. It looks as though Entenfuß might just have bankrupted Maulbronn, but more for his lavish apartments than for the strange company he kept.

The Court Magician
(1519–1522)

After Maulbronn the trail runs cold. A smattering of legends and historically datable incidents put Faustus in the company of nobles, high-ranking clergy and even the Emperor himself in the role of something like a court magician. He appears in Heilbronn, in Boxberg, in Frankfurt, in Bamberg and in Innsbruck, wandering the roads of the Empire again in search of fame and fortune. The sightings are often mere hearsay. Rumours were rife and out of such fertilizer legends grow easily.

The Violet Garden

A story passed by word of mouth tells of Faustus in Heilbronn and nearby Boxberg castle. There is no date for this story, but Heilbronn is relatively close to Maulbronn, indeed could even be a misinterpretation of the latter, which leads us to place this story next to the events of Maulbronn.

Boxberg lies some sixty kilometres to the north of Heilbronn by modern roads and roughly double that distance away from Maulbronn. A castle was raised sometime in the twelfth century and by the thirteenth it is likely that the surrounding settlement already had town and market rights. Towards the end of the thirteenth century the town and castle came under the control of the Knights of St John from Wölchingen and held the status of a commandery. After a century the Knights sold it to the noble von Rosenberg family. Due to a cavalier regard for the law, the von Rosenbergs became something of a problem to their neighbours during the fifteenth century. In 1470 the Electoral Palatinate (*Kurpfalz*), Electoral Mainz (*Kurmainz*) and the High Chapter (*Hochstift*) of Würzburg allied themselves against the predatory family and destroyed their castles, including Boxberg. The von Rosenbergs eventually got Boxberg back and repaired it, but the family was set upon its career. In 1523 the Swabian League marched against the outlawed Melchior von Rosenberg and destroyed Boxberg castle for a second time and the Electoral Palatinate took possession of it. It was not until after Faustus's death that Albrecht von Rosenberg brought Boxberg back into his family's hands in 1548. It was finally sold to the Electoral Palatinate in 1561, which retained possession until the early nineteenth century. A seventeenth-century map shows a fairly imposing castle sitting on a hill above a walled town.[1]

If Faustus ever did visit Boxberg castle, then before 1523 he would have been the guest of the family von Rosenberg, perhaps of Melchior himself. After that date he may well have been enjoying the hospitality of the Elector Palatine, perhaps arranged through Virdung. Writing in 1940, Karl Hofmann dated the events of his poem 'Dr. Faust auf Burg Boxberg' to 1523. Unfortunately he gave no reason, but the destruction of the castle provides good grounds to suppose that Faustus must have visited before 1523.

The story, first published by Franz Joseph Mone in 1838, presents Faustus as a frequent visitor to the castle. On one occasion, whilst walking with the lords and ladies of the manor on a cold winter's day, he chivalrously leapt to the ladies' defence when they complained of the frost and conjured up a summer's day complete with fruiting trees and blossoming flowers. The ladies delighted in stepping through the masses of violets, but Faustus could not resist a practical joke. He caused ripe grapes to appear on the vine and invited his companions to reach out and put their knives to the purple bunches, ready to cut them on his command. When all were holding sharp blades to grapes he revealed that they were in fact holding their knives to each others' noses, a story we encountered earlier in Erfurt. The part of the garden where this took place has ever since been called 'the violet garden'.

That was not the end of his adventures in Boxberg. Another story recorded in 1838 told of Faustus and his 'Ghost Carriage'. In a rush to get from Boxberg castle to a banquet in Heilbronn before the clock struck midnight, Faustus hitched his carriage to four black horses and drove like the wind. Even so, he was not going to cover the sixty kilometres in the fifteen minutes he had left without some magical intervention. It is said that a man working in a field saw him speeding past with horned spirits furiously paving the way before him, whilst others lifted the slabs after him.

The demonic road-builders are an ingenious explanation to account for such a fast journey over heavily-rutted, slow-going roads. Magical journeys covering great distances in an impossibly short duration of time are, like the magical deceptions, another mainstay of the Faustian legends. A variation of the legend adds that some of the stones remained behind after the journey as an eternal reminder that evil spirits had been at work there. The story is a familiar type of folk explanation for unusual features in the landscape.

A final legend about Faustus and Boxberg adds another reason to place this location before Frankfurt and legends connected with Faustus's supposed visit there. According to this legend recorded by Hofmann in 1940, Faustus was travelling with a party of merchants *en route* to the Frankfurt Fair. Faustus's connection with the castle is forgotten (or not yet established) and it is through one of the merchants being a cousin to the castellan that the party was invited to enter Boxberg. They sat down to a feast and became so engrossed in the meal that they scarcely took any notice of the heavy rain that had started falling. When the time of their departure arrived – no doubt realising that the roads would now be all but impassable – Faustus leant out of the window, telling his companions that he intended to pull a rainbow towards them. Standing at the window with his hands apparently full of prismatic light, Faustus offered the rainbow as a form of transport to the others, magnanimously waiving any fee. Unsurprisingly, no one was keen to put their faith in the insubstantial beams to carry them the 146 kilometres to Frankfurt. Faustus let go of the rainbow and it returned to its former place in the heavens, explaining that he did not want to travel alone. And so the party set out on foot for faraway Frankfurt.

Trouble in Frankfurt (1519)

As plague ravaged France, Erasmus wrote enthusiastically of an impending Golden Age. There were few signs of it: war, witchcraft and disease were riding high. In 1518 von Sickingen was on the warpath, conquering the town of Gernsheim and besieging Darmstadt, and forcing the inexperienced Philipp I (1504–1567), Landgrave of Hesse, to pay heavy compensation. A new book out of Antwerp told the story of Mary of Nijmegen, or Nemmegen, concerning what is often seen now as a type of female Faustus. She makes a pact with the Devil but is saved by confessing her sins to the Pope. It was a conventional tale of wrong-doing and repentance. Closer to home there were executions for witchcraft in Waldsee, west of Heidelberg. Hope, if there was any, lay in the election of a new emperor.

When Maximilian I died in 1519, his failure to force through the appointment of Charles V as his successor left the field wide open. The office of Emperor was an elected one and Charles was not the only contender. Henry VIII, King of England, François I, King of France, Ludwig II, King of Hungary and Bohemia, and two or three of the Electors themselves were also in the running. It was known that Pope Leo X did not favour Charles and, despite all his titles, Charles could project no military force into Germany. The Electors looked divided in their sympathies, after all, three of them were archbishops whose ultimate interests lay with the Holy See. There was everything to play for.

The day of reckoning would take place in Frankfurt on 28 June 1519. A convocation of electors and their extensive retinues would mean an influx of wealthy nobles and courtiers – rich pickings that would have drawn many from far and wide. Faustus would have found his services in demand: divinations were wanted, miracles sought.

Ludwig II and Henry VIII were in similar cash-strapped positions and their bids were never more than opportunistic ones. France was the richest kingdom in Europe and François I had pledged half its annual income to the venture. He also had the Pope's blessing and thus some influence over the archiepiscopal Electors. To win over the German lords he added blood to the promise of cash, claiming that he was a German descended from Charlemagne. It is unlikely whether anyone was much impressed by François's new genealogy, just as few people would have thought of Charles as particularly German. In 1519 Charles had never set foot in Germany and knew nothing of the language, but like François he was proclaimed the 'German' candidate.

There were, however, some real German candidates to contend with. Friedrich III (1463–1525) 'The Wise', Elector of Saxony, appeared strong, but played a cautious game. He had some solid support within the Empire, but never openly revealed his intentions, letting others suggest that he was a candidate right up until the end. The other prime challenger was Trithemius's old patron, the Elector Joachim I von Brandenburg. His vote was eagerly sought by the supporters of both François and Charles, whilst he was himself coveting the imperial crown.

It was not just the electors that the candidates tried to woo. Knights like von Sickingen were also important powerbrokers. In an attempt to win von Sickingen over, François I invited him to Sedan, sending as ambassador Robert III (1491–1537), Count de la Marck, Duke of Bouillon, Seigneur of Sedan and Fleuranges, to escort him. Von Sickingen accepted the invitation. From Sedan he travelled on to François's court at the Château d'Amboise on the Loire.

The offer was 30,000 kronen-thalers cash and another 8,000 a year for life. The dramatist Lassalle portrayed von Sickingen as manfully turning down François's bribe, yet Lassalle would have been disappointed to learn that von Sickingen kept what cash François was able to pay him. German banks would not honour French promissory notes and German towns opposed to François's bid threatened to execute merchants bringing such notes into the Empire. The deal was all but worthless.

On the other hand, Charles's credit was good. Having the guaranteed revenues of Castile and the Tyrol behind him he was able to secure the services of Maximilian's old bankers, the Fuggers. Against François's uncertain promise, Charles was able to pay out 40,000 florins to von Sickingen. In characteristic style, von Sickingen raised a troop of several thousand *Landsknechte* and marched on Frankfurt. With him was the legendary Georg von Frundsberg (1473–1528), Baron zu Mindelheim, the 'father of the *Landsknechte*'.

The troublesome Ulrich von Württemberg had decided that the run-up to the election was an opportune moment to attack the city of Reutlingen. The rumour was that he was acting in French interests. The Swabian League swiftly mobilised and occupied Württemberg – and von Sickingen, ostensibly working with them, exploited the situation to plunder Maulbronn monastery. Charles's agents bribed the League to remain in the field under Habsburg colours, threatening the Elector Palatine in nearby Heidelberg. Another 30,000 florins brought the Swiss onto Charles's side, helped by their distrust of Ulrich. With von Sickingen, the League and now the Swiss, Charles had at last secured a powerful military presence in Germany.

François now over-played his hand with disastrous results. The untimely death from syphilis of Lorenzo di Piero de' Medici, Duke of Urbino, decided François to assert his rights over the Duchy of Urbino in the Papal States. The Pope was furious and withdrew his opposition to Charles. The archiepiscopal electors were given a clear signal and were not now troubled by their conscience in accepting Charles's bribes.

With the electoral college effectively besieged in Frankfurt, feelings were running high. Riots broke out amongst the townspeople over the impending decision. There was also plague in the city and the electors were keen to depart as quickly as possible. Ludwig II's vote as an elector was complicated by his young age and, at the last moment, his pro-French advisor was replaced by a pro-Charles one. The Elector Palatine was cowed by the Swabian League on his doorstep. Charles's enemies now coalesced around Friedrich of Saxony. The English diplomat Richard Pace (1482–1536), in Frankfurt for the election, reported that 'Friedrich was elected Roman King but ... declined the title believing himself not powerful enough to hold it'.[2] With rumours of the Swiss army just over the horizon and the very real threat of von Sickingen encamped just three kilometres away, it was the show of arms that cast the deciding vote.

With a thick wad of Fugger bills in their purses and a signed agreement from Charles to implement the imperial reforms that Maximilian had rejected, the Electors voted in Charles, and quit the pestiferous, mutinous city post-haste. Charles may have been jubilant when the news eventually reached him in Spain, but he must have dearly wished for an alchemist. The campaign had cost him over 835,000 florins with almost half of that going into the Electors' coffers. As Pace wrote only days after the election, the title had been 'the most dear merchandise that ever was sold; and after mine opinion it shall be the worst that ever was brought to him that shall obtain it.'[3]

For his crucial role von Sickingen was made Imperial Chamberlain (*kammerherr*) and councillor. Where von Sickingen was, we might conjecture that there also was Faustus. Von Sickingen would truly have lived up to his later reputation if he had not abandoned his former protégé because of a little local dispute, shocking though it no doubt seemed to the good burghers of Kreuznach. Faustus may have played some role in von Sickingen's attack on Maulbronn, perhaps signalling a change in the relationship between the alchemist and the monastery after the dismissal of Entenfuß. But more than that, the election of a new Emperor, especially in a situation where so many contenders circled the ring, was a prime opportunity for a magician. Predictions of the future would have been in high demand as Electors and lords tried to determine which would be the winning side. This tentative connection with von Sickingen puts Faustus in the right place at roughly the right time to agree with at least one of the many legends about him.

The Frankfurt Fair

Amidst all this drama of war and politics we lose sight of Faustus. With Entenfuß run out of office it would not be surprising to learn that Faustus was no longer welcome in Maulbronn, assuming he ever was. It is possible that Faustus may have moved on to Wittenberg. Lercheimer refers to him visiting Melanchthon there and Melanchthon did not arrive until 1518, but the evidence points to him being in Wittenberg at a later date: 1527 or 1530. A return to Kreuznach was out of the question and, despite Trithemius's demise, Würzburg was probably similarly disinclined to admit him through its gates. The Empire was a large place and trying to find Faustus is like looking for a wand in a woodpile.

A legend connected with Bamberg makes reference to 'loot from Frankfurt' and a document dated 1520 puts Faustus in Bamberg at that time, tentatively suggesting that Faustus was in, or believed to be in, Frankfurt before 1520. The legend is not an historical source and cannot be relied upon, and Faustus could also (or instead) have visited Frankfurt after 1520, but by skating over this thin ice we can bring in a story about Faustus in Frankfurt to fill the annoying gap in the historical record.

The story concerns professional rivalry and ends in murder. It is striking in this point, since the other dupes and deviousness that infest the Faustbook tales are comic rather than criminal (apart from his habitual stealing from the rich, but even this has a note of popular justice about it). There is also a glimpse here of the sort of illusionist trick that may well have been performed by travelling magicians.

According to the legend as told by P.F., Faustus arrived at the fair during Lent and discovered that four 'jugglers' had arrived earlier and were entertaining the crowds by cutting each others' heads off and sending them to the barber for a haircut. Faustus was annoyed by this 'for he meant to have himself the only Cock in the Devils [*sic*] basket' and set out to find them.[4]

Faustus observed that when the magicians struck off the head of the first of them, a lily appeared in a glass of water, which the chief magician named 'the tree of life' – the lily being a common symbol for the Resurrection. The decapitated head was washed and combed by the barber before the magician placed it back on his colleague's body and miraculously welded the two back together again and into life. As he did so the lily vanished from the glass. The trick was repeated with the other magicians. Faustus bided his time until it was the turn of their chief. Like the others, his head was also struck off and brought to the barber. Stealthily, Faustus cut off the head of the lily and when the other magicians brought their chief's head back to restore it to his body, found that he was dead.

The story appeared as early as the 1580s. The version that Spies published in 1587 added the moral observation that just as the chief magician was killed, so 'the Devil gives all his servants such an end at the last and makes away with them'.[5] In the Faustbook the conjuring trick is recounted as if it were achieved through supernatural means, and of course for the superstitious that meant the intervention of the Devil. It was also the case that there were travelling magicians or conjurers performing illusions in much the same manner as stage magicians today. In *Saint James and the Magician Hermogenes* of 1565 Pieter Bruegel the Elder shows us, amid a tumultuous scene of cavorting spirits, a body sprawled on a table, a sword separating it from its head which lies on a nearby platter.

In 1584 Reginald Scot published his account of how this trick, called 'the decollation of John the Baptist', could be performed. It required two associates, one to play the body and the other the decapitated head, and a specially prepared table with two holes in it. Scot added that the trick could be enhanced by having the 'head' boy inhale brimstone to turn his skin a deathly hue and sprinkling his face with blood. One can imagine how grisly this spectacle must have appeared and how similar methods could have been used by the Frankfurt jugglers. Suddenly, the fabulous nonsense of the legends can be seen to have a possible basis in reality.

This is not the only story of Faustus in Frankfurt. Roshirt (*c.*1570–75) told two more tales and other local Frankfurt stories persisted for some time. In the eighteenth century a traveller called Rudolph Lang wrote about some stories he had heard whilst in Frankfurt concerning a picture or image of Faustus.[6] The popularity and importance of the Frankfurt Fair certainly makes it a possible destination for Faustus and the surviving store of legendary material related to his being here make it a little more probable, but we will never know for sure.

One of the Roshirt stories ended up in the Wolfenbüttel Manuscript and later appeared in Spies 1587 and P.F.'s 1592 version. The location of Frankfurt was lost in the transmission until the story was appended after the wedding in Munich incident, which we will discuss presently, without any sort of narrative reason for its being there. It is a fairly typical story casting both Jews and magicians in a bad light. The deceptions of charlatans were clearly a cause of concern for certain sections of society and such moralising tales tended to feed that fear.

Faustus was at an inn frequented by Jews and for sheer devilment decided to play a trick on one of them. Borrowing money against his leg, which he let the Jew take away as surety, Faustus contrived to extort further recompense for the lost leg when the Jew threw it away, fearing that it would rot and pollute his house. It is a rather lame joke, if you will excuse the pun, but evidently a popular one to have survived three different retellings, not including variations such as that involving a horse dealer in Pfeiffering. Who is not to say that a magician never played such a trick?

Astrology for the Bishop (1520)

Slightly more than 200 kilometres to the east of Frankfurt the next piece of the jigsaw falls into place in the shape of an entry in the accounts of the Bishop of Bamberg. Drawn up by his chamberlain Hans Muller from Walpurgis 1519 to Walpurgis 1520, we read in an ornate hand an entry for 12 February 1520 under the heading 'Miscellaneous':

> Item. Ten gulden given and presented to honour Doctor Faustus, philosopher, who made for my Lord a nativity or judicium. Paid on the Sunday after [St] Scholastica's [Day] by order of his reverence.[7]

This 'nativity or judicium' was some sort of astrological prognostication and the chamberlain's uncertainty in describing it could point to a lack of knowledge concerning such things, or a lack of knowledge concerning this item in particular due to some element of secrecy. Given the hostile letters of Trithemius (1507) and Mutianus (1513) it is a surprise to find Faustus doing business with a bishop. It also shows that despite the best efforts of his enemies, Faustus was able to command respect and win the favour of the high and mighty, an echo of which is perhaps heard in the Faustbook amidst all the moralising verbiage: 'he had the most famous name of all the Mathematics [astrologers] that lived in his time.'[8]

The office of bishop of Bamberg was an important one, more important than any other bishopric in Germany. After Heinrich I von Bilversheim (r.1242–57) secured the title of Prince-Bishop and several rights of sovereignty from the Emperor for himself and his successors, the bishops of Bamberg came directly after the archbishops in ecclesiastical precedence. Faustus's client was not just any bishop, but the foremost bishop in Germany at that time.

In 1520 the fortieth Bishop of Bamberg was Georg III Schenk von Limpurg. Born in 1470 to a noble family, Georg was not much older than Faustus and well-educated. He had registered at the University of Ingolstadt when he was sixteen and already the canon of the cathedrals of Bamberg, Würzburg and Strassburg. For the summer term of 1490 he enrolled at the University of Basel. There is no record that Georg left with a degree from either institution, and in 1505 he acceded to the bishopric.

Since 1251 the Bishops of Bamberg had resided in the Altenburg overlooking the city of Bamberg. Walking across the narrow bridge over the deep defensive ditch, Faustus would have entered the gatehouse under the watchful eye of the tower looming above him. In the inner courtyard, the palace to his left would have been his obvious destination. The sum Faustus received for his services gives a clue to his reception. Here was an honoured guest, an astrologer of high esteem. No tradesman to come by the side door, but a scholar to be received in the Bishop's court.

In many ways the Bishop was an unlikely client. Most obviously his high ecclesiastical position would lead us to expect a disinclination towards retaining the services of an astrologer, especially one who been denounced as a necromancer. Beyond this problem of office, Georg III was directly involved in the Church's war on magic. In 1507 he had issued new laws with strictures against magic prominent amongst them. Georg III made the practice of magic a capital offence, authorised the use of torture and established the punishment as death by burning. Faustus, it might be thought, was walking into the lion's den.

The apparent inconsistency between Georg III's persecution of magic and his employment of Faustus leads one to suppose that Faustus was not seen as, or not proven to be, a practitioner of that sort of magic by Georg III. It is not the case that these laws were not enforced or enforceable. In the early seventeenth century they would be put into devastating effect. Nor should we assume that Georg risked his own reputation to consult this particular astrologer when Bamberg was teeming with them. The only conclusion we can arrive at is that the sort of things Trithemius reported Faustus as saying about himself in 1507 were taken at face value by Georg III in 1520 – we might suppose that Faustus stressed his philosophical and astrological credentials over his necromantic and blasphemous ones. In the intervening thirteen years, Faustus proved himself to be more successful than his enemies' campaign against him.

Despite his new laws against magic, Georg III was an unusually enlightened prelate. His court in the lofty Altenburg became a haven for intellectuals and artists, such as the Humanists Lorenz Beheim and Ulrich von Hutten. Von Hutten even collaborated with Georg III's *Hofmeister* (chief administrator) Johann von Schwarzenberg to produce a German translation of Cicero. He later dedicated the 1518 publication of his speech on the Turkish problem to the Bishop. The brothers Andreas and Jacob Fuchs, Humanists and former pupils of Crotus Rubeanus, were both Church officials in Bamberg and closely associated with Georg III's court. Georg sponsored the arts by employing Hans Wolf as his court painter and gave commissions to both Loy Hering and Albrecht Dürer. His bookbinder was the respected geographer and astrologer Johannes Schöner (Schonerus, 1477–1547), who would go on to become professor of mathematics and astrology in Nuremberg.

Schöner was an alumnus of the University of Erfurt and had pursued his own studies into astronomy and astrology in Nuremberg. An undated woodcut shows him wrapped in his doctor's gown, his fringe cut short over a high forehead, hair growing long over his ears at the sides to meet an unpleasant-looking beard of rats' tails, with heavy bags under his eyes, presumably the result of many a sleepless night gazing at the heavens. When he moved to Bamberg he produced globes showing the latest discoveries in the New World and began printing his own books, dedicating his first work on geography to Georg III in 1515. Schöner's great interest was astrology and most of his later printed works were devoted to exploring the secrets of the celestial influences. Schöner was also something of a loose cannon. He had fathered a daughter with his mistress and was so altogether lax in his church duties that he was deprived of a benefice in Bamberg. But the Bishop liked him and continued to offer his patronage. One of his undoubted privileges was that he enjoyed access to the Bishop's library where there were manuscripts already thought to be antique in the sixteenth century.

Schöner was not the only astrologer in Bamberg at this time. Lorenz Beheim was also noted for his skill at astrology as well as his legal acumen and Humanist interests. Willibald Pirckheimer thought him the most learnéd man of his circle and the two corresponded at length on alchemy and astrological medicine. Beheim had met Reuchlin while studying in Italy and had learnt the mysteries of the cabbala from him.

With such skilled proponents of astrology on hand, it is surely of significance that the Bishop instead turned to Faustus, an outsider. There is no record that Georg III ever consulted Schöner or Beheim on the subject of astrology, but as members of his court they may have supplied their advice informally or on a *quid pro quo* basis. Both Schöner and Beheim had better reputations than that usually attributed to Faustus, but the fact that the Bishop preferred Faustus in 1520 is a glowing endorsement of the much maligned necromancer.

A Princely Sum

Two things are immediately striking about the payment: that it was 'given and presented as a testimonial', and that it was made on a Sunday. Both of these suggest a public ceremony, at least in the sense of being conducted in the court. In addition, an official record was made of the payment, so this was not some secretive transaction. Then there is the sum paid itself.

Ten gulden was a lot of money in 1520. To put it into perspective, a labourer earned less than two gulden, a craft apprentice three or three-and-a-half gulden, and a soldier received between three and four gulden a month in wages. At mid-sixteenth century prices, a balanced diet would have emptied a *Landsknecht's* purse and left nothing over for beer. Even the wealthy Basel printer John Amorbach could only afford sixteen to twenty 'crowns' per annum for his son's board and lodging whilst at university. Looking at the local economy, Faustus's fee was more than a bookbinder or artist in Bamberg could make per commission. Johannes Schöner received just under four gulden for a single book-binding order. Hans Wolf made about two gulden by helping Dürer paint his portrait of Georg III. Faustus's contemporary astrologers could earn more, or at least some of them said they could. The Italian Girolamo Cardano (1501–1576) claimed to have once turned down 200 'crowns' for a horoscope. Virdung gave a more reliable account when he noted the expense of four Hungarian gold pieces paid to Albertus de Brudzewo for his help with a review of the subject of astrological nativities.

The exact value of ten gulden was difficult to measure in the sixteenth century. The coin could be called a gulden, guilder, or florin – all names that refer to the first gold coins minted in Florence in 1252. Made of silver rather than gold by the sixteenth century, the coin had no standardised value and mostly circulated within localised economies. Generally, the gulden was the currency of the southern imperial states: in the centre it was the thaler, whilst in the north we find the marck. In the contemporary record and the legendary material concerning Faustus, gulden, florin and thaler are all met with, but are not always exactly the same thing. It was not until 1559 that the Holy Roman Empire had an official currency.

If the uncertainties over how much Faustus's payment was worth have us scratching our heads, then the problem of what he was paid for will have us pulling our hair out. Hans Muller was no doubt an able *Kammermeister* but we could have wished for a little more detail in his curt entry in the accounts.

Previous research has been hampered by a critical misunderstanding. Most other accounts interpret Faustus's service as an '*Indicium*', but are then at pains to explain exactly what this is. After re-examining the original, I argue that the Bishop's chamberlin wrote '*Judicium*'.[9] *Judicium* means 'judgement', as in usage recorded from at least 500 CE of *Judicium Dei* ('Judgement of God'), the practice of trial by ordeal, and from the mid-fourteenth century of *Judicium Pillorie* ('Judgement of the Pillory'), but more significantly as in the title of Nicolaus de Shadek's *Judicium Astronomicum* of 1524. This latter use specifically refers to the practice of *astrologia judiciaria*, or 'judicial astrology'.

Judicial or divinatory astrology was concerned with man's fate, what we might think of as the 'Judgement of the Stars', as distinct from *astrologia naturalis* ('natural astrology'), which was a sort of astrological weather forecasting. This type of astrology was forbidden by canon law because it denied free will, although if the Bishop was happy to commission such work, his attitude to canon law must have been individual, to say the least, and, anyway, Faustus could easily work his way round the problem with recourse to the old get-out clause that the stars 'inclined without constraining'. Later in the sixteenth century, Pope Sixtus V would issue a bull outlawing judicial astrology along with the entire gamut of magical arts.

Schöner was quite capable of providing this sort of service. A copy of his horoscope of Johannes Carion survives and he would go on to draw up Luther's horoscope with his friend Melanchthon. In 1547 he would publish a book dedicated to judicial astrology, *De Ivdiciis Nativitatum*, with a foreword by Melanchthon. Could this Lutheran connection be the reason why Georg III turned to an outsider for his glimpse into the future?

The Horoscope

Faustus would have begun like any other sixteenth-century astrologer, and by looking at the practices of others we can follow his steps. The sixteenth-century horoscope was quite different in construction from its modern cousin. Instead of the planets plotted on a wheel with the constellations marked at the rim, it was drawn up in a square – the so-called quadrant system – with the twelve houses marked in triangles around a central box and the signs of the zodiac marked on the outside edge, three to each side, or more often within the triangular houses themselves. Each house was thought to govern a particular area of one's life and so

the presence of the planets and their relationships to the others around them determined how these facets of existence would be formed and directed.

The complex tables of the Middle Ages were gradually being replaced by easier to use
ephemerides, essentially astronomical almanacs showing the predicted positions for the
heavenly bodies. The positions of the planets would be described in terms of degrees,
minutes and seconds, placing them within a zodiacal sign. Thus for 23 April 1466 we
would find the position of the sun given as 11° 7´ 33´´ of Taurus. However, the astrologer
would still need to make adjustments for place and time. The printed ephemeris was usually calculated for a large town at twelve noon and any variation from this would have to
be taken into account.

Having drawn out his quadrant, Faustus could determine a number of things. With
the Bishop's place of birth and the exact day, hour and minute of birth, he could construct a complete natal chart showing the course of his life. But Georg III already felt
himself to be approaching *Domus Mortis*, the 'House of Death'. It is possible that Georg
III may have employed Faustus to produce just such a chart as a testament to his life in
the same way that Melanchthon sought to demonstrate Luther's greatness by casting a
birth chart for his hero. However, the astrologer was not restricted to birth charts.

Horoscopes were also drawn up to determine the outcome of specific events, such
as commercial transactions and even invasions. The chronicler Matthew Paris reported
that Emperor Friedrich II (r.1215–1250) used astrologers to forecast the outcome of
his plans and even when to consummate his marriage. It has been calculated that
more than 200 events in the reigns of the Habsburgs, from coronations, marriages,
battles and the signing of treaties, were dictated by the astrologers' calculations.

The question then is, what problems were pressing on Georg III's mind? The year
1520 exhibited all the usual turbulence of disaster and war that we have come to
expect of the Renaissance. The religious mind must have been preoccupied by the
series of events begun in 1517 and Georg III in particular was known to be greatly
troubled by Luther's rebellion against Rome. Many of his advisors at court had sided
with Luther and one of them, Lazarus Spengler, had already written to the influential
Willibald Pirckheimer saying that the Bishop was with them. Spengler himself would
be threatened by a Papal Bull. Georg III perhaps saw this as a strike too close to home,
as Spengler would report with disappointment the Bishop's changed attitude in a
letter of 5 November 1520. Georg III had already commissioned Loy Hering to produce his epitaph and tombstone in 1518–19, so it might be that the Bishop's thoughts
were directed more to the hereafter, no doubt exacerbated by his vacillation between
Luther and Rome. Georg III was only fifty years old in 1520, too young, one might
suppose, to be contemplating the end, but he was to die only two years later.

If Faustus's prognostication related to the Lutheran rebellion, then his conclusions
did not induce the Bishop to renew his support for the rebels; perhaps they even
made him change his mind. Also, if Faustus's prognostication was about Luther or the
Reform movement, then this may explain why Georg III sought an outsider, especially as his most prominent astrologer, Schöner, was a staunch Lutheran. The status of
'judicium' as outlawed or at best theologically dubious astrology is another compelling reason to turn to an outsider. If this theory is correct, then this could also explain
why such a sensitive document has not survived.

'Good, Fat Pigs'

As well as the official record, Bamberg also has its tales about the magician. According to Roshirt, when Faustus came to Bamberg he was warmly welcomed and entertained in one of the inns. It also happened that there was a swineherd there who was talking to the landlord, bemoaning the fact that he did not know where to get his hands on a herd of good, fat pigs. For the Faustus of the legends it was an unmissable opportunity to beguile a country bumpkin, especially since 'the loot from Frankfurt' was nearly all gone – no mention was made of the Bishop's generosity. Faustus conjured up a herd of pigs and sold them to the swineherd, warning that he should take care not to drive them through water. Of course, the swineherd disregarded the advice and found that his pigs turned to straw when he attempted to ford a river.

It is a typical and fairly unremarkable magical story. There is something more innocent in the magician's simple duping of the swineherd than his typical image as a diabolical pact-maker. Faustus's magic is taken for granted: it is a simple thing for him to bewitch the pigs. However, the tale still makes the implicit acknowledgement that magicians are cheats and should be avoided.

With the Bishop's gold in his pocket, Faustus had little need of defrauding swineherds, but the early death of Georg III deprived Faustus of one of his most influential and important clients. It not only took from him the possibility of future contracts, but removed a pillar from the edifice of his reputation. Amidst the growing crowd shouting him down, there was now one less voice to potentially add its support. In time there might have been a more permanent place for Faustus in the Bishop's court, but now there was only the open road.

A Wedding in Munich (1521–1522)

The year 1521 opened with the excommunication of Luther. In a letter written from the Wartburg he raged that all his enemies were inspired by Satan and that he was engaged in a direct struggle with the Devil. Undeterred, he would go on to publish his translation of the New Testament. This was not the only threat to Rome. Suleiman I 'The Magnificent' (1494–1566), only twelve months into his sultanship, would lead the Ottoman Turks to capture Belgrade, marking their farthest inroad into Christendom. As if to signal defeat or resignation, Pope Leo X died. Paracelsus was in Constantinople where he would later claim to have discovered the Philosophers' Stone. The fear of witches was of course still in the air. In his *De Strigimagorum Daemonumque Mirandis*, Sylvester Prierias cited a wealth of contemporary cases of witchcraft that lead the reader to suppose that the belief in witchcraft was flourishing in Rome and central Italy during the early years of the sixteenth century.

Faustus probably cared little for the plight of Luther and was most certainly unaware of Paracelsus's discoveries. As a learnéd magician he undoubtedly thought himself above the mere station of 'witch'. Few magicians have ever shed a tear over the death of a pope and there is no reason to suppose that he was in or near Belgrade, or otherwise much involved at this time with the Turkish problem. Many of the 'world events' that occupy historians now had little immediate impact on everyday life, and Faustus must have had concerns of his own. Georg's money was surely all used up. He needed a new client, a new cause, a new source of income.

In April 1521 François I declared war on the Empire and by summer von Sickingen was fighting in northern France on the Emperor's orders. He saved himself the trouble of assaulting Sedan's formidable fortress by concluding a truce with Robert de la Marck. Nearby Mouzon on his flank fell after a brief siege, leaving the way open to Mézières. He had 35,000 men against 2,000 and victory seemed assured, but, according to legend, a deception by Pierre Terrail, Seigneur de Bayard, broke the siege and scattered von Sickingen's forces. Recalled to the Imperial Court in Brussels, von Sickingen was accused of treason and only received the vaguest promises from Charles V to reimburse his campaign costs. Had Faustus marched with von Sickingen to divine the career of the campaign, or given him astrological advice before he left?

Still spoiling for a fight, von Sickingen marched against the Archbishop of Trier to settle a personal feud, an event that is now seen as part of the wider Knights' Revolt (1522–23). If Faustus was with him at Mézières, then he could have been with him here. However, added to the possible estrangement over Kreuznach, von Sickingen's new-found Protestantism could have driven a further wedge between the two men. For the adventurous, the promise of riches to be won in Italy was as strong a siren call as ever, and 1522 is chiefly remembered for the Battle of Bicocca, although we should not overlook the siege of Rhodes, as will become apparent later.

Faustus, so the story goes, was at the Duke of Bavaria's son's wedding in Munich. If Faustus did indeed go to Munich, and let us suppose that he did, then it could only have been on 3 October 1522, time enough to have accompanied von Sickingen on his campaign in France.

According to the Faustbook Faustus was sought out by 'three worthy young dukes', students of the university, who were agog at the thought of the sumptuousness, 'pomp and bravery' that would attend the wedding of the Duke's son in.[10] Faustus conducted the noblemen into a garden and spread his cloak, bidding them to sit upon it. Faustus turned to his travelling companions with a warning. On no account should they talk to anyone, even if spoken to by the Duke himself. Faustus cast his spell and they flew up into the air.

There is no sign of Faustus's earlier demon horse. He was not, like Luther's sorcerer, content to ride a common goat or broomstick; he employed a more commodious magical cloak to convey the young noblemen to Munich. We are reminded of the legendary hole in the roof of that house on the Schössergasse in Erfurt, said to have been made to accommodate Faustus on his magical cloak.

The spurious *Black Raven* (supposedly Lyon, 1469) attributed to Faustus included instructions for performing this feat, but despite the early date given to this text it probably derives from the story in the Faustbook rather than the other way round. Called 'Doctor Johann Faustis Coat Ride' the magician is instructed to spread a large red coat on the ground and trace a magical figure in the middle of it. The magician is then told to walk backwards onto the coat – holding tightly another representation of the same magical figure – until he is standing in the middle of the magical figure. The instructions warn 'do not step your feet outside this symbol, otherwise the trip will not be a happy one.' The magician must then call upon the spirit Aziel three times, with the final piece of important advice: 'If you want to leave a room, be sure that the windows are open.'

Luther, of course, had his own opinion on such cloak rides from which the later story of Faustus's journey in the Faustbook may have derived. 'As for flying through space on a cloak,' he said 'without doubt it can be done for a short or a longer distance.'[11] But he also wondered if it was an illusion created by the Devil.

Faustus's cloak would have conveniently transported the group over the imposing fourteenth-century gates and walls that encircled sixteenth-century Munich. The motto of the city was not then *München mag Dich* ('Munich likes you'). Like every other city of the Empire, Munich was suspicious of you. To gain admittance within those walls one was required to show proof of having a relative, friend or place to stay inside.

Founded in 1157/58 by Duke Heinrich (1129–1195), 'The Lion', to control the trade route across the River Isar, Munich had recently become the capital of a reunited Bavaria after a bloody war of succession. Faustus and his noble tour group flew over the walls and across the rooftops of, as P.F. puts it, 'a right princely Town' that 'appeared as if it were new, with great streets therein, both of breadth and length.'[12] The enlarged town hall and the twin spires of the comparatively new *Frauenkirche* (constructed 1468–1488) – as yet devoid of their characteristic brass onion-domes – would have been easily distinguishable landmarks.

The old Duke, Albrecht IV (1447–1508), known as 'The Wise', had had three sons by his wife, Kunigunde of Austria, daughter of the Holy Roman Emperor Friedrich III: Wilhelm IV (1493–1550), Ludwig X (1495–1545) and Ernst (1500–1560). Ernst had gone into the church and in 1522 was an ecclesiastical official in Passau; he would go on to become Archbishop of Salzburg. Wilhelm and Ludwig both reigned as dukes of Bavaria, despite the fact that their father had willed the everlasting succession of the firstborn (primogeniture). With the support of his mother and the States-General, Ludwig had forced Wilhelm to accept him as co-regent in 1516. Ludwig died without leaving an heir, but Wilhelm's marriage to Marie von Baden-Sponheim on 3 October would, in time, give Bavaria its next duke.

It is a sign of its general unreliability that the Faustbook refers to the marriage of the Duke's son, since the son was then the Duke. In 1522 Albrecht had already been lying for many years in the *Frauenkirche*. It is also an indication of the story's dubious veracity that the three noblemen of Faustus's party are 'not here to be named'.[13]

Flying over the market, the cloak-riders would have been drawn by the blazing torches and sounds of merriment coming from the *Neuveste*, built in 1385 on the site of today's *Residenz*. We might suppose that Ernst put aside the affairs of the Church to attend the ceremony and the pushy Ludwig was surely not one to be left out as Wilhelm and Marie were wed. When they arrived, Faustus and his company were given a warm, if somewhat perplexed welcome on account of their silence.

Of course, it could not have been the 'good old Duke' who greeted them, as P.F. had it, but the twenty-nine year-old Wilhelm.[14] A group portrait of Wilhelm and his family from 1534 shows a man in his early forties. A broad black hat sits rakishly on a cushion of neatly trimmed hair. He stares purposefully at nothing in particular somewhere over the viewer's right shoulder. His wife looks pale and somewhat full in the face. Dull eyes stare out above thin, pursed lips. In contrast to her bland expression, her clothes gleam with gold thread. There is sumptuousness in this portrait, but the display of wealth is balanced by a tone of seriousness and restraint.

Faustus, with a wary eye out for possible trouble, advised his companions: 'if anything happen otherwise then well, when I say, sit up, then fall you all on the cloak.' His earlier warning proved in vain and the jaunt was cut short by the politeness of one of the young noblemen who, being given a bowl of water to wash his hands, asked his friend to wash first. Faustus cried 'sit up' and the noblemen leapt onto the cloak, but as it took to the air, the one who had spoken fell off and 'was taken and laid in Prison'.[15]

The prisoner was interrogated. Who was he? Who were the others who had vanished so mysteriously? But he kept his mouth shut and the Duke ordered that the recalcitrant guest be racked the next day. Facing the slow and excruciatingly painful dislocation of his limbs, the prisoner reasoned that 'I shall be constrained by force to tell more than willingly I would do.'[16] Faustus had not abandoned him and before daybreak he reappeared, throwing the guards into a heavy sleep and springing the locks with his magic, perhaps with a charm like the 'Key of Pluto' from Codex 849.

It was not foolish young students, however high-born, who needed his help, but his old patron von Sickingen. In August 1522 he had led around 8,000 men against Richard Greiffenklau von Vollrads (1467–1531), Archbishop of Trier, but finding himself deprived of the reinforcements he expected was compelled to retreat on the Ebernburg, assaulting some of the Archbishop's possessions on the way. Alarmed by his boldness, the *Reichsregiment* placed von Sickingen under the Imperial ban. Pamphlets appeared decrying that he was in league with the Devil – one even included a supposed letter from von Sickingen to Satan. Von Sickingen sent the Elector Palatine a letter of feud and conducted a series of raids against Otterbach, Lützelstein and Kaiserslautern. It was a knight's way of giving the *Reichsregiment* two fingers.

With the edges of the Christian world falling before the Ottomans, the mighty of the Holy Roman Empire were at each others' throats. The rulers of Trier, Hesse and the Palatinate mobilised against von Sickingen. Having secured help from the Swabian League, they cornered him at Burg Nanstein in Landstuhl with a combined army of 3,000 men. Shortly after the siege began, von Sickingen was mortally wounded by falling masonry during a bombardment and was forced to capitulate. He died the next day on 7 May 1523. Faustus had lost another powerful patron, perhaps also a friend.

12

The Planets Collide
(1523–1525)

Contrary to usual opinion, the astrologers proclaimed that the solar eclipse of 23 August 1523 would be beneficial. The benevolent Jupiter would dominate the maleficent Saturn and all would be well. It was only to be the calm before the storm.

In 1523 a new Pope was in Rome: on 18 November Giulio di Giuliano de' Medici (1478–1534), a Knight of Rhodes and Grand Prior of Capua, took the name Clement VII and became the second of the Medici popes. In one of his most characteristic portraits by Sebastiano del Piombo we see a fleshy face, the heavy lidded eyes of a libertine, a hint of a sneer playing upon his lips and a sidelong glance that conveys the deviousness for which he would long be remembered.

Inspired by the mass torture and execution of alleged witches conducted by the Inquisitor of Bologna, Pico della Mirandola gave his full support to the Christian atrocities. In his book *Strix* he recounted endless details of the horrors witches supposedly indulged in, especially revelling in reciting details of sexual intercourse with incubi and succubi. At the same time, Bartolommeo de Spina, similarly inspired by some recent witch-burning in Ferrara, wrote his *Quaestio de Strigibus* refuting those who contended that the witches' sabbat was an illusion. De Spina argued that the high number of people burned for witchcraft in the diocese of Como alone was proof that witchcraft existed.

Grimoire

In 1523 a little book of magic making great claims for itself was supposedly published in Rome. Like many others this book was attributed to the Supreme Pontiff himself. *The Enchiridion of Pope Leo III* was not a book of ceremonial magic in the grand tradition, but rather a catalogue of charms and an extended magical devotion called

'The Seven Mysterious Orisons'. The *Enchiridion* was said to have been presented by Pope Leo III to Charlemagne after his coronation in Rome – an unlikely event. Although it has attracted the reputation of black magic and been condemned as such, the *Enchiridion* is relatively innocent.

There was, however, a more sulphurous book on the market. Attributed to Faustus, the *Doctor Johannis Fausti Manual-Höllenzwang* was reputed to have been printed in Wittenberg in 1524. A black bird adorns the cover and, like the *Black Raven* purported to have come out of Lyon in 1469, the *Manual-Höllenzwang* begins with a stern warning:

> Without a circle read me not out loud,
> For then I spell great danger.[1]

Butler believed the book to be the original *Harrowing of Hell* – thus actually coming before the *Black Raven* with its unfeasibly early date of publication. However, the date of 1524 is not to be trusted either. It would appear to have been produced after the name of Faustus was irrevocably connected to the idea of the pact in the last half of the century, and yet the naming of Faustus's familiar as Aziel instead of Mephistopheles and that the book actually leaves out Mephistopheles altogether, points to the sixteenth century and especially before Mephistopheles exclusively filled the role of familiar. It is, however, the use of the name 'Johannis' instead of Georgius that suggests most strongly that this is not an original work. As with all these texts, we can never trust the place and date of publication given to them.

In the Sign of Pisces

Whether Faustus really was working on his *Manual-Höllenzwang* or not, we can be sure that one event had not escaped his notice. The conjunction of seven planets in Pisces predicted for February 1524 was the source of almost universal alarm and an astrologer of Faustus's fame could not have avoided the subject. Terrible things were expected. It was believed that the conjunction of Saturn and Jupiter in Scorpio in 1484 had led to the dreadful scourge of syphilis. That such a great conjunction was taking place in the sign of the fish, Pisces, was the cause for many to predict widespread flooding of biblical proportions.

As early as 1499, Johannes Stöffler and Jacob Pflaum had foretold terrible catastrophes for 1524 in their *Almanach nova*, warning of:

> Certain changes and transformations for the whole world ... changes such as we have hardly heard of for centuries before our time, either from historians, or from our elders.[2]

Stöffler and Pflaum's prediction went through successive editions, but it was couched in general terms and largely restricted to academic circles. It was instead the famous

Italian astrologer Luca Gaurico (1476–1558) who really put the cat among the pigeons with a publication sent to the Reichstag at Trier in 1512. Gaurico drew a much more vivid picture of looming disaster, being the first to talk explicitly of a flood caused by the conjunction in his *Prognosticon ab incarnationis*. Alarmed, Ludwig V commanded Stöffler and Virdung to investigate, whilst Leonardo da Vinci was inspired to paint psychedelic swirls of watery chaos.

Faustus may have discussed the subject with Virdung back in Heidelberg all those years ago – certainly Virdung had written about the matter in 1520 whilst discussing the signs over Vienna. He returned more fully to the subject in his *Practica* of 1521. Virdung believed that the effects of the conjunction would be felt as early as 1523 with an intemperate amount of water destroying the fruits of the earth and ships at sea in 1524. He was not of the Noah camp, however, and settled for a partial deluge with long-lasting effects. Virdung deduced that the repercussions of the conjunction would last for forty years with a timed series of after-effects being felt at precisely calculated intervals until 1563.

One of the more influential books at the time was the *Mirabilis Liber* sometimes ascribed to Johannes Lichtenberger (1440–1503), astrologer to the Emperor Friedrich III, but it was a later work incorporating much of Lichtenberger's earlier *Prognosticatio* of 1488, as well as extracts from Savonarola's *Compendium revelationum* of 1495. Lichtenberger's *Prognosticatio* was a major success: thirty-two editions and some 10,000 copies appeared in the years to 1530. First published in 1522, the *Mirabilis Liber* was swiftly reprinted by Jehan Besson of Lyon in 1523 (although it bears the date 1524) and many more editions followed. Disaster was a common theme. A chapter described as 'Another Prophecy from Jean de Vatiguerro', who flourished in the fourteenth century, predicted that 'Many towns and strong military posts on the Po, the Tiber, the Rhône, the Rhine and the Loire shall be razed by extraordinary floods and earthquakes.'

On the cover of Leonhard Reynmann's astrological *Practica* called *On the Great and Manifold Conjunction of the Planets* (1523) an illustration shows the planets gathered in the giant figure of a fish to denote Pisces as a great stream of water descends upon the earth where houses, a church and dead bodies bob upon the waves. Even those of a more sober temperament predicted unusual quantities of rain and snow. Only a few stood against the general opinion. As early as 1519 Pico della Mirandola's nephew Agostino Nifo had written *On the False Prognostication of a Deluge*, arguing that the eclipse of 1523 would have a palliative effect on the coming conjunction. Nifo hoped that his counter-prediction would break the stranglehold of terror. He hoped in vain. Was Faustus a doom-monger or a moderate? Whatever prognostications he made, they have gone unremembered.

The prophets had had twenty-five years to spread their message of doom and the people just as long to worry about it. The invention of printing made it possible to carry this message of impending catastrophe from one end of Europe to the other with unprecedented speed. As many as sixty different authors produced 160 pamphlets during the peak publishing years from 1519 to 1523, putting an estimated 160,000 copies into circulation.[3]

According to that famous nineteenth-century chronicler of 'popular delusions' Charles Mackay, London in the sixteenth century 'swarmed ... with fortune-tellers and astrologers, who were consulted daily by people of every class in society on the secrets of futurity.'[4] As early as June 1523 a consensus had been reached amongst these diviners that 1 February 1524 would see the muddy and pestilential River Thames gradually overflow its banks and drown the entire city, washing away 10,000 houses in the process. If that was the case, then they were using foreign literature to make their point: no English astrological writing was produced on this subject.[5] Nonetheless, the prediction caused widespread panic, growing as the appointed time drew nearer, and the trickle of families who packed up their belongings and retreated to Kent and Essex swelled into a steady torrent. By the beginning of 1524 the exodus was reaching biblical proportions.

By mid-month as many as 20,000 people had fled London – in 1500 the city only had a population of around 40,000. Those with money relocated to the high ground of Highgate, Hampstead and Blackheath. Tented villages appeared from Waltham Abbey in the north to Croydon to the south of the river. At Harrow-on-the-Hill, the Prior of St Bartholomew's in Smithfield, a man called Bolton whose wealth equalled his great credulity, built himself a fortress and provisioned it with enough for two months. He laid in a fleet of boats and a team of expert rowers on standby in case the rising waters threatened him in his lair. A week before the day of reckoning Bolton retreated into his fastness.

The sun rose on 1 February to find curious crowds gathered along the banks of the Thames. As the prediction had specified a gradual rise in the waters, the bolder sort thought it safe to watch the beginnings of the disaster and still have time to make good an escape. They must have stood there for some time, watching the Thames flow by in its accustomed manner; slowly, as the sun climbed higher in the sky and the Thames stared back at them unperturbed, a sense of foolishness began to set in. Even as the sun set over the placid waters, people were still too afraid to go to sleep in case the deluge should catch them unawares and many stayed at their vigil until dawn. The next day they went back to their everyday lives. As panic gave way to embarrassment, then relief, rage followed. The whole caste of astrologers came close to a ducking in the Thames, but some quick thinking kept them dry. It was claimed that there had been an error in their calculations: the flood was due in 1624.

Similar scenes must have been played out across Europe. The *Mirabilis Liber* had singled out Paris for 'despoliation and devastation'. In certain parts of Italy deforestation had already caused severe flooding in past years and the promise of more to come was a very real threat. The message was carried throughout the land by apocalyptic preachers, wandering astrologers and *cantastorie* (street-singers), and panic was born in every heart. Penitential processions and civic rituals took place to ward off the coming catastrophe. The rich fled to the high ground just as they had tried to escape the plague in Giovanni Boccaccio's day, whilst others started building arks. The rich were no different in Germany and also fled to the mountains. Johannes Carion had considered the problem as early as 1521 and advised his employer Prince-Elector Joachim I von Brandenburg to seek the high-ground of the Kreuzberg before the waters inundated them. People began selling off their possessions and the fields went untilled. Even Luther was talking about it, managing to turn a sermon on circumcision into a discussion about astrology and omens.

Mephistophiel.

1. Statue of Faustus in Knittlingen. (*Author's collection*)

2. Mephistopheles as depicted in
Magiae Naturalis et Innatural, Passau, 1505
(eighteenth century). (*Johannes Scheible,* 1849)

3. The 'Geburtshaus Doctor Faust', locally held to be the birthplace of Faustus.
(*Author's collection*)

4. The man who started the legend. Statue of the Abbot Trithemius in his home town of Trittenheim. (*Author's collection*)

5. The first historical reference to Faustus: Trithemius's letter to Virdung, 20 August 1507. (*Biblioteca Apostolica Vaticana*)

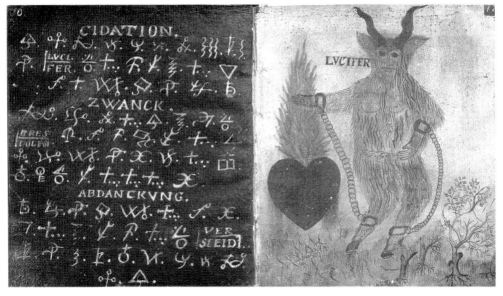

6. Faustian grimoire: *Doct. Faust Hollen Zwanck* [*sic*]. (*Národní Muzeum, Prague*)

7. Mutianus calls for the theologians to rise against Faustus, 3 October 1513.
(*Universitätsbibliothek Frankfurt am Main*)

8. Franz von Sickingen, Faustus's sometime patron. (*Ludwig Bechstein,* 1854)

9. According to the legend, Faustus signed his first pact on 23 October 1514. (*Hermann Faber,* 1888)

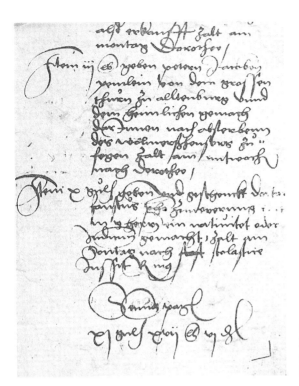

10. The account book of the Bishop of Bamberg for 1520, showing the payment to Faustus. (*Staatsarchiv Bamberg*)

11. Rebdorf monastery where Faustus stayed in 1528. (*Author's collection*)

12. Faustus's Commandery of 'Hallestein', the Grad Komenda, first mentioned in 1528. (*Destinacije.com,* 2004)

13. Records of the City of Ingolstadt expelling Faustus, 1528. (*Stadtarchiv Ingolstadt*)

14. Refused safe conduct to Nuremberg, 1532. (*Nürnberg Staatsarchiv*)

Anno 1539 ist im Leuen zu Staufen Doctor Faustus so ein wunderbar= licher Nigromanta gewesen, elendiglich gestorben und

15. Wall mural on the Zum Löwen inn, Staufen, depicting Faustus's death, said to have taken place here. (*Author's collection*)

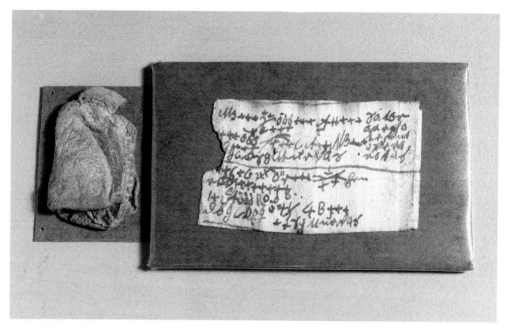

16. Charm fragment found in the 'Geburtshaus Doctor Faust', Knittlingen, unknown date. (*Faust Museum, Knittlingen*)

17. Rembrandt's so-called *Faust in his Study*. (*Rembrandt, c.1652*)

Here, too, the weather stayed fine. The forewarned disaster had not struck, but at the end of the year the astrologers were able to weigh their predictions against their observations. The meteorological record kept daily by an astrologer in Bologna indicated that 1524 had indeed been a rainy year, but fell short of the tsunami that had been prophesied. Cardano later wrote smugly of his own opposition to the flood theory espoused by Stöffler, commenting that 'the weather was perfectly calm' and congratulating himself that, aged only twenty, he had predicted rightly.[6]

As the year turned the corner, it was relief that flooded the populace. In Italy, the carnival-goers of 1525 delighted in making the flood the object of obscene humour. In Venice in particular, the public storytellers were causing the maidens to blush and the men to slap their thighs with their ribald tales. In retrospect it has been concluded that such antics had 'an enormous negative effect on the figure of the astrologer'.[7] The more accurate predictions of Nifo and Cardano did little to assuage the general ire directed against anyone bearing the name of 'astrologer', but astrology was far from over. They may have failed to predict a flood, but 'certain changes and transformations' were still to come and couched in such general terms could not fail to pass.

A Land Full of Murder and Bloodshed

There was more on the cover of Reynmann's *Practica* than deluge. On a hill two men sound the muster on fife and drum. Below them a group of peasants armed with scythes, flails and pitchforks confront representatives of the Roman Church. Along with a depiction of heavy rainstorms, Johannes Carion's pamphlet of 1521 showed a knight and a peasant putting a group of clergymen to the sword. Carion's 1522 edition showed women and children meeting the same fate. On the front of Johann Copp's 1523 *Practica Teutsch* siege cannon bombard a city. Still more of de Vatiguerro's prophecies published in the *Mirabilis Liber* predicted that 'stars shall collide with each other, and this shall be the sign for the destruction and massacre of nearly all mankind.'

Pisces was a shark and the heavens would rain blood. Terrorised by the prophecies of doom, driven to desperation by two years of poor harvests, aggrieved anew by the old complaints of high taxes and social injustice, inspired by revolutionary religious teachings, and seizing the chance to settle old scores, the common people raised their banner of war, the *Bundschuh*.

The *Bundschuh* was the rough rawhide footwear of the German lower classes and because of the striking contrast of this humble shoe to the noble spurred boot, it came to symbolise the popular rebellions that history has come to know as the Peasants' War. It was also a play on words. The *Bundschuh*, common to all working men, implied their common bond, their *Bund*.

'Nobleman, may a cow shit on you' ran one of their slogans, but there was more to this than class conflict.[8] It has been called the Peasants' War, but it was an uprising of more than just peasants. Crippling taxes and political disenfranchisement were the common complaints of both poor artisans and peasants. Rising prices, the curse of the age, hurt everyone and even some of the middle classes and lower nobility joined the conspirators. Unemployed or disillusioned *Landsknechte*, many of whom came from peasant or working-class backgrounds, swelled their ranks. It was revolution.

The sixteenth century is so often divided between Renaissance and Reformation, between the arts and religion, when at the heart of the Empire it was rebellion and divisiveness between the people that defined the age. This was an age when politics and religion were edges of the same sword, but it was not Luther who was leading this popular revolt, it was people like Hans the Piper. In 1476 crowds of up to 40,000 had turned out to listen to this young shepherd and musician tell them how the Madonna of Niklashausen had spoken to him. The message was one of revolutionary communism inspired by a religious vision and deeply moved those who heard it. It moved the priests deeply enough to denounce Hans's visions as sent by the Devil. Hans called a huge army to his side, but he was arrested and his army outmanoeuvred by trickery. Luther came after, a late entry to a long-standing struggle, and one who preached against the peasants in favour of feudal obedience. He was not a revolutionary.

As a boy Faustus would have heard stories of the many uprisings, and perhaps seen mutilated exiles begging for bread. As a young man he may have seen it first hand during the 'Poor Conrad' uprising. Since then the rebellion had smouldered for thirty years, flaring up periodically in Speyer, in the Breisgau near Stuttgart, in the Upper Rhine Valley, until the final reckoning in the bloody battles of 1524–6.

In Germany, a country of only ten or eleven million, roughly one person in thirty-three, according to the highest estimates, was marching under the *Bundschuh*. Contemporary estimates of their numbers varied wildly of course. When Archduke Ferdinand wrote to his older brother the Emperor about the rebels, he numbered them at 300,000, although Mario Sanutos only recorded a figure of 200,000 in his diaries and another source suggested 100,000. Modern estimates based on incomplete figures give a total of 151,500 accounted for and another 30,000 not unlikely.[9]

The trouble began in June 1524 during the harvest in the county of Stühlingen, south of the Black Forest and far beyond Faustus's known sphere of action at this time. Folklore attributes this to the whim of a Countess who had her peasants collect snails instead of bringing in the harvest. Enraged by this latest abuse of noble privileges, over a thousand peasants raised a banner of war and elected the *Landsknecht* Hans Müller von Bulgenbach to lead them; the rebellion spread.

Ferdinand mobilised the Swabian League, but circumstances forced them into negotiating with the rebels. The bulk of its fighting force was earmarked for Charles V's campaign in Italy and many of the remaining *Landsknechte* had gone over to the other side. The League tried to buy time with sham negotiations as its agents worked to undermine the movement, offering double pay to those who agreed to fight in Italy. Other towns seeing the rebels marching towards their gates set up special courts to hear their grievances, but again, all they wanted to do was stall for time. As summer turned to winter, the tactic worked and the icy wind blew many of the discontented back to their firesides.

The deposed Duke Ulrich now saw his chance to retake his forfeited lands in Württemberg. Adopting the ridiculous title of 'Ulrich the Peasant' and waiving aside his previous oppression of the peasantry, Ulrich presented himself as a new man, a friend to the lower orders and a champion of their cause. Over the winter he raised a mercenary army, bolstered by a peasant band under von Bulgenbach, and by late February 1525 he was marching on Stuttgart.

Ulrich stood more than a fighting chance, but his attempt to reclaim his Duchy was suddenly cut short. Following the French defeat in Italy, the Swiss mercenaries in his service were recalled and the remaining peasant militias were unable to stand against the professional soldiers of the Swabian League. After only a few heady weeks he was again a fugitive. This setback did not bring peace. Discontent was still waving her banner high.

The League continued trying to buy more time and had involved Ulrich Schmid and his 10,000 strong Baltringen Band in negotiations. Believing that they now had a chance to be heard, the Band compiled a massive list of over three hundred grievances. At the beginning of March, Sebastian Lotzer put these complaints more succinctly in the famous Twelve Articles. They covered such things as the appointment of pastors, the grain tithe due to the Church, serfdom, the hunting of game, wood-cutting, excessive services, the relationship between lord and peasant, ruinous rents, the multiplication of new laws, the erosion of commons and the death tax. The document was couched in pious terms, giving the political demands a religious character and in the process making them twice as strongly felt. Within a short space of time 25,000 copies were in circulation. In all these lists and articles the core demand was simple: the abolition of serfdom. This was nothing less than the overthrow of the establishment.

Further peasant bands sprang up in March and April from the shores of Lake Constance to the walls of Würzburg. Their numbers swelled anew with *Landsknechte* returning from the Italian campaign. There were many victories against only a few setbacks, morale was high, but by now the League was ready.

The dull thud of thousands of marching feet, the discordant rattle of arms and the whinnying of horses carried on the wind. In the distance a banner could be seen flying above a forest of *Landsknechte* pikes. It bore three black lions on a field of gold. The rebels grew uneasy as they recognised the armorial insignia of Georg III, Truchsess von Waldburg (1488–1531), leader of the Swabian League army. He had seen off the truculent Duke Ulrich at Stuttgart and was now intent on smashing the peasants.

Known as *Bauernjörg* ('peasant George'), Truchsess von Waldburg had also been conducting sham negotiations with the peasants to enable him to deploy his forces. Spring flowers were crushed under the feet of fighting men and the bodies of the dead as Truchsess opened his campaign with a series of skirmishes against the Baltringen Band before moving against the Leipheim Band. On 4 April 1525 the first decisive battle of the Peasants' War was fought and the peasants lost.

Truchsess quickly followed up with further victories, but the war was far from over. The peasants continued to capture cities and castles, and more joined their numbers. As many as a thousand castles and religious buildings were destroyed in 1525 alone. Heilbronn, Stuttgart and Erfurt and other major towns fell into their hands. Although Truchsess had shown that he could more than match the rebels in the field, there was widespread panic amongst those who did not share their cause. Luther, for one, became hysterical in his denunciations of them. Returning to Wittenberg to preach, the rebels drowned him out with a tumultuous peel of bells and he was pelted with copies of the Twelve Articles. Luther expected that they would win and feared for his own safety. He derided the revolutionaries with his usual recourse to Satan and called upon the nobles to slaughter them mercilessly.[10]

The momentum of the uprising was finally checked in a rapid series of bloody battles throughout May and into June 1525. Some groups still held out and there were further uprisings, but decimated and leaderless, the peasants' dream of a better world had been drowned in the blood of their dead.

Although numerically superior to the League, the rebel bands were locally deployed and scattered over a wide area. Lack of a unified command and bickering between radical and liberal factions internally weakened the rebels who were already disadvantaged by their relative lack of soldiering experience, in spite of the *Landsknechte* in their ranks. Against them the League deployed duplicity and might backed by Fugger and Welser money, and carried out by the ruthless Truchsess and other seasoned campaigners such as Georg von Frundsberg. The peasants' willingness to negotiate constantly saw them outwitted and their readiness to meet superior forces in the field, whilst a credit to their bravery, was a tactical mistake.

The conjunction of the planets may not have augured a biblical flood, but to the astrologer with hindsight they had unleashed a deluge of blood and tears: 'A land full of murder and bloodshed' in Luther's words.[11] As many as 100,000 are thought to have perished and not all of them died on the field of battle. There was no Geneva Convention in the sixteenth century. Atrocity was the norm. Captives were publicly burnt alive, staked to the ground, beheaded, disembowelled or hoisted on wheels. The cry of freedom ended in the scream of summary justice. Crushed and ground firmly back into the dirt, the peasants would continue to bear the heavy yoke of serfdom for another two hundred years.

Given what we know of Faustus it is difficult to assess where his sympathies would have lain. Association with the rebels would have damaged his career and perhaps it did. The historical record charts a more troubled course after the events of 1524–1526. Whilst Faustus seemed to hold the commonality in awe, his sometimes high brow pitch was also aimed at the intellectual community and those who sought its services. Before the uprising he had sought out noble patrons or clients like von Sickingen and the Bishop of Bamberg, and later claims would reveal, if not a noble lineage, then at least noble aspirations. Against this we have seen that some nobles did take up the commoners' cause and his earlier association with the rebellious von Sickingen may have radicalised his politics. It was easy for the educated to despise the peasants for their rudeness and illiteracy, and social justice was not the concern of sixteenth-century students and scholars. If he played a part it was surely as an astrologer divining the outcome rather than as a partisan, but later claims would reveal that he did involve himself in the business of war. If it is unlikely that he joined the revolution, he certainly could not have avoided it – the countryside was a charnel house – but by 1525, according to the legend, Faustus was many miles away.

Auerbach's Cellar

Made famous by Goethe and thus irrevocably attached to the name of Faustus is the incident at Auerbach's Cellar in Leipzig. Today two bronze statues flank the entrance to the cellar, marking a moment in the building's history when it almost vanished forever. A rich suitcase manufacturer called Anton Mädler bought Auerbach's Hof in 1911, intending to demolish it and build a new exhibition pavilion in its place. The vehemence of the local reaction to his plans caused him to reconsider and instead of the wrecking ball he brought in art. The sculptor Mathieu Molitor was commissioned to embellish the entrance and in 1913 his *Faust and Mephistopheles* and *The Enchanted Students* were unveiled. The projecting left foot of Faustus in the *Faust and Mephistopheles* group has been buffed to shining gold by the hands of countless people rubbing it for good luck as they passed. In 1999 two smaller sculptures by Bernd Göbel were completed showing *Faust and Margaret* and *Mephistopheles and Marthe* after Goethe. Both women are naked and apparently trying to fend off the advances of the diabolical duo. Even this crowd of brazen characters fails to reveal the truth of Faustus's visit to Auerbach's Cellar.

Goethe contrived a riotous scene at Auerbach's Cellar, drawing on the Erfurt legend of tapping wine from the table and the Erfurt/Boxberg tale of attempted nose cutting. But he also included a story we have not found elsewhere, extricating his hero from a dangerous situation on the back of a barrel.

A story made famous by the incomparable Goethe and immortalised in bronze seems unshakable, but did it really take place? Faustus's contemporaries made no references to him being in Leipzig. The story appeared for the first time in a 1588 edition of Spies's 1587 *Historia* and Auerbach's Cellar was not mentioned by name. However, on the walls of the Cellar are two murals depicting the legendary event and bearing the date 1525, and there is a mention in the seventeenth-century Leipzig Chronicle, a late source admittedly, placing Faustus there for that year.

It is no surprise to find Faustus in a wine cellar. We often meet Faustus in the inn or tavern, especially in the Faustbooks where he seems to be almost constantly carousing in the company of riotous students. There have been some who have taken this report at face value and used it as yet another mark against Faustus's name. However, whilst the stories are clearly exaggerated even if true, the Germans as a nation were, by the common report of many, excessive drinkers. P.F. was rather amusing on this point, calling Faustus 'the God *Bacchus*' before describing how he threw a feast 'after the manner of Germany, where it is counted no feast except all the bidden guests be drunk.'[12] It was even something acknowledged by some Germans themselves, such as Matthäus Friedrich in 1522: 'Germany is and always has been plagued, more than all other countries, by the devil that drives people to drink.'[13]

But the censorious tone of both Friedrich and P.F. is that of the religious moraliser – we must not forget that P.F.'s version of the Faustus story is a religiously motivated tract and Friedrich may have studied under Luther at Wittenberg. P.F. is also talking about 'foreigners' and hence inclined to exaggerate through prejudice. Yet we should not underestimate the role alcohol played in Faustus's lifetime. The culture of drinking in early sixteenth-century Germany was at the heart of society. The drinking establishment was an institution that rivalled the church in its importance. Men met here to conduct business, concluding deals with a traditional contract toast, and define their social roles.[14]

Tavern and inn also provided additional avenues of power beyond the official and tightly controlled venues of guildhall and town council. As a popular, secular powerbase it is natural that we should find someone like Faustus seeking business here. Paracelsus, for example, broadcast his religious views in the inns and taverns and faced similar accusations of drunkenness, pointedly when his views did not accord with those of the authorities. What becomes for later writers a sign of Faustus's delinquency and charlatanry was for Faustus the obvious sphere in which to pursue his career. There were other stories of Faustus in inns. On one occasion he silences a roomful of noisy peasants,[15] but it was the barrel-riding in Auerbach's Cellar that was to prove the more enduring tale. But why in Leipzig?

Even then Leipzig was an old university town. The *Alma mater Lipsiensis*, officially endorsed by Pope Alexander V, opened its doors on 2 December 1409. Simon Pistoris the Elder (1453–1523), doctor and professor of medicine at the university, was also a proponent of the use of astrology in medicine. Perhaps more to the point, Pistoris's rival in Nuremberg at that time, the former astrologer Polich von Mellerstadt remarked in 1510 or earlier, with more than a hint of irritation, that 'because astrological judgements are sold at higher prices in Leipzig than in Nuremberg, astrologers are esteemed more highly there than here.'[16] A wandering scholar like Faustus would have found his way naturally to the doors of this august institution with its astrological tradition and higher prices. And where there is a university there are students, and where there are students there is drinking, and so we return full circle to the cellar.

The town was bustling when Faustus arrived, if he did. Famous for its fairs since the twelfth century, Leipzig was a flourishing city in the sixteenth century. The earliest fairs had been held by long tradition over the Easter period and on the Feast of St Michael (29 September), but there was also a New Year fair established in 1458. Since 1507 they were officially recognised as imperial fairs (*Reichsmessen*). Drawn by learning, the fair or the good fortunes of the Lords of Rochlitz, industrious at their nearby castle, the town was filled with scholars, merchants and artisans. Many of them would have found their way to a heterogeneous group of buildings by the market square owned by a certain Dr Heinrich Stromer from Auerbach (*c.* 1478–1542). Here a special passageway was given over to the fair where, according to the Leipzig Chronicle, 'a great variety of goods is sold and much money invested and spent'.[17]

Dr Stromer, or Auerbach as he is commonly called, was a doctor of philosophy and medicine, dean of the medical college, a member of the town council, and later the personal physician to Elector Friedrich III of Saxony. The buildings that have become known as Auerbach's Court began life slowly and in piecemeal fashion. Auerbach bought the main building in 1519 from the heirs of town councillor Hanns Hommelshain. This substantial four-storey half-timbered dwelling probably dated to 1438, when the judge Dr Nicolaus Schulthess was its owner. Over the next few years he bought up several neighbouring buildings and in 1530 began building work that would take another eight years to complete. When it was finished it comprised a hundred vaults for use by merchants during the fair, additional stalls within the vaults, two galleries, 'pleasant rooms, lounges and lodgings', and a fine stable for the merchants' horses. In 1525, the time of Faustus's supposed visit, Auerbach had but recently opened his new wine cellar.[18]

The Leipzig Chronicle records that 'some people say that the famous Dr Faustus stayed with him [Auerbach] when he was in Leipzig', although this is contested.[19]

Whether Faustus stayed with the owner or not, the legendary deeds enacted here continue to grace its walls. Two paintings bear the date 1525, but they were not painted then, and a cask preserved in the cellar is believed to have been that very same ridden by Faustus. However, if Auerbach ever met Faustus, he chose not to commemorate the fact.

In the Faustbook we find Faustus sampling the wines of the Rhineland, admiring those of Budapest in Hungary, stealing all the beer and wine from an innkeeper in Ravensburg, and ransacking the wine cellars of the Dukes of Saxony and Bavaria and the Bishop of Salzburg, but never touches so much as a drop in Leipzig. During his magical world tour he calls into Leipzig where he marvels at a 'great vessel' in the castle, but this was not the property of Auerbach.[20]

In the course of the Faustbook, Mephistopheles outfitted Faustus and his assistant with only the finest fashions, notably calling in Leipzig to collect some pieces, suggesting that the city was also known for the sumptuous stock of its mercers. Faustus was also said to have a friend in the town, a certain 'Jove Victori', a physician by profession and formerly a fellow student at Wittenberg, to whom he wrote about cosmology and his world tour. While the first reference places Faustus in Leipzig – at least according to the sixteenth-century legend – neither of these references are directly concerned with marvellous cask-riding exploits.[21]

Widmann notably added a chapter – 'Dr Faustus gives the students in Leipzig a cask of wine as a present' – in his retelling of the legend in 1599. Pfitzer revised Widmann, changing the cast a little and reducing the size of the cask, and republished the tale in 1674. Another version appeared in 1728 and a folk legend was recorded in 1839 that repeated the same course of events. A regular patron of the cellar whilst a student in Leipzig, Goethe found a copy of the tale, according to one tradition, chained to the wall and with it the inspiration for his famous scene.[22]

The adventure began much like Faustus's trip to Munich. He was in Wittenberg when he was approached by students from Hungary, Poland, Carinthia and Austria, or simply Polish noblemen according to Pfitzer, who wished to see the Leipzig Fair. Some desired only to satisfy their curiosity, others wanted to try and make money. Faustus's motives were unclear. An 'old folk legend' recorded in 1839 had Mephistopheles cajole Faustus: 'Why do you live like a broody owl in the wilderness, wasting your life in desolate loneliness?'[23] The solution was to whisk him off to Leipzig.

In the earlier tales, like a magical taxi-driver, Faustus delivered his demanding friends to the town. In Widmann the party simply set out to walk the seventy kilometres, whilst in Pfitzer Faustus 'procured by his art' a peasant's cart and horses in which they 'mounted in good cheer and drove on rapidly.' Widmann's journey was uneventful, but Pfitzer threw in the alarum of a hare running close by – an omen of bad luck that 'induced them to conceive timorous thoughts'. However, they spent so long debating whether it was an evil sign for their journey that before sunset they found themselves, 'to their great astonishment', at Leipzig.[24]

Wandering through the Fair the next day they came by a cellar where the wine porters (called 'shooters' or 'whitecoats' on account of their long white coats) were struggling to extract a large barrel. Widmann tells us that this cask could hold sixteen or eighteen 'buckets', but Pfitzer was content with only seven or eight. Whatever size it was, the shooters found that they could not shift it. The 1728 version of the story has Faustus and his companions laughing 'long and loud' at their predicament. In Pfitzer, Faustus, 'nearly sneering', said to the men, 'how do you set so awkwardly about it, yours are so many, and you can not force such a cask out of the cellar? Yet an only one might do it, if he managed it properly.'[25]

One can imagine the effect: 'the shooters, like useless knaves, were very angry at such a language, used foul words.' They challenged him to do it, if he could, 'in the Devil's name'. The cellar-master appeared on the scene and extended the challenge, offering the barrel as a reward to the one who could bring it up, convinced it was beyond any of them. A crowd gathered to see the fun, for surely a miracle or a fight was promised. Faustus descended into the cellar. The next moment he popped out like a champagne cork, riding astride the troublesome barrel. The cellar-master 'much aghast' and objecting that 'such was not done naturally', grudgingly kept his word. For once Faustus was shown in a good light, sharing his bounty. He threw an enormous party that lasted for several days until every last drop has been drained from the cask.[26]

13

All the Victories in Italy
(1521–1527)

The whole world was now in warfare.
– Cellini[1]

A remark supposedly made by Melanchthon suggests that Faustus was neither holding court in a Leipzig inn nor in Germany at all to witness the peasants' uprising, but
farther south with those much needed soldiers of the Swabian League. To be sure, the
sporadic nature of the Italian campaign would not necessarily prevent either of these
possibilities, but Manlius reported that Melanchthon had said that 'the same magician
Faustus, a wicked beast and a sewer of many devils, lyingly boasted that all the victories of the Emperor's armies in Italy had been won by means of his magic.'[2]

Up until the 1520s there were not many victories to lay claim to. Despite a flair
for self-promotion as 'the last knight', Maximilian I's campaigning had been largely
unsuccessful. During the War of the League of Cambrai from 1509 to 1515, the French
had won the majority of the battles. But under Charles V the imperial generals would
win their laurels. From 1522 to 1530 Charles and his allies would wrest a series of victories from the French, all of which Faustus could have laid claim to having magically
guaranteed. In particular, the Empire struck a resounding blow against the French at
the Battle of Pavia, inflicting a loss on their enemy such as the French had not suffered since Agincourt. Where Maximilian had waged an ineffectual and ramshackle
campaign, it did indeed seem as if magic had suddenly and decisively changed the
fortunes of the Imperial armies.

Of course, Manlius said that Melanchthon did not believe a word of Faustus's
claims: 'This was a vain lie … I, truly, tell this because of the young men, that they do
not immediately give flattering assent to such vain men.'[3] But nor should we accept
Melanchthon's (or Manlius's) view. What is important is that the statement ascribed to
Faustus is related as some sort of lesson to his students, which means that it is unlikely
(but not of course impossible) that he is simply making it up. He may have heard it
second hand, but the location of this passage in his text after recounting Faustus's

adventures in Wittenberg does present the possibility that Melanchthon may have had it first-hand from Faustus himself. Indeed, Lercheimer was to later make the claim that Faustus had been acquainted with Melanchthon whilst the two were in Wittenberg.

If Faustus actually did make this claim, then what sort of magic might he have been referring to? Given what we know of his career so far, we can form a reasonable impression of what occult services he may have rendered. The association with von Sickingen – believed to have never attempted any move without consulting an astrologer – and then the documented judicial astrology for Georg III, Bishop of Bamberg, suggests an astrological role, perhaps divining auspicious times of action for the Imperial army. Melanchthon, however, specifically mentioned magic. With demonic steeds, flying cloaks and magical armies at his command – according to the legends – the Prince of Necromancers could draw upon a wide repertoire of forbidden practices, perhaps including the alchemical manufacture of gold to assist his Emperor in foreign wars.

In Italy, Faustus would find that her men of war were, like his compatriot von Sickingen, greatly interested in the arcane arts. As an astrologer used to high society and one who sought its patronage, Faustus would have made himself known to the leaders of this campaign, for how else was he going to promote his art and win himself honours and riches?

One of those men was Alfonso d'Avalos, Marquis del Vasto, who would later govern Milan (1538–1546) and be immortalised by Titian. Del Vasto is known to have consulted Cardano about his horoscope sometime after 1543 and showed a keen interest in the occult. He supported Giulio Camillo Delminio (1480–1544), usually known as just Giulio Camillo, the architect of the *L'idea del theatro* or 'memory theatre', an ingenious amphitheatre designed to give access to the entire works of Cicero by word and phrase, and organised according to the perceived structure of the universe. A life-size model of the project was constructed that could accommodate several people. Viglius Zuichemus wrote to Erasmus in 1532, describing it as 'a work of wonderful skill' enabling people inside it 'to discourse on any subject no less fluently than Cicero'.[4] But it was also a lot more than just a device to induce rhetorical eloquence.

Camillo belonged to the Hermetic-cabbalistic tradition of Pico della Mirandola and constructed his theatre on those principles. This intricate system of spatial mnemonics was built to represent the order of eternal truth with depictions of the creation, from the first cause through the angels, the planetary spheres, and down to man. It was also an enormous magical machine. The theatre was decorated with planetary images that acted as astral talismans, drawing down the celestial influences so that they could be channelled and put into action. In theory the operator could harness the magical powers of the universe by mastering the proportions of cosmic harmony replicated in the theatre's elaborate structure. Camillo's *L'idea del theatro* was published in Venice in 1550 and had seen ten editions by 1584, such was its popularity. Italy, the source of the Hermetic tradition, was rich ground for the Renaissance magician. Faustus, as it were, was coming home.

Faustus was not unique in claiming to have used his magic for military purposes. There are precedents to consider that may give us insight into his possible activities at this time. Hartlieb recounted meeting a famous soldier in 1455 who told him that the Teutonic Order always planned their campaigns according to the prognostications of the breastbone of a goose, which was especially valued as a weather oracle. The conjuration of magical armies was part of the standard repertoire of the magician. In *The Sacred Magic of Abramelin the Mage* there is just such a formula for their invocation. The magician can chose from invoking an entire army to an unspecified number of 'armed men', or even 'cause a Siege to appear' through the intervention of the spirits. Abraham, the supposed author of the *Sacred Magic*, described once having had cause to use just such a spell himself. According to Abraham, he rescued Friedrich I (1369–1428), Duke-Elector of Saxony, from a tight spot during the Hussite Wars by the timely invocation of 2,000 knights.

While the tales of Abraham may be a late composition merely posing as fifteenth century, the better authenticated Codex 849 also has a prescription for summoning an instant fighting force. The spell 'For obtaining a castle' adds a fortress to Abramelin's host of armed men, but still comes with a number of useful defenders and can indeed be used solely for 'summoning countless legions of armed men'. The compiler of the Codex, like Abraham, also claimed to have put the spell to use, although in this case he brought forth an 'innumerable horde' of demonic knights to assault the Emperor and his entourage while they were out hunting in a gloomy forest and erected the magic castle as their refuge. The compiler of the Codex describes his magical operation as a test to see if it worked, but the Emperor and his knights surely felt that a practical joke had been played at their expense when the castle and besiegers vanished to leave them standing in the middle of a marsh. In the Faustbooks there are several examples of Faustus raising troops of supernatural soldiers, but it is the case of Conrad Kyeser of Eichstätt (1366–c.1405) that best shows how Faustus may have provided specifically martial advice to the generals.

Kyeser was a physician by training, a soldier by choice and a diplomat by preferment. He was also an astrologer and likely a sorcerer to boot. He served under Stephan III, Duke of Bayern-Ingolstadt, amongst others, until he fell from favour. In an attempt to set his career back on track he wrote a huge volume on warfare and other subjects called *Bellifortis* (c.1405).[5] Generally admired today for its technological illustrations, *Bellifortis* went beyond engineering to explore how the dark arts could be employed against the enemy. Kyeser gave instructions on how to manufacture inextinguishable torches, how to use the hide of a deer to protect against being wounded in battle, and how to use the feathers and hair of animals killed in the hunt to produce target-seeking arrows. With some of his recipes he strayed onto the dangerous ground of witchcraft. The book spawned numerous copies, imitations and adaptations that continued to have an influence as late as the seventeenth century. It is feasible that Faustus could have come across *Bellifortis* and used it in his own pitch to potential clients.

If Faustus was in the field with the imperial forces and not conjuring from afar, then, to make his alleged claims stand up, we would expect him to have made his way south. We must suppose that Faustus cast his charts and gave his prognostications for the 'top brass', since it would make no sense for him to make his claims if he had been advising anyone of lesser rank. Perhaps he met with Georg von Frundsberg, who raised most of the mercenaries bound for the Italian campaigns. Von Frundsberg was no stranger to Italy or to war. He had fought against the French at Milan in 1499. He had been involved in the war of the Bavaria-Landshut succession in 1504, fighting for Maximilian I. He had led his men against Ulrich von Württemburg in 1519. In 1521 he had been with von Sickingen at the walls of Mézières, opportunity enough, one supposes, to have heard of Faustus, perhaps even to have met him. The year afterwards he distinguished himself at the Battle of Bicocca. Amberger Memmingen's portrait of him shows a stout character in black armour, a halberd grasped in his mailed fist, but the open visor reveals a friendlier face than his accoutrements suggest. He is without the extravagant plumage of the *Landsknechte*, a sober, more serious man of action. Stern though he no doubt was, even the hard men of the Teutonic Order were eager for the advantage magic promised, as Hartlieb testified, so we should not suppose that he was disinclined to listen to a necromancer, especially one connected with his old comrade-in-arms von Sickingen.

The Four Years War (1521–1525)

While Emperor Charles V was strengthening his position through alliances with Pope Leo X and Henry VIII, Robert de la Marck had been harrying the borders of the Low Countries in league with Charles, Duke of Gelders, and Henri d'Albret had crossed the French border into Spain. For a time things looked black for the Empire and, notwithstanding the successes of von Sickingen and the Spanish levies, it was largely the fault of the French themselves that began their reversal of fortunes in Italy. Given the vagueness of Faustus's reported claim – 'all the victories' – it is here that we should start.

François I's captain Odet de Foix (1485–1528), Vicomte de Lautrec, could not be said to have much enjoyed his occupation of Milan. De Foix owed his office to his sister, currently in François's favour, and in 1521 he would come to regret it. To the north German *Landsknechte* had crossed the Alps and were advancing via Trent. To the south the Italian *condottiere* and Lieutenant of the Emperor, Fernando de Avalos (1489–1525), Marquis of Pescara, was marching out of Naples. Siege was thrown round Parma, but abandoned when Alfonso d'Este (1476–1534), Duke of Ferrara, threatened. It seemed as if the Imperialist advance would be checked, but Ferrara was defeated and the Pope's *condottiere* Giovanni de' Medici (1498–1526) struck hard at France's Venetian allies, clearing the road to Milan.

As the Imperialist and Papal armies met up it brought the Swiss into conflict with each other, as mercenary contingents now fought for both the French and the Imperial alliance. Disquieted by this development, the Swiss Diet ordered the recall of all Swiss units. To the dismay of de Foix he found his Swiss decamping in droves, whilst those on the Papal payroll stood firm. De Foix fell back on Milan, but here he found that his oppressive measures had not subdued the populace and an uprising flared up as soon as the banners of the Empire were seen over the horizon. De Foix, his Venetian allies running before him, retreated on Como.

As usual it came down to money. The substantial funds voted by the Low Countries in 1521 were exhausted by the end of the year. Still revelling in his diplomatic success in England and the Treaty of Windsor pledging both rulers to a massive invasion of Italy in 1524, Charles V was nevertheless forced to disband much of his army – and any freelancing necromancer would find himself in a tight spot. To salt this self-inflicted wound, the death of Leo X caused the Swiss to transfer their allegiance to the French *en masse* and François I of France found the unemployed German *Landsknechte* only too ready to accept his coin. The balance of power had shifted suddenly and dramatically yet again.

In spring 1522 de Foix marched back towards Milan, intent on recapturing it. However, he found that new defensive works now rendered the city nigh impregnable and the fiery Milanese were eager to bloody French noses again. To add to de Foix's troubles, unrest had been growing amongst the Swiss mercenaries as their pay fell into arrears. On 26 April unrest boiled over into mutiny. It was still a soldierly mutiny with the Swiss demanding to be allowed to attack what they thought was a weak Imperial position at Bicocca just outside Milan. Scenting an easy victory over the much smaller force, the Swiss were keen to get their hands on the spoils. On the 27th de Foix reluctantly led them into battle. The French assault was stopped in its tracks by withering fire from the Imperial harquebusiers and cannon.[6] As many as 3,000 of de Foix's Swiss did not return from the field of battle that day.

With their tails between their legs, the Swiss returned home to lick their wounds. 'They went back to their mountains,' said Guicciardini, 'diminished in numbers, but much more diminished in audacity.'[7] De Foix had no option but to abandon his designs on Milan and retreat altogether from Lombardy.

Hoisted by their own petard at Bicocca, the French next faced the Empire at the Siege of Genoa. Fernando de Avalos and Prospero Colonna (1452–1523), another seasoned mercenary and scion of the noble house of Colonna, approached the city on 20 May 1522 to find its gates defiantly shut against them. The siege lasted until 30 May when the Genoese finally surrendered. The triumphant Imperialists ran riot, looting and pillaging.

In the summer of 1522 English and Imperial fleets harried the French coast off Brittany and Normandy, but in Italy Charles was again forced by lack of ready money to lay off troops. Revenues from Castile, beginning to come in after the suppression of revolt, were already pledged and those of the Low Countries were used up. His brother Ferdinand was pressing for funds to fight the Ottomans just as lack of resources left an unrelieved Rhodes to fend for herself and lose. François I, therefore, had every hope of retaking Milan. But his aggressive legal claims upon the Duchy of Bourbon had alienated his powerful Constable of France, Charles III (1490–1527), Duke of Bourbon, who now offered his sword, 500 men-at-arms and 8,000 foot-soldiers to the Emperor. Together with Henry VIII and Charles V, he hatched a secret plan to partition France.

The plot was discovered and Bourbon was lucky to escape with his life, let alone the army he had promised. The allies went ahead with their design: the Duke of Suffolk and Count van Buren in the north marched to within 80 kilometres of Paris, the Spanish in the south advanced on Bayonne and to the east a German force threatened the border at Bresse in today's Rhône-Alps. With the element of surprise gone, a shortage of funds and an overall lack of co-ordination, the campaign quickly foundered, allowing the French once more to march into Lombardy in 1523 – although a fearful François had chosen not to lead them as originally intended.

It was Admiral Guillaume Gouffier, Seigneur de Bonnivet (*c.*1488–1525), who led the army into the Milanese. Hugely outnumbered, Prospero Colonna wisely fell back on Milan, abandoning the western part of the Duchy to the French. If Faustus was there he would have found himself in an unprepared city that, if Bonnivet had only pressed on, would have easily fallen to the French. As well as Milan, the Empire still held Pavia, Lodi, and Cremona, and Colonna now concentrated his defence on these cities. By the time Bonnivet reached Milan he found the city ready for him and settled down to starve the Milanese into submission, sending von Sickingen's old enemy Bayard to take Lodi and Cremona.

Although Lodi surrendered, Cremona successfully resisted and Bayard was recalled. The election of Giulio de' Medici as Pope Clement VII on 19 November 1523 brought money and men to the Empire's side, compelling Bonnivet to break the siege of Milan and retreat to the Ticino. Not even the death of Colonna in December offered the French an advantage as the Viceroy of Naples, Charles de Lannoy (1487–1527), and the Marquis of Pescara stepped swiftly into the breach. With reinforcements arriving from Germany and support from Venice, the Imperialists advanced against Bonnivet, driving him back to Novara in the Piedmont. Bonnivet was finally defeated at the Battle of Sesia on 30 April 1524. France's great hero Bayard was killed by a harquebus ball as he fought a rearguard action enabling the wounded Bonnivet and the rest of the army to escape.

Bourbon and Pescara pressed their advantage, advancing into Provence and laying siege to Marseilles on 19 August. Here Renzo da Ceri, the Orsini captain, put up a strong defence, aided from the sea by the galleys of Andrea Doria. François hurriedly assembled an army to relieve Marseilles. With time running out, Bourbon urged his men to an all out attack on 4 September, but Marseilles was too strongly defended. With Pescara openly against the whole expedition and the relief army on its way, Bourbon conceded defeat and marched his men back the way they had come with Anne, Duc de Montmorency (1493–1567), snapping at his heels. The Imperial army went to ground once more in its strongholds of Milan, Alessandria, Pavia, Lodi, Pizzighettone and Cremona. The strategy had worked against Bonnivet before, but, in the shifting mire of Italian politics, would it work again?

The Battle of Pavia (1525)

For some historians it would mark the end of the Middle Ages, for others it would mark a new development in warfare; certainly it would be one of the most dramatic battles of the age. The French had been encamped outside the town of Pavia since late 1524 conducting a leisurely siege: 'the king said, "Let us sit here until the bread cease"; and they died of hunger.'[8]

Since marching triumphantly back into Milan – whose garrison had been decimated by plague – the French were moving confidently through Lombardy, strong in their new alliance with Pope Clement VII and with Giovanni de' Medici now in their pay, but Pavia, that stone in their path some twenty miles to the south, would not yield. François I had somewhere between 26,000 and 40,000 men in Italy at his disposal, but this fortified town, garrisoned by only 6,000 to 9,000 men under Antonio de Leyva (1480–1536), Duke of Terranova, checked his advance.

The long siege allowed the Imperial forces to organise themselves. Bourbon was the first to arrive, marching out of nearby Lodi to the north-east. By the beginning of February the commander-in-chief of the Imperial army in Italy, Charles de Lannoy, together with Fernando de Avalos, arrived with the rest of the army. The Imperialists could now field more infantry; François I had the advantage in cavalry and cannon.

De Lannoy opened with a bombardment to distract the French from their assault on Pavia. Protected by the walls of the hunting park, the French were in a strong position. The bombardment lasted most of the month, achieving little. With food, munitions and morale running out for the defenders of Pavia, the Imperial army was compelled to step up the attack.

The battle began on a misty morning in the dark hours before sunrise. Alfonso d'Avalos was first into action leading a force of harquebusiers, whilst French and Imperial light cavalry clashed swords. François I was quick to deploy his troops, countering the Imperial advance with artillery fire so that a fog of gunsmoke obscured the rising sun. Impetuously, François led his cavalry into the fray, routing de Lannoy's centre, but he had ridden across his own guns, blocking their line of fire. François had single-handedly thrown away his advantages. Cut off and struggling on the boggy ground, the heavy cavalry was all but helpless. Turning to face advancing ranks of pikemen, heavy fire from Spanish harquebusiers tore the flower of French chivalry to shreds.

De Leyva led the garrison out of Pavia and the French were hammered on all sides. As the smoke cleared from the battlefield it became obvious that de Lannoy had won a decisive victory. François I had been captured and his army scattered and put to flight, and all on the Emperor's birthday.

Faustus would not have been surprised. As he may have been able to inform the victorious Imperial leaders, the outcome had been foretold. According to the astrologer Erasmus Rheinhold (1511–1553): 'Those that have Mars in the fourth house, in a position of dejection, are unfortunate warriors.'[9] François I had Mars in the fourth house.

Writing shortly afterwards, the Spanish Humanist, Alfonso de Valdés (1500–1532), crowed over the victory: 'It seems that God has miraculously given this victory to the Emperor.'[10] The French may have been defeated, but the war was far from over. The French had been trounced at Pavia, but before long they would be back for more.

De Valdés also expressed concern about 'the Turk', and he had good cause. Continued French aggression gave the Ottoman Sultan Suleiman I a golden opportunity and he marched out from Belgrade at the head of a vast army, numbering between 70,000 and 100,000 soldiers. With Poland and Venice declaring neutrality, Ladislas II (1506–1526) of Hungary was left to face the approaching horde on his own. Ladislas led what troops he had in a glorious cavalry charge against greatly superior forces. It was a gesture of defiance, of chivalric insouciance, and was doomed to fail. Suleiman was only compelled to delay his continued assault on Europe by the necessity of quelling revolts in Cilicia and Maramania.

A prophecy made by Augustin Bader of Augsburg in 1527 and repeated by Paracelsus foretold that the Turks would reach the Rhine, destroying the current order and subjugating all in an empire that forcibly united Christian, Jew, Turk and pagan.[11] Suleiman would be back.

The Sack of Rome (1527)

According to the Faustbook, Faustus, like the Imperial army, also made it as far as Rome. After trudging around the 'Holy City' taking in the sights, Faustus returned to the west bank of the Tiber and the Vatican complex to see the Pope's palace and 'his manner of service at his table'.[12] The palace that Faustus would have seen was a mish-mash of Nicholas III's (r.1277–1280) incomplete fortress, Nicholas V's (r.1447–1455) enlargements, Sixtus IV's (r.1471–1484) library and Sistine Chapel, Innocent VIII's (r.1484–1492) Belvedere Palace, Alexander VI's (r.1492–1503) Borgia Tower and Julius II's (r.1503–1513) huge Belvedere Court.

But Faustus was not interested in architecture. Walking under the shadow of the imposing stonework looming above them, 'he and his Spirit made themselves invisible' and slipped past the halberds of the Swiss Guards 'into the Popes Court, and privie chamber where he was'.[13] Someone like Faustus could chose from three prescriptions 'for invisibility' in Codex 849 alone.

In the inner sanctum of Clement VII (r.1523–1534), Faustus and Mephistopheles watched 'the many servants attendant on his holiness, with many a flattering Sycophant carrying of his meat'. Even the Faustus of the Faustbook, so used to clothing himself in the finest raiment and eating the choicest faire, is astounded by the 'unmeasurable and sumptuous' feast: 'fie (quoth *Faustus*) why had not the Devil made a Pope of me?'[14] The heavy satire did not end there.

Faustus, looking around, saw many like the Faustbook's version of himself: 'proud, stout, wilful, gluttons, drunkards, whoremongers, breakers of wedlock, and followers of all manner of ungodly exercises.' Marvelling at such a debauched crew, he turned to Mephistopheles and complained that 'I thought that I had been alone a hog, or pork of the devils'. Feeling quite at home, Faustus decided to stay awhile.[15]

In the Faustbook he stayed three days, watching the Pope throw one sumptuous party after another. Roused by the author's Protestant disgust at the Pope's habit of continuously blessing and making the sign of the cross over his mouth, the invisible Faustus slapped him on the face and burst into a fit of loud laughter. The startled Pope quickly composed himself and explained the incident away as a damned soul, 'commanding a Mass presently to be said for his deliverie out of Purgatory'. The Pope waved his hand and it was done, while he continued to sit at his dinner table. When the next dish was brought in Faustus snatched it up, saying 'this is mine', and rushed out. Faustus ordered Mephistopheles to bring him wine and the Pope's own goblet to 'make good cheer in spite of the Pope and all his fat abbey lubbers'.[16]

Robbed of their wine, the Pope and his companions blamed the damned soul again. Mass was ordered to be said in every Church and the bells to be rung in every belfry throughout Rome, and in addition that the spirit be cursed with 'Bell, Book, and Candle'.

Bell, book, and candle; candle, book and bell,
Forward and backward, to curse Faustus to hell.[17]

'Bell, book and candle' is the popular phrase for ceremonial excommunication from the Church of Rome. A bishop attended by twelve priests would recite the terrible formula before the altar. It is as close to a curse as Christianity gets. The victim is denied the succour of Father, Son and Holy Ghost, and is condemned to hell where Satan will mortify his body.

The bishop rings a bell to symbolise the death knell, closes a holy book to symbolise the excommunicant's separation from the church and snuffs out a candle or candles, knocking them to the floor, to symbolise the excommunicant's soul being extinguished and removed from the light of God. In effect it is a sentence of spiritual death and anyone thus excommunicated who does not seek absolution within one year is automatically suspected of heresy. For all the gravity of the ceremony, Marlowe could not resist satirising the peevishness of the Pope and his gang, having them chant: 'Cursed be he that took away our holiness' wine' (III.2.101–110). In the Faustbook Faustus was nonplussed by the din of bells and chanting priests, and instead 'made good cheer' before summoning up a terrifying thunderstorm and taking his leave of the Holy City.[18]

It is the incident not mentioned in the Faustbook that Faustus surely claimed responsibility for. It was another great victory for the Imperial army, but it was also their disgrace. The so-called 'Sack of Rome' of 1527 by the troops of Charles V was, to his chagrin, the culmination and crowning victory of his Italian campaigns. Pope Clement VII's double-dealing to try and free himself from Imperial domination had finally led to his ruin.

With the French king François I now his prisoner, Charles V constrained him to sign the Treaty of Madrid (14 January 1526), to confirm its terms by his solemn oath and swear to abide by it upon his honour as a knight. Under its conditions François agreed to marry the Emperor's sister, Eleonora, to renounce all his rights over Milan, Naples, Genoa, Asti, together with the suzerainty of Flanders, Artois, and Tournai. He ceded to Charles the Duchy of Burgundy, excluding its traditional dependencies. The Duke of Bourbon was to be pardoned, all of his confiscated lands to be restored, and to be reimbursed for his expenses. François was to cease to be the ally of the Duke of Gelders and retract all the claims of d'Albret to Navarre. He agreed to hand over his two sons as surety and to surrender himself in the event of non-fulfilment. Satisfied by his word of honour, Charles released François in February 1526.

As soon as François was safely back in Paris he reneged on his promises to the Duke of Bourbon, broke the terms he had sworn by the Treaty of Madrid, denied that he had been defeated at Pavia and sold off the Duke of Bourbon's lands to other French nobles, notwithstanding the fact that he had handed over his sons as hostages. On 22 May, together with Rome, Venice, Milan and Florence he concluded the League of Cognac against the Empire. Charles V's army would soon be facing him again on the field of battle.

The Duke of Bourbon, once more betrayed by his perfidious king, asked Charles V for financial help, but the Emperor had more pressing matters to contend with and granted Bourbon the title of Duke of Milan and the command of another large army with which to occupy northern Italy. In the summer of 1526, as the money ran out, Bourbon's control over this army began to deteriorate. Unable to provide for his troops in any other way, Bourbon began selling off the last of his family heirlooms and jewels to pay the soldiers.

Charles V had meanwhile sent an envoy to the Pope, but obtaining no satisfaction from that quarter, sought out the disaffected Colonna family and renewed old alliances. Lulling the Papal army into a false sense of security by pretending a reconciliation, Pompeo Colonna led an unexpected assault upon Rome on 20 September 1526. He cornered Clement in the Castle of Sant'Angelo whilst his followers plundered the Vatican. Charles distanced himself from the action, but took advantage of the situation. Clement was lost. With no idea what to do he turned from the League to the Empire and, following a minor victory, back to the League again. Finally, he signed an eight month truce with Charles on condition that he pay an immediate indemnity of 60,000 ducats.

By early 1527 the Duke of Bourbon had sold off all of his treasures and was forced to turn a blind eye while his soldiers looted neighbouring towns. From February to May Imperial soldiers ravaged the northern Italian countryside with impunity, all the time on the verge of open mutiny. Churches were stripped of any gold and silver that could be melted down to pay the mercenaries as Bourbon's pleas for funding went unheard. Even von Frundsberg was having problems controlling his men. Elderly and in poor health, he resigned his commission and returned home. Now, on hearing of the 60,000 ducats, the soldiers' threats of mutiny became louder. The Imperial commissioners went back to Clement VII and squeezed 40,000 more ducats out of his coffers.

The promised ducats did not reach the men whose prowess in arms had made it all possible. In April Bourbon had little choice but to accede to the wishes of his men to attack and loot the fabulously wealthy city of Rome. Pope Clement VII thought that he was safe behind his wall of treaties and promised gold, safe in the belief that no one would ever dare to storm the inviolable capital of all Christendom, but as the hungry Imperial army approached Rome, he hastily ordered the inhabitants to rally to the city's defence. Only a few thousand answered the summons to meet the 20,000 strong army when it arrived on 5 May. Thinly spread along the walls and with only a few old cannons, the citizen levies must have had little hope in resisting the coming attack. It did not take an astrologer to divine the outcome, but Faustus might have comfortably made his prediction. Rome's star was in the descendent.

There was a comet that year; astrologically it portended terrible things: war, plague, famine, earthquake, fire and flood. There were other signs for Faustus to interpret. Parhelia, a phenomenon in which light intensifies at the rim of the solar halo to give the appearance of up to two additional suns in the sky, was seen prior to the battle. The numerical significance of three was often connected to the Trinity and hence indicated a Christian victory. But the coming battle was Christian against Christian, which one would prevail? Who was the more Christian? The heretical Protestants, or the debauched, idolatrous Romans? Providence, as always, was on the side of the big guns.

On the morning of 6 May, as thick fog swathed the walls, Bourbon gave the order to attack. His men took up the cry 'kill, kill, blood, blood, Bourbon, Bourbon'.[19] Leading gallantly from the front, Bourbon was almost immediately struck by a harquebus ball fired by one of the defenders and killed. The Italian artist, musician and goldsmith Benvenuto Cellini (1500–1571) later claimed credit for the fatal shot. Despite the loss of their general, the army easily overwhelmed the city's meagre defences, and leaderless were freed to vent the darkest cruelty of their hearts upon the city and its people in a murderous rampage and orgy of rape.

The Swiss Guard put up a brave defence on the steps of St Peter's Basilica, allowing Clement VII to scurry to safety down the *passetto*, the secret passage linking the Vatican to the Castel Sant'Angelo. His escape was short lived. Without any further secret passages to lead him out of the city, he managed to hold out in his castle until 5 June. The Castel Sant'Angelo now became his prison, but 400,000 ducats bought a comfortable confinement.

Of the 55,000 men, women and children in Rome many had fled the city. Of those unlucky enough to find themselves without the convenience of a secret passage, thousands were put to the sword by the rampaging soldiers. One sober estimate put the number of dead at 4,000. Their religious differences aside, Catholic and Protestant soldiers united in desecrating the Eternal City. Thomas More (1478–1553) described captives having their genitals torn off. Women, even those in religious orders, were violated, ambassadors were robbed, cardinals were ransomed, ecclesiastical dignitaries and ceremonies were mocked, and the soldiers squabbled over the spoils of war. Churches, shrines and other historic monuments were looted and in some cases destroyed. 'Luther' was scrawled upon the walls of rooms decorated by Raphael. The great library of Bishop Egidio di Viterbo was ransacked and lost. From the battlements of Sant'Angelo, Cellini and others watched 'the indescribable scene of tumult and conflagration in the streets below'.[20] Only the Sistine Chapel, not long redecorated by Michelangelo and where Charles de Bourbon's body had been taken to lie in state, was spared their fury. The Trinity of this parhelia was one of greed, lust and murder.

When news of the sack of Rome reached Charles V, he quickly sent his deepest apologies to the Pope, claiming that Bourbon's renegade army had acted without his approval. Charles may have been embarrassed by the sacking and by his inability to control his army, but he could not have been displeased by the fact that they had struck decisively against Clement VII.

The propaganda machine was soon cranking out its version of events to excuse Charles V from the horrors of the sack. Alfonso de Valdés in his *Dialogue* put all the weight of condemnation on the Pope, whilst portraying Charles as dutifully defending his subjects against a despicable warmonger.

When Charles V visited the city after its conquest, the *Via Sacra* through the ruins of the ancient forum was repaved to facilitate his triumphal entry to the Capitol in time-honoured tradition. It may have been Charles V's crowning victory, but it marked the end of the Renaissance in Italy.[21]

Bicocca in 1522, Sesia in 1524, Pavia in 1525, Rome in 1527 – these were the victories to which Faustus alluded. Pavia was the defining moment – two giants locking horns – whilst the sack of Rome was like the squashing of a cockroach, unpleasant and infinitely less heroic. Taken together, these four battles between the foremost powers of Europe represented a great accomplishment for any magician to claim – a bold assertion, but, being unverifiable, a safe one too. It could only have been made later, when he returned from the fighting (supposing that he did in fact go to Italy). Between 1522 and 1527 he may have come and gone in Italy, following the ebb and flow of the *Landsknechte* moving between battlefield and wheatfield, and the inner call of the habituated wanderlust of the travelling scholar.

There were still more victories to win in Italy, still more trophies Faustus could claim with his magic. However, we have a handful of references to suggest that he was elsewhere than Italy after 1527.

14

On the Road to Exile
(1527–1528)

The Sack of Rome cast a heavy pall across Europe. Even Lutherans like Melanchthon regretted the indiscriminate mayhem of the philistine soldiery. Leonardo da Vinci had spoken prophetically when he wrote that 'Creatures shall be seen upon the earth who will always be fighting one with another with very great losses and frequent deaths on either side.'[1] The cannon smoke had hardly cleared when France and England allied themselves against Charles V and declared war. Three months later, Odet de Foix was leading yet another army into the Milanese. As if she was not troubled enough, a typhus epidemic was ravaging Italy that by the end of the year would claim tens of thousands of lives. While the European powers resumed their old games, the armies of Suleiman the Magnificent were gathering for the final assault on Christendom.

It was witchcraft and magic that was epidemic in Germany. Another victim was burned in Waldsee – the fourth in a witch-hunt that would send more than forty-three people from Waldsee to prison or more often the flames in the course of the sixteenth century. The Visitation of the Saxon Church (1527–8) had uncovered the ecclesiastical underworld that produced and harboured such works as Codex 849. As Luther would angrily recall in 1543, the Visitation had found a large number of books of magic in the possession of village pastors and churchwardens with such 'evils' inscribed in them as the Tetragrammaton and prayers in Hebrew.

Around this time another of those curious Faustian manuals was claimed to have been produced. Butler called it *Praxis Magica Faustiana* and gave it a date of 1527 or 1577 and its place of publication as Passau, but said no more about it. Her source was Johannes Scheible's extraordinary collection and this is undoubtedly the same document called *Praxis Magica Fausti* of 1571 that Scheible published in 1847. In 1875 a Major Herbert Irwin translated the work into English but did not publish it – a situation that continued up until the late twentieth century. The occult scholar A.E. Waite (1857–1942) acquired Irwin's manuscript and briefly described it in *The Book of Ceremonial Magic* in 1911. In 1924 it fell into the hands of the lawyer John G. White

(1845–1928) who finally bequeathed it to the Cleveland Public Library in Ohio where it remains to this day.

On stylistic grounds Waite thought that it was probably composed in the seventeenth century. The claim appearing in the work to have come from an original manuscript in the Municipal Library of Weimar is disputed by Waite on the grounds that there was no Municipal Library in Weimar in 1571. It cannot be ruled out that there was some sort of library existing at this time, but the word 'municipal' is entirely misleading.

The whole was pithily summed up by Waite as consisting of 'a few curious plates … and a few unintelligible conjurations, all exceedingly brief.'[2] The entire ritual is directed towards the invocation of a spirit called Rumoar – a new addition to the Faustian pantheon. We do not find him in the so-called *Black Raven* attributed to Faustus, nor do we find this spirit listed by Wierus in his *Pseudomonarchia Daemonum*. The spirit is placed under the jurisdiction of Lucifer, but from the ritual it is not clear what the conjurer expects from him and no hints as to his character or sphere of influence are given. Like most of these rituals, its frame of reference is Judaeo-Christian, with God, Jesus and the Tetragrammaton invoked to command the spirit.

It is unlikely that Faustus ever wasted his time in composing such a thing, but we readily see how the name of Faustus became popular among the compilers and peddlers of dubious black magic rituals in the centuries that followed.

If 1528 was a dark year for Europe and the Empire, the stars were not favourable for Faustus either. In 1528 he was destined to be maligned and thrown out of one of the principal cities of Bavaria, but only after he had revealed some astonishing new information about himself. First, however, a mysterious letter from Agrippa suggests that he may have spent early 1528 in Paris.

The School of Wickednesses (1528)

The Ancients were wont to brand notorious folly with this proverb, *viz.* To bring Owls to *Athens:* but it is not a part of less folly, but of most great impiety, to send devils to hell. You know what I call hell, *viz.* that *School* of wickednesses.[3]

So the indignant occultist Agrippa wrote from Paris on 13 February 1528. The letter was written to 'a certain friend of the King's Court' who has been tentatively identified as the French royal physician Jean Chapelain.[4] It was a certain member of that 'school of wickednesses' that had roused Agrippa's ire, a member, who although unnamed, is often identified as Faustus.[5]

Agrippa had been in Paris since January that year, trying to extricate himself from royal service and secure papers and a military escort to the border with the Low Countries. Travelling north from Lyon where he had left his family, Agrippa, impecunious and desperate, was trying to reach Antwerp and a new life. However, he still found time to associate with a circle of men interested in the occult and was evidently hanging on news of events at court. In his letter he said that 'there was sent for out of

Germany with no small charges a certain master of Spirits, that is a Necromancer, who possesseth a power over spirits.'[6]

The connection with Faustus is tenuous. The only clues are that this magician comes from Germany and makes extravagant claims. His identification as a necromancer stands in favour of the argument. Faustus had after all declared himself to be the source of necromancy. But there must have been other necromancers in Germany at that time besides Faustus – Agrippa himself was thought to have been one of them.

Paris, the city Balzac called 'the ante-chamber to hell', had a long history of association with the dark arts.[7] One thinks of the notorious Chambre Ardente affair of the seventeenth century, but Parisian diabolism extends still further back. William of Auvergne claimed to have seen forbidden books of necromancy when he was a student in Paris in the early thirteenth century. Some years later in 1277 the Archbishop of Paris officially condemned all necromantic writings. A hundred years on, the University of Paris showed a similar inclination in declaring all witchcraft to be heresy. There was a strong interest in the problem of witchcraft. At least two editions of the *Malleus Maleficarum* had recently been published in Paris by the printer Jehan Petit (around 1507 and 1510) and another by Joanne Parvo in 1517.

But the talk in Paris would have been of the recent eruption of demonic possession at the convent of St Pierre in Lyon. A bishop and three priests had been called in to exorcise the cloister, running the demon to earth in a nun, Sister Alexis de Thesieux, whence they finally returned the spirit to hell. A dramatic account was published by Adrien de Montalembert in Paris in 1528. It was a story to discuss in context with the trial and execution for witchcraft of Catherine Peyretonne at Montpezat in 1519 and the two cases of lycanthropy and cannibalism investigated at Besançon in 1521.

Although Agrippa was writing from Paris, in 1528 the royal court was some nineteen kilometres up the Seine at the Château de Saint-Germain-en-Laye. Robert de la Marck described it vaguely as 'a very fine château five leagues from Paris, with a fine park in a fine hunting forest'.[8] Unlike many other more occasional residences it was permanently furnished and a favoured winter retreat. It was another medieval fortress that would be remodelled by François's Loire architect Pierre de Chambiges, and in 1528 work had already begun.

Having perhaps only heard the name of this king until now, Faustus – we shall assume it was he – now met him face to face. François prided himself on his accessibility. His personality was like that of his totem animal, the heraldic salamander, politically slippery and emotionally fiery. Jean Clouet the Younger's famous portrait of around 1530 shows us narrow, self-satisfied eyes above a long, crooked nose. It was a nose to challenge the jib of Charles V's Habsburg chin. The eyebrows arch superciliously, the small lips reject any hint of a smile, yet do not quite develop into a sneer. His costume is extravagant. His sleeves are puffed out to such an extent that they grossly distort the shape of his upper torso, giving him the shoulders of Hercules, an exaggeration which has the unfortunate consequence of making his head look disproportionately small.

What would this king have made of Faustus? Did he see in him a new Jambres, as the Devil saw in Cyprian? The 'James and Jambres' that Agrippa alluded to in his letter were the Egyptian magicians Jannes and Jambres (or Mambres) who contested

Moses and Aaron as related in the New Testament (2 Tim. 3:8). Agrippa suggested as much when he said 'as *James* and *Jambres* resisted *Moses,* so he should oppose *Cæsar*' – Caesar being Charles V in this context. François was not looking for parlour tricks and fairground hokum, but news of 'all things to come' and an insight into 'all secret counsels', according to Agrippa. This reminds us of the sorts of claims Trithemius was making for his steganography all those years before. Had Faustus acquired a copy of this precious manuscript or developed similar techniques of his own?

There was much going on in the world that François would have been desirous to learn. On 17 February 1528, just a few days after Agrippa's letter, the Imperial army left Rome under the command of Philibert de Châlon, Prince of Orange – after making sure that they had taken all that was valuable – and was moving to counter de Foix who had so far been successful in taking Alessandria and Pavia, but had bypassed Milan to march straight for the prize, Rome. Imperial losses had been slight in taking Rome, but little more than half, about 11,000 men, marched out again – presumably the others were busy hauling their loot home. De Foix enjoyed a numerical advantage and so François surely hoped that here was another opportunity to defeat Charles once and for all.

Did Faustus use his magic to divine what Philibert de Châlon's secret counsels were? He would have seen that in the coming months Prince Philibert would be helplessly besieged in Naples while the relief force coming down from Germany would be emasculated once again by lack of funds, but not only that. When the bills finally arrived there was no one to cash them and still less to buy, so depleted was the country. Nevertheless, François's designs on Italy would be dashed within little more than a year.

Beyond merely showing the future, Faustus may have been claiming to be able to influence it. In his letter Agrippa talked of 'mountains full of horsemen' and 'fiery Chariots' with reference to Elisha in Dotham (Dothan) from 2 Kings 6:13–17. The besieged prophet Elisha prayed to his God 'and behold, the mountain [was] full of horses and chariots of fire round about Elisha'. Such astonishing feats were certainly within the scope of current magical manuals, so it would not have been at all impossible for Faustus to have made such a claim. He may have taken the opportunity to inform the French king – as he had apparently informed Melanchthon – that all the victories that had been won in Italy were down to his occult intercession.

As well as mentioning the Siege of Pavia, there is also another clear reference to contemporary events in the letter. Agrippa stated that this magician claimed 'he could bring back the King's children through the air'. As we know, François's two eldest sons were still in hock to Charles after he had reneged on his word of honour given in Madrid. The heir-apparent François (1518–1536) and his brother, the future king of France, Henri (1519–1559), returned home not through the air by magic in 1528, but by treaty and the promise of two million crowns in ransom in 1529.

Agrippa said that this necromancer claimed to be able to 'fetch up the treasures of the earth' – claims that would not have fallen on deaf ears given the extraordinary outlays in expenditure that the Italian campaign was costing François. Expertise in love magic was also hinted at, which would have warmed François's womanising heart – a proclivity said to have been belied by that pendulous nose. Finally, Agrippa's reference to this necromancer claiming to be able to 'cure all desperate diseases', although universally useful, was again particularly apt. François was widely rumoured to have syphilis. The story went that he had been deliberately infected by the jealous husband of one of his mistresses, passing it on to him through her. Paracelsus, that other Faustus, turned his fickle genius to the problem, so why not Faustus himself?

Of course Faustus visited Paris in the Faustbook, but his trip was fleeting and unverifiable. He apparently 'liked well the Academy', but the University of Paris would not have cared for Faustus, given what we know of its conservatism and earlier condemnation of Reuchlin.[9] Agrippa used the excuse of the appearance of this unnamed necromancer to decry what he saw as the decadence of the royal courtiers who 'run to the invocations of evil spirits'.[10]

Whatever François made of this necromancer's claims, his courtiers at least seemed to have thought highly of him and been eager for his audience. Agrippa painted the 'school of wickednesses' in the blackest of colours. Its members were nothing short of Satanists, abandoning their faith in God and believing this magician able to command all things.

Agrippa, of course, needed to add an escape clause for himself or run the danger of being damned by his own words. He affirmed that there were 'Occult Ingenuities' that did not offend God and could deliver a whole host of benefits to health, wealth and wisdom.[11] But for all of the 'school of wickednesses' and their supporters, Agrippa prophesied damnation.

Agrippa went on at length to recount how the 'wicked' shall 'gnash their teeth' and so on, but he had made his point.[12] The tone of this diatribe against the 'German Sorcerer' is reminiscent of his sometime master Trithemius's own invective against Faustus, which perhaps gives us another clue to the identity of the unnamed necromancer. There is also an element of sour grapes here. Reading between the lines, Agrippa was annoyed that a competitor had won the position and no doubt coveted some of the largesse that accommodated those 'no small charges'.

At the time he wrote this letter, Agrippa had been out of royal favour for two years. Religiously he was too much of a radical and his political scheming contributed to make him *persona non grata*. Ostensibly, his decline can be charted from the offence he gave to Louise de Savoie, the Queen Mother, after refusing to draw up a horoscope for François at her request. He may have done so to avoid being the bearer of bad news. He wrote to Seneschal Bohier that the stars favoured, not François, but the Duke of Bourbon. Furthermore, Claude Bellievre recorded that sometime in May 1527, Agrippa had said that the malign influence of the heavens would kill the king within six months.[13] Prophecy of the monarch's death could be construed as constructive treason. Although François had outlived those six months by the time Faustus supposedly arrived, he may have wanted a second opinion. He may even have heard of Virdung's gloomy prophesy for his predecessor Louis XII and welcomed the chance to discuss its apparent accuracy with one of his colleagues.

After Agrippa's cryptic letter we briefly lose sight of Faustus again. The next year, 1529, Agrippa was attached to the court of Margaret of Austria after turning down impressive offers from Henry VIII and the Imperial Chancellor Mercurino Gattinara, and wrote no more letters about expensive German magicians. The next reference appears four months later and almost 800 kilometres away.

The Meteorological Monk

The name Faustus curiously appears in the meteorological notebook of a monk. It seems so incongruous: a monk interested in science receiving a call from a necromancer. But this monk, called Kilian Leib, did indeed record in his journal some fragments of a conversation he had had with Faustus on 5 June 1528. Was Leib referring to a letter from or about Faustus, a conversation with someone else about Faustus, or was Faustus with him in person? Events later in the month point to the two having met.

Kilian Leib was the prior of the monastery of Rebdorf near Eichstätt, to the north of the Danube in Bavaria. From Eichstätt one passes by the formidable fortress of Willibaldsburg looming from a nearby bluff overlooking the river to find the monastery sitting directly alongside the road in the *Altmühltal* nature park. Now home to the Knabenrealschule Rebdorf, it is a stout, regular building, punctuated by the double spires of the church.

Rebdorf lies in the Diocese of Eichstätt, which was founded by St Boniface in the eighth century CE. The Bishopric of Eichstätt was a powerful position, controlling not only Rebdorf but also Ingolstadt. Like other German principalities in the thirteenth century, the Bishopric of Eichstätt was granted sovereignty and emerged in the fourteenth century as the independent ruler of a territory that at one time encompassed over 700 square kilometres and 56,000 subjects. In the sixteenth century the von Huttens also exercised some power here. When Faustus was there, Gabriel von Eyb (1496–1535) presided as Bishop, to be succeeded in 1539 by Moritz von Hutten (1503–1552).

The Augustinian monastery at Rebdorf was founded in 1159 largely through the intercession of Friedrich I Barbarossa. A Romanesque church was soon constructed on the site. A nave and two aisles were built in an Italian style that was at that time fashionable in Bavaria. The two towers that still stand today were added in the second quarter of the thirteenth century and altered in the fifteenth century. A cloister added in the second half of the fifteenth century was decorated with stained glass and gave a final resting-place to the good and the great of Eichstätt. As a consequence of changing tastes, the buildings were remodelled in the late Baroque style that one sees today.

Leib had entered the monastery at the age of fifteen in 1486. He quickly rose to prominence, managing the economic interests of the monastery from 1497. From 1499 to 1503 he took a leading role in the reformation of the monastery of Schamhaupten near Altmannstein. In 1505 he was elected Prior of Rebdorf. His good management of the monastery finances enabled him to distribute generous alms, but more importantly, politically speaking, to lend money to the Bishop of Eichstätt and various needy princlings.

He developed a close friendship with Willibald Pirckheimer and wrote to many other famous Humanists of his day, such as Erasmus, Johannes Reuchlin, Christoph Scheurl, Thomas Venatorius and Jacob Wimpfeling. But it was his connection with Daniel Stibar that may explain his meeting Faustus.

Daniel Stibarus or Stibar (1503–1555), was a judge, city councillor and canon in Würzburg and a distant relation of Georg III's successor as Bishop of Bamberg. In 1536 Joachim Camerarius referred to a friendship between Stibar and Faustus, but beyond that curt reference we have nothing more. Stibar was an influential friend to have, as Leib would have known. A tentative web of connections spins itself between Faustus, the Bishop of Bamberg, Stibar and Leib, but it is impossible to determine who may have introduced whom, if at all.

Leib's interest in astrology inspired him to start recording meteorological observations and the corresponding positions of the planets in the margins of Stöffler's *Almanach nova* from April 1513 onwards. This became his so-called *Wettertagebuch*, or weather-diary, that he would faithfully keep for 28 years. The planetary conjunction in Pisces in 1524, said to portend an impending catastrophic flood, offered him a prime opportunity. Leib made careful note of the weather that year and found nothing out of the ordinary. This led him to interpret the conjunction as an omen of religious rebellion, the new Reformed religion. In January 1528 he wrote the *Gründtliche Anzaygung* attacking the Reformation, and because of Pirckheimer's support for Luther, broke off their friendship.

He was a self-taught man, never having attended university, but was a celebrated linguist and an avid reader of classical literature, digesting works in Latin, Greek, Hebrew and even Aramaic. He was also an avid writer, recording the events of his time in two historical works: *Annales maiores* and *Annales minores*. However, it is for his *Wettertagebuch* that he is chiefly remembered today.

In an age before barometers, thermometers and modern agricultural practices, the weather was an unpredictable and often harsh master. The weather's changing moods could stop armies in their tracks, bring the merchant to poverty and the peasant to starvation. This made it a magnet for superstition and magic, like the goosebone weather divination of Hartlieb's Teutonic knight.

Leib stood out because of his scientific approach to the problem. Although a believer in astrology, he wanted to find the evidence that it had an influence and to determine just what that influence was, but his interest in weather extended beyond the stars. Using the voluminous *Ephemerides* of Regiomontanus, Leib cross-tabulated natural phenomena with planetary movements. He recorded when the first swallows arrived, when the first buds appeared and when he could eat his first dinner without candles. He observed the starlit sky and the changing patterns of sunshine and rain. He discovered that good visibility of the Alps was a sign of imminent rain. He listened to the different tones of the bells of neighbouring villages, the song of frogs, the howling of wolves and noted when bees swarmed at unusual times. He observed the hoarfrost and how quickly it melted on different surfaces. He made observations about violent thunderstorms, droughts, downpours, epidemics, crime, rising food prices, the deaths of his fellow brothers and famous contemporaries, and registered anything out of the ordinary. Amongst all these jottings Faustus appears as if he too were a natural phenomenon or celestial body.

Another Prophet

When Faustus arrived at Rebdorf he found a wealthy and well-connected monastery run by an able and intelligent Humanist theologian. It was not the backwater that it is today, but a centre of Humanism and an economic power-base. Faustus was paying a visit to an important man.

In his scrawling hand, Leib recorded two things about Faustus that we have yet to examine: one of his astrological theories and his occupation or status at the time. Faustus and Leib must have sat of an evening debating the pros and cons of astrology. Leib with his careful note-taking, following the predictions and observing the actual conditions; Faustus with his noble clients and some degree of social success. One of the topics under debate may have been the great fuss stirred up by Luther and his followers. In his anti-Lutheran book Leib had discussed the influence of the stars on the development of this new movement, which was to him utterly heretical, and he may have sought Faustus's opinion on the matter. However, what was really of interest to Leib was the matter of conjunctions. Leib recorded part of their conversation in his weather-diary:

> Georgius Faustus Helmstet on the fifth of June said, that when the sun and Jupiter are together in the same degree of a sign, then are born prophets (namely such as himself).[14]

While Leib no longer believed that conjunctions had a direct effect upon the weather, like Faustus he still thought that they had an effect upon the affairs of men. Leib and Faustus were not alone in this view; the theory of conjunctions was an important cornerstone of Renaissance astrology. Conjunctions were graded as great, medium and small. The conjunction of the sun and Jupiter was ranked as great and correspondingly signalled momentous events.

As related by Leib, Faustus drew upon the common ground of interpreting conjunctions. Leib's bracketed aside – 'namely such as himself' – adds a biographical element to this information. Leib is telling us that Faustus thought he was astrologically ordained to be a prophet because he was born under just such a conjunction. Melanchthon would try and do the same thing in his sycophantic interpretation of Luther's horoscope.

Faustus's stay with Leib must have led to a dispute between them. Leib had come to several conclusions that struck at the heart of astrology. Firstly, on the basis of the observations recorded in his *Wettertagebuch*, he argued that it was impossible to predict the weather using astrology or any other means. Secondly, he argued that it was against God's will for man to foresee the future for his worldly benefit. He went further to state that it was improper for a Christian to use the stars to determine his future, drawing on the authority of the Bible and Pico della Mirandola, although he thought that it was both proper and possible to use of the stars to foretell of a heresy like Luther's. Finally, he concluded that astrologers could not accurately calculate the positions of the planets and so could only make erroneous predictions.

However, this last conclusion also cut against Leib, as Faustus may have pointed out. If astrologers could not accurately calculate the positions of the planets, then the astrological charts he had used in his experiments were inaccurate and the conclusions he had reached on the strength of them were likewise false. Leib both undermined his own conclusions and equivocated on whether one really could tell the future using astrology. He had taken a step along the path of science, but his position was weak and open to attack, and Faustus had ten gulden from the Bishop of Bamberg to attest to the value of his predictions.

The Unlikely Knight

Leib had more to say about Faustus, more indeed than was probably recorded. After noting Faustus's views on conjunctions and his destiny as a prophet in the *Wettertagebuch*, Leib continued:

> He claimed that he was the commander or preceptor of a house of the Hospitallers on the border of Carinthia which is called Hallestein.[15]

Commander or preceptor was the usual title given to the leader of a commandery, but prior, procurator or master might also be used. The commandery itself was a small, usually fortified outpost or waystation with attached church, manned by a garrison of variable size. It was not the high rank that any crank might lay claim to, but a middling, though important, position.

Out of the hundred or so military orders that Christian zeal has spawned, that of the Hospitallers of St John of Jerusalem is generally held to be one of the most important.[16] The Order of St John is most immediately thought of in connection with the islands of Malta and Rhodes, but their network spread throughout Christendom. The first official mention of the Order was the Papal Bull of Paschal II in 1113, although the tradition of maintaining hospitals or hospices in Jerusalem dates back to the seventh century. By the thirteenth century the Order owned 19,000 manses or manors across Europe.

The organisational structure that developed from the fourteenth century, following the Order's successful conquest of Rhodes, saw it divided into tongues or nations, priories, bailiwicks and commanderies. There were eight tongues, each governed by a bailiff or pillar and each reserving to itself one of eight supreme offices or dignitaries: to Provence, that of the Grand Commander; to Auvergne, that of Marshal; to France, Grand Hospitaller; to Aragon, Standard-Bearer; to Castile, Grand Chancellor; to Italy, Admiral; to Germany, Grand Bailiff; to England, Turcoplier. Each tongue was divided into priories, further subdivided into bailiwicks and finally separated into the individual commanderies. Above this structure presided the Grand Chapter with supreme authority resting in the Grand Master – a term introduced in 1489. The Order's mission was encompassed in its motto *Tuitio Fidei et Obsequium Pauperum* – to protect the faith and serve the poor.

Knights were recruited from amongst the nobility (proof of which was carefully scrutinised) and before being eligible for a commandery were required to complete three 'caravans' or campaigns, equivalent to a modern soldier's tour of duty. As a knight of a religious order, vows of poverty, chastity and obedience would also be required. In practice these vows seldom carried much weight among the worldly warriors. Once a knight had secured a commandery in Continental Europe (as opposed to any of the besieged islands) he acted almost entirely independently, caring little for the orders of his superiors.

In 1528 the forty-fourth Grand Master of the Order was Philippe Villiers de L'Isle-Adam (1521–1534), an able soldier and leader, but one whose career would be ever marred by the loss of Rhodes. The Order had driven off the Turks before; in 1480 they had repulsed the onslaught of Mahomet II. But in 1522 Suleiman I renewed the attack with an Armada of between 400 and 700 ships and an army of some 140,000 to 200,000 men against a garrison of no more than 6,000 knights and auxiliaries. Suleiman was confident of victory.

For six months the knights heroically withstood this ferocious assault until they were finally defeated by the exhaustion of their supplies and, most shamefully, the failure of the European powers to provide reinforcements. Villiers de L'Isle-Adam and his knights were offered exemplary terms: the remaining 180 knights and 1,500 assorted mercenaries were allowed to withdraw with their lives, under condition never to return, and in recognition of their bravery Suleiman even ferried them safely to Europe in his own ships.

Strange stories became attached to the Knights of St John. It was rumoured that the English alchemist George Ripley made gold for them on Rhodes, producing £100,000 per annum. But there was nothing more extraordinary than this valiant defence against a force that outnumbered them so greatly. When the news of the fall of Rhodes reached Charles V he exclaimed, 'Nothing in the world has been so well lost as Rhodes!' For all his admiration of the defenders' valour, he refused to assist Villiers de L'Isle-Adam in his plans to recapture the island. In 1528 the Order was effectively homeless and had been for six long years, although petitions to Charles V for Malta would eventually bear fruit in 1530.

If Faustus really was a knight of the Order and preceptor of a commandery, then he must have come from a verifiable noble lineage and have completed his three obliga-tory 'caravans'. Leib's reference to 'helmstet' may be intended to mean that he was a scion of the noble house von Helmstatt. The German Tongue was known for its strict application of the rules, requiring a formidable sixteen quarters of nobility for admis-sion, but he may also have received some special dispensation. After the fall of Rhodes and the significant losses that the Order incurred, especially amongst the German Tongue, the requirements of membership were loosened.[17]

This claim to a military title reminds us of Melanchthon's remark that Faustus had been involved in winning the Empire's victories in Italy. If Faustus had done what he is reported to have said he did in Italy, then he may have been rewarded with this position or with the ennoblement necessary to secure it. It is also possible that it was this position that got him involved in the Italian campaigns in the first place, perhaps during one of his required caravans.

It also meant, if true, that he was Roman Catholic, at least nominally, or more specifically a member of the 'Religion of St John'. This is no great revelation – until the Reformation almost everyone in Europe was a Catholic, even if they could not write their name or understand the Latin Mass. However, to be a Catholic in 1528, over ten years after Luther had allegedly nailed his theses to the door of the castle-chapel in Wittenberg, meant taking sides in the great debate of the age. Even within the Order, the Reformation caused dissent and division. The master and knights of the bailiwick of Brandenburg, which had long exerted its near independence from the Grand Priory of Germany, accepted the Reformed religion, although stopped short of breaking off all connections with the Order. Furthermore, demonstrating his

Catholic loyalty surely put Faustus in good stead with the anti-Reformationist Leib and may have been contributory to his staying in Rebdorf.

Faustus may also have been lying. As lies go, it was a good one. It was not overly grandiose and it was difficult to verify – the commandery he claimed lay hundreds of kilometres away in dangerous country. But the rewards were considerable: it gave Faustus the status of a nobleman and potential (if risky) access to the Order's extensive network and the protective shield of their reputation. However, it is a claim that can be checked.

According to the usual interpretation, Faustus told Leib that his commandery was called 'Hallestein on the border of Carinthia'. In the sixteenth century the Duchy of Carinthia was ruled by the Habsburgs and enjoyed some degree of independence under the umbrella of the German Holy Roman Empire. However, there appears to be no place called Hallestein there. Schottenloher, who deciphered Leib's hand as 'Hallestein', thought the place meant must be Heilenstein, but there is no reference to this place on modern maps.

If the Order of St John had a commandery in Carinthia, it would have been within the Grand Priory of Bohemia under the German Tongue. Records, assuming there were any, of Faustus's appointment would logically have been made at the Grand Priory's headquarters in Prague. Enquiries revealed that there were indeed records of a 'Kommende Haillenstein' held by the State Archive in Prague. Unfortunately these were only kept, or had survived, from 1564 onwards and there was no information relating to Faustus. The trail has not ended yet, since the central archives of the Order are kept on Malta. The director of the archives there, then Brother Joseph Mizzi, consulted the *Libri Bullarum* for the years 1526–34 where the official chancery copy of the document appointing Faustus to the position of preceptor of Hallenstein would be found, if it existed. Mizzi wrote 'I regret to inform you that I did not come across any notice relating to Dr Faustus.'[18]

However, if 'Faustus' was a title and not a family name, then it is unlikely that Mizzi would have found it even if Faustus's claim was true. Suggestively, the first recorded mention of Faustus (Trithemius, 1507) puts him in Gelnhausen, a town long connected with the Order of St John, and he did claim the title of 'Master', which may have been military instead of academic. However, there is simply not enough evidence here to either confirm Faustus's claim or judge it fraudulent.

I had all but given up when I discovered the photograph of an old ruined manor house in today's Slovenia. It was identified as 'Grad Komenda/Heilenstein/Hallenstein'.[19] The problem was that this Heilenstein was not within the bounds of the old Duchy of Carinthia. Instead it lies near the city of Celje (called Cilli in the sixteenth century) on the River Savinja in what was in Faustus's time the Duchy of Styria.

The word Schottenloher deciphered as 'Carinthia' is an almost unintelligible scrawl in the original text. However, the crucial point is that Leib wrote 'on the border of' and Schottenloher thought he indicated 'Carinthia'. If the Carinthian interpretation is correct, then a place not in Carinthia itself, but near it could still be referred to as 'on the border of Carinthia'. The commandery of Hallenstein/Heilenstein in Styria does lie close to the old border with Carinthia. At the time, the Duchy of Styria was Habsburg land within the Kingdom of Bohemia and part of the Holy Roman Empire. The Hospitallers also organised the region under the Grand Priory of Bohemia.

Made spine-chillingly infamous in Sheridan Le Fanu's vampire novel *Carmilla* (1872), the Duchy of Styria had been created out of a part of Carinthia in the tenth century. First known as the Carinthian Mark or Windic Mark, the region eventually became known as the Steiermark after the ruling family who took their name from the castle of Steier. In the twelfth century under Margrave Ottokar II (1164–92) the area was raised to a duchy. After its ruling families became extinct, the Duchy passed into the hands of the Habsburgs from the thirteenth century onwards. Lying at the edge of the eastern Alps, the region is mountainous – the highest peak, the Dachstein, soars to almost 3,000 metres. Like Carinthia it was heavily forested, breathtakingly scenic and rich in mineral ores. The hills around Cilli were not noted for the iron-ore deposits that were being exploited in the north of the Duchy, but the town lay on the important trade route running from Pettau on the eastern border of what was left of Hungary to Triest on the Adriatic and on into the Republic of Venice via Görz and Udine where it joined the main commercial artery flowing from Villach and Gastein in Carinthia.

The Grad Komenda lies above the town of Polzela in pine-forested mountainous country. Today, a broken stone lion guards the entrance to a stout stone building with staring black window holes framed with shattered glass. It was mentioned in 1170 as the property of Degnardus de Helenstein and stayed in the family's hands for around a hundred years. The name of Hartwig, a dean or vicar of the area, was associated with it in the second part of the thirteenth century. From 1323 until 1780 ownership was in the hands of the Knights of St John.[20] There is still no documentary evidence to prove that Faustus governed this commandery, but at least we have discovered that the place referred to is real.

If Faustus was at Rebdorf – as it appears from Leib's journal – then it seems natural that he should mention his Catholic credentials to the Prior Kilian Leib. He might even have arrived wearing the black cloak and white eight-pointed cross of the Order, with tales of far away 'Hallestein' and ruinous war against the enemies of Europe.[21]

At Hallenstein Faustus would have been on the front line against the hordes of Suleiman. Although the Battle of Mohács (1526) that saw the defeat of Hungary and the death of King Ladislas (Lajos) II had been fought some 400 kilometres away, the Duchy of Styria would find itself increasingly near the fighting as Suleiman pursued his territorial ambitions. Its hard country was its best defence, but even so, Styria suffered repeated incursions of Ottoman troops. But Faustus was not there in 1528.

Banished from Ingolstadt (1528)

It was the year of haricot beans, brought back from the New World by Hernando Cortes, of the Austrian evangelist Jacob Hutter's 'community of love', of the burning of the Anabaptist Balthasar Hubmaier (1481–1528) in Vienna, of Baldassare Castiglione's (1478–1529) *The Book of the Courtier*, of Paracelsus's *De Kleine Chirurgia*, of Melanchthon's proposed educational reforms and of the banishment of Faustus. When he stayed with Leib, Faustus was clearly *en route* for Ingolstadt. Twelve days after Leib's conversation about prophets and Knights of St John in his *Wettertagebuch* we find Faustus again being mentioned in writing, this time in the records of the city of Ingolstadt:

(a) Minute on the actions of the city council in Ingolstadt.
Today, the Wednesday after St Vitus' Day, 1528. The soothsayer shall be ordered to leave the city and to spend his penny elsewhere.
(b) Record of those banished from Ingolstadt.
On Wednesday after St Vitus' Day, 1528, a certain man who called himself Dr Jörg Faustus of Heidelberg was told to spend his penny elsewhere and he pledged himself not to take vengeance on or seek redress from the authorities for this order.[22]

St Vitus' Day in 1528 fell on Monday 15 June, making Wednesday the 17th. Faustus had spent less than two weeks in Ingolstadt, but it was long enough to get into trouble and be called before the city council. What is interesting here is the insight into Faustus's career. He is described as a 'soothsayer' (*Wahrsager*), that is, a fortune-teller or diviner. This clearly tallies with Trithemius's earlier report of his various divinatory proficiencies and the commission from the Bishop of Bamberg, and shows what sort of services he was offering in the town. It is significant that it was the town council that judged his case, rather than the university or ecclesiastical courts. This could be interpreted to mean that the university did not recognise his degree and, additionally, that his transgressions were not deemed to fall under the jurisdiction of the church – it was not, then, a case of heresy or witchcraft. The formulaic repetition of 'spend his penny elsewhere' seems to hint at a financial scandal.

Writing in 1539 Begardi said that many people had complained to him that Faustus had cheated them and 'left many to whistle for their money'.[23] It is possible that Faustus was suspected of coining or passing off counterfeit currency. It would be relatively easy for an experienced alchemist to make his gold go a little further, perhaps using a staining technique, and coining was certainly a widespread crime at the time. The Jesuit Delrio, writing not later than 1599, claimed that both Faustus and Agrippa were notorious for paying innkeepers in bewitched coins that afterwards turned to valueless leaves and filth. Perhaps here is the origin of that tale. Certainly, what Reginald Scot (1584) called the conveying of money was a known and practised art of deception. He detailed the methods of legerdemain by which one may seemingly make money appear and disappear, to be thrown away and still kept, and transformed from one denomination into another. Using such sleight of hand, it would be no great deal to appear to pay for one's board and lodging whilst actually giving the innkeeper something worthless. However, the phraseology of the judgement was standard legalese for the period. The Carmelite prior Andreas Stoß (1480–1540), for example, was banished from Nuremberg in 1522 with the same wording.

On this bare skeleton of fact, later legends grew up around Faustus's activities in Ingolstadt. In 1900 Tille published twenty-six references to Ingolstadt, although most of these derived from a very few sources, usually Roshirt or Widmann. An anecdote recorded by Roshirt almost fifty years after Faustus's visit told of the magician lecturing on philosophy and chiromancy at the university, and Number 7 on the Harderstraße is known locally as 'Wohnhaus Fausts'.[24]

Although the official records are quiet on the subject of his employment there, Faustus may have at least attempted to teach at the university, or may have held unofficial classes at the students' own expense or as a loss-leader for his soothsaying practice. If we are to believe Paracelsus, he would have found Ingolstadt a 'university of some old scholastics' and like Celtis may have come to despair of the bad beer and endless turnips on the menu.[25]

Others contend that Faustus actually studied at the university himself. Writing in 1676, Durrius argued that Faustus had been awarded a doctorate in medicine, while an eighteenth-century Faustbook – the anonymous *Christlich Meynenden* – stated that he had been awarded the degree of Master by the University of Ingolstadt and was generally known for his good conduct. Neither idea should be seriously entertained. There is no record of Faustus having studied here; Durrius is a late source and the Faustbook is both a late and a legendary one. It is conceivable that Faustus's name has become confused with that of Johannes Reuchlin who did teach Greek and Hebrew here from 1520 to 1521 before moving to Tübingen. Greek and Hebrew were languages whose aura of mystery among the uneducated may well have led to rumours of magic.[26]

A story is preserved that combines elements of Roshirt's anecdotes about the unfortunate Jewish moneylender of Frankfurt and the Bamberg swineherd swindle. Unusually for the Faustbooks, the location of this incident is named. P.F. (1592) called the town 'Pheiffring', but there are earlier references to 'Pffeffering' (Wolfenbüttel, *c.*1580) and 'Pfeiffering' (Spies, 1588). None of these places can be found on a map of Germany today, but the town in question is undoubtedly Pfifferling, some sixty-five kilometres to the east of Ingolstadt.

At the market in Pfifferling, Faustus allegedly sold a horse to a dealer, warning him not to ride it through water. More curious than wary, the dealer galloped his mount into a pond where it was transformed into a bale of hay. Half-drowned, the angry dealer tracked down Faustus. Finding him asleep in bed, he tugged violently at his foot to wake him, but to his consternation he pulled off the whole leg. Faustus screamed blue murder and the terrified dealer ran off.

We should never read the legends as factual, but they do provide us with suggestive possibilities. In this case we see that the legend is located close to an area historically documented to have been visited by Faustus and involves the sort of activities that would certainly have had him barred from a city like Ingolstadt if he had tried them there. And banished he most surely was.

15

Entertaining the Emperor
(1529–1530)

While Faustus was dealing with Ingolstadt councillors, the Treaty of Cambrai had brought temporary peace between France and the Empire, but Charles V was almost immediately embroiled in countering the increasing militancy of the Reformists. At the Reichstag of Speyer that year, Charles argued for the withdrawal of all concessions made to the Lutherans, but six princes and fourteen cities protested against this action, thereby giving the name of 'Protestant' to their cause. Just as it had been during the Peasants' War, it was the question of self-determination that proved divisive. The Protestants moved to consolidate their position and in 1530 the League of Schmalkalden was formed, threatening the future of Catholicism in Germany.

Elsewhere in 1529 the talk was of more mysterious signs and portents. In Breslau (Wrocław) Michael Behaim recorded that 'a most terrifying sign' had been observed in the sky. It was described as a huge star showing the figures of an old man and an old woman. Over Liegnitz (Legnica) there was 'the appearance of a great multitude of armoured soldiers bearing bloody swords in the sky', but Behaim offered no interpretation.[1] There was much work to be had for a professional astrologer like Faustus.

In Germany controversy raged over the Carthusian Prophecies. Discovered on a wall in the Carthusian Monastery in Nuremberg, they foretold the fall of the Pope, the nobility and the merchant classes and the coming of the Kingdom of Christ. There was even an undisguised attack on Luther and his ideas. Then there was Paracelsus. He had turned up in Nuremberg where Sebastian Franck (1499–1543) called him a 'peculiar and wondrous man', but noted that 'he stands alone against nearly the whole medical guild'. Paracelsus insulted the city's doctors and their 'buxom, fat wives', and ostracised himself through his quarrelsomeness.[2]

After being thrown out of Ingolstadt it is anyone's guess where Faustus went next. In a time of astrological wonders he could be sure to find his services welcomed somewhere. There were still battles being fought under Italian skies and victories to claim for the Empire. He could not have been at the Battle of Landriano with Antonio de Leyva on 20 June 1528 unless he put that demon steed to good use again, but the Siege of Florence (24 October 1529) and the decisive Battle of Gavinana (3 August 1530) could have become candidates for his catch-all claim of having won Italy for the Emperor. Sifting through the hints and traces, legends and lies, we can construct a tentative series of events for the next few years of Faustus's life.

Cannibal Magic (Vienna, 1529)

In the sixteenth century, Vienna was everything. It was the gateway to the Empire. Suleiman's invasion of Europe had so far been facilitated by a lack of cohesion between her kingdoms. Despite all the talk of a new crusade, Europe's princes had so far been content to squabble amongst themselves and let Hungarian blood douse the ardour of her enemies. But the plan, or rather lack of one, had backfired. Suleiman's bloodlust was not sated. During the period 1516–17 the Ottomans had swelled their Empire with Syria and Egypt. With the fall in 1522 of the island bastion of Rhodes, their power extended over the eastern Mediterranean to the detriment of southern Europe's shipping routes. From the east they had been relentlessly crawling closer to Europe's heart. Belgrade had fallen in 1521 and Ottoman raids pressed deep into Poland as far as Lvov and beyond in 1524. In 1526 they captured Buda, looting the city and carting off Matthias Corvinus's incomparable library. Now Suleiman's armies were marching on Vienna. If Faustus laid claim to having won all the victories in Italy, why stop there? If he had won Italy for the Emperor, would he not also have tried to save Christendom from the Turk?

Vienna is noted today for its cultural refinements – all cafés and classical music. It is a reputation rooted in the sixteenth century. When Charles V's brother Ferdinand arrived in Austria to take up the administration of the family's possessions there, he was just eighteen. Born and bred in Spain, it was the first time he had set foot in his ancestral lands. He brought with him a Spanish court and introduced a southern way of life. However, Viennese culture was not all due to Ferdinand and his courtiers. Regiomontanus had lectured here and the Danubiana society had successfully sown Humanistic ideas.

After years of decline during the fifteenth century due to the Ottoman threat, a plummeting currency and changing trade routes – the new sea-route to the East Indies and the discovery of the Americas – Vienna was not about to welcome this Spaniard with open arms. The burghers revolted against Ferdinand, but as usual were crushed, and were forced to concede a large part of their former autonomy.

In all the 1,152 pages in Tille's monumental catalogue of *Faustsplitter* there is only one reference to Vienna and a short one at that. But it was a reference that Manlius claimed had been made by Melanchthon, who has generally been held as reliable by Faustus scholars. Not only that, it is also a reference made by a contemporary – a contemporary Faustus may have met – and so is highly significant. On the face of it, it is a silly story and few people have bothered to enquire into it. The story is undated and was told ten to twenty years after Faustus was dead, but it *was* told.

It was a long way from the comfortable jostle of houses in Helmstadt to the world-stage in Vienna. But Faustus was in his prime and an experienced traveller. He may have arrived from his commandery in Styria to the south, but given his last known position at Ingolstadt, it is more likely that he would approach from the west. *En route* he may have stopped at the Faust-Schlössl (or Fauststöckel) near Aschach in Austria, giving rise to the local legends that survive there.

A large box-like structure built around a squat central tower with red roofs and yellow painted walls, the Faust-Schlössl is now a hotel and restaurant. It sits on a small bluff overlooking the Danube; forested slopes rise up behind it. One legend even claims that Faustus had the Devil build it for him and today guests may spend the night in the 'Dr. Faust Suite'. According to Adalbert Depiny, during his supposed stay there Faustus put the Devil to a number of challenging tasks: high-speed road building, bridging the Danube in front of his galloping horse and even setting up a bowling-alley on the river. The so-called *Jochenstein* is said to be the remains of one of his skittles. A new element enters the legend – all the outrageous tasks are part of Faustus's plan to fox the Devil and break the pact. Local traditions disagree whether he was successful or not, either escaping, drowning in the Danube, or being torn to pieces on a nearby mountaintop.

In the Faustbook he took the road out of Augsburg, seventy-four kilometres south of Ingolstadt, following the trade route to Munich and on to Salzburg – another location with its store of Faustus legends. Here the road divides, running south into Carinthia and on to Venice, and snaking north-east to Linz before following the course of the Danube east, past the Faust-Schlössl to Vienna. It is a trek of more than 500 kilometres. But the thirsty traveller would be well rewarded. P.F. reported that there was more wine than water in Vienna.

During Melanchthon's excessive commentaries on the Scriptures delivered between 1549 and 1560, he related a peculiar tale concerning the Devil, tinged with grudging admiration for the Archfiend:

> The Devil is an amazing artificer: he has a power to accomplish things that are natural but which we do not understand. For he can do more than man. … Faustus the magician devoured another magician at Vienna, who was discovered a few days later in a certain cave. The Devil can perform many wonderful things; nevertheless the Church has its own miracles.[3]

Speaking in a babble of Latin and German, Melanchthon nonetheless clearly placed Faustus's abilities within the sphere of Devilry. The tone of censure is apparent, but he gave away little of what he thought about Faustus's magical feat. Did he think that it was only a trick, or did he really believe that it had taken place as described? His attributing it to the Devil would tend to suggest that he did indeed believe that Faustus had swallowed a fellow magician.

In the Faustbook we read of Faustus eating an improbable quantity of hay at Zwickau and making it reappear again, but he refrains from devouring any of his companions. However, the trick was well known. In 1389 at the court of Wenceslas IV of Bohemia, according to the chronicler Dubravius, the magician Zyto swallowed a competitor called Gouin, all bar his muddy shoes. Whether Faustus swallowed a competitor or a confederate we will never know, but such a deception could not be accomplished without the complicity of the apparent victim.

Melanchthon (through Manlius) gave no indication when this event was supposed to have taken place, still less why it took place in Vienna. His concern, after all, was not historical accuracy, but religious propaganda. Faustus could have performed this feat at any time and in any other place, but it is notable that he did not, at least according to what little we know of his career.

Local Viennese legends preserve strange memories or imaginings of Faustus in the city. He is said to have built a triangular shaped house at Flossgasse 7 – the birthplace of the composer Johann Strauss (1804–1849) – but it is the legend connected with an inn on Am Bühel near the Tiefer Graben that has particular resonance. The legend, first published by Carl Calliano (1932–36) with later variations from Gustav Gugitz (1952), leads us down the stairs of a small house into a cellar bar full of students, artists and travelling entertainers. His reputation for magic and practical joking had preceded him and when Faustus walked through the door he found a warm welcome. The drinkers were clamorous for some display of his art, but first there was a thirst to quench. A servant brought him a large glass, filled almost to overflowing with wine. He clumsily spilt it, whereupon Faustus jestingly retorted that if he spilt it again he would eat him skin and hair. Grumbling with annoyance, the servant returned with another overfull glass and, not quite as accidentally as before, spilt it again. Faustus stretched his mouth wide and swallowed him whole, washing him down with a bucket of cold water. The drinkers gasped in shocked amazement, whilst the innkeeper begged for his servant back. Faustus calmly replied 'open the door and look at the stairs.' The innkeeper did as he was told and there was the servant dripping wet and teeth-chattering from the cold water, sitting at the top of the stairs.

The servant stomped back into the inn and exclaimed 'I don't want anything to do with you, for you are surely in league with the Devil.'

'Devil here, Devil there,' Faustus replied, 'but just beware pouring the wine like that again!'

The whole inn fell to muttering about 'the God be with us', a euphemism for the Devil. Inspired or provoked, a painter and engraver from Nuremberg called Hirschvogel stood up and offered to paint the Devil on the wall. The other drinkers, who had evidently been spilling too much wine down their necks, raised a cheer and made way for him. Hirschvogel took a piece of charcoal from the stove and sketched the figure of a nobleman on the wall, sitting cross-legged, a short cloak like a dragon's wing over his shoulders and a cap sporting a cockerel's feather on his head. The face glowered scornfully. When he had finished, Faustus stood up and said, 'now you see the Devil on the wall, but I will show you the same alive.' Darkness stole over the cellar and the drawing started to move. The clothes became fiery red and slashed with sooty black. The cloak turned green. The eyes glowed like embers in an unnaturally pale face. With a thunderous crash he leapt from the wall amongst the drinkers.

The joke had gone too far and with wild screams everyone ran out of the cellar. Faustus roared after them 'you shouldn't paint the Devil on the wall!' The legend has it that this was the source of the popular saying and the inn was ever after known as *Zum Roten Mandl*, 'to the Red Man'.

The magical eating trick clearly echoes Melanchthon's earlier tale, but there are inconsistencies. We are once again in the inn where so many of Faustus's legendary exploits took place, but there is no sign of Melanchthon's other magician or cave. Augustin Hirschvogel (1503–1553) was real enough, but he only moved to Vienna in 1544 and although we cannot rule out a brief trip, his role in the story is surely as legendary as that of Faustus.

Meanwhile, the largest army Europe had yet seen was bearing down on Vienna under the banner of Islam. Estimates vary wildly concerning its size from anywhere between 120,000 to 350,000 men. One thing cannot be doubted. When Count Niclas von Salm (1459–1530) and his force of around 12,000 to 22,000 men saw them swarming over the horizon, they knew that they were heavily outnumbered.

Charles V was in Bologna with Pope Clement VII, trying out the Iron Crown of Lombardy for size, whilst Ferdinand had retreated to Linz in Austria to wait out the result. Vienna's defensive walls were in need of repair and an old soldier who had just turned seventy led the garrison. The city had been all but abandoned. It looked as though the disaster of Rhodes was about to be repeated. Only something like magic could, it seemed, possibly save them. Even if Faustus was not in Vienna, it is likely that, as an astrologer, he was asked about events taking place there.

Suleiman I had begun his advance westward late in the year. Heavy rains had washed out bridges and turned the roads into quagmires, and it was late September by the time he reached his target, having abandoned his heavy siege artillery along the way. Vienna's walls held the invader up into October with the weather worsening all the while. There was little need of a goosebone to tell the defenders who the victor was going to be. At the end of an extended supply line over difficult terrain, it was the weather that got the best of Suleiman's army. His men threw themselves at Vienna's walls and were slaughtered in their thousands. By December, Suleiman was back in Istanbul.

The Return of Alexander (Innsbruck, 1530)

A tale is told of Faustus at the court of Emperor Charles V in Innsbruck. The story appears in the Wolfenbüttel Manuscript of around 1580, Spies printed it in 1587 and the mysterious P.F. translated it in 1592, whence it ended up in Marlowe's *Faustus*. There is no contemporary record of Faustus having been there, but Melanchthon did place him in Vienna, still within the borders of present day Austria although almost 500 kilometres away by modern roads.

What is interesting about the Faustbooks here is that reference is made to Charles V and not anyone else. It would have been easier to look back to his predecessor Maximilian I and the stories that had already accumulated around Trithemius and his supposed feats of necromancy at his court. Charles's successor Ferdinand I (r. 1558–1564) could also have been a candidate as could his successor Maximilian II (r. 1564-1576) and it would have been certainly more current, although probably politically unwise, to mention the reigning Emperor, Rudolf II (r. 1576–1612). Rudolf would have been the natural choice. The melancholic and occasionally insane Rudolf once declared that he belonged to the Devil. As a champion of the counter-Reformation he was also much more of a target for Protestant hacks like P.F. and Spies. And yet the Faustbooks chose Charles V, an actual contemporary of Faustus.

It is a chance detail that points to stories that must have been told more than a generation before Spies and P.F. plied their trades. Neither Spies nor those who came after him showed any real knowledge of when Faustus might have been born or died. They gave no dates, with the exception of Battus's Dutch Faustbook, and named few of the characters. Amongst all this vagueness the name of Charles V clearly stands out.

The unmistakable naming of Charles V can also be interpreted in another way. For a Lutheran like Spies, Charles V was an enemy of the Reformation and by consulting an irreligious black magician like Faustus he is shown with partisan intent as a patron of the diabolical arts. If this was his intent, then Spies played a dangerous game himself. To attack one Emperor, and one not long committed to the earth, was to attack the throne itself. Rudolf II could hardly be expected to welcome such a slander upon his forebear and the Frankfurt authorities, who held such tight reigns on the publishing industry, were cognisant of the respect owed to their ruler. Spies either took an unusual risk or was faithfully reproducing earlier stories told about Faustus. Spies may well have wanted to implicate a Catholic Emperor in stories of black magic, but the extent to which he invented parts of the story to suit his agenda has to be ruled out in this case. Spies's religion could have had no influence on the earlier Wolfenbüttel Manuscript in which the name of Charles V also occurs. We cannot rule out the possibility that whoever wrote the Wolfenbüttel Manuscript named Charles for political reasons, but it was certainly not Spies.

In the Faustbook this incident appears before Faustus's trip to Munich, which if it did take place, must have been on 3 October 1522, suggesting a prior date for his meeting with the Emperor. However, the Faustbook is such a chaotic document that the order of its contents can hardly be taken as an accurate chronology.

Although Charles had been elected Emperor in 1519, he did not arrive in Germany to personally acknowledge this tribute until 1520. From 1522 to 1529 Charles resided entirely in Spain. This would give us two 'windows' in which Faustus and the Emperor might have met in Innsbruck: sometime between 1520 and 1522, or after 1529. We have Faustus definitely placed in Bamberg for early 1520 and Ingolstadt for 1528, but this still gives him plenty of time to make the long journey south.

In October 1520 Charles V was in Aachen being crowned King of the Romans. It was the first time he had set foot on German soil. In January 1521 he was in Worms convening the Reichstag and alarming the nobles with his foreign dress and less than fluent German. After discussing the important matters of state, Charles was also called upon to judge in the case of a troublesome monk called Martin Luther. The discussions and hearings lasted well into April until a sorely tried Charles issued the Edict of Worms, banning Luther and his supporters.

In 1522 Charles was in Brussels where he nominated his brother Ferdinand as his regent in Germany – in the so-called 'Compact of Brussels' – before leaving once more for Spain by way of England. Once in Spain, Charles was so preoccupied by revolt and later the consolidation of his Spanish power-base that he left Germany and her problems entirely in Ferdinand's hands. Given such a full schedule it is unlikely that Charles could have found the time to be entertained by Faustus, supposing that he was. If we are to seriously consider this possibility then we must concede that a later date, at least after 1529, is more probable.

Charles was only twice more in the Empire within Faustus's lifetime: from April 1530 to January 1531 and from January 1532 to October 1532. After being crowned

Holy Roman Emperor by the Pope in February of 1530, Charles travelled north, passing through Trent and Innsbruck *en route* to Augsburg. This was the only time in Faustus's lifetime that he stayed in Innsbruck. If Faustus did meet the Emperor in Innsbruck, then it could only have happened in April 1530.

The Conjuration at Innsbruck

Innsbruck was the final resting place of Charles V's father, Maximilian I. Under Maximilian, Innsbruck had become an important political and military centre. Strategically placed at the gateway to the Brenner Pass just thirty kilometres to the south, Innsbruck formed the pivot in Maximilian's Italian campaigns as an advance camp and refuge. The armourers and gunsmiths of the Tyrol equipped his forces. The silver and copper mines supplied valuable materials and the mint in Halle turned it into currency. Between campaigns Maximilian had indulged his favourite leisure pursuit of hunting in the well-stocked countryside.

As P.F. told the tale the 'Emperour *Carolus* the fifth of that name' was holding court at Innsbruck where, as luck would have it, Doctor Faustus was also residing. It is not implausible that he should have been following the Imperial court. Cardano reported that Charles had in his train a juggler when he visited Milan who was so skilful that he was widely regarded as a magician. 'Being there well known of divers Nobles and gentlemen' Faustus was invited to the court, even into the presence of the Emperor himself, to dine with them. Charles 'looked earnestly on him, thinking him by his looks to be some wonderful fellow.' The magician could have employed an operation 'for gaining dignity and honour' from Codex 849 to his advantage here. Certainly the Emperor was intrigued. After dinner he called Faustus into his private chambers. 'Faustus,' said Charles, 'I have heard much of thee' but Charles demanded proof – not withstanding all those Italian victories Faustus had allegedly won for him.[4]

Faustus put himself at the Emperor's disposal, 'To cast his magic charms that shall pierce through/The ebon gates of ever-burning hell' as Marlowe (IV.2.20–1) so eloquently put it. Charles lamented that 'mine elders and ancestors', were unapproachable in their greatness – a confession perhaps of his own failings as Emperor – and requested that Faustus should conjure the shade of Alexander the Great 'and his Paramour' to appear before him. Well practised in raising ancient Greeks since his Erfurt show, Faustus consented, but had something more to add. He could only conjure spirits who had seen Alexander and his paramour, and hence able to take their shapes, but not those personages themselves.[5]

It is an interesting change in perspective. The Erfurt stories assumed that he brought forth the real heroes from out of Hades, but here the influence of contemporary demonologists is felt. It is not the dead who return, but supernatural simulacra. It is part of the attempt to circumscribe the power of the magician: all of his works are illusions of the Devil, thus invocations of the dead must also be illusory. It is not a theory that Faustus himself would have ascribed to and even if he had, it is unlikely that he would have communicated it to his clientele.

The *Malleus Maleficarum* used the example of Simon Magus, reputed to have caused the head of a dead man to move, to illustrate the argument that the raising of the dead was accomplished by illusion and specifically railed against the necromancers, with reference to the Witch of Endor, who, 'when they think that they call the dead from hell to answer their questions, it is the devils in the likeness of the dead who appear and give such answers'.[6] The *Malleus* had not convinced everyone and the invocation of the dead was still a live issue in the sixteenth century.

According to the tale, Faustus added the condition that Charles must not attempt to speak to the spirits. Charles agreed and Faustus opened a door to admit 'the great and mighty Emperor *Alexander magnus*'. The antique marvel entered the room, his costly armour dazzling their eyes, to offer a 'low and reverent curtesy'.[7] Faustus intervened to prevent Charles from returning the salute; to greet a demonic spirit as a royal equal would have been a serious breach of etiquette. The two watched on as Alexander made another bow and exited. Now his 'Paramour' came in, making her curtsies in a dress of blue velvet embroidered with pearls and gold – perhaps that same blue dress worn by the spirit conjured at Maximilian's court in Hans Sachs's *Historia* of 1564. She was tall and thin, but with a face as round as an apple and 'excellent fair like Milk and blood mixed'.[8]

Charles decided to test the visions shown to him and in a manner that is too reminiscent of Maximilian I testing the apparition of his Mary of Burgundy to be more than mere coincidence. Charles said that he has heard that Alexander's paramour had a distinctive mark on the back of her neck, and finding that the spirit had one in the same place was 'well contented'.[9]

As a boy Charles had eagerly read Olivier de La Marche's stories and would have found amongst his writings La Marche's 'proof' that the Habsburgs of Austria were descended from a prince of the royal house of Troy. He would have seen the ancient world in some regards as his homeland and the heroes his ancestors. Foremost amongst these heroes was Alexander the Great.

Already legendary in his day, Alexander's exploits became popularised through the *Alexander Romance*. Once thought to have been written by Callisthenes of Olynthos, the historian who accompanied Alexander on his campaigns, but since attributed to an unknown Pseudo-Callisthenes, the *Alexander Romance* was one of the bestsellers of the Middle Ages, going through translation into every major language and more than a few minor ones. Plutarch, widely read and greatly esteemed in the Renaissance, wrote of Alexander in his *Parallel Lives*, placing him alongside Caesar. Quintus Curtius Rufus's *History of Alexander the Great* (*c.*1470) was also hugely popular: the Bibliothèque Nationale of France alone holds ten Latin editions printed before 1550.

Alexander's astonishing triumphs endeared him to the myth-makers, and magical legends accrued around the romances. There were stories of enchanted gems and fabulous automata, and tales of the magical feats of Alexander's tutor, Aristotle, and of the pseudo-Aristotelian grimoire, the *Secret of Secrets*.

The name of Alexander was a title of the highest praise. Through successive victories against the Ottomans in Serbia and Bosnia in the years 1479 to 1483, the King of Hungary, Matthias Corvinus, won renown and direct comparison to Alexander the Great. When he became Pope in 1492, Rodrigo Borgia took the name of Alexander VI as a purposeful identification with the ancient Macedonian king. In his address to the new Pope, the ambassador of Savoy, Pietro Cara, called him 'a new Alexander the Great'.[10] He decorated his living quarters in the Vatican (the *Appartamenti Borgia*) with a relief portrait in plaster of his illustrious namesake. In the first half of the sixteenth century, the Villa Farnesina in Rome was monumentally embellished with Alexandrian motifs. François I likewise decorated his palace of Fontainebleau. Alessandro ('Alexander') Farnese, Pope Paul III (1534–1549) chose scenes from the life of Alexander the Great to adorn his apartments (the *Sala Paolina*) in the Castel Sant'Angelo in Rome.

Alexander the Great was not just another ancient hero, but a popular figure in the literature and art of the day and a role model for the princes of the Renaissance. It was no accident then that Charles should have asked Faustus to produce such an icon of the chivalric virtues of courage, generosity, magnanimity, self-restraint and, in those days when the threat of the Turk loomed large, victory over the infidel.

The similarities with the earlier Innsbruck tale told by Hans Sachs and the rumours that the conjuror was Trithemius are clear. Consequently, students of the history of literature have tended to view such tales as the repetition of a type with only the names changed. This is plausible, but such an argument overlooks one important aspect in this case. Faustus was a self-declared necromancer, even the 'font of necromancy'. Is it not to be expected that he should have attempted such feats as described at Erfurt and Innsbruck? A necromancer who does not invoke the dead is not worth the name.

After impressing the Emperor with his invocation of the spirits, the Faustbook added a further adventure, descending yet again to farce. After invoking Alexander, Faustus wandered off, presumably leaving Charles to reflect upon the marvels he had just witnessed. In a gallery he leaned out to admire the garden and observed the Emperor's courtiers strolling about, but he also espied a knight slumped fast asleep at one of the windows of the great hall. Faustus conjured a pair of stag's horns to grow out from his head. The knight woke up and tried to pull his head in, shattering the glass in the windows. The courtiers in the garden looked up and added their laughter to that of Faustus. The Emperor, on hearing the disturbance, came out to learn its cause and also found the poor knight wedged in the window with his antlers to be worth a laugh. The Emperor congratulated Faustus on such a merry jest and with a bow the magician relieved the butt of the joke from his cumbersome headgear. But the knight would remember him.

For unexplained reasons of his own Faustus now left Innsbruck, but not before being heaped with 'many rewards and gifts'. A league and half outside the city walls, perhaps even before he had finished singing Heinrich Isaac's (1450–1517) *Innsbruck, ich muss dich lassen* ('Innsbruck, I must leave you'), Faustus came into a wood and was ambushed by the disgruntled knight. The knight and his companions charged Faustus with lowered lances. Faustus turned some nearby bushes into horsemen and sent them at the gallop against his foes. Luckily for Faustus there were more bushes in the wood than angry knights and he soon had his enemies outnumbered, surrounded and pleading for clemency. A merciful Faustus spared them, but not without adding a set of goat's horns to each knight's brow and ox's horns to their steeds as 'their penance'.[11]

Marlowe added the name of Benvolio to bring this anonymous dupe to life, but the evidence may suggest that this was the unflattering portrait of a real person. Not only was this Benvolio humiliated in front of the Emperor, but he was further trounced by a mere illusion in front of his comrades-in-arms. The unnamed knight is introduced in a manner that suggests that his name is being withheld, but a note in the margin of Spies's 1587 edition gives the name of Baron von Hardeck. This von Hardeck has been identified as Ferdinand von Hardegg (1549–1595), an obscure Austrian count who later became infamous for abandoning his command of the fortress of Győr in Hungary to the Ottomans for which he suffered execution for treason. However, von Hardegg was all but unknown when Spies printed his *Historia* in 1587 and his naming seems to have been a tactical move to forestall a libel case from what one historian has argued was the real target.[12]

The year after publication, Spies was accused by Baron Fabian von Dohna of trafficking in libellous books. Von Dohna was advisor and military commander to Count Johann Casimir in Heidelberg, and his charges carried weight. Spies was compelled to write a letter of apology to von Dohna and after the deletion of the offending passages, the city council considered the matter closed. However, the roots of this went further back. Von Dohna had led Casimir's mercenary army into France to support Henri III of Navarre (later Henri IV of France), but returned in humiliation after the army deserted him. Von Dohna was held responsible for the failure. He instigated a pamphlet war with his critics and claimed that there was a conspiracy against him, which led to the libel charges being brought against Spies. Spies and von Dohna thus had some 'history', but the cause was more than a failed military jaunt in France. The Calvinist von Dohna had been instrumental in driving out the Lutherans from Heidelberg, which was seen as an act of revenge after he himself had been expelled by the Lutherans.

It is a plausible connection, but is that all there is to it? There is little that could be considered original in Spies, so why credit the printer with this hidden attack on von Dohna? In fact, we find the same stories in the earlier Wolfenbüttel Manuscript. While it might be thought that Spies was settling some scores on his own account, he clearly did not invent the stories themselves.

The practical joking with stag's horns and windows had been performed earlier by the fourteenth-century Bohemian sorcerer Zyto, suggesting that it was a fairly typical tall story or magical trick. Luther told a story about an unnamed magician who ridiculed Emperor Friedrich III (1415–1493) with a pair of antlers and Michael Lindener had a magician conjure horns on the heads of people looking out of their windows into the market square in his *Katzipori* of 1558. But the conjuration of magical armies was part of the standard repertoire of the magician, as we saw earlier.

What look like the wildest tales to the modern reader can often be traced to the authentic tradition of magic. Summoning the dead and invoking magical armies were known to the magician and, if we are to believe the grimoires, practised by him. However, the evidence for Faustus having met the Emperor in Innsbruck rests entirely on the unreliable Faustbooks.

The Fugitive
(1530–1534)

While war still raged in northern Italy, in the Coliseum in Rome, Benvenuto Cellini witnessed a dramatic and terrifying invocation of demons. But it was not Faustus who was invoking them. Cellini's experiments aside, 1530 was a bad year for occultists generally. Agrippa had published his *De incertitudine*, an apparent recantation of the occult philosophising of his youth. Friedrich Peypus's underground edition of Paracelsus's book on syphilis – the *French Disease* – caused such a great hue and cry that Paracelsus was forced to flee Nuremberg. Further publication of his books was banned.

One can imagine that Nuremberg was not well disposed to receive any other vagabond philosophers that year. Ingolstadt had already closed its doors to Faustus. The Klinge faction would surely have him arrested if he returned to Erfurt. Kreuznach was out of the question. His old patrons were dead. For Faustus, Germany was shrinking. Perhaps he had found some employment interpreting the strange signs of 1529 and earned some favour at the Emperor's court, but now what was he going to do?

The Faustbook has Faustus almost continually at Wittenberg, living with his uncle there, studying there, setting out to a wedding in Munich from there, visiting the Leipzig Fair from there, but the historical sources are far fewer in number. In 1591 Moryson was told that Faustus had lived there about the year 1500, which is too early to tally with what we know of his career. In his lectures at Wittenberg as recorded by the faithful Manlius, Melanchthon makes the first mention of Faustus being in Wittenberg at some point, but omits to supply a date.

Zacharias Hogel, drawing on a mid-sixteenth-century source, mentioned that Faustus lived in Wittenberg, oddly while lecturing at the University of Erfurt – an event we can date to 1513. In 1585 Augustin Lercheimer also claimed that Faustus had been in Wittenberg. It is not reasonable to think that Faustus actually lived in

Wittenberg while lecturing at a city over 200 kilometres away. Not even a magician renowned for his magic flights by demonic horse or cloak would consider such an inconvenient arrangement. Lercheimer solves the problem by bringing Faustus and Melanchthon together.

Escape from Wittenberg

Melanchthon did not arrive in Wittenberg until 1518, giving us the earliest possible date that Faustus could have been here. Bar some visits here and there, Melanchthon stayed in Wittenberg for the next forty-two years – that is until 1560 – long after Faustus's presumed death. This gives us a long span of time – twenty or more years – in which Faustus could have visited Melanchthon in Wittenberg. There are no clues in Lercheimer's account to allow us to date this encounter, if it did in fact take place.

Melanchthon (through Manlius) supplies another clue by mentioning the important role played by the 'great prince Duke Ioannes'.[1] This was Johann (1468–1532) 'The Steadfast', who succeeded his brother Friedrich III to become the Elector of Saxony from 1525 until his death in 1532. This gives us a much narrower range of only seven years.

In 1530 Melanchthon was preoccupied with the so-called 'Augsburg Confession', attempting to demonstrate that the Protestants still belonged to the Catholic Church, which was presented at the Reichstag in Augsburg that year. Johann would also be at that fateful meeting, proclaiming his Reformed beliefs and winning the enmity of the great lords gathered there. In 1531 Johann seems to have been embroiled in intrigues. While 1530 and possibly 1531 seem too busy, the principal players too preoccupied, the incidents involving Faustus are so brief as to present no serious interruption to their other affairs. Sometime in the late 1520s or early 1530s does appear plausible.

When Faustus arrived he would have found Wittenberg bustling. An artist would have been drawn to the busy workshop of Lucas Cranach and his son, but the wandering scholar had other reasons for his visit. Melanchthon's theology lectures were drawing crowds, initially of between 500 and 600 students, eventually of 1,500. Like those other students, Faustus may have been drawn by the popularity of Melanchthon's classes; he would not have been interested to hear Melanchthon discourse on philology – his official subject. Hardly anybody bothered to attend Melanchthon's lectures on philology. Melanchthon also promoted astrology in his lectures, telling his students that it was both a legitimate field of academic study and an important instrument in the affairs of state. Faustus may have felt that he would receive a warm reception such as might be expected from one astrologer to another.

Friedrich the Wise had but recently completed a twenty-one-year building project on the castle and its adjoining *Schlosskirche*, 'Castle Church' (1490 to 1511). Also serving as the university's chapel, the Castle Church quickly became famous both for its artistic interior and for Friedrich the Wise's unique collection of relics. By 1520 Friedrich had amassed 18,970 of them. The Church must have been piled high with holy bones, fragments of the 'true cross' and other tattered remains of dubious origin. Fire destroyed the building in 1760 during the Seven Years War and what we see today dates from the nineteenth century. According to the story, Luther nailed his 95 theses to the door of the Castle Church in 1517 – generally used as the university notice board – and Wittenberg became the centre of the Reformation.

When Faustus arrived, assuming that he did, Wittenberg was a frenetic centre of missionary activity. Luther was an almost constant presence, installed in the former monastery with his ex-nun Katharina von Bora, the press rattling off his tracts and hymns, and his disciples swarming in and out through the city gates, pausing to admire the sooty spot where their leader had burned the Papal Bull. These zealots had little time for the stargazer who walked amongst them and Lercheimer, writing in 1597 painted a rather squalid picture of Faustus in Wittenberg:

> He had neither house nor courtyard in Wittenberg or elsewhere; he stayed nowhere, but lived like a villain, was a parasite, a gourmandised drunkard, and fed himself by his jugglery.[2]

Lercheimer was compelled to take issue with the opinion that Faustus had lodgings in the town, arguing that he could not have 'a house and courtyard at the outer gate in Scheergasse' because there was no outer gate and no Scheergasse.[3]

Lercheimer graduated from Wittenberg University in 1546 and had heard all the local tales about Faustus. In his day 'the doings of this magician were still remembered by many there'.[4] However, his denunciation had an agenda. In the third edition of his *Christlich bedenken* published at Speyer in 1597, he spoke out vigorously against the Spies history of 1587, decrying the fact that Faustus had been brought up in Wittenberg, had studied at Lercheimer's *alma mater* and had later lived in his town. Lercheimer was surprisingly open about his ulterior motive of trying to clear his university and religious heroes, Luther and Melanchthon, from the stain of association with the necromancer.

Lercheimer appeared to contradict himself when he confessed that 'the doings of this magician' were still well known when he himself studied there in the mid-1540s. As well as being shown the blackened tree where Faustus supposedly performed his magic, Moryson also saw Faustus's alleged house in 1591. Writing in the nineteenth century, Gustav Schwab (1792–1850) recorded that Faustus, nearing the end of the term of his pact, drew up a will in which he left 'the house and garden with the iron gate in the Scheergasse by the city wall' and more besides to his assistant, Christopher Wagner.[5] Another local tradition has Faustus living in the Bürgermeistergasse in Wittenberg beside the former residence of Hans Lufft, the man who printed Luther's new Bible. Katharina von Bora, the nun who escaped in a fish-barrel and later married Luther, also lived for a time on the Bürgermeistergasse. Placing Faustus on the same street as Luther's publisher and future wife sounds artificial, but there is no proof to decide the matter either way. To complicate matters, a bookshop at 31 Collegienstrasse today proudly bears a plaque above the door with the name of 'Johann Faust' on it.[6]

Wherever Faustus lived, he did not stay there long. Both Melanchthon and Lercheimer were agreed upon that. Lercheimer said 'he carried things so far that they were on the point of arresting him' and according to Melanchthon it was Johann who had given the orders, but with the sound of boots clattering in the Scheergasse, Bürgermeistergasse, or Collegienstrasse Faustus made good his escape.[7]

Melanchthon himself did not mention their supposed meeting, but Lercheimer recounted it in some detail.

> The obscene, devilish knave Faust stayed for a while in Wittenberg … He came sometimes to Mr Philipp Melanchthon, who gave him good words, berated and forewarned him that he should desist in time, or else he would come to an evil end, as did happen. But he gave no thought to it.[8]

It is hard to imagine the frail looking Melanchthon berating anyone, let alone such an infamous necromancer as Faustus, and it is an indication of the severity and authority of that rebuke that Faustus 'gave no thought to it'.

> Now one day about ten o'clock Mr Philipp left his study to go down to the table. With him was Faust, whom he had forcefully scolded. He spoke against him: Mr Philipp, you always ride me with smouldering words. One day, when you go to the table, I will make all the pots in the kitchen fly up the chimney, so that you and your guests will have nothing to eat.[9]

It is not much of a threat, but equal, perhaps, to the seriousness in which Faustus held Melanchthon's rebukes. Lercheimer has the mild man of the Reformation rouse himself against the calamity of going without his evening meal:

> Whereupon Mr Philipp answered: this you shall not do, I shit on you and your art. And he did [not] whatsmore: the Devil could not rob the kitchen of this saintly man.[10]

In 1868 Grässe published a similar story about Melanchthon and Faustus, drawing most of his details from Lercheimer, but in the same context he added another incident. The story has no date and involves Faustus and an unnamed man. It is an attempted conversion story that could be told about Melanchthon or the earlier Dr Klinge. Faustus responded by sending a demon to scare him at bedtime, but the 'God-fearing man' gets the better of it through ridicule and it stalks back to its master to complain.[11]

It was a sorry excuse for a demon, but still yet a more sorry excuse for another story about the power of faith. The tale turned up in the Faustbooks, set in Wittenberg as always.[12] However, Grässe also added another anecdote. Again we are left wanting a crucial name, but this time the authority of Lercheimer himself is added, dating the story to sometime within Lercheimer's own lifetime from 1522 to 1603:

> Dr Faust, however, did lead a student astray. Dr Lercheimer himself knew one of his friends well into an advanced age. This man had a crooked mouth. Whenever he wanted a hare, he would go out into the woods, make his hocus-pocus, and a hare would run right into his hands.[13]

The hare, of course, is one of the Devil's creatures and would be expected to run to one of his servants. The crooked mouth is taken as a sign of inner crookedness: physiognomy – judging character from the face – was widely considered reliable at the time. If Lercheimer did claim to know one of Faustus's 'friends' it almost adds a little more weight to the stories he told about him.

The Second Pact

A streak of fire blazed across the heavens all through August and September of 1531 to the consternation of many and the excitement of a few. It was what we call Halley's Comet today that was making the fearful cross themselves as they gazed skywards. Luther was sure that the sign was a portent of great events to come. Melanchthon wrote excitedly to several correspondents about it, asking for news and relaying the observations of others. The astrologers of Nuremberg – Johannes Schöner and Joachim Camerarius – tried to decipher its meaning with a morass of words as clear as they were inky black. Camerarius wrote to Daniel Stibar in Würzburg in October to warn that the comet presaged pestilence. In late December, Camerarius had finished writing his *Norica sive de ostentis*, interpreting the phenomenon of the comet with the support of a multitude of classical sources. Paracelsus also produced his own interpretation, predicting bloodshed. He dedicated it to the Swiss Reformation leader Huldrych Zwingli (1484–1531) and sent him a copy. Two months later Zwingli lay dead on the field of battle at Kappel. Zurich's militant Reformation had been decisively defeated by the combined forces of the Catholic Cantons. The victors desecrated his corpse: quartered by the public hangman, it was burnt on a heap of dung.

It was a year for devilry. In Battus's 1592 Dutch edition of Spies 1587, Faustus signed his second pact of seven years duration on 3 August 1531. In P.F.'s translation the pact is dated 25 July. We have no reason to suppose that he really did sign a second pact, but fiction outsells the truth. It is now that the Faustbook introduces the 'old man' who tries 'to persuade him to amend his evil life, and to fall unto repentance'.[14] If not actually Melanchthon or Dr Klinge, he is cut from the same sanctimonious cloth.

This old man is of course a Christian, honest and virtuous, and a lover of Scripture. Seeing that many students made their way to Faustus's door, the busybody immediately 'suspected his evil life', as if a few students was a sure sign of satanism. Feigning friendship, he beguiled Faustus to step into his house and dine with him. It was a trap and once the meal was over the old man rounded on him, accusing him of defying God, selling his soul to the Devil and of being 'worse than a heathen person'.[15]

After being subjected to an exhausting monologue, the Faustus of the Faustbook thanked the old man, confessed that he had been persuaded and departed. Whilst we might wish that Faustus stood firm in his beliefs, there are other examples to show – Agrippa foremost amongst them – how occultists wrestled with their conscience over the implications of their art in the face of the oppressive dogma of the Church. In the Faustbook, Faustus has a dark night of the soul, thinking over the words of his neighbour, until at last he decides to repent. Resolved now, he will renege upon his promise to the Devil.

As might be expected, Mephistopheles was not pleased and, suddenly appearing, gave Faustus a beating. He reminded him that he had signed up with Lucifer and vowed himself an enemy to God and all men: 'and now thou beginnest to harken to an old doting fool'. Mephistopheles informed him that it was too late to renege on the deal and forced him to write out another pact on pain of death. Again Faustus seated himself at his desk and, dipping his quill in a vein, wrote 'I once again confirm, and give fully and wholly my self unto the Devil both body and soul', specifically swearing that 'I will never give ear unto any man, be he spiritual or temporal, that moveth any matter for the salvation of my soul.'[16]

The whole incident is another invention of the Faustbook. Faustus did not sign a first pact and he did not sign a second, but the pestering of 'good Christians' must have been real enough. There were others they were pestering with far greater effect. In 1531 the sky above Waldsee was black with smoke from the burning faggots and the body of Elsbet Muellerin, tried and condemned for witchcraft. Faustus lived his life on a knife edge of heresy: the Inquisition on one side, the bigots of Reform on the other. As he made good his escape from Wittenberg he must have wondered if he would always be so lucky.

Unsafe Conduct (Nuremberg, 1532)

In the records of the city of Nuremberg for 10 May 1532 the deputy *Bürgermeister* made note of an undesirable character refused entry:

Doctor Fausto, that great sodomite and nigromancer, at Furr refused [safe conduct].[17]

Hieronymous Holzschuher, the official responsible for this information, was obviously not a fan. We know Faustus was not allowed entry to Nuremberg, but where was he when he made the request? Holzschuher wrote '*zu Furr*'. Unfortunately, there is nowhere of that name in Germany. Franz Neubert, writing in the first half of the twentieth century, reasoned that this place must be 'Fürth'.[18] It is a plausible interpretation; Fürth is a small town just nine kilometres outside Nuremberg.

Tucked safely between the confluence of the River Regnitz and River Pegnitz, there had been a settlement here from at least 1007. Since 1440 Fürth had also become a centre of Jewish settlement. The town lost out to nearby Nuremberg in 1062 when Heinrich IV transferred the right to hold a fair and coin money from Fürth to Nuremberg. The town had been under the jurisdiction of the diocese of Bamberg since 1307 by the command of Count Konrad II, but the city of Nuremberg and the counts of Nuremberg all had their competing claims. The Bamberg connection might tie in with Faustus's work for the Bishop there, but it is impossible to say for sure.

Enclosed within triple walls behind a dry moat, its eight gates overlooked by 200 towers, Nuremberg was an impenetrable fortress. In the Faustbook Faustus's magical journey takes in the sights of Nuremberg, unhindered by the deputy *Bürgermeister* and the formidable defences. It is possible that Faustus made it within the walls at some point, although probably not in the 'sumptuous apparell' that Mephistopheles had purloined for him there (and elsewhere), according to the Faustbook.[19] Melanchthon (through Manlius) recounted a story of how Faustus had, at an unknown time, narrowly escaped from Nuremberg, just as he had from Wittenberg:

When he had just started breakfast he became agitated and at once got up and paid the host what he owed. Scarcely was he outside the gate when the bailiffs came and searched for him.[20]

If this story is true, we can imagine Faustus either escaping to Fürth and then requesting re-admittance, or else, cautioned by his previous narrow escape, writing in advance to test the waters. Safe conduct was an early form of passport granting freedom of travel without fear of harm. Luther was issued with a safe conduct to allow him to travel to the Reichstag in Worms in 1521 and in 1528 we find Agrippa seeking safe conduct to leave France. It is clear that safe conduct was only sought in situations of real and present danger and that Faustus had reason to fear for his safety. One interpretation is that Faustus was specifically denied protection from arrest by the city authorities, suggesting that he had been there before.[21] Unfortunately, what Manlius tells us of Melanchthon's account is a jumble of hearsay with no consistent chronological order.

Nuremberg was a natural destination for Faustus; it was one of the great cities of Germany. In the mid-fifteenth century the town had a population of around 20,000, which was considerable for the period. At the beginning of the sixteenth century it reached the height of its magnificence. New possessions were gained after the War of the Landshut Succession – Nuremberg had backed Duke Albrecht of Bavaria-Munich – so that it could lay claim to more land than any other Imperial free city. Its political importance, industrial power, and superior culture earned it the title of the Empire's Treasure Box.

The children of Nuremberg were some of the most productive and influential people of the day, such as Hans Sachs and Albrecht Dürer. The city's fame also attracted many of the foremost figures of the times, such as Conrad Celtis and the brothers Willibald and Charitas Pirkheimer. The great mathematician and astrologer Regiomontanus went there in 1471. As Faustus sat in Fürth awaiting a decision on his application, Johannes Schöner and Joachim Camerarius had already established themselves in Nuremberg since 1526. Both were professors at the University: Schöner of mathematics; Camerarius of Greek and history. Both were practising astrology.

It is possible that with the Bishop of Bamberg's sometime astrological advisor knocking at the gates of their own little patch of turf, Schöner and Camerarius conspired to keep the competition at bay. The deputy *Bürgermeister* Holzschuher was an acquaintance of Camerarius's and it seems likely that he would have informed him of Faustus's request. Camerarius and Schöner were friends as well as colleagues, so it is reasonable to suppose that they would jointly defend their interests. Camerarius and Faustus would lock horns later – we have the documents to prove it – so the suggestion that presents itself is that their rivalry began here, or if it began earlier, then first demonstrated itself here.

Camerarius had taught Greek at the University of Erfurt in 1518, not long after Faustus was supposedly there, and had no doubt heard the tales in circulation concerning his magical feats. He had gone to Wittenberg in 1521 and there befriended Melanchthon. He was a better philologist than Melanchthon and would garner an international reputation.

Now in Nuremberg, Camerarius was busy cutting out a fine career for himself. Towards the end of 1532 he published his *Norica sive de ostentis* about the comet of 1531. He was editing and translating from the Greek the works of Hephaestion of Thebes, Hermes Trismegistus and Vettius Valens for his book *Astrologia*. He had the handwritten manuscripts of Regiomontanus from Schöner's library to help him. Schöner's library proved to be a rich mine. From it Camerarius published the commentary of Theon of Alexandria on Ptolemy's astronomical writings. He was also working on a Greek edition of Ptolemy's *Tetrabiblos* with translations and notes, which was eventually published in Nuremberg in 1535. Alongside this academic work, Camerarius was also providing private astrological consultations for the aristocracy. It was a lucrative business – as the Bishop of Bamberg's payment to Faustus shows – and Camerarius would surely not have wanted any outsiders cutting in on it.

It was also a Reichstag year for Nuremberg. After the Protestant princes and cities formed themselves into the mutual protection pact of the Schmalkaldic League in 1531, Charles V was forced to treat with them. The result was the Religious Peace of Nuremberg signed on 23 July 1532. The Protestants were granted an amnesty until the next Reichstag, while Charles was reinforced in his campaign against the Ottomans. Nuremberg sent double its quota of combatants and by September the Ottoman army was on the retreat. Was the Reichstag the reason for Faustus trying to get to Nuremberg? Given his former association with the Bishop of Bamberg, were there politico-religious reasons for keeping him out?

In Nuremberg the old charge resurfaced against Faustus. He was the 'great sodomite'. We are reminded of Trithemius's libels all those years before. Here we find evidence that the rumours had now disastrously caught up with him. Was he 'the great sodomite', or were Camerarius and Schöner laughing up their sleeves to see the gates barred against their rival?

The Great and Powerful Sea Spirit

According to a story printed by a seventeenth-century publisher, Faustus was already dead by 1532. He had left all his worldly goods to his assistant – the publisher called him Werner, but he is more usually known as Wagner – including the magical book that the publisher was now presenting to the public. However, this Werner had lost the book. It passed from hand to hand until it came into the possession of a man who used it to procure a vast fortune for himself. Perhaps fearful of its power, this man then buried the book in 1532. It was rediscovered in 1661 and now in 1692 the publisher was setting it before the public as the most effective and least complicated of the Faustian rituals.

Published in Amsterdam as *Doctor Faust's Great and Powerful Sea Spirit*, the book's centre-point is the invocation of Lucifer himself and of course the sea spirits, Forneus, Vepar and Zaleus. An additional spirit called Paymon, although not invoked, makes an appearance as Lucifer's attendant. With this unholy crew now present,

> You can now demand from Lucifer as much gold and silver and jewels or any other useful treasure that lies in the sea, grows in the sea or has been cast into the depths of the sea by shipwreck, as you like.[22]

Although the work is very doubtfully that of Faustus to say the least, and probably dates from the late seventeenth rather than the sixteenth century as its publisher claimed, there are nevertheless authentic Renaissance spirits involved here. The four demons were listed by Wierus in 1563 and their characters faithfully reflect the descriptions given by the latter.

What all this really suggests is that the publisher of the *Sea Spirit* had a copy of Wierus or something similar at hand. It also gives us an insight into the demonology of the period. Lucifer needs little introduction, but his spirits Forneus, Vepar, Zaleus and Paymon demand some explanation. Wierus claimed to be working from a manuscript called the *Liber officiorum spirituum (Book of the Offices of Spirits)*. Some of the spirits named by Wierus, and hence presumably also found in this earlier *Liber spirituum*, are also to be found in Codex 849. The Codex contains conjurations involving both Lucifer and Paymon, but not Forneus, Vepar, or Zaleus.

Forneus is given the rank of marquis in hell's hierarchy, in command of twenty-nine legions drawn from the orders of thrones and angels. He is described as being 'like unto a monster of the sea'. His special commissions are to endow those who invoke him with facility in rhetoric, an enhanced reputation, knowledge of all languages and to turn enemies into friends. Vepar, also known as Separ, is a duke, and like Forneus he commands twenty-nine legions of inferior demons. Although referred to as a 'he', Vepar takes the form of a mermaid and is described as 'the guide of the waters, and of ships laden with armour'. His powers extend to making the sea 'rough and stormy' and to appear to be full of ships. On a less savoury note, he can also 'killeth men in three days, with putrefying their wounds, and producing maggots into them'. Zaleus, named as Zaleos or Saleos in the text, is an earl of hell who curiously takes to wearing a ducal coronet. No legions are listed as being under his command; instead he comes forth alone in the appearance of a well endowed soldier astride a crocodile. Forneus and Vepar are clearly 'sea spirits', while the crocodile is the single element to connect Zaleus to the water.[23]

The central theme of the operation is, like so many others, the finding of hidden treasure. What makes the *Sea Spirit* unique is that the scene of the operation has shifted from land to the ocean. Presumably having exhausted the hoards of land lubbers with more run-of-the-mill conjurations, the magician is now forced to turn to new avenues of wealth. However, contrary to the book's publisher, in 1532 Faustus was not dead.

Magic for the Archbishop (1532)

If Faustus could not get into Nuremberg, or had just narrowly escaped, then where did he go? There is nothing else to suggest that he remained in Fürth, indeed Fürth, so close to Nuremberg and, for Faustus, so far, was a less than ideal location to practice his art. Where were the wealthy patrons? Where were the gullible crowds? Where was the money to be made? All in Nuremberg.

A clue turns up in a letter written in 1583 from the papal legate Minucci to Duke Wilhelm of Bavaria. Minucci told the Duke that 'count Hermann von Wied had Fausto and Agrippa in his presence in the time of his apostasy, because he wanted to learn from the most famous people in the magic art.'[24]

Hermann von Wied (1477–1552) was an Elector and Archbishop of Cologne. The 'apostasy' that Minucci referred to was his acceptance of the Reformed faith. The fourth son of Count Friedrich von Wied, he was virtually born into the Church. At the age of six he was given a benefice in the cathedral chapter of Cologne, later becoming Archbishop-Elector of Cologne in 1515 and Bishop of Paderborn from 1532 to 1547. He is remembered by some as having governed his electorate with energy and intelligence, although that is disputed. He was at first hostile to the Lutheran teachings, creating the first martyrs of the Reformation, but a quarrel with the papacy contributed to a change of mind. He still held out hope that reform would come from within the Church rather than from without.

With the assistance of his friend John Gropper (1503–1559), he began, around the year 1536, to introduce reforms in his own diocese. This move was welcomed by the Protestants and the League of Schmalkalden promised to defend him. However, the victory of Charles V over William, Duke of Cleves, and the hostility of the people of Cologne significantly checked his ambitions. Gropper was more of an Erasmian than a Lutheran and eventually found himself opposing the direction being taken by von Wied. In 1542 von Wied brought in von Sickingen's old chaplain Martin Bucer (or Butzer, 1491–1551), who leaned more towards Zwingli than Luther, to manage the Reformation and in 1543 invited Melanchthon to join him. Both the Emperor and the Pope summoned him to appear before them in Brussels and Rome respectively to answer for his conduct. He was excommunicated by Paul III in April 1546, and in January 1547 he was deposed by Charles V and replaced by Count Adolf von Schaumburg. He retired to his castle of Burg Altwied where he died on 15 August 1552.

The particulars of von Wied's career should make us suspicious of any report from a papal legate. Minucci may have been trying to smear von Wied's name, but with von Wied dead for more than 30 years there was little point. It is difficult to judge Minucci's motives or the sources of his information. However, we do know that the Archbishop possessed a copy of Agrippa's *Occult Philosophy*, among other books of magic. If the Archbishop read Agrippa, then why not meet him? And if he met Agrippa, then why not Faustus?

If we work on the assumption that the meeting could have taken place, the logical question is when? Minucci vaguely said 'in the time of his apostasy', which as we see from von Wied's career could have been as late as 1536. The key to dating this may lie with Agrippa. His connection with von Wied is proven and he was known to have been a guest at von Wied's country estate in Poppelsdorf.

At the beginning of 1531 Agrippa was in Antwerp overseeing the printing by John Grapheus of the first edition of his *De Occulta Philosophia*, volume one. He dedicated it to Hermann von Wied with the most flowery and convoluted language imaginable. Prolix and sycophantic, Agrippa was clear in his aim: he wanted von Wied's favour.[25]

In early 1531 Agrippa left for Queen Margaret of Austria's court at Mechelen, near Brussels, working for a time as court historian. It was from here in January that he wrote the supplicatory letter to von Wied. The approach was successful and in 1532 he was invited to Poppelsdorf.

Poppelsdorf today is a smart suburb of Bonn, full of wonderful Art Nouveau houses, yet, overlooked by the Venusberg, still retains something of its country past. This is nowhere more true than in the botanical gardens that encompass the site of the Archbishop's old residence. Now called Schloss Clemensruhe, the medieval moated castle was transformed in the sixteenth century into a more suitable abode and entirely rebuilt in the eighteenth century in the French palatial style.

Agrippa's move paid off. The Inquisitor of Cologne, the Dominican Conrad Köllin (or Colyn), delayed publication of the remaining two volumes, but with the Archbishop's intercession and some compromises on Agrippa's part, publication was resumed and the whole book appeared in 1533. If Faustus was there at the same time as Agrippa, then 1532 is the most plausible date. Even if they were not there at the same time – and Agrippa's hostility to that German sorcerer in France who may have been Faustus, suggests that they would hardly have been overjoyed to meet again – it seems that von Wied's interest in the occult was at its highpoint and so increases the likelihood that he also met Faustus around this time.

The townspeople may have once thrown a suspected witch from the top of the city walls, but the Archbishop preferred to bathe with magicians. Agrippa enjoyed a warm reception from this man of the cloth. The last surviving letters of his printed correspondence reveal that he and von Wied were relaxing in Bertrich's baths in Bonn in the company of friends and good books. Faustus may not have been one of those friends, but if he and the Archbishop met, then we can expect that he was similarly entertained.

The Prisoner of Batenburg

Johannes Wierus told a curious story about Faustus that took place in a small town called Batenburg in today's Netherlands. Batenburg lies on the River Maas, the same river that, under the name of the Meuse, flows through Mouzon, the town that von Sickingen had captured all those years earlier. It is possible that Faustus came here by river or overland from a town like Cologne, 165 kilometres to the south-east, or Münster, some 190 kilometres to the east. Previous historians have dated this particular adventure to 1530, whilst others are inclined to think it took place in 1532 or 1533.[26] We have reason to believe that Faustus was in the vicinity of Cologne around the year 1532 and we have better reason to believe that he was in Münster in 1536, so the later date is plausible. The event could have taken place as late or later than 1536, but after Münster the references tend to locate our magician much further south. For the sake of establishing some sort of coherent chronology, we are going to risk dating this to 1532/3.

Wierus was not complimentary about Faustus, but then we are hardly surprised by that, so few have been sympathetic to this maligned figure. Wierus began this particular story about Faustus by saying

> There was nothing he could not do with his inane boasting and his promises. I will give one example of his art on the condition that the reader will first promise not to imitate him.[27]

Faustus had been taken prisoner at 'Batenburg on the Maas, near the border of Geldern', that is, Guelders or Gelderland.[28] Why that should have been so we are not told, nor is Wierus in the least curious. It is as if he expected Faustus to be routinely arrested. Apparently a certain Baron Herman was away at the time, evidently the master of this place. This must have been the Guelders nobleman Herman van Bronckhorst and Batenburg who flourished around this time. He plays little part in the tale, which centres instead upon his chaplain, Dr Johannes Dorstenius.

In custody under some unknown charge and facing who knows what judgement – the accusations of sodomy and necromancy usually flung at Faustus could both spell his death – Faustus attempted to gain the upper hand. He promised Dorstenius 'knowledge of many things and various arts' and Dorstenius being 'good but not shrewd' agreed to become his pupil. Dorstenius 'kept drawing him wine, by which Faustus was very much exhilarated, until the vessel was empty.' Dorstenius announced that he was going to the nearby town of Grave to have his beard shaved whereupon Faustus 'promised him another unusual art by which his beard might be removed without the use of a razor, if he would provide more wine.' Dorstenius agreed and Faustus told him to rub his beard with arsenic, although omitting details of the correct preparation of such a potentially dangerous depiliative. The chaplain happily smeared the poison all over his beard and sat back to await the results, but to his horror and great pain 'there followed such an inflammation that not only the hair but also the skin and the flesh were burned off.' Wierus tells us that 'the chaplain himself told me of this piece of villainy more than once with much indignation.'[29]

We learn no more. For Wierus the whole point of the story is to show how malicious Faustus was and Faustus scholars have in the past swallowed it whole and regurgitated it.[30] As we saw in the introduction, Wierus is a late and biased source who cannot be taken uncritically. If we trust Wierus that he did indeed hear this story from the chaplain Dorstenius, then the attribution adds authenticity to the telling, but it could just as easily be a ploy on Wierus's part. The story itself is a mere fragment, undated and thrown in to reveal his subject's bad character. That Faustus turns on his jailor rings true: what prisoner would gladly suffer incarceration awaiting summary justice if he thought he could incapacitate at least one of his guards and possibly engineer his escape? Instead of showing up Faustus as a scoundrel, this incident reveals ingenuity when hard pressed. Wierus is not concerned to say what became of Faustus in Batenburg. It is only clear that he did not remain there. With Dorstenius clawing at his burning face, it would have been a simple thing to lift the keys from his belt, assuming there is any truth in the tale at all.

A contributory reason for Faustus's refused admission to Nuremberg and perhaps even an explanation for his enforced stay in Batenberg, was the change in criminal law introduced by the Emperor. In 1532 Charles V promulgated a new criminal code for the Empire called the *Carolina*, taking care to make provision for the crime of witchcraft. For causing harm or making trouble the penalty was death by fire, and even when no harm or trouble had been caused, some punishment, left to the judge's discretion, should be meted out.

Faustus could well have been languishing at some judicial authority's pleasure while it was decided what to do with this self-confessed necromancer who, Dorstenius aside, had not yet harmed anyone with his magic. However, there are other dimensions to this situation.

Guelders is a relatively unprepossessing region today, but it was a different matter in the sixteenth century. It had been a thorn in the Empire's side for some time. The 'Achilles of Guelders' to some, the 'bane of the Netherlands' to others, Charles of Egmont (1467–1538), Duke of Guelders and Count of Zutphen, was no friend to Charles V. Egmont had, with French military aid, successfully led a revolt in Guelders in 1492 to wrest the territory from Habsburg control. He had allied himself with France during the Four Years War, and with Robert de la Marck had wrought havoc in the Low Countries. He was a general sponsor of turmoil in the area, encouraging his pirate chief, Long Peter, the self-styled 'King of the Zuider Zee', to terrorise the coastal waters. In the early 1530s he had recently signed the Treaty of Gorichen (1528) with Charles V, but relations remained tense and erupted into a prolonged war of succession from 1534 to 1538. Given this situation, there are distinctly political reasons why a German in Guelders might be arrested. Whether incarcerated or not, Faustus was free to wend his way possibly to Würzburg and the company of nobles.

The Fortunes of von Hutten (1534)

In early 1540, Philipp von Hutten wrote to his older brother Moritz from Venezuela, telling him the latest news of his expedition:

> Here you have a little about all the provinces, so that you may see that we here in Venezuela are not the only ones who have been unlucky up to now; all these aforementioned Armada that left Sevilla before and after us perished within three months, insomuch, I must admit that the Philosophus Faustus hit the mark, for we struck an evil year.[31]

Von Hutten knew the odds were against him and Faustus's predictions must have weighed heavy on his heart. But the rewards were high. Shimmering before the young adventurer's eyes was the fabulous wealth of El Dorado.

The legend of El Dorado, Spanish for 'the gilded one', arose in the first half of the sixteenth century to lure men across the vast ocean to the steaming, pestiferous jungles of a place that was as much like the moon to them as it was another place on earth. The name was first given to the king or high priest of a South American tribe who was said to cover himself with gold dust at a yearly religious festival held near Santa Fe de Bogota. In the retellings, El Dorado became a whole city of gold (also called Manoa or Omoa), and finally an entire country in which gold and precious stones were to be found in fabulous abundance.

A few years before von Hutten's expedition in 1531, a man called Martinez, lieutenant to Diego de Ordaz, claimed to have been rescued from shipwreck, taken inland and entertained at Omoa by El Dorado himself. To the people of the time such reports as this made El Dorado a reality. In 1534 the name 'El Dorado' glowed on the horizon as real as the setting sun, just as golden and just as enticing. What young man in his early twenties could resist the adventure?

Philipp had grown up close to the sources of power. He had spent his formative years at the court of Charles V under the tutelage of Duke Heinrich von Nassau (1483–1538), for whom he later carried out numerous missions. In 1534 his adventurous spirit was captivated by the Venezuelan expedition being proposed by the wealthy merchant-banking family of Welser. The Welsers had been granted the right to colonise and exploit Venezuela in 1526 as repayment of the debts Charles V had run up during his election campaign. On 22 August 1534 von Hutten had an audience with Charles V to discuss the expedition. On 19 October he sailed from Spain for the New World with Georg Hohermuth von Speyer (1500–1540) and Nikolaus Federmann (1506–1542). Stormy weather drove them back to port four times before they finally departed on 8 December.

They would have left with all due pomp and ceremony; princes of the Empire embarking upon a great adventure. A miniature from Jerome Coeler's (or Köler) account of his travels in 1533–1534 shows four brightly-attired fighting-men, one blowing upon a trumpet, another carrying an enormous banner, during a procession at Sanlucar in Andalucia before the expedition to Venezuela. Another scene shows a galleon setting out with the wind full in her sails and cannon bristling along her sides; the port is a mere speck in the distance and sea monsters swim alongside her.[32]

In February of 1535 Philipp's ship *La Santa Trinidad* arrived in the *Mundus Novus* ('New World'), sailing into the harbour of Coro and the country known to the colonists as *Klein-Venedig* ('Little Venice'; in Spanish, 'Venezuela'). It seemed a lush and verdant land, abundantly decorated with the yellow flowering Araguaney, which would later become the country's national tree, and the Prima Vera or Gold Tree whose masses of golden-yellow flowers seemed like a promise of the precious metal under its roots. But death hung heavy on the sweet-scented air. The previous governor, Ambrosius Ehinger (also Dalfinger, *c.* 1500–1533), had died two years earlier from a poisoned arrow and von Speyer now found himself taking his place.

Von Hutten was under no illusions that this would be anything other than a life or death struggle. Federmann had been here before and even written a book detailing the hardships. The dangers brushed aside with Renaissance bravado, they set off on a long and hazardous expedition into the interior in search of gold.

The young adventurer had not just sought his Emperor's blessing before the fateful expedition, but had also enquired of certain astrologers whether the stars were propitious for his planned mission. Von Hutten was by no means unusual in turning to astrology for a guide to the future. Before him the great explorer Magellan consulted an astrologer on the location of the Spice Islands and Columbus would later attribute all his achievements, not only to geometry, navigation and arithmetic, but also to astrology.

Camerarius now elbowed his way in. He was acquainted with both Philipp and Moritz von Hutten. With Moritz he shared an interest in Humanism and astrology, and had encouraged Moritz in the publication of his cousin Ulrich von Hutten's manuscripts. In 1529, whilst passing through Nuremberg, Philipp had called in to see Camerarius and give him news of his brother Moritz's health. In 1535 he published *Erratum*, ostensibly a reply to Erasmus's criticisms of his work that also revealed his interest in the von Huttens with a poem dedicated to Moritz. The opening lines of this poem concerned the future of Philipp's expedition.

The poem eulogised Philipp, stressing the glory that his expedition would win for his family, the Emperor and the Empire. Camerarius was vague about the exact details of his prediction, but did give the impression that he had made some sort of prognostication for Philipp before he set off and that from such comments as appear in the *Erratum* we may conclude that it was a favourable one.

In 1536 Camerarius wrote to Daniel Stibar, confidently predicting the outcome of Philipp's expedition. Philipp was 'a youth destined for fame' he said, adding 'I desire and prophesy an entirely propitious outcome.'[33]

Faustus predicted an entirely different result. Although Philipp did not say whether judicial astrology was involved, Faustus's career to date would suggest that it was. Philipp had valued Faustus's advice – he called him 'the Philosopher' – so Faustus was no mere mountebank as Camerarius would have us believe. Philipp did not say where or exactly when he met Faustus, if he ever did. Several references to Würzburg in his letter to Moritz suggest the possibility that this was the place. In the letter he asked his brother to extend his greetings to Stibar and his other friends at the Würzburg court. In addition, Philipp was born at Schloss Birkenfeld, not too far from Würzburg – it is possible that he returned home one last time before leaving for Spain and the New World. Philipp's and Faustus's mutual friendship with Stibar may have been the factor that drew them together, again making Würzburg a likely location for any meeting.

To Philipp's cost, events would prove which of Faustus and Camerarius was the better diviner. By December of 1540 von Speyer was dead and von Hutten had become captain-general of Venezuela. Soon after he mounted a new expedition into the interior. Returning after five years of wandering he found that a Spaniard, Juan de Caravazil (also known as Caravajil or Carabayal) had been appointed governor in his absence. By 1545 the Welsers had failed to abide by the terms of the arrangement with Charles V and the Emperor had revoked their rights, claiming the territory for himself. In April 1546 von Hutten and fellow explorer Bartholomäus Welser VI the Younger were arrested and executed on Caravazil's orders.

In the chapel of Mariasondheim near Würzburg there is a monument carved with an elaborate relief showing two figures kneeling before the cross. They are Moritz and Philipp. Behind them, the artist Loy Hering has laid out upon the cold alabaster the tragedy of Philipp's Venezuelan adventure. The epitaph is believed to have been composed by Camerarius. Despite his inaccurate prognostication, he still managed to have the last word.

17

Baptism of Blood (1534–1535)

The Empire seemed as though it were being compressed in a vice, its internal flaws and tensions threatening to explode it at any moment. The French and the Ottomans were exerting tremendous external pressure, whilst religious upheaval in the German states seemed like the prelude to open war. Luther had completed his translation of the Old Testament into colloquial German and now issued a complete Bible. Germany was swarming with French agents and French support promised to the Lutheran princes made them bold in their opposition to the Emperor.

The dissolution of the Swabian League offered another opportunity for Ulrich von Württemberg to reclaim his Duchy, and with the support of Philipp I, Landgrave of Hesse, and other Protestant princes he invaded Württemberg in April 1534. In May he won a decisive victory at Lauffen and a few weeks later was grudgingly restored to his title of duke with Württemberg ostensibly under Austrian suzerainty. With the Duchy in his hands once more he vigorously pursued a policy of Reformation, violently seizing all the ecclesiastical possessions that he could to swell his impecunious exchequer. One of the casualties of this aggressive *Klosterordnung* ('monastery order') was Faustus's former haven of Maulbronn. The monks and abbot were forced to flee, finding refuge in the Cistercian priory of Pairis in Alsace. Ulrich's insatiable greed caused him to extort an excessive tax that undermined his renewed popularity, again sowing seeds of dissension. The world Faustus had known in his youth had changed forever.

The End Times

The Lutherans were not the most threatening of the new religious groups. Luther called them *Schwärmer* ('enthusiasts', or 'fanatics'). Even Zwingli, whom Luther thought too extreme, had denounced them as *Wiedertäufer*, *Täufer*, or *Catabaptistae* ('drowners'). Even the name we know them by today was one bestowed by their enemies. From the Greek *ana*, 'again', and *baptizo*, 'baptize', we know them now as the Anabaptists, although they called themselves simply Christians, believers, or the brethren. Marx may have thought that religion was the opiate of the masses, but to the Anabaptists it was their crack cocaine.

Many had come before them. Waldensians, Petrobrusians, Henricians, Albigensians, the Brethren of the Common Life, the Hussites, and the fifteenth-century Bohemian reformer Peter Chelcicky, all held many of the beliefs later found in the Anabaptist movement. It was an old problem. The idea of rebaptism is documented at least since the second century, whilst many Anabaptists themselves point to the first-century example of the Apostle Paul (Acts, 19). In the second and third centuries, Montanus, and his followers the Montanists, and Tertullian denied infant baptism, practiced adult baptism and re-baptised those baptised by 'heretics'. The Donatists in the fourth century re-baptised those who had been baptised by bishops who were deemed 'traditors' (those who had recanted their faith or who had handed over the Scriptures to pagan authorities), or who were from churches stained by fellowship with 'traditors'. Re-baptism was criminalised under the Justinian Code (529 CE) and punishable by death because of its political implications.

To Luther's consternation the Zwickau Prophets had spread the message in Wittenberg in 1521. However, it was the Swiss Reformer Conrad Grebel who, in 1523, formulated the tenets of what became known as Anabaptism. Grebel preached that it was impossible to be born into belief or have it conferred upon you. Belief was a voluntary act that could only be demonstrated by responsible adults through the ceremony of baptism. Infant baptism was therefore meaningless. Neither Grebel nor his followers used the term re-baptism or anabaptism because they denied that pouring water over a child's head constituted any sort of Christian baptism at all. Added to this were a primitive communism and a millenarianism that directly challenged the political system and social stability.

Over the next few years the sect grew and spread across the Empire. By 1529 Charles V ordered its extermination by any means possible. Consequently the movement was driven underground. Its followers met covertly, recognised each other by secret signs and became even more of a threat to the authorities. The Anabaptists were convinced that the end was coming – and for the Anabaptists of one town in northern Germany they were right. Faustus, too, would be drawn into the tragedy and madness that was the Siege of Münster.

A New Jerusalem

Münster was a town of lofty gabled houses and arcades, whose skyline bristled with monuments to its holiness. Its 9,000 or so citizens slept safely behind stout fortifications that were only dismantled in the eighteenth century. Its documented history begins in the ninth century when Charlemagne installed his newly-appointed Bishop of the Saxons, Ludger, in a monastery here about the year 800, but it was an isolated and uneconomical location. Too far from a navigable river or important trade route, the settlement that was then called Mimegardevoord or Mimegerneford grew with painstaking slowness. Sometime in the eleventh century the name of Münster (from the Latin for monastery) came to replace the earlier name. In the twelfth century the town received a charter and during the thirteenth and fourteenth centuries developed into one of the most prominent members of the Hanseatic League. Its growing wealth had fattened the Church and Münster became covered with its buildings. A cathedral, 10 churches, 7 convents, 4 monasteries and 4 charitable foundations jostled for space in its crowded streets.

Church and town enjoyed an uneasy relationship – easier for the Church than the town, as usual. The Church communities were exempt from taxation, its members exempt from military service, and their self-sufficiency contributed nothing to the local economy whilst offering the local farmers, artisans and merchants serious competition. Following the upheaval of the Peasants' War in 1525, Münster had made itself independent from the Church, grudgingly granted by the Prince-Bishop Friedrich von Wiede, and enjoyed self-rule through the offices of a council and two mayors.

The first signs of religious mania were evident in 1531 when the former priest Bernard Rothmann, enthused by radical Lutheran ideas, led a mob to destroy the 'idols' in his old church of St Mauritz. He had studied under Melanchthon, but found the teachings of the mild-man of the Reformation too passive, too academic. Melanchthon was known to have remarked to Luther that Rothmann would either turn out to be 'extraordinarily good or extraordinarily bad'.[1] He was not wrong.

Rothmann left Münster to evade the consequences, but returned again in early 1532 to resume preaching. Anabaptist themes crept into his sermons, alarming Catholics and Lutherans alike. Fearing that civil order was being undermined, von Wiede ordered him to desist. Rothmann gave in, but his obedience lasted only a few short weeks. This time the Bishop ordered Dirk von Merveldt, Bailiff of the Cathedral, to make the council expel this troublemaker. But there were those on the council, like the merchant Bernard Knipperdolling, who supported Rothmann.

Having secretly pledged their allegiance to the cause in Knipperdolling's house, Rothmann, Knipperdolling and others marched into the church of St Lambert's and destroyed the stone sarcophagi that held the mouldering bones of long dead clerics. Excited by their desecration, the mob rampaged through the streets, burning piles of votive candles, priestly vestments, paintings, tapestries and books. Rothmann threw his own sermons into the fires, exclaiming, 'The truth of Holy Scripture shall triumph'.[2]

Von Wiede's retirement forestalled the armed conflict that seemed inevitable. The ailing von Wiede was succeeded by Franz I von Waldeck (1491–1553), welcomed by the Catholics of the town as a 'brave and righteous knight'.[3] The Lutherans' opinion of him was diametrically opposite. They saw him as a whoring, hunting, drinking, swaggering noble, not a 'bishop' in any sense of the word. It was true that he was not an ordained priest and had had several children by his mistress, but his sympathies were inclined towards the Lutheran cause.

His portrait shows a heavily-jowled and bewhiskered man, his fat right hand closed tightly round a sword, his bishop's crosier pulled protectively to his chest. There is a look of sullen stupidity mixed with an aggressive possessiveness about him. History has remembered him as having lived a dissolute life.

The new Bishop prevaricated, awaiting the Emperor's ruling on the situation. Knipperdolling seized the initiative. He organised an illegal armed guard for

Rothmann and forced the council to effectively deny Roman Catholics the right to practice their faith. Rothmann reigned from the pulpit of Münster's grandest church, St Lambert's, enjoining his congregation to enjoy the God-given delight in feasting and the flesh. A witness to these events, Herman Kerssenbrück, later described Rothmann's religious services as being closer to the rituals of Baal or Satan than to Christianity.

At his court in far-away Regensburg, the Emperor received report of the disturbances and furrowed his brow. He suspected that von Waldeck's indecision was more than mere weakness and a sign of secret sympathies. He demanded that strong action be taken against the troublemakers.

The town council ignored the Emperor's message and von Waldeck retaliated with a blockade. With their prosperity threatened, the townspeople turned to neighbouring Landgrave Philipp I, a known Lutheran sympathiser, to intercede on their behalf. The councillors also put out appeals to their neighbouring cities, but their support was not forthcoming. Philipp intercession fell on the Bishop's deaf ears. There was nothing for it but to hire mercenaries.

On Boxing Day 1532, a force of 900 armed men stormed the Bishop's stronghold of Telgte in a daring midnight attack. They had hoped to surprise the Bishop at home, but von Waldeck was holidaying at his residence of Billerbeck. They returned instead with eighteen hostages, some of them high-ranking ecclesiastics.

The Bishop was forced to parley. The town was granted full religious liberty in return for its promise of obedience and tolerance of Catholic worship. Rothmann himself was forbidden from public preaching, but paid little heed. Other preachers gave him their support and he again began to publicly spread his views.

Tensions in Münster had momentarily distracted the Emperor from the more pressing problems posed by François I and the Ottomans. The news of the stand-off must have travelled far and been the talk at every inn and castle court. Knipperling's basement printing press had been churning out Rothmann's sermons and leaflets for months. His message of the common ownership of all goods was one that not just the religiously inclined could be moved by. Rothmann wrote that the poorest were now the richest in their town, once despised they were now the most distinguished. To this carrot he added a large stick, warning that because God was about to 'punish the world' everyone should 'get ready to go to the new Jerusalem'.[4]

These leaflets and rumours of the new preaching at Münster were drawing large numbers of pilgrims, the poor and many others who believed they had nothing to lose and everything to gain. All along the highways of the Empire, religious fanatics and the destitute were on the move, seeking the road to a better life as one of the Company of Christ in Rothmann's new Kingdom of Zion. In the opposite direction went the oppressed Catholics and others who did not need an astrologer to tell them that this growing throng of the dispossessed boded ill.

News must also have reached Faustus's ears. We have no information on his religious persuasions: his associations with the Lutheran von Sickingen and the Catholic Georg III suggest that this was a matter of indifference to him, at least so far as his clientele was concerned. As a philosopher versed in the Greek and Latin classics, as a Hermeticist steeped in occult lore, as an astrologer learnéd in the motions of the stars, and as an alchemist who had separated and recombined the elements of the earth, he did not need wild-eyed preachers to interpret the world or the Word for him. But as one who claimed to be able to recreate the miracles allegedly performed by Jesus, even to better them, he too, might have made that journey north. His fellow Faustians, Agrippa and Paracelsus, did not seal themselves within Hermeticism but also joined the religious debates of their day – neither of them much to their advantage.

The influx of new disciples tipped the balance in Münster. Radicals replaced the moderates on the council. Draconian and summary punishments were introduced against morally objectionable behaviour. In late 1533 mass baptisms, conducted by hordes of newly arrived preachers such as Jan Bockelson (1509–1536), the tailor's apprentice from Leyden (and more usually known as Jan van Leyden), started taking place. In one week alone, 1,400 people were re-baptised. The poor were put to work strengthening the city's defences. The able-bodied were organised into militias. The freedom the citizens had won was beginning to turn into another tyranny, but they would not feel the weight of this new yoke until it was too late.

Tensions between the different factions within Münster were also escalating. Lutherans and Anabaptists were not seeing eye-to-eye. As usual the trouble centred on Rothman. When the Lutheran co-mayor ordered Rothmann and his most vocal acolyte Henry Roll to be arrested and expelled from the city, hundreds of armed supporters turned out ready to defend them. Anabaptist women, demanding the reinstatement of Rothmann, chased the Lutheran preacher out of St Lambert's and pelted the councilmen with dung when they tried to reprimand them.

The Bishop despaired at the mounting chaos and sent furious letters hither and thither, to Landgrave Philipp I, to the council. He demanded that the Anabaptists be expelled, but was again rebuffed. Rumours circulated that the Bishop had amassed an army and was preparing to attack. Using this as a pretext the Anabaptists now moved against the Lutherans and the remaining Catholics, striking first at the council. The councillors barricaded themselves inside the Overwater Church, defended by their own militia of armed supporters. Meanwhile armed peasants entered the city, ready to defend the Bishop's cause and the Catholic faithful. Stalemate ensued, broken only by the treachery of co-mayor Tilbeck. Sent to parley with the Bishop, he burnt their offer of truce and told his fellow councillors that the only option was to side with the Anabaptists. The peasants withdrew without a fight – pacified by an innkeeper's liquid incentive – and the council surrendered to the Anabaptists. At sunset the phenomenon of parhelion split the sun into three burning orbs and set the clouds on fire. Münster was bathed in golden light. The triumphant Anabaptists took this as a sign of God's grace and celebrated with wild abandon: 'Nothing could have been more frightful, more insane, or more comic' reported Kerssenbrück.[5]

Messengers were sent out urging other Anabaptists to join them, for the time had come. Over the following days more zealots flooded in. Amongst them was Jan Matthias. A former baker from Amsterdam, Matthias was in his fifties, a tall, stooping figure, dressed always in black, with the beard of a prophet and the burning eyes of a 'true believer'. He was regarded as another Enoch sent to herald the Second Coming. By his side was the beautiful runaway nun Divara, younger by some twenty 20 years, dark-haired and always dressed in white. If Münster had become a tyranny, then its tyrant had arrived.

Faustus would not have found a welcome within Münster's gates now. Matthias frothed during one of his sermons that 'Everywhere we are surrounded by dogs and sorcerers and whores and killers and the godless and all who love lies and commit them.'[6] Matthias had all those who would not be re-baptised expelled – Knipperdolling's intervention saved them from a worse fate. Faustus, if he had been here, would now have been thrown out and undoubtedly glad for it. The indications are that he was here, if not in Münster itself, then nearby.

A Mighty Fortress Is Our God

As the exiles trudged out through the city's ten gates, beyond the double walls and across the two moats to who knows what future, the Bishop was laying his siege. He had already executed several Anabaptists in neighbouring towns and confiscated their belongings. Such summary actions betrayed his weakness: he was not yet able to move against heavily defended Münster. He lacked artillery and had to borrow Landgrave Philipp's prized siege cannons known colourfully as the Devil and the Devil's Mother. From the Princes of Cleves and Bentheim, and the Archbishop of Cologne came forty smaller cannons. Wagon convoys brought in supplies from near and far: almost 300 barrels of black powder from Brabant and Amsterdam, salpetre and sulphur from Mengen, iron shot for the harquebuses from Deventer, cartloads of halberds, spears and fire-arms, and wheelbarrows and shovels for the engineers. Then there were the soldiers, almost all of them mercenaries, some 8,000 men marching from the Rhineland, Saxony, the Low Countries and Denmark with their trains of camp followers, to hire out their lives for a few gulden. The Bishop negotiated loans from his allies and extorted more tax from his subjects to meet the expenses – the *Landsknechte* alone cost 34,000 gulden a month.

Although the later legends always situate Faustus in the company of students and scholars, in the historical documents we often find him in the company of knights and princes, boasting of winning all the Emperor's victories in Italy and claiming title in the warlike Order of St John of Jerusalem. It is perhaps now with the *Landsknechte*, rather than the zealots, that Faustus takes the road to Münster. From experience he knew that military men also looked to the stars, to the signs and portents, and thus to the astrologers during their campaigns.

Marching to the fife and drum of some mercenary band, perhaps in the company of old friends from the Italian Wars, or picking his own way north through the bad roads and inclement weather, Faustus would have arrived to find the Bishop's army already encamped outside Münster. Divided into seven compounds, the camp stretched across four miles, pennants fluttering from the white tents. Soldiers drilled while wives did the washing and children played in the fields. Local merchants arrived and set up shop. The camp had become a second Münster, made of canvas and rope instead of seasoned wood and stone.

Two months of inactivity passed, stretching the patience of the Archbishop of Cologne and the Emperor. Von Waldeck was already falling behind with his payments to his soldiers and slowly some of them began to desert. Gert von Münster, known as 'the smoker' for his enthusiastic addiction to the new drug of tobacco, deserted with a troop of his men to the Anabaptists. The Bishop's soldiers marched up and down, maintained watches and patrols, and fought off night forays and surprise attacks from the Anabaptists. Behind the impassive walls, sounds of the Anabaptists' preparations could be heard as the defences were strengthened, black powder and charcoal manufactured, lead roofing melted down for bullets, iron hammered out by the blacksmiths into spearheads and sword blades, and pitch and quicklime made ready in cauldrons along the ramparts. They would also have heard their trumpets and singing. A snatch of a hymn like 'A Mighty Fortress Is Our God', taken from Luther, drifting on the air, reminded all that this was no ordinary siege. They would have seen smoke rising from continued mass book burnings as Matthias purged his people of every written word except that of the Bible.

We should not picture Faustus sitting with the *Landsknechte*, sharing their boredom and money worries, but rather seeking out the Bishop, his commander-in-chief Ulrich von Dhaun, or his lieutenants, Johann von Buren, Hermann von Mengerssen and Eberhard von Morrien. Prasser's *Waldeck Chronicle* mentioned a Hensel Hochstraten as the military leader. Only these noblemen and officers of rank could afford his services, or required them.

On 5 April 1534 Faustus may have watched as a divinely inspired Jan Matthias and a bodyguard of a dozen at best rode out of Münster's Ludger Gate to challenge von Waldeck's army to single combat. There would be no toying with this token gesture. The Bishop's finest cavalry, 500 men-at-arms in black armour mounted on black horses, charged this sixteenth-century David and cut him to pieces. A black rider paraded Matthias's head before the walls of Münster before it was stuck on a spike and set up in view of the city, and that night the bloody lump of the Prophet's genitalia was nailed to the wooden doors of the Ludger Gate.

With their leader gone, and so ignominiously, von Waldeck must have been confident that Münster would fall, but it did not. Neither Knipperdolling nor Rothmann were charismatic enough to fill his place; instead it was the young Jan van Leyden who now stood up and donned the mantle of power (as well as marrying – his third concurrent marriage – the newly widowed Divara).

The Bishop still did not act – a bold move now would have taken advantage of the chaos that enveloped Münster after the death of its prophet and which van Leyden was now bringing to order. Sieges are often won by inactivity, the aggressor simply waiting until the defenders are starved into submission, but Münster enjoyed a high degree of self-sufficiency and, as any competent commander would have seen, would not easily succumb to hunger.

Faustus may have stood with the Bishop and watched the clouds of dust rising up from Münster as they pulled down the steeples – symbols in stone of the Pope's power and that of his Bishop. The Anabaptists turned the 'Jewel of Westphalia' into ruins, except the spire of St Lambert's and a few other towers that were saved for use as artillery platforms.

After some preliminary mining to try and drain the moat, the Bishop eventually began the siege in earnest on 22 May. He opened with an artillery barrage, firing, it has been estimated, around 700 cannonballs a day for four continuous days. Equipment for storming the walls – grappling hooks and long ladders – and straw mats to cover the muddy bottom of the exposed floor of the moat were made ready in anticipation. But the soldiers had started drinking earlier on the afternoon before the planned dawn assault. Waking up to see a sun glowing red on the horizon, they mistook its setting for its rising. Screaming *Attacke!* they staggered forward in a chaotic, drunken charge. They forgot the straw mats and became bogged down in the moat, easy targets for the defenders. About 200 were either killed or wounded with little or no losses to the other side.

Towards the end of July the sounds of shots and cries from within the walls could be heard, all that was evident to the besiegers of the failed coup led by the blacksmith Henry Mollenheck. It was another missed opportunity for the dithering von Waldeck.

After months of mining to try and re-drain the moat – it had filled once more – the Bishop was ready to mount another offensive. Did he turn to Faustus and ask, 'Are the stars propitious?' The answer was lost in the roar of cannon-fire as 'the Devil' and his 'Mother' and their numerous offspring bombarded the city. The main gate of St Mauritz took a heavy pounding and the walls were breached, but answering fire from the Anabaptists prevented the Bishop's men from pressing their advantage. That night the walls were shorn up and torrential rain turned the ground to mud, bringing von Waldeck's army to a wet and boggy standstill.

When the rain finally stopped at the end of August, the Bishop attacked. The seasoned veterans, professional men of violence, were repulsed by the determined defence of the mostly civilian Anabaptists. Their assault driven back from the inner wall by boiling pitch and quicklime, the retreating mercenaries were ambushed and massacred. The Bishop lost forty-two officers and hundreds of men; the Company of Christ, only fifteen. Van Leyden had held the city and his people once again raised their voices to sing 'A Mighty Fortress Is Our God' – had they not proven it?

The Bishop's army, once 8,000 strong, was reduced to less than half its former size over the next few months. Whilst some had been frittered away in useless and occasionally comic assaults on the city, most were simply deserting. These men were mercenaries who had not been paid, why should they stay? They owed nothing to the Bishop, who, on the contrary, owed much to them. By late October there were only 3,000 left, hoping that their employer would eventually make good his promises. If Faustus was also in the Bishop's pay, then he too was undoubtedly feeling the pinch.

Meanwhile, the Anabaptists had sent out secret missions to preach the word to the surrounding towns. Cocooned in his religious mania, Jan van Leyden, or King Jan as he was now, was convinced that the countryside would rise up at their call. Twenty-seven men in all left the city gates at daybreak. In Coesfeld, Osnabrück and Warendorf they readily found sympathisers and performed baptisms. But the Bishop cowed the towns by threat or force of arms into surrendering the Anabaptist preachers. Only one escaped death, returning to Münster bound in chains and barely alive. Somewhere in the Bishop's camp, or in one of these neighbouring towns, Faustus too would have been aware of the situation: that only by the Bishop's alacrity and readiness to do violence had the Anabaptist plague been prevented from spreading further.

Part of the Bishop's alarm must have been due to the realisation of how permeable his cordon round the town really was. Faustus would have observed the increased haste in constructing the planned ring of seven blockhouses with connecting ramparts. By December, Münster was finally sealed in. Even so, the Anabaptists still managed to send out copies of Rothmann's works to Landgrave Philip I, Luther and Melanchthon. Philipp responded with equanimity and tolerance, suggesting that a peaceful solution was still within everyone's grasp. Luther for his part replied with typical fury in his tract *Concerning the Devilish Sect of Anabaptists in Münster.* A thousand copies of Rothmann's newly finished diatribe *Revenge* were sent out to rouse the Anabaptists of the Low Countries to join the war against the Bishop.

These were dangerous times. The Anabaptists were not confined to Münster alone. Their network spread out across the Empire, but so too did that of their opponents. Strangers must have been suspect wherever they appeared, for who could tell if they were agents of the Bishop or of King Jan. Law and order was maintained only by the vice-like grip of summary execution. Someone like Faustus, already used to narrow escapes from the authorities in less dangerous times, must have been especially exposed now. It was a dangerous profession. In 1535 his fellow magician Agrippa died under mysterious circumstances in Grenoble, aged just forty-nine.[7]

Faustus was already a radical figure, making claims that the Church, the Lutherans and the Anabaptists would consider blasphemous and heretical. He had no friends among the religious and few among the Humanists. Frightened by the rumours of necromancy, the towns were inclined to close their gates against him. Only by being under the shield of one of the powerful lords could he hope to survive; his previous work for the Bishop of Bamberg, his calling card and surety.

Reports that Münster was slowly but surely eroding its supplies convinced the Bishop to sit out the siege. Comfortable in his castle at Iburg (Bad Iburg) and safely forty-one kilometres away, he let winter take its toll on Münster's morale. Still the city did not fall. Facing greater and greater daily privations, the Anabaptists nonetheless continued their defiance. 'When will it end?' must have been his constant question, and if he had retained Faustus's services it would certainly have been directed at the diviner.

From mid-April 1535, van Leyden had allowed the starving to leave the besieged city if they so wished. They left in their hundreds. He warned them that on no condition would they be allowed to return. It seemed like no warning at all: they did not want to return. The Bishop, however, ordered his soldiers to shoot the men and drive the women and children back to the city gates. His calculated ruthlessness saw in these starving people a weapon he could use against the Anabaptists: to bite into their morale, or, if allowed back within the gates, to eat up their reserves.

Not everyone was as Machiavellian. Count Ulrich von Dhaun protested to the Bishop against such cruelty. Ignoring him, the Bishop planted no-man's-land with dead Anabaptists tied to posts and wagon wheels. By early June there were approximately 800 men and women and a great number of children trapped between Münster's walls and the Bishop's ramparts. The butchers were busy, despatching up to fifty men a day, but it was clearly going to take some time – and an excess of inhuman cruelty – to hack through this mass of desperate humanity.

The Bishop took to his bed with a fever and eventually von Dhaun could stand no more. He took all of the refugees into custody, releasing the foreign women on condition that they swore to keep the peace and holding the others until the end of the siege. This humane action came too late to save the 600–700 unarmed men who had already been put to death.

After fifteen months of expensive, wearisome siege, von Waldeck was handed the keys to Jan's kingdom on a plate. A group of guards who had had enough, deserted their watch and escaped under cover of darkness. Two of them independently revealed, not only the entire condition of Münster's defences, but also a secret way through the city walls. The Bishop still did nothing. He still thought that Münster would surrender. It was a fool's hope. By massacring all those who had so far tried to surrender (only von Dhaun or the information they carried had saved some of them from that fate) he gave the city's defenders more than enough incentive to fight on until their last breath.

Enter the Necromancer

After sixteen months of siege, the Bishop finally decided to take the city. As von Dhaun made arrangements, especially forbidding the consumption of alcohol after the last debacle, a stranger arrived in camp.

> Franciscus [Franz] I, by the grace of God, son of Philipp II by his second marriage born, Bishop of Münster, in the year 1535, 25 June, besieged and surrounded the city of Münster which had been occupied by the Anabaptists and, with the support of imperial princes led by Hensel Hochstraten, captured it ... At which time the distinguished *Nigromanticus* Dr Faustus, himself turning aside from *Corbachii*, predicted that, without doubt, the city of Münster would be captured by the Bishop that same night.[8]

The *Waldeck Chronicle* from which this quotation comes is a late source, written around 1650 by Daniel Prasser, and often overlooked. Despite this lateness, the reference is both dated and geographically located, unlike almost all of the legendary material that grew up after Faustus's death. On this basis we should not dismiss it out of hand, even though it is impossible to verify its accuracy.

He seemed to arrive at just the right time from a town called 'Corbachii', which is modern Korbach some 148 kilometres away by today's roads. It might be expected to take almost a week to cover that distance, depending on how Faustus travelled, and there is no hint of a demonic horse or flying cloak here. It seems that he had stayed a safe distance away from the troubles in Münster, but – if we are to believe this account – was clearly well aware of the situation. During the course of this extraordinarily long siege, it is entirely conceivable that Faustus made the journey more than once and may have visited other locations in the area during that time.

Korbach is in the county of Waldeck, lying on the intersection of the Cologne-Leipzig and Frankfurt-Bremen trade routes. It was a flourishing trading centre, a member of the Hanseatic League and safe behind a double wall with five well-guarded gates. Korbach was also the seat of Franz I's brother, Philipp III (1486–1539), Count of Waldeck.

One can imagine Faustus strolling by the Gothic *Spukhaus*, the so-called 'haunted house', dating from 1335. With its steeply crow-stepped gable facing onto the street and punctuated with sinister black holes for windows, this old warehouse looks like it easily lives up to its reputation. Local tradition records that he stayed in the Hanxleden Manorhouse on Kirchstraße, which was unfortunately torn down in 1965 and only one wall remains.[9] Mixing with the *Feldhühner*, or 'partridges' as the people of Korbach were called, and avoiding the night watchmen, known as 'gunpowder heads' because of their zealous over-attention to duty, Faustus would have found an eager audience amongst the travellers and traders, not to mention the Bishop's brother.

Arriving in the Bishop's camp, he prophesied rightly. Using the secret entrance, a group of soldiers gained entrance to the town during a vicious downpour, easily overpowering the guards who had taken cover from the rain and fallen asleep. These commandos occupied the Anabaptists until von Dhaun's main force scaled the outer walls and swarmed through the streets. The Anabaptists' secret weapons, the rolling fortresses, were immobile – the horses had been eaten – and the commander who took refuge behind them with 200 armed men was bought off by the offer of his life.

Expecting rich bounty, the *Landsknechte* were sorely disappointed. For more than a year they had sat out winter cold and summer heat, and endured the impecuniousness of the Bishop only to plunder an empty coffer. They reacted as sixteenth-century soldiers do, leading one contemporary, Dietrich Lilie, to write 'the murder was too horrible to describe'.[10] The ringleaders were rounded up and cast into prison while the Bishop dreamt up the most terrible way to execute them. Prasser's *Waldeck Chronicle* has a brief account of it:

> The farcical Johann of Leyden, who named himself King of Israel and Zion, was humbled togther with Knipperdolling and Kretching, their bodies being torn with glowing, burning-hot pincers, confined in iron cages and suspended from the tower of St Lambert's, the 23rd of January in the year 1536.[11]

Each man was publicly tortured for a full hour before being stabbed through the heart. A contemporary, the Lutheran theologian and inquisitor Antonius Corvinus, recorded 'the courage with which [Jan] proved himself, giving only once a cry against the pain', but any admiration of this stoicism was countered by his belief that 'it is certain that Satan is able to lend strength and courage to those he catches in his web'.[12] This was not an isolated view. People, especially Luther, really did believe that the forces of good and evil had waged war over Münster.

The broken bodies of the three leaders were then taken to the foot of the west tower at the north end of the *Prinzipalmarkt* and hoisted 200 feet for all to see. Ravens gathered to pick their bones clean, their raucous cries the only funeral lament for these heretics. The cages are still there today and in the city museum one may see the pincers that were heated until they glowed white hot.

Beyond the Black Forest
(1535–1536)

Old antipathies between France, the Empire and Venice split Christendom
and invited Europe's ancient foe, the Turk, to plunder her. War was everywhere,
but where was Faustus? Would he again lend his wand to the Emperor's cause as
he had allegedly claimed before? Faustus was now in his late sixties. He had
seen many of his former clients and possibly friends die before him. He needed
to find security and that meant money, a position, or another wealthy patron.
At this stage in Faustus's career we begin to see a cluster of locations around the
place generally identified as Faustus's final destination. There would be no more
adventuring in Italy or in the dangerous borderlands abutting the Ottoman Empire.
Towards the end of his life he seems to have travelled south, into the Black Forest
and beyond.

The Restless Guest

During his wanderings across Europe Faustus must have found himself occasionally calling upon the kindness of strangers for shelter. There was an extensive
network of private inns along the major trade routes, but one alternative to the
notoriously flea-ridden inns was the monastery. Christianity had spread its long
tentacles throughout Europe and where there were a few monks, there was a roof
for a stranger. There are two accounts of Faustus seeking such refuge. The first
was told by Johannes Gast (d.1552) and published in the second edition of his
Sermones Convivales in 1548. The story told by Gast has a certain authority because
he claimed to have actually met Faustus, but unfortunately there is no date or
location ascribed to it. In spite of his own claims, we should approach Gast's testimony with a degree of caution. He was, after all, writing a book of anecdotes to be
told after dinner rather than an historical treatise.

Under the title 'Of Faustus the Necromancer', Gast related his tale:

> He puts up before night at an exceedingly wealthy cloister, to stay the night there.
> A brother sets before him vile wine having no quality. Faustus asks that, from the
> other cask, he draw the best wine, which is customarily given to nobles.[1]

We should remember that Faustus had claimed to be a Commander of the Order
of St John, a position that ordinarily required nobility. His request, then, would be
entirely in keeping with his status. The problem was that the monk did not have
the keys. The prior kept those himself and, as the monk explained, 'it is a sin to
awaken him'. However, Faustus had espied them lying in the corner: 'Take them
and open that cask on the left and give me a drink' he ordered. The monk refused;
the prior had not given him permission to serve any other wine. Faustus now lost
his temper: 'In a short time you shall see marvels, you inhospitable brother.'[2]

Faustus left early in the morning without saying goodbye, but that was not the
end of the matter. He sent a 'furious demon' to pester his hosts that Gast said moved
things about in the church and the monks' cells.[3] This 'furious demon' is clearly what
we would call a poltergeist today. What is interesting is that Faustus is able to send this
entity to plague the monks and, in a fashion, possess the monastery. It is the threat
allegedly made to Melanchthon realised.

How could Faustus send such an entity? In the third book of his *Occult Philosophy*,
Agrippa divides necromancy into two classes: one which he calls necromancy and
concerns 'raising the carcasses' and the other he calls sciomancy, which is 'the calling
up of the shadow'. Forced by incantations and the use of their remaining physical substance, these shadows could aid the necromancer in a variety of operations to 'kindle
unlawful lusts, cause dreams, diseases, hatred and such like passions'.[4] If Faustus, a
supposedly self-styled necromancer, was to invoke a 'furious demon', then this could
have been the method he chose.

According to Gast the problem grew so great that the monks seriously debated
leaving or even destroying the monastery. The prior wrote to the Count Palatine
for help and he generously took the monastery under his protection and threw
out the monks. Gast noted that from time to time the Count sent the monks some
supplies. The Count reported no problem with troublesome spirits, but Gast maintained that whenever a monk set foot inside there was such a commotion that he
could not stay.

The only clue to a location is reference to the 'Count Palatine'. At the time this
would have been Ludwig V (r. 1508–1544), son of Philipp 'The Upright', whom we
encountered earlier. He ruled a large, irregularly shaped mass of land extending along
the Rhine south of Mainz and reaching out far to the west. The size of this territory
helps little in pinpointing the scene of the drama related by Gast, beyond establishing
a rough idea that Faustus was somewhere in the southwest of Germany.

In the sixteenth-century *Zimmerische Chronik* we read a remarkably similar account,
this time with a named location.

> The monks at Lüxhaim in the Wassichin had a ghost that he [Faustus] sent
> to their cloister, which they could not get rid of for many years and greatly

molested them, only because at one time they had not wanted him to stay over-
night, that is why he sent them a restless guest.[5]

There is today a town called Lüxheim near Bonn, but the mysterious region of
'Wassichin' is thought to be the Vosges mountains, some considerable distance from
Bonn. Bonn is furthermore several hundred kilometres to the north of the Palatinate,
whereas part of the Vosges mountain range did lie within Ludwig V's territory.
Looking for somewhere that could conceivably be this 'Lüxhaim', I came across the
very similarly named Lixheim, a small town west of Strassburg in the Vosges region
in today's French Lorraine.[6] Triangulating the points of agreement in Gast and the
Chronik, Lixheim must be 'Lüxhaim'.

There has also been a Benedictine monastery, or priory, there since 1107. One
hopes that by the time Faustus arrived the monks had repaired the damage inflicted
on it during the Peasants' War. It was secularised in 1550–1551 and finally destroyed
during the Thirty Years War. Up until the nineteenth century there were two houses
in Lixheim known as the 'remises' (sheds) of Doctor Faustus.[7]

In the *Zimmerische Chronik* there is no attempt made to date this story; it is just
another tale of Faustus. In Gast, the story's textual proximity to his Basel story and
both Basel's and Lixheim's relative geographical proximity to Staufen – the town
generally acknowledged to have been the place where he died – suggests a date
towards the end of Faustus's life. It is possible that he may have stayed in Lixheim
monastery whilst making his way south from Münster, the last dated reference we
have for him. Thus at the earliest it could be late 1535, or at the latest 1538.

Dinner in Basel (*c.*1535)

After recounting his tale of devil-summoning in Lixheim, Gast continued with
'Another Story about Faustus':

> At Basel I had dinner with him in the great college and to the cook he gave
> various kinds of birds to roast. I am ignorant as to how they were obtained, or
> who gave them away, at this time there were none for sale. Furthermore, I had
> never seen them in our region. He led a dog and a horse, I believe them to have
> been demons, that were ready to follow him to the end. The dog sometimes
> assumed the likeness of a servant and carried the food, so I was told.[8]

The action has moved further south into new territory, but there are familiar elements, like the magical banquet and the demon horse that remind us of Erfurt and
Prague. The addition of the dog finds echo in stories circulating about Agrippa and
later we find its role solidified in the fictions of Marlowe and Goethe. Melanchthon
also told the story and linked it with the name of Agrippa, possibly for the
first time: Faustus had a dog who was the Devil, just as Agrippa had a dog who was
the Devil.

Gast reveals a close association with the necromancer. He did not meet him in an inn like Mutianus, but actually dined with him in 'the great college' (*collegio magno*). The University of Basel had been founded in 1460 with a charter granted by Pope Pius II. The model was a familiar one: a faculty of arts leading to the faculties of law, medicine and theology. Paracelsus had been through these doors, stirring up trouble, so the university was used to controversial visitors.

Then a city of around 10,000 inhabitants, bustling round the twin spires of the cathedral, Basel had become a centre for printing, pharmacy, Humanism and reform. Once a part of the Upper Rhenish Imperial Circle (*Reichskreis*), Basel had since allied itself with the Swiss Confederacy and broken away from Rome. Johannes Froben (1460–1527) had set up his press here and had published the works of his sometime lodger Erasmus. When Paracelsus arrived in the 1520s he cured Froben of a troublesome leg complaint. Basel had embraced Zwinglism and Gast himself was a Protestant clergyman in the city. His reputation, however, rested principally on the popularity of his *Sermones Convivales*, a collection of anecdotes and tall tales.

In the Faustbook, Faustus made a visit here as part of his whirlwind world tour, pausing just long enough to learn of an interesting legend. As usual, he took the time to visit 'many rich Monuments' and admired the brick wall and 'great trench' that surrounded it.[9] However, the name struck him as unusual and he enquired of Mephistopheles its origins:

> His Spirit made answer and said, that before this City was founded, there used to be a Basiliscus, a kind of Serpent, this Serpent killed as many men, women, and children, as it took a sight of.[10]

Of course there was a gallant knight on hand to do battle with the perilous beast. The knight surpassed his courage with cunning, having a suit of crystal fashioned for him that covered him entirely. Over this he wore a black mantle and set out to find the monster. Scenting another easy victim, the basilisk crept out of its lair to meet him. With the creature rearing up before him, the knight pulled off the mantle. The basilisk had not even time to utter a cry at its undoing and shattered into a thousand pieces.[11]

Fabulous tales were no anomaly in Basel. Towards the end of the 1530s Basel society was treated to the pagan revelations of a curious work by the Swiss scholar Gilg (or Aegidius) Tschudi (1505–1572). His *Die uralt warhafftig Alpisch Rhetia* published in Basel in 1538 detailed what he described as pagan fertility customs still being performed in the Swiss Alps. Tschudi told of yearly rituals in which groups of masked men called *Stopfer* ('Piercers') journeyed from village to village, carrying huge clubs and leaping dramatically into the air to collide violently with one another. The Reformer Durich Chiampel later added his own recollections of similar rites held to ensure the fertility of the harvest. What Tschudi and Chiampel dismissed as pagan superstition and the worst sort of nonsense was then still a living tradition in the remote mountains. Faustus and the *Stopfer* were worlds apart – high magic and folk custom were never comfortable bed-fellows – but the extermination of these folk practices by Protestant and Catholic priests echoes the transfiguration of Faustus from magus to diabolist. History was being rewritten and not by sympathetic hands.

As they sat together in the refectory of 'the great college' perhaps Gast and Faustus discussed Tschudi's work or the recent witch trials.

Some years earlier in Pfeffingen, a township within the demesne of the Bishopric of Basel, three women had been tried for witchcraft. The trial records state that 'without being subjected to duress or to torture' Agnes Callate, Ita Lichtermutt and Dilge Glaserin had all confessed to having been seduced by demonic ravens who granted them whatever they wished to eat and became their lovers.[12] The abundance of produce – cherries, birds and wine – delivered by the ravens is uncannily similar in effect to the fertility of the land ensured by the leaping *Stopfer*. At a distance, twice removed, we think of Faustus's own magical banquets and out of season produce, faint echoes perhaps of similar fertility rites.

Such an interpretation would not be against Renaissance thinking. In 1561 Conrad Gesner (1516–1565), the Swiss teacher, physician and scholar, wrote to his friend, Emperor Ferdinand I's 'Physician in Ordinary', Johannes Crato von Kraftheim, about a celebrated wandering scholar called Faustus. Gesner had some interesting ideas on the origins of the 'prohibited arts' that people like Paracelsus and Faustus practised. 'I suspect indeed' he said 'that they derive from the Druids who among the ancient Celts were for some years taught by demons in underground places. This has been practiced at Salamanca in Spain down to our day.'[13] Known as the 'Swiss Pliny', Gesner's scholarly output was enormous, covering the fields of zoology, botany, philology, medicine and the Classics. His most popular work was a treatise on the 'secret remedies' of alchemists and empirics, and he had been in Basel in 1537 about the time Faustus may have been there.

At that time Basel was the home of another Renaissance man, the unparalleled Erasmus. Now past his prime, aged and in poor health, Erasmus was glad to accept the offer of Mary of the Netherlands of a living in Brabant. As he packed his bags and made ready for the journey his good fortune was interrupted by a severe case of dysentery. He did not recover and died soon after. Against the usual custom he did not receive the last sacraments. He was buried with great ceremony in Basel cathedral in 1536. Anyone in the town or with connections to it could not have been unaware of the passing of this giant of the Renaissance.

Erasmus had kept Agrippa at arm's length, despite Agrippa's overtures towards him, and it is unlikely that he would have received Faustus. But Basel was a small town and local gossip was the continuous news broadcasting of the day. Gast's circle probably included the likes of Sebastian Münster (1488–1552), Hebraist and geographer, Ottomarus Luscinius (Otmar Nachtgall, *c.* 1478–1537), Humanist, musician and theologian, and the priest and dramatist Valentin Boltz (d. 1560). Whilst Boltz did not arrive in Basel until after Faustus's time in 1546, Faustus may well have met the others. These were convivial times and it is unlikely that Gast dined alone with Faustus in the university. However much he may have enjoyed Faustus's stories, Gast ended his account on a familiar and less than sympathetic note: 'God preserve us lest we become slaves of the Devil.'[14]

Slaves of the Devil (1536)

In 1536 Joachim Camerarius was in Tübingen, having been called there to reform the university, but his mind was much preoccupied with other matters. As we saw, he had been determined to make a positive prediction for the outcome of Philipp von Hutten's expedition to the New World. Part of the reason for that could have been competition from a rival. He wrote defensively to Daniel Stibar warning him about other astrologers and trying desperately to bias him against them:

> Do not think that one should accept any divinations of astrologers or haruspices with greater faith than those of men who have discovered the essence of prophecy, not steeped in some kind of superstition, but endowed with a certain instinct and divine power.[15]

In another letter to Stibar, written three months later, he revealed the target of his attack.

> When the moon stood in Pisces in opposition to Mars, on the 4th of August, I endured a very difficult night. I owe to your friend Faustus the pleasure of discussing these affairs with you. I wish he had taught you something of this sort rather than puffed you up with the wind of silly superstition or held you in suspense with I know not what prestidigitator's tricks. But what does he tell us, pray? For I know that you have questioned him diligently about all things. Is the Emperor victorious? That is the way you should go about it.[16]

So, Camerarius had heard of Faustus. Philipp's letter to Moritz von Hutten shows that he had consulted Faustus on the subject of his expedition and Camerarius was clearly unhappy about the intrusion of a competitor. Much has been made of 'your friend' (*tuus*) with some suggesting that a particularly close relationship existed between Faustus and Stibar. The reference to juggler's or conjuror's tricks was a common form of abuse. Prince-Bishop Franz von Waldeck used the same words when writing about the Anabaptists to the town-council of Warendorf in 1534.[17]

Dismissing Faustus's work as 'silly superstition', Camerarius sought to defend and exalt himself by reference to his own higher abilities, what he called 'a certain instinct and divine power'. Camerarius supplemented his astrology with the ancient arts of the *sortes Homericae* and *sortes Virgilinae*, a method of bibliomancy involving the works of Homer and Virgil. The diviner would open a suitable text such as the *Iliad* at random and interpret the passage he alighted on as having special bearing upon the question at hand. To answer his own question posed to Stibar, 'Is the Emperor victorious?', Camerarius reported that the *sortes* drawn from Homer were favourable: 'His honour is from Zeus, and Zeus Allwise cares for him.'[18] He reminded Stibar of the *sortes* he had cast for Charles V years before when he was still a boy. This time he had opened Virgil's *Aeneid* and read: 'Because of his arrival even now the Caspian kingdoms and the Scythian land dread the divine oracles, and the mouths of the sevenfold Nile are alarmed.'[19]

Camerarius's concern about the exploits of the Emperor must have been widely shared. Old enemies had unfurled their banners of war and the Empire again found itself ringed with naked steel. In the autumn of 1534 Charles V laid out his plans for a campaign in North Africa, at the same time sending out emissaries to sue for peace with France. But François I was intent on causing mischief. His own emissary, de la Forêt, was with the corsair Barbarossa (*c.*1478–1546) in Algiers and then at the Ottoman Court, looking for cash and allies in the war against the Empire. Barbarossa had been successfully raiding the Italian coast and had captured Tunis from Mulay Hassan, an ally of the Spanish, proving himself an irksome thorn in Europe's side. When another of Charles's emissaries met François in the spring of 1535, he found the French king unresponsive, but uncovered a conspiracy involving several of the German princes. Venice meanwhile was entreating Suleiman to abandon his campaign in Mesopotamia and counter Charles in the Mediterranean.

On 30 May 1535 Charles sailed out of Barcelona to be joined by the fleets of Andrea Doria (Genoa), the Knights of St John (Malta), Portugal, Sicily and the Italian States to lead a combined force of over 400 ships towards Tunis. By August he had conquered the city and whipped Barbarossa back to his Algiers lair, but news may not yet have reached Camerarius. After his victory Charles had taken his forces to Italy, over-wintering in Naples and spending Easter of 1536 in Rome.

Italy at that time was in the grip of several witchcraft panics. As Reginald Scot told the story, events unfolded at Cassalis in Salassia (possibly modern Casali near Firenze). A gang of witches was believed to be behind a resurgence of plague in the district. Similar cases emerged at Genoa and Milan amidst devastating plague outbreaks that continued into the seventeenth century. In the fourteenth century in France and elsewhere, lepers had been accused of the same crime and exterminated *en masse*. The Jews were blamed for inciting them and behind the Jews the conspiracy theorists saw the Muslims. Little had changed. Acting on Luther's advice, the Elector of Saxony, then Johann Friedrich I, expelled the Jews from his domain in 1536. Mixing misfortune, minorities and ignorance was like mixing saltpetre, charcoal and sulphur. Sociologically, such panics are often linked with wider social crises.

In Rome, Charles V warned Pope Paul III that if François I continued to reject his peaceful overtures then it must come to a final battle that could only end in the Turk's conquest of Europe. In February 1536 the treacherous François had allied himself with Suleiman. In March he invaded Savoy and by early April held Turin. Charles responded by challenging François to single combat. Being far from a model of chivalry, François declined. Abandoning plans to besiege Algiers (and ultimately Constantinople), Charles found himself leading an army of between 50,000 and 60,000 men into Provence, up to the very gates of Marseilles.

Had Camerarius been right? To an extent Charles's campaign was successful, particularly against the Ottoman's North African allies, but having taken Aix-en-Provence, he found himself stalemated by Montmorency. The French commander had split his army between the heavily fortified towns of Avignon and Valence, and refused to come out, leaving to the invader a systematically devastated countryside. Charles hesitated before Marseilles to the south and Arles to the west, and on 13 September decided to turn back. The mouth of the Golfe du Lion might have been alarmed, but

Camerarius was wrong. The Emperor was not victorious. By December he had sailed back to Barcelona – he had already considered abdicating.

In his correspondence with Stibar, Camerarius was simply blowing his own trumpet and crying down Faustus at the same time. His towering conceit is reminiscent of Trithemius and Mutianus before him. However, his letter does reveal something of how the troubles of the period were discussed in intellectual circles.

If Faustus really was a Commander of the Knights of St John, then he could hardly have avoided being swept up in the conflicts of this period, especially as Turkish raiders were probing frontier areas like Styria. Charles V's settlement on the Knights at Tripoli and Malta (1530) had been intended to provide a bulwark against the corsairs, and their ships had joined the campaign against Tunis. The evidence, such as it is, suggests that Faustus was in southern Germany. The fighting days, if he had any, of the seventy year-old magician were over. He may have lost his commandery – preceptors were appointed for periods of five or ten years and could resign – or have been travelling abroad to seek support for the war against the enemies of the Empire. Even if he took off the distinctive cloak of the Knights, he was still the one-time astrologer to the Bishop of Bamberg and was doubtless looking for another wealthy client. The shifting power balance in Württemberg may have made his home region too dangerous for an itinerant magician and the principal towns of Bavaria had already shown him the door.

The Faustbook of course made no mention of the politics of Faustus's day. Instead we find the magician conjuring up a bevy of lovelies to entertain him in the autumn of his years. As the end of the pact approaches 'he began to live a swinish and Epicurish life', although according to the Faustbook he seems to have done that from the beginning. He commanded Mephistopheles to bring him seven of the fairest maidens he has seen in all his extensive travels. According to P.F. he was duly supplied with 'two *Netherlanders*, one *Hungarian*, one *English*, two *Wallons*, one *Francklander*.' In the Wolfenbüttel Manuscript the ladies from Walloon were originally from Swabia and we should note that the 'Francklander' hails from German Franconia, not France.[20] With this extensive harem he lived as Jan van Leyden might have done: 'and with these sweet personages he continued long, yea even to his last end.'[21] The Faustbook gave the date of this as in the twentieth year of Faustus's pact, which would give us 1534 using the dates in the Dutch edition, but of course this dating is hardly reliable.

To lust, the Faustbook added avarice to Faustus's list of deadly sins. With a rudimentary banking system that was available only to wealthy merchants and nobles, burying one's money was still seen by many as the best way of safeguarding it against theft. Consequently many like those unfortunates at Jena and the deluded Leipzig serving-boy John George E., dreamt of finding a hidden hoard, much as people today discount the fourteen million to one odds and squander their money on the lottery. The Faustus of the Faustbook was not immune to this obsession and turned to finding buried treasure in the twenty-second year of his pact, or 1536 by our rough reckoning of the dates in the Faustbook.

The Faustbook had Faustus back in Wittenberg, skulking around the ruins of an old chapel less than a kilometre outside of town. The Devil pointed out the spot for him to dig and presently he uncovered the treasure trove 'like a huge light burning' and guarded by a 'mighty huge serpent'. Faustus charmed the serpent and heaved up the treasure. He was unpleasantly surprised to find that he was digging up 'nothing but coals of fire' and 'there also he heard and saw many that were tormented'. Not to be put off by this preview of damnation, Faustus persevered in recovering the coals and back in his den found that they were transformed into silver and gold. According to the Faustbook, Wagner found this hoard after Faustus's death and estimated it to be worth in the region of a thousand gilders.[22]

We see that the Faustus of the Faustbook was too busy with what the Wolfenbüttel Manuscript called his 'devilish concubines' and the pursuit of buried treasure to take much interest in the affairs of the day. However, the real Faustus could hardly have been ignorant of them. His presence in south-western Germany may have been a result of instability in Württemberg and the hardening of attitudes towards him in Bavaria, as we see from the official records of Ingolstadt, Nuremberg, and Saxony-Anhalt. The fallout from the suppression of the Anabaptists in the north may also have made this region too dangerous for someone regularly perceived as unconventional. Faustus may have used the waterways to travel much of the distance from Batenburg, lying on the River Meuse (Maas), to Lixheim, bypassing turbulent Württemberg altogether, and the Rhine would have taken him directly into Basel. Using these routes he could have travelled swiftly from the last dated reference to him in Münster in 1535 to the locations given by Gast for around the year 1535.

The Devil's Brother-in-Law

The fantastical stories gathering about Faustus even penetrated Luther's religious cocoon. In 1537 Antonius Lauterbach made a record of a conversation he and others had had with Luther:

> Mention was made of magicians and the magic art, and how Satan blinded men. Much was said about Faustus, who called the Devil his brother-in-law, and the remark was made: 'If I, Martin Luther, had given him even my hand, he would have destroyed me; but I would not have been afraid of him, – with God as my protector, I would have given him my hand in the name of the Lord.'[23]

A sense of fear is tangible in Luther's words. If he had given Faustus his hand, by which he may mean to imply agreement rather than simply physical contact, then he believed that he would have been 'destroyed' (*vorterbet*). This confession immediately led him to state that he would not have been afraid, suggesting either that he was indeed afraid (by a counter-intuitive psychological reading of this passage), or was concerned that his remark would be interpreted in that way. Luther then changed his tack and asserted that he would have given Faustus his hand because God would have protected him from anything that Faustus could throw at him, including association with the forces of darkness. He acknowledged that the likes of Faustus possessed some power – in this case the power to destroy Luther – and struggled to assert that his God-given authority was greater.

Wierus told a story with a similar element. Continuing his beard theme after recounting the story of Dorstenius, Wierus wrote of 'another acquaintance of mine, whose beard was black and whose face was rather dark and showed signs of melancholy (for he was splenetic)' who 'approached Faustus'. On seeing this foreboding individual, Faustus hailed him, 'I surely thought you were my brother-in-law and therefore I looked to your feet to see whether long curved claws projected from them'. Wierus took care to explain to his readers that Faustus was 'comparing him to the Devil, whom he thought to be entering and whom he used to call his brother-in-law.'[24] It sounds more like a joke at the expense of Faustus's wife – the reference to an in-law would suggest that he had one – or perhaps a sixteenth-century mother-in-law joke. It hardly deserves the sinister connotations that Wierus gave it, making it look as though he is grasping at straws.

Luther and Wierus would certainly have been aware of a similar line from the Bible. During Jesus's disputation on the Mount of Olives, he insulted his opponents by saying 'Ye are of your father the Devil' (John, 8:44). By reporting that Faustus himself called the Devil his brother-in-law, a similar form of rhetorical device was being employed to blacken his image. The implication is that Faustus was so thoroughly aligned with the Power of Darkness that he was in effect related to it.

However, the exact wording used by Luther is open to another interpretation. When Luther said '*welcher den Teufel seinen schwoger hies*' he could also have meant that the Devil was Faustus's coach-driver, meaning that he was the one who led him on. The word *Schwoger* – usually *Schwager* – can mean either 'brother-in-law' as it is everywhere translated, or 'coach-driver', especially the driver of a post coach, in old fashioned usage. To be driven by the Devil makes much more sense in this context, but Wierus had evidently heard 'brother-in-law' stories and wrote about them in less ambiguous Latin.

The death of clients and possibly patrons like Georg III and von Sickingen and the multiplication of religious zealots like Trithemius, Mutianus and Dr Klinge might account for the changing attitude towards Faustus. The Humanists were being overwhelmed by the bigots. Where once Reuchlin had faced the Inquisition because of his promotion of Hebrew, Luther would grow frothy mouthed with his venom against the Jews. The Reformation was slowly strangling the Renaissance.

The developing Protestant antagonism towards Faustus could also account for his apparent migration southwards. Curiously, it had always been Catholic prelates, like Georg III and possibly von Wied and von Waldeck, or Humanist nobles, like von Sickingen and Philipp von Hutten, who had sought his services. It is a tentative suggestion; after all, Basel was no stranger to Reformation thought and yet apparently Faustus received some degree of welcome there, if we are to believe Gast. The *Klosterordnung* had destroyed his onetime haven at Maulbronn and the Lixheim story suggests that he was still using the services provided by the monasteries. Later references would indicate that he found his final refuge in Swabia, deep in the vast tracts of the Black Forest.

19

The Wages of Sin
(1537–1538?)

It is a common proverb in *Germany*, that although a Conjurer have all things at commandment, the day will come that he shall not be worth a penny: so is it like to fall out with Doctor *Faustus*, in promising the Devil so largely.
– P.F.[1]

As the end drew near, the Faustus of legend turned to women for comfort, and to one woman in particular. His lusts unsated by those devilish concubines, there was still one woman yet who could outdo them all. According to the Faustbook, in the twenty-third year of his pact, Faustus invoked Helen of Troy and made her his wife. What were the wages of sin for Faustus? He had wealth and women, and the most beautiful woman of all. The wages of sin were the same as they are for all of us: death (Romans, 6:23).

The male view of womankind in the sixteenth century was a witch's cauldron of fear and desire heated to boiling point. This was nowhere more obvious than in the art of the period. When Hieronymous Bosch (1450–1516) depicted the creation of woman, he saw it as part of a continuum from the fall of Lucifer and the rebel angels from heaven to the expulsion of Adam and Eve from the Garden of Eden: Lucifer fell because of man and man fell because of woman. Hans Baldung Grien (*c.* 1484–1545) wove the contradictions of longing and loathing together in his paintings *The Three Ages of Woman and Death* completed in 1510 – the same year he executed his famous *The Witches' Sabbath* woodcut – *Eve, the Serpent, and Death* (*c.* 1520–1525) and *Death and the Maiden* (1518–20). These works contain a moralising message of *vanitas*, of the transience of life, that challenges female beauty with the death mask we all must wear.

There are no contemporary references to Faustus having a wife or mistresses, except that curious remark he is reported to have made about the Devil being his brother-in-law, which scarcely balances the oft-made accusation of sodomy. Both are as trivial and as false as the other, culled from the sixteenth-century repertoire of insults. The legend has its own answers. Marlowe's Faustus demands of his spirit 'let me have a wife, the fairest maid in Germany, for I am wanton and lascivious, and cannot live without a wife.'[2] In the Faustbook he cannot marry, is forbidden to do so by the monkish Mephistopheles, because 'wedlock is a chief institution ordained of God' and Faustus has contracted to defy God.[3]

Religious rhetoric is at work again. In the lines of the Faustbook we read an inversion of the Lutheran directive that every man should marry and a deliberate attack on the Catholic ideal of a celibate (unmarried) clergy. The barb against Rome was made all the more obvious coming out of the mouth of a devil in the form of a monk. Faustus must have heard such things in his own day. He may have read Johann Eberlin von Günzburg's (1465–1530) pamphlet published in 1522 with the long-winded explanatory title 'How very dangerous it is, if a Priest has no Spouse. How Unchristian and Harmful to the general well-being those People are, who prevent Priests from attaining the State of Matrimony'. Or he may have been subjected to such diatribes from someone like the Nuremberg preacher Osiander who put the Reformist position forcefully when accosting a young audience in 1533: 'Thus, my dear little children, you must not think that it is up to your own free will whether to marry or not … For God has commanded that we should all marry.'[4]

That Mephistopheles appears as a monk in the Faustbook amplifies this critique of Catholicism. The Reformer Urbanus Rhegius (1489–1541) told anyone who would listen that 'every monk is a whorer either in secret or in public.'[5] The Holy See was itself the Whore of Babylon. Even the enlightened Erasmus advocated marriage in no uncertain but clearly polemical terms: marriage was divinely ordained but contradicted by monastic vows.

However, it was not just a Lutheran perspective that praised wedlock. Looking at a wide range of sixteenth century pamphlets produced in Germany, we find that both Protestant and Catholic writers saw marriage and the family as the bedrock of social order, and consequently attributed both religious and political crises to the breakdown of marriage and the family.[6] Thus Faustus's unmarried status is a further challenge to the social order. It reinforces his threat as an outsider. It is a threat that is also amplified in his choice of mistress. After wallowing in the pleasures of a harem of devilish concubines, the Faustus of legend desires something even more delectable: 'he had a great desire to lie with fair *Helena of Greece*.'[7]

Mephistopheles was obliging – now that the tricky question of marriage was behind them – and Faustus was smitten: 'Sweet Helen, make me immortal with a kiss' (Marlowe, v.1.104). Helen of Troy, as we know her now, seems to have reciprocated and, as the Faustbook puts it, 'in time she was with child'.[8] A miraculous son was born with the gifts of prophecy and divination, and Faustus named him 'Justus Faustus'.

Helen is a classical Eve, 'the face that launched a thousand ships', as Marlowe put it so well, whose actions wrought the destruction of the heroes Hector and Achilles – 'And burnt the topless towers of Ilium' (Marlowe, v.1.102, 103) – engulfing the Greek world in war. She is also the epitome of the breakdown of marriage. Married to Menelaus, King of Sparta, she was seduced by Paris, son of the King of Troy, and eloped with him. The motif of the apple even occurred at the beginning of the myth when Paris was commanded to judge which of the goddesses Hera, Athene and Aphrodite was the most beautiful and present the winner with a golden apple.

The relationship between Helen and Faustus little occupied the attention of the Faustbook. She appeared, they (or Faustus at any rate) fell in love, a son was born – that is the sum of it. Yet she was the crowning glory. When Faustus had all the world's knowledge, all the riches he desired, Helen was his final trophy. Goethe's humble Gretchen is a poor substitute for this exotic, classical queen. Through the German association of death and women in the sixteenth century, Helen also becomes a sign of the end. Where the maiden is, there also is death.

As the hour of doom approached in the legend, Faustus called for 'a Notary and certain masters' and set down his will, making everything over to his faithful Wagner. The spurious document listed a house and garden, a farm, 1,600 'gilders', a gold chain, plate and 'other household stuff'.[9] As a reward for his loyal service, Faustus granted Wagner a final wish. Wagner asked for Faustus's 'cunning'. Faustus granted it, along with all of his books, on the condition that he 'love and peruse my books well'. Faustus also added a familiar spirit for Wagner, called Auerhanen in the Wolfenbüttel Manuscript, but later changed to Akercocke by P.F. He placed another condition upon his servant, that he 'publish my cunning, and my merry conceits, with all that I have done (when I am dead) in an history.'[10] It was an ingenious device of the Faustbook. Added to the first-person pacts it gave the legend the greater appearance of reality. An incautious sixteenth-century reader would have been entirely gulled by the subterfuge. Even the publisher himself may have truly believed that he was bringing Faustus's own account of his life to the public.

If Faustus had anything to bequeath to another in his last days, then nothing of it remains. The tools of his esoteric trade, like the ephemerides he must have used to prepare his predictions for the Bishop of Bamberg and Philipp von Hutten, are no longer to be found. Such curiosities as have turned up over the years in the Knittlingen Fausthaus cannot be proven to have belonged to Faustus himself. The mundane stuff of his life has all been lost through neglect, wilful or not.

Helen and Justus were not to outlive him. As suddenly and strangely as they had come, so they vanished, leaving the world of men as the last breath left the body of Faustus. Where Spies was silent in 1587, Widmann felt compelled to add more in 1599 and had Justus make a parting address as if by way of explanation: 'I must hasten away, for my father is dead, and therefore my mother can have no abiding-place here, and must hie away too.'[11] Perhaps it was Widmann's explanation why that for all the thousands bearing the surname Faust or Faustus there is not to be found one legitimate descendent of Georgius Sabellicus Faustus.

For all its subtle tricks, the Faustbook cannot persuade us of the truth of Helen and little Justus, or of the will. In reality, like so much else of Faustus's life, we know little of his last days.

The Trial of Dr Faustus

There is something that did not happen to Faustus that by its absence becomes more meaningful. Faustus was never tried in a court of law, ecclesiastical or secular, for practising the magical art. Magic implied a pact with the Devil because the learnèd theologians refuted the fact that the magician could be independently powerful. The pact was also implied in all cases of witchcraft and the trial records are full of instances of accused witches confessing (usually under torture) how they had bound themselves to the Devil. Faustus practised magic, as he himself seems to have admitted, therefore Faustus must have made a pact with the Devil in support of which are his alleged additional and whimsical references to the Devil as his brother-in-law. Having formed a pact with the Devil, Faustus was as guilty as the witches of having fallen into heresy, even apostasy; why then did he not meet their fate?

One suggestion is that the Inquisition – and presumably everyone else – were too afraid to prosecute Faustus because of his close association with the Devil.[12] However, fear was what usually started the Inquisition lighting the faggots in the first place. We have seen how the reaction of some his contemporaries led them to call for extreme punishment. Thrown out of Ingolstadt, incarcerated at Batenburg and narrowly avoiding the authorities at Wittenberg, it was not fear that kept Faustus from the stake or the hangman's noose.

As a doctor, Faustus was of the patrician class, as a commander of the Knights of St John, he was a nobleman, and we know that he moved in aristocratic circles (von Sickingen, von Hutten, the Bishop of Bamberg), so could this association with the powerful have sheltered him from accusations of witchcraft? The historical record shows that witchcraft accusations have been made against popes, kings, queens and their courtiers, so the lords whether spiritual or temporal were not exempt and this would have been all the more certain for someone lower on the feudal scale. Social class was not protection enough, even in an age when most witches were drawn from the ranks of the poor.

However, holding the title of doctor, whether he was or not, may have conferred professional immunity upon Faustus. Writing in 1983, Leland Estes was astounded that he could find no evidence of a university-trained medical man having been executed for witchcraft in Europe. Christina Larner's close inspection of the record of witch-hunting in Scotland revealed that whilst almost every other occupation group and social category produced accused witches, there was not one physician, surgeon or apothecary on the list. It was not the title of doctor alone that had this special effect. For example, a doctor of theology in 1453 and a doctor of law in 1589 were both tried for witchcraft. It was being a doctor of medicine, or being involved in the officially sanctioned medical treatment of others that was the deciding factor. Medical professionals enjoyed a level of immunity that not even those higher in the feudal hierarchy benefited from: professional status was more important than social class.

Although he was described by Begardi as having claimed great skill in medicine, so far as we can deduce from the contemporary records, Faustus was not a doctor of medicine but of philosophy, if he was a doctor at all. Undoubtedly this meant that he enjoyed less shelter under the aegis of the profession. It could be the case that Faustus simply eluded capture. More than once we read of his making a hasty departure and in one case there is definite reference to an attempt to arrest him. Unfortunately, we do not know on what charges. Then there is the more or less legendary account of his imprisonment at Batenburg. Similarly, the perception of Faustus as a nigromancer and sodomite was enough to keep the gates of Nuremberg barred against him in 1532.

Another factor closely allied to this is Faustus's itinerant career. Most accusations of witchcraft are made by acquaintances and neighbours of the accused within relatively small social groups as a reprisal for misfortune or as part of a repertoire of female verbal violence and are usually only subsequently extended by the torture of the accused. As a scholar wandering between university and court, Faustus played no role in the petty squabbles of village politics (even when they were enacted in larger towns). The gender bias amongst those accused tends to reflect concerns over socially marginal and especially economically unproductive women, and were usually expressed by women themselves. Being a man made it statistically less likely to be accused of witchcraft, but far from impossible. Of far more importance is the fact that Faustus appears to have operated almost entirely outside of this social process of community conflict resolution. No fishwife or washerwoman held enough of a grudge against Faustus to denounce him. Instead such accusations as were made and have survived occurred within Faustus's own sphere of academia and Humanism.

Faustus was not an exception. Agrippa, Paracelsus, even Trithemius himself, all had reputations that could easily have given rise to accusations of witchcraft. Even as Trithemius was casting his aspersions he was defending himself against the rumours of black magic started by the alchemist and numerologist Carolus Bovillus and others, yet despite that, he was consulted by the Emperor on theological and magical matters. Court astrologers like Virdung were common; astrology was fashionable. Alchemy was also of interest to lordlings with cash flow problems and impoverished scholars looking to turn their knowledge into hard currency. Like Faustus, Agrippa and Paracelsus were wandering scholars, and Trithemius was safely cloistered for most of his life. They were not likely to be accused of having curdled a neighbour's milk.

Conceptions of social power flowing from gender and professional status contrived to make Faustus and those in a similar position less likely to be tried for witchcraft. Where witches were generally held to be ignorant women by a structurally misogynistic society, the magicians made great store of their learning. The magicians themselves constructed a protective discourse in which they clearly demarcated themselves from the witches.[13] Someone like Trithemius could invoke that considerable learning in his defence, showing how the possession of magical books did not taint him and demonstrating that his was a natural magic entirely compatible with Humanistic Christianity. Unlike the village gossips who used the accusation of witchcraft, the Humanists and Humanist-magicians such as Trithemius employed a rhetoric of folly and sexual misdemeanour to attack their opponents. It is only later in the discourse of the Reformation that the situation changes, notably when the Devil-obsessed Luther broaches the subject and by then Faustus was nearing the end of his natural life, if not actually dead.

The case is not cut and dried and things might have gone differently for Faustus. In 1594 the Cologne newspaper *Warhafftige newe Zeitung* reported a recent case of witchcraft, describing a 'leader' or 'king' of the witches, a learnéd doctor who practised 'diabolical magic', and directly compared him to Faustus.[14] In 1589 Dr Dietrich Flade (1534–1589) had been tried and convicted of witchcraft. Could Faustus have ended up like Flade?

Flade was a doctor, but a doctor of law, not medicine or philosophy. He was professor of law at the University of Trier and later dean of the faculty and rector. He was head of the civil courts in Trier – one of the highest judicial positions in Germany – and advisor to the Archbishops of Trier. Flade not only held high office, but was also one of the wealthiest men in town; his annual income was greater than that of the whole city. Neither professional immunity – granted that Flade was not a medical man – nor social rank were sufficient to save him. Not even his own legal acumen served. His sophisticated defence crumbled under repeated torture and corroborative evidence was tortured out of others until there could be no doubting the guilty verdict. However, there are several key factors to consider: there were political motivations behind this case and the trial itself occurred late in the sixteenth century, well after Faustus's own lifetime. The times had changed. Flade only resembled the legend put forth in the Faustbooks, not Faustus himself.

In the early sixteenth century, Europe experienced an overall lull in witch-hunting. The years from about 1490 to 1560 were relatively quiet and certainly after 1517 the Reformation movement pushed witchcraft into the background as it struggled to assert itself. Luther himself noted the change in 1535, saying:

> When I was a child there were many witches and sorcerers around … But now that the Gospel is here you do not hear so much about it.[15]

He ended by making a polemical thrust against the Roman Church as 'spiritual sorcery' with its worship of saints and sale of indulgences, and everything else he railed against – most of it not actually what we would consider to be witchcraft at all. However, there really was an underground movement that sought to overthrow the established social and religious order, and that practised the Black Mass, that is, a deliberate parody of the Christian Mass (at least once). It was called Anabaptism. It has often been overlooked that the years 1520 to 1565 saw large numbers executed for heresy. Of some 3,000 executions for heresy in this period, about two-thirds of them were Anabaptists. The Anabaptists were both themselves accused and accused others of crimes familiar in witchcraft trials, especially Satanic conspiracy. Despite this discursive overlapping between religious heresy and witchcraft accusations, the two forms remained relatively discrete. The Anabaptists may have been accused of being in league with Satan, like the witches, but they were executed because they were Anabaptists, not witches. Nor should we overlook the upheaval of the Peasants' War, the motivation behind much of which was religiously inspired, or, at the very least, couched in religious language. All those who died fighting for a peasants' Christianity of primitive communism and self-determination had also strayed from the straight line of orthodoxy.

The reasons for these patterns are complicated, but there is a sense in which we can see the increase in witch-hunting towards the end of the century as a sublimated response to the division of Christendom into Protestantism and Catholicism. Following a comparatively mild period of Catholic censure of the Reform movement under Charles V, circumscribed as it was by the political necessity of retaining the support of the Lutheran lords, Protestantism had moved beyond academic theology to new levels of popularism where reasoned debate gave way to the arguments of the mob. Witch-hunting was a displacement of aggression towards the 'witchmongers', the Catholics, as Reginald Scot called them, or the 'heretic' Protestants, as well as an exaggerated and violent means of establishing group identity for both parties. By the mid-1560s the Anabaptist 'threat' had been neutralised through mass murder in the same way that the millenarian peasant movements had been crushed by force of arms, leaving the path to the courtroom free for all those petty complaints and wild accusations that are the bane of close-knit communities. The courts were also now equipped with a procedure and the experience of trying heresy that fitted well with the theorisation of heretical witchcraft that had begun a hundred or so years earlier, exemplified by the *Malleus Maleficarum*.

We also have to take into account the criminal legislation on witchcraft. Article 109 of the *Carolina* promulgated in 1532, prescribed the death sentence only for those crimes of witchcraft that resulted in the harm of another. Although Article 44 stated that association with anything that implied witchcraft was sufficient justification for the use of torture, Article 21 expressly removed divination from this list. While Faustus could have been accused of practising witchcraft – he was a self-confessed necromancer – we have no evidence that he harmed anyone. Poor Dr Dorstenius, shaven too close for comfort, and the pesky poltergeist of Lixheim are neither historically verified nor verifiable. It was only later in the century that witchcraft *per se* became the crime, regardless of whether anyone caused harm by it or not. If we look at the Criminal Constitutions of Electoral Saxony for 1572 we find that a pact or any sort of truck with the Devil becomes the crime, not the misuse of magic. The Palatinate revised its criminal code along similar lines in 1582. In the earlier part of the sixteenth century the limited criminalisation of witchcraft no doubt explained, in part, the relatively few witch trials leading to execution during this period.

Within his lifetime Faustus was accused of being a fraud, not a diabolist. He was branded a sodomite – a capital offence – but not a witch. He was denounced as a necromancer, but not a heretic (although Trithemius came close). The combination of several factors ensured that he did not end up like the unfortunate Flade. He lived in a time of relatively low witch-hunting and leniency towards magic; he enjoyed the privileged status of a scholar and lived outside the social conditions that commonly produced accusations of witchcraft. The wandering life alone was not safeguard against accusations of witchcraft as the numerous cases brought against beggars attest, but in combination with the scholarly life brought the individual the dual benefits of professional immunity and social distance. Such records as we do have show that his clients (the Bishop of Bamberg and von Hutten) sought his astrological services. Despite Trithemius's accusations, others took Faustus seriously, reinforcing the protective effect of his professional status.

That Faustus was not tried for witchcraft is one of the principal questions raised by his life. Writing in 1563, Wierus expressed his exasperation that Faustus and other 'infamous magicians' went unpunished, while hundreds of deluded old women were sent to their deaths. Even in the later legend material that sought to revise this apparent escape from punishment, Faustus was made to answer, not to the judge, but to the Devil.

The Devil's Due

No one knows exactly when or where Faustus died, or how. The generally accepted date to be found in dictionaries and encyclopaedias is 1540, but that is only an approximation, rounded to the nearest convenient decade. The death of Paracelsus on 24 September 1541 has perhaps confused the actual death of Faustus. According to Battus's Faustbook of 1592, Faustus's end comes on 23 October 1538. For once the Faustbook may not be entirely wrong. In 1539 he was mentioned, unflatteringly, in the *Index Sanitatis* of Philipp Begardi in such a way as to suggest that he was already dead.

Begardi probably wrote his *Index* in 1538 – the dedication is dated 8 January 1539, although it was published 20 August 1539 – and so the crucial passage 'several years ago' may indicate that Faustus died in the mid to late 1530s. Begardi's information may not have been accurate. People were often reported to have died when they had not and news of a death could take some time to circulate. Begardi's references to Faustus's wide travels and the divinatory arts rings true, and Begardi appears to have known people who had met Faustus. The real problem is that Begardi did not explicitly state that Faustus was dead.

Wierus provided a similar dating to Begardi's, although writing in 1568, when he said 'a few years prior to 1540 he [Faustus] practised [i.e., magic]'.[16] When Conrad Gesner wrote to his friend Johannes Crato in 1561 he only vaguely referred to 'a certain Faustus, who died not long ago'.[17] The *Zimmerische Chronik* said that Faustus had died 'around this time', which from the context is interpreted as 1541 from reference to the Regensburg Reichstag of that year.[18] The range of dates spans the three years from 1538 to 1541, but none of the sources is specific and all point to a date earlier than that given or inferred. Faustus probably died sometime between the last dated reference to him as being alive in 1535 and the earliest reference to his demise in 1538.

Everyone who has written about Faustus has been more concerned with the question of how he died. In 1548 Gast gave details of the manner of his end – or as Gast imagined it:

> Nevertheless, he was alloted a miserable, lamentable end, for he was suffocated by Satan, whose dead body on its bier continually turned its face to the ground, notwithstanding that it was five times turned back.[19]

Gast was the first to write of the death of Faustus, but assuredly not the last. In 1563 Manlius published the words of his master, Melanchthon, delivered sometime between 1554 and 1557, notably getting Faustus's name wrong:

> A few years previously this Johannes Faustus, on his last day, sat wholly dejected in a certain village in the Duchy of Württemberg. The host asked him why he was so gloomy, which was against his character and habits (he was otherwise a disgraceful good-for-nothing who led a corrupt life and was again and again nearly killed because of his libidiousness). Thereupon he said to the host in the

village: 'Do not be terrified this night.' In the middle of the night the house was shaken. When Faustus did not get up in the morning and by now being nearly midday, the host summoned others and entered his chamber to find him lying near the bed with his face turned round. In this way the Devil murdered him.[20]

There is no reason to suppose that Gast and Melanchthon (or Manlius) were known to one another, but their stories share a common element: the strange condition of Faustus's body. Manlius's version became the better known tale. Wierus, writing in 1568, gave almost exactly the same account of Faustus's death:

Here, at last, in a village in the Duchy of Württemberg, he was found dead close by his bed, his face turned about, and in the middle of the night before the house was shaken, that is how it was reported.[21]

It is clear whence Wierus derived his information, but his retelling was adding authority to the story. Philipp Camerarius (1537–1624), the son of Joachim Camerarius, repeated these details some years later, citing Wierus as his source.[22]

We can see that these separate accounts of Faustus's death somewhere in Württemberg are in fact all derived from Melanchthon. Melanchthon's account, in both Manlius's book and Andreas Hondorff's excerpts, was published frequently and widely in the late sixteenth century, giving his version greater force through repetition. The popularity of Spies's *Historia* of 1587 would imprint this violent death on people's perceptions of Faustus's final days.

A Magician and his Penance

In 1555 Melanchthon delivered another of his popular Sunday lectures, this time choosing as his subject 'a magician and his penance'. The story concerned an unnamed nobleman of Regensburg and is a piece of barefaced propaganda for Melanchthon's religious views. The story contains many points of similarity with his account of the death of Faustus and no doubt contributed to a certain confusion between the two accounts, leading to rumours that it was Faustus himself who died in Regensburg. We find the same dissolute life, the practice of magic, a pact with the Devil and a twisted corpse.

The nobleman 'led an extremely wicked life' practising magic, but when the Reformed faith reached Regensburg he started going to church and became remorseful. He transformed himself into a model of piety and lived to an old age. On his deathbed he called his friends round him and confessed that he had made a pact with the Devil. He was confident that his new found piety would deliver his soul out of the Devil's clutches, but consequently warned his friends that the Devil would 'rage against my body and deform it'. As he breathed his last 'there was rumbling and such disturbance that the house appeared to collapse'. Terrified, his friends ran off, returning later to find that the Devil had 'twisted the dead man's face against his back'.[23]

It is of course a comfort to the Christian, and especially the Protestant in this case, to think that magicians and sorcerers would eventually tremble before God and repent of their former ways. Even today the sentiment is held as a vouchsafe of the righteousness of the Faith and the Christian fold is duly full of those who claim to have been saved from a life of wickedness in the practice of magic.

What we see here is that the reports of Faustus's death in fact conform to a type. They should not be seen as in any way accurate, but simply versions of the same desire to vindicate the writers' belief and punish, with a rod of words, those who infringe their arbitrary morals. As we read in Psalms (146:9): 'the way of the wicked he turneth upside down.'

Even though Melanchthon (through Manlius) had padded out the spare scene described by Gast, his vague mention of a village in Württemberg leaves us scratching our heads. It is left to the relatively late *Zimmerische Chronik* of around 1565 to give us the name of Faustus's final destination: 'finally, in the manor of Staufen in Breisgau, at a great age, he was slain by an evil spirit.' While many have taken the town of Staufen itself as the place intended, the *Zimmerische Chronik* was less certain: 'Faustus died in or not far from Staufen, a town in Breisgau.'[24]

Today Staufen is part of Baden-Württemberg, but in historical maps of the mid-1500s Breisgau is shown as a separate region. Breisgau was a Habsburg possession and part of the Austrian Circle that included Styria. Melanchthon's testimony may or may not be taken as supporting evidence for the *Zimmerische Chronik*'s identification of Staufen (or near Staufen) as the location of Faustus's death.

The essential problem with the *Zimmerische Chronik* is that it is already party to the legend formation around Faustus. There are also textual similarities to other stories about both Faustus and other magicians that are often seen to discredit it. The *Chronik* cannot be dismissed on these grounds alone. Almost all of the sources we have are part of the legend formation and provide a less than objective view of Faustus. That there are similarities with other stories told about Faustus and other magicians may indicate, not derivation, but that the *Chronik* is drawing on the same magical tradition as revealed in the grimoire. There are also reasons to suppose that the author of the *Chronik* knew what he was talking about. He was something of a black magician himself.

The *Zimmerische Chronik* was written by Count Froben Christoph von Zimmern with assistance from his secretary Hans Müller (d. 1600). He had acquired part of Archbishop Herman von Wied's book collection, including his copy of Agrippa's *Occult Philosophy*, and as hinted earlier, there is a possibility that the Archbishop had been personally acquainted with Faustus. Christoph's father Johann Werner II (1488–1548), a contemporary of Faustus, was also interested in the Dark Arts. Before his death he had burnt his magical books and warned his sons Johann Christoph (1516–c. 1553), Froben Christoph and Gottfried Christoph (c. 1524–c. 1566) against following the left hand path. Both Johann and Gottfried evidently took heed and entered the church, becoming canons in Strassburg and later Cologne, while Froben became intrigued. Froben, like his father, would eventually abandon the occult, and some of that late fear of the forbidden arts entered into his *Chronik*. It is unlikely that Froben and Faustus crossed paths. In the 1530s the young student was to be found in Tübingen (1533), Strassburg and Bourges (1533–1534), Cologne (1536–1537), Louvain (1537–1539) and Paris (1539–1540), where he is believed to have attempted some alchemical experiments.[25]

Lercheimer repeated the location given by Gast and Wierus, although he was forced to try and refute an idea that was in circulation and would acquire dominance through Spies in 1587:

> He was strangled by the Devil in a village in Württemberg, not at Kimlich near Wittenberg, because there is nowhere a village of that name. For after he ran away to avoid capture, he was never allowed to return to Wittenberg.[26]

All of the Faustbooks are generally agreed that Faustus was in the vicinity of Wittenberg and was carried off by the Devil in fulfilment of his pact. The Wolfenbüttel Manuscript, Spies and P.F. all gave Rimlich, not Kimlich as Lercheimer thought, but in any case Lercheimer was right: there is nowhere called either Kimlich or Rimlich. The English traveller Fynes Moryson had heard the story, too, when he visited Wittenberg in 1591, but despite exploring the surrounding villages could find no one to verify it.

Alexander Tille listed fifty references to the death of Faustus in his colossal *Faustsplitter*. Although many were literary references, it is not surprising to find that there are other traditions that give other final locations for Faustus. Amongst these we find Prague, as we saw earlier, Cologne, Regensburg, Königsberg (Kaliningrad), Cappel on the Baltic coast, and the castle of Waerdenberg (Wardenburg) in Holland even has the 'evidence' of an indelible bloodstain to support its claim. Other Wittenberg traditions maintain that the place in question was a small village called Pratau, some three kilometres away. Here in a tavern called 'Freischütz' Faustus met his end. Even Knittlingen and Maulbronn are mentioned.[27]

Like all of the suggestions we have examined so far, none of these other alternatives is entirely credible. However, there is a geographical similarity between the report of Melanchthon and the *Chronik* that is suggestive. Given what biased, unreliable and incomplete reports we have, I am more persuaded by Melanchthon and especially the *Chronik*, than the Faustbook or any of the other legends.

On a steep knoll the imposing ruins of a castle perch dramatically like a ragged old eagle. Vineyards crawl down the slopes, adding to the romantic charm, to find the town of Staufen nestling at their foot. The castle had been raised in the thirteenth century by the Lords of Staufen, Bailiffs of St Trudpert's monastery. In its shelter a settlement had prospered and in the fourteenth century was granted the right of calling itself a town. A defensive wall and ditch once enclosed it with two gates – the Bürgerturm in the north and the Malefizturm in the south – controlling access. Staufen today still has a prosperous air, but gone are the days when silver mining made it rich. Documented as early as the eleventh century, the silver mines in the surrounding Münstertal were the prized possession of the von Staufens. In the thirteenth and fourteenth centuries the family was extracting approximately 230 grams of silver per ton annually, a fifth of all the precious metal yield of the Black Forest. But by about 1535 the once rich seams were petering out.

Witchcraft trials are documented from 1523 to 1632, raising once more the phantom of a judicial end to Faustus's life. However, the belief is that Faustus was invited to the town by the local lord Antonius von Staufen (1523–1567) and a connection has been made between the declining family fortunes and Faustus's reputation as an alchemist.[28]

According to the late sixteenth-century *Schwäbische Chronick* of Martin Crusius (1526–1607), Antonius von Staufen was well-educated and intelligent. The account is eulogistic and should be taken with a pinch of salt; nevertheless, we find someone who had attended university and taken definite steps to broaden his mind.

At university he shared the lecture hall with Nicolai von der Stroß from Basel. In 1537 Nicolai purchased a book printed in Basel by Heinrich Peter (or Petri, 1508–1579). It was Sebastian Münster's treatise on designing sundials bound together with a 1532 edition of the *Quadrans Apiani*, a scientific work on astronomical instruments printed by Peter Apian (1495–1552). On the leaf facing the title page of the *Quadrans* is a mysterious inscription written in a hand other than Nicolai's: '*Zwanzig, Zwanzig nahest wan*'. The writing trails off as if something devilish had overcome the writer. It was found many years later in the attic of a house on Staufen's Spitalstraße. The reference to the number twenty (*zwanzig*) has been related to Faustus's supposed twenty-four year pact and it has been suggested that it was Faustus himself who wrote it in 1537 with just four years left to run.[29]

As attractive as that is, the supposition is based on two things that are less than true: that Faustus signed a pact, and that he died in 1541. In addition, the script requires considerable powers of imagination to be decipherable at all and there appears to be more written than can be easily transcribed. Still, a connection with a scholar who had come from Basel is not out of the question given Faustus's probable visit to the city in the mid to late 1530s.

Nicolai did not study at Basel as far as we can tell, but at the University of Freiburg. His name appeared in the same list as Erasmus – a professor of theology there in 1533 – and 'Wernherus Wÿga de Zÿmern', identified as a presbyter in the diocese of Konstanz. Antonius von Staufen, through his father's marriage to his second wife Agnes, was related to the von Zimmerns. Both Antonius (matriculated 1534) and Nicolai (matriculated 1533) had studied together with another of Froben's relatives, Gottfried von Zimmern (matriculated 1535), in Freiburg. Wilhelm Werner von Zimmern had held the post of rector. Thus we can trace ties of kinship and friendship that bring the families of von Staufen and von Zimmern together, suggesting the possibility that Froben got the information he needed for his *Chronik* either from Antonius or through one of his relatives.

Antonius was in his teens when he apparently issued his invitation to Faustus, but after the death of his father in 1523 he and his brother Hans (1523–1545) were the sole heirs to the estate and responsibility was thrust early upon them. For whatever reason, Faustus was not invited to stay with Antonius in the castle. The inn where he supposedly stayed dates from 1407 and more or less took its present shape in 1536, so it is clearly old enough to have received its infamous guest. Things did not go according to plan. According to local folklore Faustus died in an explosion shortly after arriving and the so-called Devil's footprint in the town hall is all that remains. Whether he was successful in producing gold or not – and it seems not – Antonius was forced to pawn his possessions in 1549 for a large loan to meet his mounting debts.[30]

Certainly the people of Staufen firmly believe that Faustus died there. In a corner of the market square, under the sign of a leaping lion, is the inn *Zum Löwen* where almost 500 years earlier, as local folklore has it, a certain Dr Faustus died under mysterious circumstances. According to tradition, Faustus stayed in room no. 5 and died downstairs in the *Fauststube*, the room reputed to have been Faustus's laboratory. It is a cosy room, three-quarter panelled in a mock medieval, Gothic revival style of the early twentieth century. Six painted scenes are set above the wainscoting depicting the life and death of Faustus with captions. On the outside of the lobster-pink inn is a large mural. Above a towering mass of black letter Gothic recounting his terrible end, it shows a man falling to his hands and knees. A Devil the colour of putrid flesh with extended bat wings reaches up to grasp the man whilst another figure stands above him, hands fastened to his neck.[31]

The Devil's Polemic

But he is not quite dead yet. In the Faustbook the final moments are drawn out with relish. Faustus laid on another banquet and filled his guests up with wine before announcing that 'he had many wonderful matters to tell them'. He delivered a lengthy and impassioned speech in which he revealed that he had promised 'body and soul' to the Devil for all that he had achieved in his life and that now 'this dismal day those twenty-four years are fully expired, for night beginning my hour-glass is at an end.'[32]

It was just the sort of confession an inquisitor could have wrung from him on the rack. Faustus's purpose in inviting his friends to his end, according to the Faustbook, was to bid them a final *adieu* and warn them against following a similar path. He delivered a gushing sermon about having God always before one's eyes and visiting church a lot. He ended with the familiar advice about paying no heed to any strange noises in the night and requested that his friends give him a Christian burial: 'and so I wish you a quiet night, which unto me notwithstanding will be horrible and fearful.'[33] It was a fine speech, surely stirring to Christian hearts, but utterly false. There are clear echoes of Gast's account and Melanchthon's Regensburg nobleman.

His shocked guests called upon him to repent, but Faustus countered their efforts by saying that, like Cain, his sins were too great for God to forgive. Furthermore, there were the contracts themselves, sealed with his own blood. His guests prayed for him and left the room weeping.

Faustus lingered, reflecting on his life. His friends lay in their beds, wide-awake in expectation of the end. The clock relentlessly ticked on, their terror mounting, until between midnight and one o'clock 'there blew a mighty storm of wind.' The students rose and comforted one another, but as yet did not dare to venture forth, while 'the Host of the house ran out of doors, thinking the house would fall.' With the storm raging around them they next perceived 'a mighty noise and hissing, as if the hall had been full of Snakes and Adders.' The door to Faustus's room burst open with some unseen force and they heard his plaintive cries of 'Murder! Murder!' The voice sounded strangely hollow and after a while was heard no more.[34]

In the morning the students summoned enough courage to venture into the hall where they had left Faustus the previous evening. P.F.'s description is wonderfully gory. The hall is spattered with blood, globs of brain are stuck to the walls, in one corner lie his eyes, in another his teeth. His body, 'most monstrously torn, and fearful to behold', is found outside on a pile of horse dung.[35]

There are few today who would so readily believe that the Devil had beaten him to death, so it is not idle to speculate on other possible causes. In 1930 Harold Meek tried to fathom the mystery, considering the various guises the Grim Reaper might have assumed, from the natural – epidemic, arteriosclerosis, kidney failure and syphilis – to the unnatural – murder, accidental explosion and suicide by strychnine poisoning. He concluded that after suffering from syphilis for years – the cause of his bombastic outbursts and decline of his career – he had taken his own life with a lethal dose of strychnine. Meek's diagnosis is colourful. The effects of syphilis might explain some of his reported behaviour (and the source whence he contracted it) and the administration of strychnine could account for the contorted state of the dead body. A verdict of suicide could also explain why there is no known grave. More recently, but less convincingly, Thomas Weber suggested that Faustus was strangled and robbed by a beggar, for which there is not the slightest evidence. While these theories are at least plausible, there is a simpler and more convincing explanation.

We cannot trust the reports of Faustus's behaviour or of the condition of his body after death, so neither of these factors give any substance to Meek's theory. In reality, there was no pact and the Devil did not come for him; nor did he have need of the strychnine bottle. Old age was cause enough. In the *Zimmerische Chronik* he is described as having died at a 'great age'.[36] Faustus was at this time aged about seventy and living without the ministrations of modern medicine. The reputation he subsequently acquired is sufficient to explain the absence of a grave marker.

The world has been blinded by the more dramatic fictions that surround the life and death of this magician. When such an obviously devout man as Trithemius could so easily and quickly acquire a sulphurous reputation, how much more likely that someone like Faustus, operating outside the Church, would be seen as an agent of the Devil? In death Faustus had completed his transformation from Renaissance magus to Reformation bogeyman.

In the writings of the times, the Devil became a pawn in a game of religious retribution, the so-called *Teufelspolemik*. Just as Melanchthon could gloat on the details of Faustus's death at the hands of the Devil, so the forces of Counter-Reformation meted out the same fate to the Reformers. For example, Guazzo reported that 'It was noted as a fact that when Martin Luther died at Eisleben, the demons flew to his funeral from those who were possessed.'[37] More pointedly, Guazzo wrote that 'in 1566, through the mouth of a demoniac woman at Laon, a demon in the hearing of all mocked at the Calvinists, crying out that he had nothing to fear from them since they were his friends and allies.'[38] In an age when both Catholics and Protestants portrayed each other, and others such as the Anabaptists, as the Devil's disciples, someone like Faustus operating on the verges of heresy and outside the protective circle of organised religion was a safe and obvious target for the same accusations. When we further consider how like religions both alchemy and especially astrology were at this time, we find another cause for Faustus's denouncement. He was clearly seen to belong to a group, Wierus's 'infamous magicians', that professed their own enchanted worldview and in doing so contested that of all the others.

For all the obvious propaganda that embellishes the story of Faustus, it really is as if the Devil had carried him off to hell. No tomb shelters his mortal remains, no epitaph is inscribed to his memory, no grave marks his end. His final moments have been subverted by his enemies. We do not know for certain where and when he died, or under what circumstances. 500 years on he still lives in legend as the greatest, most notorious magician of the Renaissance. Perhaps now we can remember him for different reasons, for reasons more truthful than the stories that have chased his memory like furies down all those long years.

Epilogue: A Damnable Life?

During his lifetime Faustus had acquired a black reputation, but it was nothing to the one he would acquire after death. In life he was the Prince of Necromancers, the Second Magus, an equal of Jesus, a philosopher ranked amongst Plato and Aristotle, who could foretell the future better than any other astrologer of his age – as he apparently told his audiences. In death he became the blackest of black magicians.

The diabolical Faustus was born in the *Tischreden* of Luther and his circle, raised in the *Erfurt Chronicle* (Reichmann-Wambach, *c.*1570–1580), augmented by Christoff Roshirt (*c.*1570–1575), expanded in the Wolfenbüttel Manuscript (*c.*1580), revisited by Lercheimer (1585), codified in Spies (1587), 'Englished' by P.F. (1592) and engorged by Widmann (1599). When Marlowe added his genius to the story its essential elements were carved in stone. It was a sixteenth-century blockbuster combining the energy and restless curiosity of Renaissance man, the religious fear and fervour of Reformation and the expansionism of the Elizabethan age. But for all the popular appeal and literary fireworks, it was still a witch-hunt against a dead man.

It has been a long overdue task to try and uncover the man behind the myth. Many have fallen into the endless rut of literary criticism, arguing over how many Fausts can dance on the nib of Goethe's pen, leaving the sixteenth century sources dusty and unread. The few other writers who have turned their attention to the historical Faustus have often, disappointingly and uncritically, been only too willing to acquiesce in the character assassination begun by Trithemius.

On the basis of all we have discovered here we can say that, in all probability, Faustus was born in Helmstadt or Heidelberg on 23 April 1466, that he studied at Heidelberg University from 1483 to 1487, completed his obligatory two years of teaching and afterwards sought his fortune as a wandering scholar engaged in the great projects of his day – astrology, alchemy and magic – and that he died in the vicinity of Staufen in 1538, at the latest, his name already blackened by the libellous, ignominious ink of his foes.

He was not called Johannes Faust or Faustus. His real name was variously recorded by the university authorities of Heidelberg as Georgius Helmstetter, Jorio de Helmstat,

Jeorius de Helmstat, Georio de Helmstadt and Jeorius Halmstadt. Some years later he adopted the nom de plume of Georgius Sabellicus Faustus Junior. This was a Renaissance code linking him with two popular Humanists of the period: Marcus Antonius Sabellicus and Publius Faustus Andrelinus. In time this became shortened to just Doctor Faustus.

He lived on his wits and enjoyed certain successes as well as defeats, but only briefly benefited from the security of an official position. What we know of Faustus shows that during his lifetime he travelled widely throughout Germany with a possible foray here and there into other countries, that he had some illustrious clients and that theologians and their ilk reviled him. It is unlikely that he ever tried to conjure a spirit called Mephistopheles and almost certain that he did not sign a pact, or believed that he had signed a pact, with the Devil or any of his agents. He undoubtedly had a greater reputation than the scattering of historical references suggest. Influential men such as Trithemius – who had the Emperor's ear – and Luther and his disciple Melanchthon – all had at one time or another the name of Faustus on their lips. By all accounts he was boastful, but no more so than the people who levelled that accusation at him. In an age that excelled at defamatory polemics, we can hardly take any of the accusations made against him seriously.

History, as always, has much to teach us and the sixteenth century in particular. We see how war always leads to war until the opponents run out of resources, immaterial as well as material. We see how belief begets strife when it is unmitigated by compassion. We see how magic and science are always part of the same project to explain and predict the vagaries of fate, and ultimately master the universe. We also see the centrality of magic, both theoretically and socially, in Faustus's age. In looking for Faustus we have searched that much neglected twilight side of the Renaissance and learnt something of its secrets.

The parallels with our own times and those of Faustus are not with Nazi Germany, American foreign policy, or environmental disaster, but with the tension between religious fundamentalism and liberal pluralism. There is a striking similarity between the eclectic esotericism of the sixteenth century – that dizzying amalgam of Hermeticism, astrology, alchemy and magic – and the sprawling spirituality of the New Age today. If we can believe that sub-atomic particles can spontaneously appear and disappear, and be in two different places at once, how much closer are we to the beliefs of the sixteenth century than we realise?

We can find rational explanations for almost all of the tricks and wonders ascribed to Faustus. Blooming winter gardens, out of season produce, 'magical' banquets – all can be explained as the application of the techniques of greenhousing and refrigeration, techniques that have an ancient history. As we see in the pages of Reginald Scot's *Discoverie of Witchcraft*, the illusionist's craft was well developed in the sixteenth century with trick knives, rigged sets and all the other apparatus of deception. Even the transmutation of base metals into gold can itself be explained with reference to poorly understood techniques of purifying metals and the imprecision of assaying at the time, without condemning all of the art as charlatanry.

All of what Trithemius claimed to be able to do with the aid of spirits, we can do now with the aid of electronics. By accelerating lead atoms to enormous speeds and smashing them together we can produce gold. Other forms of magic may now be labelled under the less threatening headings of hypnosis, psychotherapy, neuro-linguistic programming and parapsychology, but they are still unexplained. We are living now in the world the Renaissance magicians dreamt of.

But there is something left over that we can never really explain. There are still those who sign pacts with the infernal powers and claim that it works, and there are still those who believe themselves tempted by the Devil. I once even met a man who claimed to have seen him. There is still a thirst for hidden and forbidden powers.

We have penetrated the sulphurous smokescreen started by Trithemius and enflamed in the Faustbooks, seen through the romantic shimmer conjured up by Goethe and the dark shadows of modernism cast by Spengler, to find the real man, as much as we could. If there is a message here, it is that truth always dies to serve political ends and partisan interests. We should always distrust the Trithemiuses of this world who seek to ruin men for their own gain. And when we remember Faustus we should not think of the pact-making diabolist, but of a Renaissance magician, both representative and victim of his age.

Notes

Chapter 1

1. Ziolkowski, 2000; Russell, 1986:58, said much the same thing.
2. Tille, 1899 and 1900; Shuh, 1952; Aign, 1975; Prodolliet, 1978; Mahal, c.1980:6; Meier, 1990: 685–820; Durrani, 2004:4.
3. For example, neither Shumaker, 1979, nor Walker, 2000, mention him in their studies of Renaissance magic; in his history of the Devil from the early modern period, Russell, 1986:58, gives only a paragraph to the historical person of Faustus and inadequately sums up his career in a sentence, and both Mebane, 1989:53, and Clark, 1997:405, make only passing reference.
4. Würzburg cod. o. Sign., quoted in Brann, 1999:105.
5. Luther, 1912–21, no. 1059.
6. For: Witkowski, 1896/7; Henning, 1959; and Mahal, 1980. Against: Petsch, 1910; Beutler, 1936; and Baron, 1983.
7. A species of chapbook (*Volksbuch* in the German), a broad genre of popular legend, referring here to the full length treatments of Faustus, beginning with the Wolfenbüttel Manuscript, Spies's *Historia* and the many works derived from it, including P.F.'s English adaptation. Generally, when I use the term it is to Wolfenbüttel, Spies and P.F. that I am referring.
8. Quotations from Mackenney, 1993:216–7.
9. Quoted in Tille, 1900:74–5.
10. I have used the form of his name as it appears in the 1587 *Historia*, but other variations are recorded.
11. Milchsack, 1892; Füssel and Kreutzer, 1988:224–33; Baron, 1992.
12. Könneker, 1991, for example, argued that it was entertainment, whilst Baron, 1992:155, convincingly argued that it would have been seen as non-fiction had such a category existed. Füssel and Kreutzer, 1988:334, highlighted its paradoxical nature.
13. Lercheimer, 1888:41–3; Baron, 1992:38, 55–8.
14. Henning, 1966:430–45.

Chapter 2

1. Durrius (also Durrii, or Dürr), 1676 (published 1726), and Neumann, 1683, for example.
2. Out of 48 sixteenth-century sources – not counting other editions of the same work (unless where different), or references to literature or plays – there are 38 references to 'Faustus' against only three to 'Faust' with the rest being indeterminate variations.

Furthermore, this is not a question of German versus Latin spelling since German texts also used 'Faustus'. It was Roshirt who first used the form 'Faust'.

3. The 'Pseudo-Clementine Literature' – the *Clementine Homilies*, the *Clementine Recognitions* and to a lesser extent the *Apostolic Constitutions*.

4. *Kaiserchronik*, attributed to Pfaffe Konrad, *c.*1141, which survives in a large number of manuscript copies; and Jacobus de Voragine's *Legenda Aurea*, thirteenth century, which by 1500 had gone through 74 Latin editions with translations into High and Low German.

5. In the *Homilies* the father is Faustus and the two brothers are Faustinus and Faustinianus.

6. Butler, 1948, sidestepped the problem. For 1478 see Mahal, 1979, and *c.*1980:72, and Hoppmann, 1998:185; Mahal, 1980:10, gives *c.*1480; Mahal, 1990b:74, suggested 26 December 1478, without giving any reasoning. Beutler, 1936, argued for 1465–8, whilst Baron, 1978:18, suggested 1466 or 1467. Battus, 1592, fol. 1ʳ gave 1491. This date also appeared in an early eighteenth-century MS catalogued by Henning, 1966:430, no.3148.

7. Hale, 1977:17, and Mackenney, 1993:21, give different figures, but neither explain how they arrived at them, especially whether they include child deaths. Not happy with this, I made my own calculations based on a sample of 133 people contemporaneous with Faustus and whose dates were fairly well established. This gave a date range of 1432 to 1590 with a mix of occupations. Almost all of these people were what we could call upper class and so clearly enjoyed the health benefits money and privilege could secure. The average age was 57.27 with a range of 20 to 90.

8. Identified earlier in connection with the usage of the name 'Faustus'.

9. Ward, 1901:n.p.

10. Sylke Titzmann, Stadtverwaltung Stadtroda, personal communication, 20 September 2006.

11. 'Hedelbergensis' is often cited as 'Hedebergensis' by other authors, e.g., Tille, 1900:5, and Palmer and More, 1936:87, but having examined the original myself I can categorically state that 'Hedelbergensis' is correct, although Mutianus did not use capitalisation. Furthermore, there is no comma separating the elements of the name as we also find in other sources.

12. E.g., Palmer and More, 1936:87; Butler, 1948:122; Bates, 1969:3.

13. Düntzer in Scheible, 1845–9, V:36.

14. Thus 'Helmstheus' and 'Helnntheus' have also been suggested. See Baron, 1978:15. Keefer's, 2007:30, n. 1, idea of a literary allusion to a garbled word appearing in a 1504 publication of the pseudo-Clementine *Recognitions* is unconvincing.

15. Working from the same material, Babinger, 1912 (not 1914 as in Palmer and More, 1965:88) came to the same conclusion; see also Beutler, 1936; Baron, 1978; and, following Baron, Grafton, 1999 and 2001, and Keefer, 2007.

16. Quotations from Manlius, 1563:44.

17. Mahal, 1980:225–6.

18. Tim Lörke, Faust Archive and Museum, Knittlingen, 1 March 2005.

19. Mahal, 1980:227, 1990:16, and 1990b:81.

20. Frank Baron, Director Max Kade Centre for German-American Studies, University of Kansas, personal communication, 1 December 2008.

21. Entries dated 1521, 1523 and 1545. Mahal, 1980:228, and 1990b:89.

22. Lang, 1985:308–15, is also critical of this document.

23. Paris, Cod. Lat. Par. 8643 (II), fol. 125ʳ-125ᵛ; Allen, 1914; Baron, 1978:92, n. 22, and 1989:297–302.

24. Baron, 1978:16.

25. Möller, 1936.

26. Toepke, 1884:370; Heike Hamberger, Director Faust Archive and Museum, Knittlingen, 2 March 2005.

Chapter 3

1. Butzbach was a classic wandering scholar who would eventually become the Prior of Maria-Laach Monastery. He first met Trithemius in 1496 and formed links with Reuchlin and many other leading Humanists. Allen, 1914:59, 76–7.

2. Quoted in Tanner, 1990:n.p.

3. Quoted in Aries and Duby, 1989:173, with corrections.

4. Cato, *Monosticha Catonis* 4.

5. Quoted in Allen, 1914:113.

6. Innocent quoted in Burns et al., 1980:353–7; de Vitriaco, 1894, II, 3: 19–20.

7. Quoted in Pachter, 1951:93.

8. Luther, 2006:n.p.

9. R. Haasenbruch, Halle-Wittenberg University, personal communication, 18 October 2005.

10. Strauss, 1989:35.

11. Allen, 1914:87; Hale, 1977:286; Mahal, 1980:212.

12. Edyta Paruch, Jagiellonian University, Kraków, (personal communications, 8 February 2005 and 16 March 2005) consulted Chmiel, 1892, and Gąsiorowski, 2004, on my behalf.

13. Of all the hundreds of German students at Kraków from 1460 to 1520 only fifty-seven have been identified. As a long shot, I also had the Archiwum Uniwersytetu Jagiellonskiego check for the name Gerlach (and variations), but although there were three who studied here none of them was our Faustus (Edyta Paruch, personal communication, 21 November 2008).

14. Waite, 1911:103; Rudwin, 1989:186.

15. I contacted all of the most likely universities, but by the time of going to press not all of them had answered (or seemed likely to answer). Of those that had, and in addition to the cases considered in the text, we can rule out Erfurt, Freiburg, Ingolstadt, Leipzig, Tübingen and Würzburg. Henning, 1959:112–4, had earlier scoured the same records and drawn a blank.

16. Quoted in Baron, 1978:16, 92.

17. Wylie, 1878, vol. 1, bk 5, chap. 2.

18. Heidelberg, H-IV-101-3-S36^v published in Toepke, 1884, I:467; Mahal, 1980:245–6. In the MS one clearly reads 'Simmern', not 'Simern' as is frequently met with.

19. Heidelberg, *Akten der Artistenfakultät*, fol. 113^v, 114^r; Toepke, 1884:370.

20. Baron, 1978:18–9.

21. Baron, 1978:19–21, 94, n. 17; Stoudt, 1995:12–8.

22. Heidelberg, *Akten der Artistenfakultät*, fol. 123^r.

23. Toepke, 1884:397; Baron, 1978:18, 93, n. 4.

24. Seuter, 1534; Baron, 1989:301; Grafton, 1999:61.

Chapter 4

1. Allen, 1914:214; Pachter, 1951:101, 178; Hale, 1977:24, 29–30; Garin, 1983:77.

2. Quoted in Hale, 1977:225.

3. Sabatini, 1912, ch. 8, and Summers, 1927:42, both draw on Francesco Guicciardini's (1483–1540) subjective account. Sabatini dismisses Guicciardini's claims and Summers is well-known for his credulity in such matters. Symonds, 1917, III:191–8, who discusses Hadrian's alleged extispicium at length, as well as the case of Manfredi, is an early critic, arguing that the Roman historian Cassius Dio began the rumours. The theory is not entertained by modern scholars.

4. Scheible, 1845–49, V:1107–116, 1124–34; Henning, 1966:438 no. 3194, 443 no. 3217.

5. The inn where Faustus supposedly stayed claims to be the oldest guest house in Germany, but problematically uses Trithemius's letter as evidence of its existence at that time. Given Gelnhausen's importance in this period it is highly likely that there was more than one inn. Similarly, there was also a Franciscan cloister where Trithemius could conceivably have stayed. Personal communications with local historians: Gudrun Kauck, 18 June 2008; Uschi Flacke, 26 June 2008; Vanessa Dippel,

26 June 2008; Axel Obkircher, 28 June 2008; also P. Rühl, the current proprietor of the Zum Löwen, www.zum-loewen-gelnhausen.de, accessed 18 June 2008; Mansfeld, 1966.

6. Trithemius, 1507 [1536:312].
7. Trithemius, 1507 [1536:312].
8. Trithemius, Würzburg cod. o. Sign., quoted in Brann, 1999:72–3.
9. Hartlieb, 1998:69.
10. Agrippa, 1651:489–90.
11. Trithemius to Count von Westerburg, 1503, quoted in Brann, 1999:120.
12. Würzburg cod. o. Sign., quoted in Brann, 1999:72.
13. Agrippa, 1651:567ff.
14. Agrippa, 1651:524. Agrippa only mentioned Zalmoxis twice in his *Occult Philosophy* compared to fourteen references to Zoroaster.
15. Quoted in Lilly, 1647:42–56.
16. Roberts and Donaldson, 1867–1872, vol. I.
17. Trithemius, 1507 [1536:313].
18. Trithemius, 1507 [1536:313].
19. Trithemius to Johannes Bracht, Würzburg, 31 October 1506, quoted in Brann, 1981:56.
20. Trithemius, 1507 [1536:313].
21. Trithemius, 1507 [1536:313].
22. Trithemius, 1507 [1536:313].
23. Trithemius, 1690.
24. For Codex 849 see Kieckhefer, 1989; Begardi, 1539:17.

Chapter 5

1. Trithemius, 1507 [1536:313].
2. Leaflet, no title, no date, Historisches Dr Faust Haus, acquired October 2005. A date carved above the cellar door has been obscured so that one can only read '15...'.
3. Trithemius, 1507 [1536:313].
4. Quoted in Brann, 1999:70.
5. Quoted in Brann, 1999:70.
6. Quoted in Muir, 1913, ch. II.
7. Julius Reisek, Heimatwissenschaftliche Zentralbibliothek, personal communication, 12 March 2007; Dr Michael Vesper, Geschäftsführer Bad Kreuznach Tourismus und Marketing, personal communication, 12 and 20 March 2007; Heinrich Laun, local historian, Bad Kreuznach, personal communication, 13 March 2007.
8. Trithemius, 1507 [1536:313].
9. Quoted in Wylie, 1878, vol. 1, bk 6, ch. 1.
10. Wylie, 1878, vol. 1, bk 6, ch. 1; Bax, 1967.
11. Lassalle, 1910:iii.
12. Trithemius, 1507 [1536:313].
13. Lercheimer, 1597:42.
14. Quoted in Manlius, 1563:44.
15. Puff, 2003:17, 28–30.
16. Kramer and Sprenger, 1485 (1996:55); Lea, 1957, I:232; Monter, 1976:135–6, 197–8 and 1985:41–55; Puff, 2003:5, 7, 23.
17. Quoted in Brann, 1999:53.
18. Hartlieb, 1998:119.
19. John of Salisbury, 1938:146–7.
20. Trithemius, 1507 [1536:313–4].
21. Quoted in Puff, 2003:131.

Chapter 6

1. Andreas Stiborius quoted in Mahal, 1980:79.
2. Vatic. Palat. Lat. 1439, fol. 39ʳ; for Virdung's MSS see Vatic. Palat. Lat. 1375 and 1391.
3. Würzburg cod. o. Sign., quoted in Brann, 1999:105.
4. Trithemius, 1518:103.
5. Letter of Trithemius to Rutger Sicamber, 12 Spetember 1506, quoted in Brann, 1981:51.
6. See Stoudt, 1995:12–8.
7. Guicciardini, 1579:405.
8. Quoted in Mackenney, 1993:91.
9. Published as *Die Emeis*, 1516.
10. Scheible, 1845–49, vol. II; Butler, 1949:159, 193, 197.
11. *Landsknecht*, sing., *Landsknechte* pl., were originally Feudal levies, but the word developed to mean mercenaries. English has retained the French form *lansquenet*, but the German is more appropriate here. Some writers Anglicise the plural as *Landsknechts*, but again the German is better.
12. Melanchthon, 1594:76.
13. Manlius, 1563:43.
14. Mathers, 1989:73, and 1997:44, 51, 57, using MSS of various dates – the earliest being late sixteenth century.
15. Kramer and Sprenger, 1996:105.
16. Kramer and Sprenger, 1996:105.
17. Erasmus wrote the book in 1509, but it was not published until 1511. The original title *Encomium Moriae* is variously given as *The Praise of Folly* and *In Praise of Folly*.
18. Quoted in Brann, 1981:117.
19. Agrippa, 'To the Reader', 1651: n.p.
20. Agrippa, 'To the Reader', 1651: n.p.
21. Agrippa, 1651:2.
22. Agrippa, 1651:355.
23. A legendary connection mentioned in the Wolfenbüttel MS. See also Tille, 1900:93, and Bechstein, 1930:285.

Chapter 7

1. Mutianus, 1513, fol. 97ʳ.
2. Quoted in Gillert, 1890:382–3.
3. Quoted in Gillert, 1890:382–3.
4. Quoted in Pachter, 1951:33.
5. Quoted in Szamatólski, 1895:54.
6. Also *Faust-Gäßchen*. Grässe, 1868:339–40; Neubert, 1932:32; Fehrle and Schrom, 1953; Durrani, 2004:29.
7. Quoted in Szamatólski, 1895:54.
8. Quoted in Szamatólski, 1895:54.
9. Quoted in Szamatólski, 1895:54.
10. Quoted in Szamatólski, 1895:55.
11. Quoted in Szamatólski, 1895:55.
12. Grässe, 1868:339–40.
13. P.F., 1592:71; Bechstein, 1930:285.
14. Quoted in Szamatólski, 1895:55.
15. Quoted in Szamatólski, 1895:55.
16. Quoted in Szamatólski, 1895:55.
17. Quoted in Szamatólski, 1895:55.

18. Quoted in Szamatólski, 1895:55.
19. Grässe, 1868:339–40.
20. Lavater, 1569:92a.
21. Kramer and Sprenger, 1996:105.
22. Jirásek, 1931; Mönikes, 2003; Holger Kempkens, personal communication, 11 May 2006.
23. Quoted in Szamatólski, 1895:56.
24. Quoted in Szamatólski, 1895:56.
25. Quoted and trans. in Kieckhefer, 1997:47.
26. Grässe, 1868:339–40.
27. Camerarius, 1591:315.
28. Camerarius, 1591:315.
29. Camerarius, 1591:315.
30. Quoted in Szamatólski, 1895:56.
31. Quoted in Szamatólski, 1895:56. The nailing up of Luther's theses has been discredited and is generally regarded as a legend spun by Melancthon.
32. Quoted in Szamatólski, 1895:56.
33. Quoted in Szamatólski, 1895:56.
34. Quoted in Szamatólski, 1895:56–7.
35. Quoted in Szamatólski, 1895:57.
36. Quoted in Szamatólski, 1895:57.
37. Quoted in Szamatólski, 1895:53.
38. Quoted in Tanner, 1990:n.p.
39. Quoted in Tanner, 1990:n.p.

Chapter 8

1. P.F., 1592:2.
2. Quoted in Walz, 1927:361.
3. P.F., 1592:2.
4. P.F., 1592:3.
5. P.F., 1592:3.
6. Scheible, 1845–49.
7. Goethe, 2001, I.3.1335–6, 1338.
8. See Beckers, 1984.
9. Bächtold-Stäubli and Hoffmann-Krayer, 1927–42.
10. Dürrius (1676, published in 1726), see Tille, 1900:234; Bächtold-Stäubli and Hoffmann-Krayer, 1927–42.
11. Dismissed by Kiesewetter, 1893. Bächtold-Stäubli and Hoffmann-Krayer, 1927–42; authoritative in Butler, 1948:132, and 1949:164, Russell, 1986:61, Empson, 1987, Füssel and Kreutzer, 1988:188, and Baron, 1992:125.
12. Burdach, 1912; Durrani, 1977.
13. See Bächtold-Stäubli and Hoffmann-Krayer, 1927–42.
14. Achitophel is the Vulgate Bible form of Ahithophel or now more commonly Ahitophel. Bächtold-Stäubli and Hoffmann-Krayer, 1927–42.
15. Oehlke, 1913:198–9, recapitulated by Radday, 1997:133–148.

Chapter 9

1. Marlowe, 1616, II.1.32; Goethe, 1949, I.4.1715.
2. Quotations from P.F., 1592:6.
3. P.F., 1592:7.

4. Mat. 26:27–8; also Mark 14:23–4 and Luke 22:20; John 5:54.
5. *Nibelungenlied* 5.2054; Bächtold-Stäubli and Hoffmann-Krayer, 1927-42, I:1430–42; Hsia 1988:8–9.
6. Scheible, 1845–49; Thorndike, 1915:123; Kieckhefer, 1989:162; Ruickbie, 2004:22–5.
7. Nider, *Formicarius*, quoted in Bailey, 2003:40, with corrections.
8. Kramer and Sprenger, 1996:76.
9. Trithemius, 1515:5; Francesco Maria Guazzo (1608 [1988:17]) quoted it with approval in support of his own argument a hundred years later.
10. Agrippa, 1651:226.
11. Quoted in Kors and Peters, 1991:238.
12. Quotations from de Voragine, 1941:312.
13. Quotations from Palmer and More, 1936:60–75.
14. Quoted in Hsia, 1988:133.
15. Baron, 1992:56–7.
16. P.F., 1592:6–7.

Chapter 10

1. The *Fürstlich Württembergisches Dienerbuch*, seventeenth century, links the two names, but the visit to Maulbronn rests on local tradition as told to me by Tobias Küenzlen, Ephorus of Maulbronn, field-trip, 1 March 2005. Mahal, 1980:197, is convinced that Faustus did visit the monastery.
2. The entry in *Fürstlich Württembergisches Dienerbuch* was copied into an eighteenth century manuscript *Maulbronner Äbteverzeichnis*, Stuttgart, Hauptstaatsarchiv, A 502 (Kloster Maulbronn), Bü 24.
3. This story was told, possibly for the first time, in 1849 by the Romantic poet Justinus Kerner (1786–1862), an old boy of the Maulbronn school.
4. Mahal, 1980:36, 196–8; Anstett-Janßen, 1999:43; field-trip, 1 March 2005.
5. Trithemius, 1507 [1536:313].
6. Kramer and Sprenger, 1996:2.
7. Ripley in Ashmole, 1652:107–193; Paracelsus quoted in Jacobi, 1988:84.
8. See British Library MS Harley 6453 for examples.
9. Oxford, Bodleian Library MS Ashmole 1487, II:26, fol. 182–196.
10. Oxford, Bodleian Library MS Rawlinson D. 893, fol. 103.
11. Dresden N 110, Nuremberg 80061, fol. 156-160^v, Munich Cgm 598.
12. Nuremberg 33733, fol. 43–47^v, *c.*1455–1457.
13. Nuremberg 33740, fol. 8^v–10^v, fol. 13^v–14^v, *c.*1556–1564.
14. Nuremberg 198353, fol. 123^v–124^r, mid-fifteenth century.
15. Nuremberg 198353, fol. 8–55^v, mid-fifteenth century.
16. Wolfenbüttel MS Extrav. 286.1, 1505-7.
17. Dated 1471, but first published 1591.
18. Quoted in Ashmole, 1652.
19. Martinón-Torres, et al., 2003.
20. Quoted in Roberts, 1994:45.
21. 'Mary the Prophetess' is the only woman recorded in the history of alchemy and was an allegory.
22. Quoted in Holmyard, 1957:245.
23. Quoted in Shumaker, 1979:163.
24. The terms used in alchemy were not standardised and showed great variation in usage. Ripley quotations here and in the following from 1471:129–40, 144-50, 173–9, 181–5, 286, 381.
25. Quoted in Brann, 1981:101. The original inscription was lost when Trithemius's resting place was relocated in 1720 to the Nothelferkapelle des Neumünsters.
26. Geber, 1928:110, and Rulandus, 1612:167.

27. Pachter, 1951:114, 116, 305, 314.
28. As suggested by Shumaker, 1979:174.
29. Quoted in Ashmole, 1652:94.

Chapter 11

1. Reproduced in Hofmann, 1940: title page.
2. Quoted in Rady, 1990:20.
3. Quoted in Rady, 1990:20.
4. P.F., 1592:66–7.
5. Quoted in Butler, 1948:134.
6. Tille, 1900:1057-8.
7. Georg III, 1520. .
8. P.F., 1592:22-3.
9. See Tille, 1900:6, Palmer and More, 1965:88–9, Bates 1969:3, Baron, 1978:44 and Mahal, 1980:365
10. P.F., 1592:52-3.
11. Quoted in Lea, 1957, I:419.
12. P.F., 1592:40–1.
13. P.F., 1592:53.
14. P.F., 1592:53.
15. P.F., 1592:53–4.
16. P.F., 1592:54.

Chapter 12

1. Scheible, 1845–49, II:853–4.
2. Quoted in Grafton, 1999:53.
3. Schoener, 2007:174.
4. Mackay, 1841, ch. 5, n.p.
5. Thomas, 1971:288. I checked the main British libraries for the years 1518–1525 and found no holdings on this subject.
6. Quoted in Grafton, 1999:55.
7. Niccoli, 1990:167.
8. Quoted in Mackenney, 1993:27.
9. Miller, 2003:8, 9.
10. Letters of Luther to John Ruhel, 4 May 1525, and Nicholas Amsdorf, 30 May 1525, in Smith, 1911:162, 164–5.
11. Luther, 1957, 46:47–55.
12. P.F., 1592:60.
13. Quoted in Roos, 1972:54.
14. See Tlusty, 2001:113; Aries and Duby, 1989:428
15. P.F., 1592:57–8.
16. Quoted in Grafton, 1999:52.
17. Quoted in Sillig, 1992:5.
18. Sillig, 1992: 3–7, 11, 63, 78.
19. Sillig, 1992:3. Sillig says that this view is 'refuted on all sides', but not by whom nor why.
20. P.F., 1592:45.
21. P.F., 1592:9, 29.
22. See Sillig, 1992:24–6.
23. Quoted in Sillig, 1992:40.

24. Quotations from Sillig, 1992:29.
25. Quotations from Sillig, 1992:31, 39.
26. Quotations from Sillig, 1992:31–2.

Chapter 13

1. Cellini, 1910:XXXIV.
2. Quoted in Manlius, 1563:44.
3. Quoted in Manlius, 1563:44.
4. Quoted in Yates, 2001:135.
5. Göttingen Cod. MS philos. 63.
6. The harquebus (arquebus) was a portable firearm usually supported on a tripod or forked rest.
7. Quoted in Oman, 1937:184.
8. Ben Joshua ben Meir, 1836.
9. Leipzig 935, fol. 15^r.
10. Quoted in Rady, 1990:51.
11. Pachter, 1951:104–5.
12. P.F., 1592:36.
13. P.F., 1592:36.
14. P.F., 1592:36.
15. Quotations from P.F., 1592:36.
16. P.F., 1592:36.
17. Marlowe, 1616, III.2.97–8.
18. P.F., 1592:37.
19. Quoted in Seward, 1974:149.
20. Cellini, 1910:XXXIV.
21. Other reasons and dates have been given, but this is not the place to go into them.

Chapter 14

1. Quoted in Mackenney, 1993:120.
2. Waite, 1911:112.
3. Agrippa, 1651:561.
4. Nauert, 1965:216.
5. E.g., Blume, 1914, and Mahal, c.1980:39.
6. Agrippa, 1651:561.
7. Quoted in Rudwin, 1989:69.
8. Quoted in Seward, 1974:34.
9. P.F., 1592:34.
10. Agrippa, 1651:564.
11. Agrippa, 1651:563.
12. Agrippa, 1651:566.
13. Nauert, 1965:94–6.
14. Leib, 1528; Schottenloher, 1913:92–3.
15. Leib, 1528; Schottenloher, 1913:92–3.
16. The Order has been known by several names and is now officially styled the Sovereign Military Hospitaller Order of St John of Jerusalem of Rhodes and of Malta.
17. Letter from Fr. Bernardinus to Fr. Georg Schilling, 2 May, 1526 (Malta, 412, fol. 183^r).
18. Quoted in Baron, 1978:47, 100, n. 14; Valeria Leonardi, Sovereign Military Order of Malta, personal communication, 17 January 2006.
19. Destinacije.com, accessed 13 January 2006.
20. See Stopar, 1992.

21. The red surcoat emblazoned with a white cross was worn over armour by a knight of St John only in war as established by Alexander IV in 1259.
22. Ingolstadt Ratsprotokolle, 1523/94, fol. 70ᵛ und 1527/30, fol 49ᵛ. I have followed Mahal's, 1980:140, interpretation based on Middle High German.
23. Begardi, 1539:17a.
24. Mahal, 1980:139, 368; field-trip, 27–28 February 2005.
25. Quoted in Telepnef, 1991:24.
26. There are no records of Faustus having studied here, as confirmed by Dr Wolfgang Smolka, Archiv der Ludwig-Maximilians-Universität München, personal communication, 24 January 2008.

Chapter 15

1. Quotations from Wilson, 2000:381.
2. Quotations from Pachter, 1951:175, 176.
3. Melanchthon, 1594, pt IV.
4. P.F., 1592:49, 50.
5. P.F., 1592:50.
6. Kramer and Sprenger, 1996:80, 126.
7. P.F. 1592:51.
8. P.F. 1592:51.
9. P.F. 1592:51.
10. Quoted in Poeschel, 1988.
11. P.F. 1592:52.
12. Baron, 1992:103–4.

Chapter 16

1. Manlius, 1563:44.
2. Lercheimer, 1597:42.
3. Lercheimer, 1597:42.
4. Lercheimer, 1597:43.
5. Schwab, 1836-7:n.p.
6. Walz, 1927:361; Mahal, 1980:368; Cordula Krause, personal communication, 1 May 2006; Kristin Pietzner, Wittenberg-Information, personal communication, 4 December 2006.
7. Lercheimer, 1597:42.
8. Lercheimer, 1597:85.
9. Lercheimer, 1597:85. Luther once recounted a similar case, see Lea, 1957, I:420.
10. Lercheimer, 1597:85.
11. Grässe, 1868:391–2.
12. See P.F., 1592:69–70, for example.
13. Grässe, 1868:391–2.
14. P.F., 1592:67.
15. P.F., 1592:67–8.
16. P.F., 1592:68–9.
17. Nuremberg, 1532, fol. 12ʳ.
18. Neubert, 1932:16.
19. P.F., 1592:9.
20. Manlius, 1563:44.
21. Dr Hirschmann, Director of Nuremberg City Archive, in Mahal, 1980:147.
22. Scheible, 1845–49, V:1142f.

23. Quoted and trans. in Scot, 1584:217–225.
24. Minucci to Wilhem von Bayern, 25 March, 1583, in Tille, 1900:56.
25. Agrippa to von Wied, Mechelen, January 1531, in Agrippa, 1651.
26. Blume, 1914; Mahal, 1980:204–5.
27. Wierus, 1568:142.
28. Wierus, 1568:143; not 'Babenberg' as in Mahal, 1980:204.
29. Wierus, 1568:143.
30. E.g., Butler, 1948:121–2.
31. Von Hutten, 1540.
32. British Library, Add. 15217, fol. 34ᵛ, 38.
33. Camerarius, 1536:5.

Chapter 17

1. Quoted in Arthur, 1999:15.
2. Quoted in Arthur, 1999:17.
3. Quoted in Arthur, 1999:18.
4. Quoted in Arthur, 1999:61.
5. Quoted in Arthur, 1999:29–33.
6. Quoted in Arthur, 1999:40.
7. Nauert, 1965:113–4.
8. Prasser, c.1650 [1921:322].
9. Again this is a local theory based on the age of the former building. See Medding, 1980.
10. Quoted in Arthur, 1999:165.
11. Prasser, c.1650 [1921:322].
12. Quoted in Arthur, 1999:178.

Chapter 18

1. Gast, 1548:280–1.
2. Gast, 1548:280–1.
3. Gast, 1548:280–1.
4. Agrippa, 1651:490–1.
5. Von Zimmern, 1881, III:529.
6. Blume, 1914, identified this place as Lüyheim by Saarburg, but there is no Lüyheim today, whilst Mahal, 1980:209-10, called it Luxeuil. I have since discovered that Karl August Barack, the editor of the *Zimmerische Chronik* (1881), had earlier identified it as Lixheim.
7. Mahal, 1980:210; Wollasch, 1984:45–61.
8. Gast, 1548:281.
9. P.F., 1592:38.
10. P.F., 1592:39.
11. P.F., 1592:39.
12. Quoted in Ginzburg, 1990:172.
13. Gesner, 1577, fol. 1a.
14. Gast, 1548:281.
15. Camerarius, 1536:4. Haruspices ('aurispicium') were Roman priests trained to divine from the entrails of sacrifices.
16. Camerarius, 1568, fol. 161ʳ–162ᵛ.
17. Ellinger, 1889:318–9; Arthur, 1999:125.
18. Camerarius, 1536:4, quoting Homer, *Iliad*, II.197.
19. Camerarius, 1536:4, quoting Virgil, *Aeneid*, VI.788–800.

20. Wolfenbüttel MS, ch. 59.
21. P.F., 1592:73.
22. P.F., 1592:73.
23. Luther, Lauterbach Extract, 1537.
24. Wierus, 1568:143.

Chapter 19

1. P.F., 1592:54.
2. Quoted in Durrani, 2004:78.
3. P.F., 1592:10.
4. Quoted in Schindler, 2002:186.
5. Quoted in Roper, 1989:105.
6. See Harrington, 1995.
7. P.F., 1592:73.
8. P.F., 1592:74.
9. P.F., 1592:74.
10. P.F., 1592:75.
11. Scheible, 1845–49, II:793.
12. Weber, 1990.
13. See the discussion in Thomas, 1971:227–31, Monter, 1976:29, and Yates, 2003:83–4.
14. Quotations from Burr, 1891:45–6.
15. Luther, 1998:n.p.
16. Wierus, 1568:142.
17. Gesner, 1577, fol. 1ʳ.
18. Von Zimmern, 1881, III:529.
19. Gast, 1548:281.
20. Manlius, 1563:43.
21. Wierus, 1568:144.
22. Camerarius, 1591:314.
23. *Exempla insignia* [etc.], Wolfenbüttel 1169, fol. 114ᵛ.
24. Quotations from Von Zimmern, 1881, III:529.
25. Jenny, 1959, passim.
26. Lercheimer, 1597:42.
27. As well as Tille, 1900, see Bechstein, 1930:113-4, and Durrani, 2004:382–3.
28. Jebens, 2001:44–7.
29. Mahal, n.d., 13; Geiges, 1981:36–38. Nicolai's book is now in the Stubenhausmuseum, Staufen.
30. Geiges, 1981:16, 21; Mahal, 1990:12; Jebens, 2001:47.
31. Information provided by the current owners and field-trip, 23 February 2005.
32. P.F., 1592:81.
33. P.F., 1592:80.
34. Quotations from P.F., 1592:81.
35. P.F., 1592:81.
36. Von Zimmern, 1881, III:529.
37. Guazzo, 1608 (1988:112).
38. Guazzo, 1608 (1988:111).

Select Bibliography

Works Attributed to Faustus

See also Engel, 1884, and Henning, 1966.

1407. *Doctor Faustens dreyfacher Höllenzwang*, Passau

1469. *Dr Johann Faustens Miracul-Kunst- und Wunderbuch oder die schwarze Rabe auch der Dreifache Höllen Zwang genannt*, Lyon

1501. *D. I. Fausti dreyfacher Hoellen-Zwang*, Rome

1501. 2nd ed., 1680. *D. Faustus vierfacher Höllen-Zwang*, Rome

1501. *Tabellae Rabellinae Geister-Commando*, Rome

1502. *D. Fausts (Original) Geister Commando*, Rome

1505. *Doctoris Iohannis Fausti magiae naturalis et innatural. Erster Theil. Der Dreyfacher Höllenzwang genannt*, Passau

1505. *Doctoris Iohannis Fausti magiae naturalis et innaturalis. Anderer Theil. Sein letztes Testament genannt*, Passau

1508. *Doctor Faust's grosser und gewaltiger Höllenzwang,* Paris

1509. *Doctor Faust's grosser und gewaltiger Höllenzwang,* Prague

1524. *Doctor Johannis Fausti Manuel-Höllenzwang,* Wittenberg

1527 or 1577. *Praxis Magica Faustiana,* Passau

1540. *Fausti Höllenzwang,* Wittenberg

1571. *Praxis Magica Fausti,* Passau

1575. *Schlüssel zu Faust's dreifachem Höllenzwang,* n.p.

1612. *Doctoris Joannis Fausti Miracul und Wunderbuch,* Passau, Überlingen MS 187

1612. *Praxis cabulae nigrae doctoris Johannis Fausti ... Magia naturalis et innaturalis oder unerforschlicher Höllenzwang ...,* Passau

1692. *Doctor Faust's grosser und gewaltiger Meergeist,* Amsterdam

Principal Sixteenth Century Sources

Agrippa, Henricus Cornelius, von Nettesheim, 1528. 'Epistolarum lib.V ep. XXVI', in Cornelius Agrippa, 1600. *Opera. Huic accesserunt Epistolarum ad familiares libri septem, et orationes decem ante hoc seorsim edita,* Bering, 239

Begardi, Philipp, 1539. *Index Sanitatis. Eyn Schöns vnd vast nützlichs Büchlin, genant Zeyger der gesundtheyt,* Sebastianus Wagner, Bl. XVIIa

Bütner, Wolfgang, and Georg Steinhart, 1596. *Epitome Historiarum,* n.p.

Camerarius, Joachim, 1536. Letter of Joachim Camerarius to Daniel Stibar, 13 August 1536, in Joachim Camerarius, 1568. *Libbellus Novus,* Rhamba, fol. 161ʳ-162ᵛ

Camerarius, Philipp, 1591 [enlarged edition 1602-9]. *Operae Horarum Subcisivarum...*, Lochner and Hoffman

Gast, Johannes, 1548. 'De Fausto necromantico' and 'Aliud de Fausto exemplum', in Johannes Gast, *Sermon Convivales,* vol. II, Nicolaus Brylinger

Georg III Schenk von Limpurg, Bishop of Bamberg, 1520. *Rechnungsbuch Georg III. Fürstbischofs von Bamberg,* 1519–1520, Staatsarchiv, Bamberg, Bestand A 231, Nr. 1741

Gesner, Conrad, 1577. Letter from Conrad Gesner to Johannes Crato von Krafftheim, Zurich, 16 August 1561, in Conrad Gesner, *Epistolae Medicinales,* Froschauer

Hogel, Zacharias, 17th century. *Chronica von Thüringen und der Stadt Erfurth insonderheit vom Jahr 320 bis 1628* (sections on Faustus derived from the lost Reichmann-Wambach Chronicle, *c.*1580), in Siegfried Szamatólski, 1895

Hondorff, Andreas, 1568. *Promptuarium Exemplorum ...*, Leipzig

Hutten, Philipp von, 1540. Letter from Philipp von Hutten to Moritz von Hutten, Coro, 16 January 1540, in Johann Georg Meusel, 1785. *Historisch-litterarisches Magazin,* Th. I, 51–117

Ingolstadt, Ratsprotokolle, 1523/94, fol. 70ᵛ und 1527/30, fol 49ᵛ, Stadtarchiv, Ingolstadt

Knittlingen, 1542. 'Kaufbrief [Bill of Sale] zur Erweiterung der Lateinschule in Knittlingen', Faust Museum und Archiv, Knittlingen

Lercheimer, Augustin, 1585 [3rd ed., 1597]. *Christlich bedencken und Erinnerung von Zauberey ...*, Müller and Auen

Leib, Kilian, 1528. 'Wettertagebuch', 1513–1531, (entry for July 1528), 4° L. impr. C. n. mss. 73, fol. 257ʳ, Bayerische Staatsbibliothek, München

Luther, Martin, Lauterbach Extract, 1537. Reference to Faustus recorded by Antonius Lauterbach, published in Ernst Kroker, 1903. *Luthers Tischreden in der Mathesischen Sammlung,* Teubner

Luther, Martin, Aurifaber Extract, 1566. Reference to Faustus recorded by Johannes Aurifaber in Martin Luther, 1566. *Tischreden oder Colloquia Mart. Luthers ...*, ed. Johannes Aurifaber, Urban Gaubisch, Chap. I, §47

Manlius, Johannes, 1563. *Locorum communium collectanea,* Oporinus

Meigerius, Samuel, 1587. *De Panurgia Lamiarum, Sagraum, Strigum ac Veneficarum, Totiusque Cohortis Magicae Cacodaemonia,* Hans Binder

Meigerius, Samuel, 1598. *Nucleus Historiarum Oder Außerlesene liebliche, denckwürdige und warhaffte Historien,* Theodosius Wolder

Melanchthon, Philipp, 1549–1560, in Philipp Melanchthon, 1594. *Explicationes Melanchthoniae,* Pars II and IV, Christopher Pezelius

Mutianus Rufus, Conradus, 1513. Letter of Conradus Mutianus Rufus to Henricus Urbanus, 3 October 1513. Cod. Lat. Oct. 8, fol. 97ʳ, Stadt- und Universitätsbibliothek, Frankfurt am Main

Nuremberg, 1532. *Geleit-Ablehnung durch die Stadt Nürnberg,* 10 May 1532. Staatsarchiv, Nürnberg, Verlässe des inneren Rates, Nr. 810, fol. 12ʳ

Roshirt, Christoff, the Elder, *c.*1570–1575. *Luthers Tischreden aus den Jahren 1535-1542, Anhang: Christoff Roshirt der Elter, Historien. Nach 1559,* Hof- und Landsbibliothek, Karlsruhe, Handschrift 437

Seuter, Petrus, 1534. Letters of Dr Petrus Seuter to Nikolaus Ellenbog, 7 October 1534, Kempten, and Ellenbog to Seuter, 12 October 1534, Ottobeuren, Bibliothèque Nationale de Paris, Cod. Lat. Par. 8643 (II), fol. 125ʳ-125ᵛ

Trithemius, Johannes, 1507. Letter of Trithemius to Johannes Virdung, Würzburg, 20 August 1507, Vatican Library, Rome, Codex Pal. lat. 730, 174ʳ–175ʳ, in Johannes Trithemius, 1536. *Epistolae Familiares,* Haganoae

Wierus [Wier or Weyer], Johannes, 1568. *De Praestigiis Daemonum et Incantationibus ac Venificiis,* 4th ed., Oporinus, 142-4

Zimmern, Froben Christoph von, *c.*1565. *Zimmerische Chronik,* Württembergische
    Landesbibliothek, Stuttgart, Cod. Donaueschingen 580 and 581a; Karl August Barack, ed.,
    Akademische Verlagsbuchhandlung von JCR Mohr, 1881, 2nd edition

Published Works

Agrippa, von Nettesheim, Heinrich Cornelius, 1530. *De incertitudine*, Grapheus
____, 1533. *De occulta philosophia libri tres*, n.p.
____, 1651. *Three Books of Occult Philosophy*, Gregory Moule
____, 1974. *Of the Vanitie and Vncertaintie of Artes and Sciences*, ed. Catherine M. Dunn,
    Northridge
Aign, Walter, 1975. 'Faust im Leid', *Jahresgabe der Faust-Gesellschaft*, I
Allen, Percy Stafford, 1914. *The Age of Erasmus*, Clarendon Press
Anon., 1589. *A Ballad of the life and deathe of Doctor FFAUSTUS the great Cunngerer*, n.p.
Anon., 1589. *The seconde Reporte of Doctour JOHN FFAUSTUS, with the ende of WAGNERs life.*
Anon., 1725. *Das Faustbuch des Christlich Meynenden von 1725*, ed. Günther Mahal, 1983,
    Faust-Archiv
Anstett, Peter R., 1995. *Maulbronn Monastery*, 2nd edition, trans. Dorothy Ann Schade,
    Deutscher Kunstverlag
Anstett-Janßen, Marga, 1999. *Maulbronn Monastery*, trans. Katja Steiner and Bruce Almberg,
    Deutscher Kunstverlag
Aries, Philippe, and Georges Duby, 1989. *A History of Private Life*, vol. 3. Harvard
    University Press
Arnold, Klaus, 1971. *Johannes Trithemius (1462–1516)*, vol. 23, Kommissionsverlag Ferdinand
    Schöningh Würzburg
Arthur, Anthony, 1999. *The Tailor-King: The Rise and Fall of the Anabaptist Kingdom of Münster*,
    Thomas Dunne Books
Ashmole, Elias, ed., 1652. *Theatrum chemicum Britannicum*, J. Grismond
Baader, Bernard, 1851. *Volksagen aus dem Lande Baden und den angrenzenden Gegenden*, Verlag
    der Herder'schen Buchhandlung
Babinger, Franz, 1912. 'Der geschichtliche Faust', *Alemannia*, 152ff
Bächtold-Stäubli, Hanns, and E. Hoffmann-Krayer, eds, 1927–42. *Handwörterbuch des deutschen
    Aberglaubens*, 10 vols, W. De Gruyter
Bailey, Michael D., 2003. *Battling Demons: Witchcraft, Heresy, and Reform in the Late Middle
    Ages*, Pennsylvania State University Press
Baron, Frank, 1978. *Doctor Faustus: From History to Legend*, Wilhelm Fink Verlag
____, 1983. 'Which Faustus Died in Staufen? History and Legend in the Zimmerische
    Chronik', *German Studies Review*, 6.2, 185–94
____, 1989. 'Who Was the Historical Faustus? Interpreting an Overlooked Source', *Daphnis*,
    18, 297–302
____, 1989b, 'Georg Lukács on the Origins of the Faust Legend', in Peter Boerner and
    Sidney Johnson, eds, *Faust Through Four Centuries*, Max Niemeyer Verlag
____, 1990. 'From Witchcraft to Doctor Faust', in Karl-Ludwig Selig and Elizabeth Sears, eds,
    The Verbal and the Visual: Essays in Honor of William Sebastian Heckscher, Italica Press
____, 1992. *Faustus on Trial: The Origins of Johann Spies's 'Historia' in an Age of Witch
    Hunting*, Niemeyer
Baron, Frank, and Richard Auernheimer, eds, 2003. *War Dr. Faustus in Kreuznach? Realität
    und Fiktion im Faust-Bild des Abtes Johannes Trithemius*, Verlag der Rheinhessischen
    Druckwerkstätte
Bates, Paul A., 1969. *Faust: Sources, Works, Criticism*, Harcourt, Brace & World
Battus, Carolus, trans., 1592. *Warachtighe Historie van Doctor Iohannes Faustus*, Dordrecht
Bax, Ernest Belfort, 1915. *German Culture Past and Present*, George Allen & Unwin
____, 1967. *German Society at the Close of the Middle Ages*, Kelley

Bechstein, Ludwig, 1930. *Deutsches Sagenbuch*, F. W. Hendel

Beckers, Hartmut, 1984. 'Eine spätmittelalterliche deutsche Anleitung zur Teufelsbeschwörung mit Runenschriftverwendung', *Zeitschrift für deutsches Altertum und deutsche Literatur*, 113, 136–45

Bernstein, Eckhard, 2003. '*Homo mysticarum rerum percupidus…*: Franz von Sickingens Interesse an Magie und Astrologie und sein Verhältnis zum historischen Faustus', in Frank Baron and Richard Auernheimer, eds, *War Dr. Faustus in Kreuznach?* Verlag der Rheinhessischen Druckwerkstätte

Beutler, Ernst, 1936. 'Georg Faust aus Helmstadt', *Goethe-Kalender auf das Jahr*, 170–210

Blume, Rudolf, 1914. 'Dr. Faustus in der Geschichte. 1914 gewidmet dem Gasthaus zum Löwen in Staufen von Dr. Rudolf Blume in Freiburg i.B.', unpublished

Bobrick, Benson, 2005. *The Fated Sky: Astrology in History*, Simon & Schuster

Borchardt, Frank L., 1990. 'The Magus as Renaissance Man', *Sixteenth Century Journal*, 21.1, 57–76

Brann, Noel, 1981. *The Abbot Trithemius (1462–1516): The Renaissance of Monastic Humanism*, E.J. Brill

___, 1999. *Trithemius and Magical Theology*, State University of New York Press

Britnell, Jennifer, and Derek Stubbs, 1986. 'The Mirabilis Liber: Its Compilation and Influence', *Journal of the Warburg and Courtauld Institutes*, 49

Burdach, Konrad, 1912. *Faust und Moses*, Reimer

Burns, Edward McNall, et al., 1980. *Western Civilizations: Their History and their Culture*, vol. 1, W.W. Norton & Company

Burr, George L., 1891. 'The Fate of Dietrich Flade', *Papers of the American Historical Association*, 5, 3–57

Butler, Elizabeth M., 1948. *The Myth of the Magus*, Cambridge University Press

___, 1949. *Ritual Magic*, Cambridge University Press

___, 1952. *The Fortunes of Faust*, Cambridge University Press

Calliano, Carl, 1926–1936. *Niederösterreichischer Sagenschatz*, 5 vols, Baden-Verlag

Camerarius, Joachim, 1536. *Commentarius captae urbis dutore Carlo Borbonio*, J. Herwagen

Cardano, Girolamo, 2002. *The Book of My Life*, trans. Jean Stoner, New York Review of Books

Cellini, Benvenuto, 1910. *The Autobiography of Benvenuto Cellini*, trans. John Addington Symonds, The Harvard Classics, vol. 31, ed. Charles W. Eliot., P.F. Collier & Son

Chamberlin, Russell, 2003. *The Bad Popes*, Sutton

Charnock, Thomas, 1557. *Breviary of Naturall Philosophy* in Elias Ashmole, ed., 1652. *Theatrum chemicum Britannicum*, J. Grismond, 291–302

Chmiel, Aadm, ed., 1892. *Album studiosorum Universitatis Cracoviensis*, vol. II, 1490–1551, Acad. Litterarum Cracoviensis

Clark, Stuart, 1997. *Thinking with Demons*, Oxford University Press

Clemen, Otto, 1912. 'Eine Erfurter Teufelsgeschichte von 1537', *Archiv für Kulturgeschichte*, 10, 455–58

Crusius, Martin, 1733. *Schwäbische Chronick*, 2 vols, Metzler und Erhard

Decker-Hauf, Hansmartin, ed., 1972–3. *Die Chronik der Grafen von Zimmern*, 3 vols, Thorbecke

Depiny, Adalbert, 1932. *Oberösterreichisches Sagenbuch*, Pirngruber

Dotzauer, Winfried, 1999. 'War Dr. Johann Faust in Kreuznach? Der Brief des Abtes Johannes Trithemius an den Mathematiker Johann Virdung vom 20.8.1507', *Ebernburg-Hefte*, 33, 453–86

___, 2003. 'War Dr. Johann Faust in Kreuznach? Der Brief des Abtes Johannes Trithemius an den Mathematiker Johann Virdung vom 20. August 1507', in Frank Baron and Richard Auernheimer, eds, *War Dr. Faustus in Kreuznach?* Verlag der Rheinhessischen Druckwerkstätte

Durrani, Osman, 1977. *Faust and the Bible*, Peter Lang

___, 2004. *Faust: Icon of Modern Culture*, Helm Information

Durrius [Dürr], Johannes Conradus, 1676. 'Epistola Ad Dominum Georgivm Sigismvndvm Führervm, De Johanne Favsto Dissertatio Epistolica de Johanne Faustosto, M. Johannis Conradi Durrii', in J.G. Schelhornius, ed., 1726. *Amoenitates Literariae*, Bartholomaei

Ellinger, Georg, 1889. 'Das Zeugnis des Camerarius über Faust', *Vierteljahresschrift für Litteraturgeschichte*, 2, 314–9

Elton, Geoffrey R., 1972. *Reformation Europe: 1517–1559*, Fontana

Empson, William, 1987. *Faustus and the Censor: The English Faust-Book and Marlowe's Doctor Faustus*, Blackwell

Engel, Carl, 1885. *Der Bibliotheca Faustiana*, Schulze

Engels, Frederick, 1926. *The Peasant War in Germany*, trans. Moissaye J. Olgin, International Publishers

Estes, Leland, 1983. 'The Medical Origins of the European Witch Craze: A Hypothesis', *Journal of Social History*, 17, 271–84

Fehrle, Eugen, and Ernst Schrom, 1953. *Sagen aus Deutschland*, Ueberreuter

Feinaug, Johannes, 1588. *Ein wahrhafte und erschröckliche Geschicht von D. Johann Fausten, dem weitbeschreiten Zauberer und Schwarzkünstler*, Alexander Hock

Flint, Valerie, 1994. *The Rise of Magic in Early Medieval Europe*, Princeton University Press

Füssel, Stephan, and Hans Joachim Kreutzer, eds, 1988. *Historia von D. Johann Fausten*. Reclam

Garin, Eugenio, 1983. *Astrology in the Renaissance: The Zodiac of Life*, Arkana

Gąsiorowski, Antoni, et al., eds, 2004. *Metryka Uniwersytetu Krakowskiego z lat 1400–1540*, vols 1–2, Towarzystwo Naukowe

Geber, 1928. *The Works of Geber Englished by Richard Russell, 1678*, J.M. Dent and Sons

Geiges, Leif, 1981. *Faust's Tod in Staufen: Sage – Dokumente*, Kehrer Offset KG

Gillert, Karl, ed., 1890. *Der Briefwechsel des Conrad Mutianus*, Hendel

Ginzburg, Carlo, 1990. *Ecstasies: Deciphering the Witches' Sabbath*, Hutchinson Radius

Godelmann Johann, 1591. *De magis, veneficis et lamiis recta cognoscendis et puniendis libri III*, Nicolai Bassaei

Goethe, Johann Wolfgang von, 1949. *Faust: A Tragedy*, trans. Bayard Taylor, Euphorion Books

___, 2001. *Faust: A Tragedy. Interpretative Notes, Contexts, Modern Criticism*, 2nd edition, trans. Walter Arndt, ed. Cyrus Hamlin, W.W. Norton & Company

Grässe, Johann Georg Theodor, 1868. *Sagenbuch des Preußischen Staats*, vol. 1, Carl Flemming

Grafton, Anthony, 1999. *Cardano's Cosmos*, Harvard University Press

Grafton, Anthony, 2001. 'Der Magus und seine Geschichte(n)' in Anthony Grafton and Moshe Idel, eds, *Der Magus: Seine Ursprünge und seine Geschichte in verschiedenen Kulturen*, Akademie Verlag

Guazzo, Francesco Maria, 1608 [1988]. *Compendium Maleficarum*, trans. E. A. Ashwin, Dover

Gugitz, Gustav, 1952. *Die Sagen und Legenden der Stadt Wien*, Hollinek

Guicciardini, Francesco, 1579. *The Historie of Guicciardin [sic] Conteining the Warres of Italie and Other Partes*, trans Geffray Fenton, Vautroullier

Haile, Harry G., 1960. 'Widman's *Wahrhafftige Historia*: Its Relevance to the Faust Book', *Proceedings of the Modern Language Association*, 75.4, 350–8

Hale, John R., 1977. *Renaissance Europe: Individual and Society, 1480–1520*, University of California Press

___, 1985. *War and Society in Renaissance Europe, 1450–1620*, Fontana

Hansen, Joseph, 1900. *Zauberwahn, Inquisition und Hexenprosesz im Mittelalter und die Entstehung der Groszen Hexenverfolgung*, R. Oldenburg

___, ed., 1901. *Quellen und Untersuchungen zur Geschichte des Hexenwahns und der grossen Hexenverfolgung im Mittelalter*, Georgi

Harrington, Joel, 1995. *Reordering Marriage and Society in Reformation Germany*, Cambridge University Press

Hartlieb, Johannes, 1998. *Das Buch der Verbotenen Künste*, trans. Falk Eisermann and Eckhard Graf, Eugen Diedrichs Verlag

Hay, Denys, 1989. *Europe in the Fourteenth and Fifteenth Centuries*, 2nd ed, Longman

Henning, Hans, 1959. 'Faust als historische Gestalt', *Jahrbuch der Goethe-Gesellschaft*, 21, 107–39

___, 1966. *Faust-Bibliographie*, 5 vols, Aufbau-Verlag

Heumann, Christian August, 1742. 'D. Christ. Aug. Heumanns glaubwürdigste Nachricht von D. Fausten, In einem Schreiben an Herrn D. Haubern', in Eberhard David Hauber, ed., *Bibliotheca, acta et scripta magica*, vol. 3, Joh. Heinrich Meyer, 184–204

Hillgarth, J. N., 1996. 'The Image of Alexander VI and Cesare Borgia in the Sixteenth and Seventeenth Centuries', *Journal of the Warburg and Courtauld Institutes*, 59, 119–129

Hofmann, Karl, 1934. 'Die Johanniter in Boxberg-Wölchingen', in *Mein Boxberg*, 23, 28–38

___, 1940. *Mein Umpferland. Jahresheft des Heimatvereins Alt-Boxberg e. V*, Kriegs-Ausgabe

Holmyard, Eric John, 1957. *Alchemy*, Penguin

Hoppmann, Jürgen G.H., 1998. *Astrologie der Reformationszeit: Faust, Luther, Melanchthon und die Sternendeuterei*, Verlag Clemens Zerling

Horst, Georg Conrad, 1821–6. *Zauber-Bibliothek*, 6 vols, Kupferberg

Hsia, R. Po-chia, 1988. *The Myth of Ritual Murder: Jews and Magic in Reformation Germany*, Yale University Press

Jacobi, Jolande, 1988. *Paracelsus: Selected Writings*, Princeton University Press

James VI and I, 1597. *Demonologie*, Robert Waldegrave

Jebens, Klaus, 2001. *Die Burg in Staufen und ihre Bewohner*, Lavori

Jenny, Beat Rudolf, 1959. *Graf Froben Christoph von Zimmern*, Thorbecke

Jirásek, Alois, 1931. *Stories and Legends of Old Prague*, trans. Mary Cochrane Vojáček, Blackie & Son

John of Salisbury, 1938. *Frivolities of Courtiers and Footprints of Philosophers*, ed. Joseph B. Pike, Oxford University Press

Ben Joshua ben Meir, Joseph, 1836. *The Chronicles of Rabbi Joseph ben Joshua ben Meir, The Sphardi*, 2 vols, trans. C.H.F. Bialloblotzky, Oriental Translation Fund

Keefer, Michael H., ed., 2007. *Doctor Faustus: A 1604 Version*, Broadview Press

Kieckhefer, Richard, 1997. *Forbidden Rites: A Necromancer's Manual of the Fifteenth Century*, Sutton

___, 2000. *Magic in the Middle Ages*, Canto

Kiesewetter, Karl, 1893. *Faust in der Geschichte und Tradition*, M. Spohr

Klingner, Erich, 1912. *Luther und der deutsche Volksaberglaube*, Mayer & Müller

Knecht, Robert, 2007. *The Valois: Kings of France 1328–1589*, Hambledon Continuum

Könneker, Barbara, 1991. 'Der Teufelspakt im Faustbuch', in Richard Auernheimer and Frank Baron, eds, *Das Faustbuch von 1587*, Profil

Konstam, Angus, 1996. *Pavia 1525*, Osprey Publishing

Kors, Alan C., and Edward Peters, 1991. *Witchcraft in Europe 1100–1700*, University of Pennsylvania Press

Kramer, Heinrich, and James [Jacob] Sprenger, 1486 [1996]. *Malleus Maleficarum*, trans. Montague Summers, Bracken Books

Kuhn, Adalbert, 1859. *Sagen, Gebräuche und Märchen aus Westfalen und einigen andern, besonders den angrenzenden Gegenden Norddeutschlands*, 2 vols, Brockhaus

Lang, Peter Thaddäus, 1985. 'Zur Biographie des historischen Faustus. Die Frage nach der Zuverlässigkeit einer Quelle aus Knittlingen', *Zeitschrift für Württemberg Landesgeschichte*, 44, 308–15

Larner, Christina, 1981. *Enemies of God: The Witch-hunt in Scotland*, The John Hopkins University Press

Lassalle, Ferdinand, 1910. *Franz von Sickingen*, trans. Daniel de Leon, New York Labor News Company

Lavater, Ludwig, 1569. *Von Gespänsten*, Froschauer

Le Roy Ladurie, Emmanuel, 1998. *The Beggar and the Professor: A Sixteenth Century Family Saga*, trans. Arthur Goldhammer, University of Chicago Press

Lea, Henry Charles, 1957. *Materials Towards a History of Witchcraft*, 3 vols, Thomas Yoseloff

Leitschuh, Franz Friedrich, 1888. *Georg III., Schenk von Limpurg, der Bischof von Bamberg in Goethes Götz von Berlichingen*, F. Züberlein

Lercheimer, Augustin, 1888. *Augustin Lercheimer und seine Schrift wider den Hexenwahn*, ed. Carl Binz, J. H. E. Heitz

Lilly, William, 1647. *The World's Catastrophe, or Europe's Many Mutations untill, 1666*, John Partridge and Humphrey Blunden

Lindsay, Jack, 1970. *The Origins of Alchemy in Graeco-Roman Egypt*, Muller

Lull, Raymond, 1953. *Le Codicille de Raymond Lulle*, Collections La Haute Science

Luther, Martin, 1524. *Ein Sermon von der beschneydung*, Jakob Schmidt

____, 1566. *Tischreden oder Colloquia Mart. Luthers*, ed. Johannes Aurifaber, Urban Gaubisch

____, 1912–21. *Tischreden*, Böhlau

____, 1930. *Werke, Briefwechsel*, vol. I, Böhlau

____, 1886. *Selections from the Table Talk of Martin Luther*, Cassell & Company

____, 1957. *Luther's Works*, 55 Volumes, ed. Jaroslav Pelikan., Concordia Publishing House and Fortress Press

____, 1998. *Commentary on the Epistle to the Galatians*, trans. Theodore Graebner, Project Gutenberg

Mackay, Charles, 1852. *Memoirs of Extraordinary Popular Delusions and the Madness of Crowds*, 2nd ed, Office of the National Illustrated Library

Mackenney, Richard, 1993. *Sixteenth Century Europe*, Macmillan

Mahal, Günther, n.d. *Zu Tode gekommen in Staufen: Wer war Dr. Faust? Betrachtungen über die historische Faust-Figur*, Kulturreferat Stadt Staufen

____, ed., 1977. *Der Tübinger Reim-Faust von 1587/88 aus dem Prosa-Faustbook "Historia von D. Johann Fausten" (1587) in Reime gebracht von Johannes Feinaug*, J. Schweier

____, 1979. *Fausts Geburtstag. Eine Hypothese*, privately published

____, c.1980. *Faust der Mann aus Knittlingen*, privately published

____, 1980 [paperback ed., 1995]. *Faust: Die Spuren eines geheimnisvollen Lebens*, Scherz Verlag

____, 1990. *Fausts Tod, Sonderausstellung 1990*, Faust Museum

____, 1990b. *Knittlingen. Versuch einer Spurensicherung*, privately published

____, 2006. *Halbgott Faust*, Attempo

Mansfeld, Markus, 1966. *Gelnhäuser Tageblatt*, Sonderausgabe, Dezember

Maltby, William, 2002. *The Reign of Charles V*, Palgrave

Marlowe, Christopher, 1604. *The Tragicall History of D. Faustus*, V. S[immes] for Thomas Bushell

____, 1616. *The Tragicall History of the Life and Death of Doctor Faustus*, Iohn Wright

Martinón-Torres, Marcos, et al., 2003. 'A 16th Century Lab in a 21st Century Lab: Archaeometric Study of the Laboratory Equipment from Oberstockstall (Kirchberg am Wagram, Austria)', *Antiquity*, 77.298

Mathers, Samuel Liddel MacGregor, 1900. *The Book of the Sacred Magic of Abramelin the Mage*, 2nd edition, John M. Watkins

____, 1989. *The Key of Solomon*, Samuel Weiser

____, 1997. *The Goetia: The Lesser Key of Solomon the King*, ed. Aleister Crowley and Hymenaeus Beta, 2nd edition, Samuel Weiser

Mayerhofer, J., 1890. 'Faust beim Fürstbischof von Bamberg', *Vierteljahrschrift für Litteraturgeschichte*, 3, 177f.

Mebane, John S., 1989. *Renaissance Magic and the Return of the Golden Age*, University of Nebraska Press

Medding, Wolfgang, 1980. *Korbach*, Wilhelm Bing

Meek, Harold, 1930. *Johann Faust: The Man and the Myth*, Oxford University Press

Meier, Andreas, 1990. *Faustlibretti*, Peter Lang

Midelfort, H.C. Erik, 2002. 'The Heartland of the Witchcraze', in Darren Oldridge, ed., *The Witchcraft Reader*, Routledge, 113–9

____, 2002b. 'The Devil and the German People', in Darren Oldridge, ed., *The Witchcraft Reader*, Routledge, 240–5

Milchsack, Gustav, 1892. *Historia D. Johannis Fausti*, Zwissler

Miller, Douglas, 2003. *Armies of the German Peasants' War 1524–26*, Osprey Publishing

Möller, Walther, 1936. *Stamm-tafeln Westdeutscher Adels-geschlechter im Mittelalter*, vol. III, Ilse Möller

Mönikes, Wolfgang, 2003. *Doktor Faust in Prag und europaweit*, privately printed

Mone, Franz Joseph, 1838. *Anzeiger für Kunde teutschen Vorzeit*, Germanisches Museum

Monter, E. William, 1976. *Witchcraft in France and Switzerland*, Cornell University Press

___, 1985. 'Sodomy and Heresy in Early Modern Switzerland', in Salvatore Licata and Robert Petersen, eds, *The Gay Past*, Harrington Park Press, 1985, 41–55

___, 1996. 'Heresy Executions in Reformation Europe, 1520–1565', in Ole Peter Grell and Bob Scribner, eds, *Tolerance and Intolerance in the Reformation*, Cambridge University Press

Moryson, Fynes, 1907. *The Itinerary of Fynes Moryson*, 4 vols, James MacLehose and Sons

Münch, Ernst, 1829. *Franz von Sickingens Thaten, Pläne, Freunde und Ausgang*, 3 vols, Johann Friedrich Cotta

Muir, M.M. Pattison, 1913. *The Story of Alchemy and the Beginnings of Chemistry*, Hodder and Stoughton

Nauert, Charles, 1965. *Agrippa and the Crisis of Renaissance Thought*, University of Illinois Press

Nelson, William, 1973. *Fact or Fiction: The Dilemma of the Renassiance Storyteller*. Harvard University Press

Neubert, Franz, 1932. *Vom Doctor Faustus zu Goethes Faust*, J.J. Weber

Neumann, Johann Georgius, 1683. *Disquisitio Historica Prior De Fausto Praestigiatore*, Fincelius

Niccoli, Ottavia, 1990. *Prophecy and People in Renaissance Italy*, Princeton University Press

Nicolle, David, 2001. *Knight Hospitaller: 1306–1565*, pt 2, Osprey

Norton, Thomas, 1477. *The Ordinall of Alchimy*, in Elias Ashmole, ed., 1652. *Theatrum chemicum Britannicum*, J. Grismond, 1–106

Oehlke, A., 1913. 'Zum Namen Mephistopheles', *Goethejahrbuch*, 34, 198–9

Oman, Charles, 1937. *A History of the Art of War in the Sixteenth Century*, Methuen & Co.

Osten, Sigrid von, 1998. *Das Alchemistenlaboratorium von Oberstockstall*, Universitätsverlag Wagner

Ostermair, Franz Xaver, 1872/73. 'Zur Faust-Sage. Doctor Faust 1528 in Ingolstadt', *Oberbayerisches Archiv für vaterländische Geschichte*, 32, 336

'P.F.', 1592. *The Historie of the Damnable Life, and the Deserved Death of Doctor Iohn Faustus*, trans. P.F., Thomas Orwin

Palmer, Philip Mason, and Robert Pattison More, 1936 [reprint 1965]. *The Sources of the Faust Tradition*, Oxford University Press

Petsch, Robert, 1910. 'Der historische Faust', *Germanisch-Romanisch Monatsschrift*, 2, 99–115

___, ed., 1911. *Das Faustbook vom Doctor Faust*, Niemeyer

___, ed., 1911b. *Lessings Faustdichtung*, Winter

___, 1914. 'Lercheimer und das Faustbuch', *Beiträge*, 39, 175–88

Peuckert, Will-Erich, 1936. *Pansophie*, Kohlhammer

Pfitzer, Johann Nicolaus, 1674. *Das ärgerliche Leben und schreckliche Ende dess viel-berüchtigten Ertz-Schwartzkünstlers D. Johannis Fausti*, Endter

Poeschel, Sabine, 1988. 'Alexander Magnus Maximus – neue Aspekte zur Ikonographie Alexanders des Grossen im Quattrocento', *Römisches Jahrbuch für Kunstgeschichte*, 23–24, 62–74

Prasser, Daniel, *c.*1650. *Waldeckische Chronik*, Nationale Forschungs- und Gedenkstätten der Klassischen Deutschen Literatur, Weimar, in *Jahrbuch der Sammlung Kippenberg*, I, 1921, 322

Prodolliet, Ernst, 1978. *Faust im Kino*. Universitätsverlag

Puff, Helmut, 2003. *Sodomy in Reformation Germany and Switzerland, 1400–1600*, University of Chicago Press

Radday, Yehuda T., 1997. 'Mephisto – hebräisch?', *Muttersprache*, 107.2, 133–148

Radermacher, Ludwig, 1927. *Griechische Quellen zur Faustsage.* Sitzungsberichte der Akademie der Wissenschaften in Wien. Phil.-Hist. Kl., Bd 206, Abhandlung 4, Hölder-Pichler-Tempsky in Komm

Rady, Martyn, 1990. *The Emperor Charles V*, Longman

Reuter, Simon Heinrich, 1715. *'Sultana a.z-.zulma [Alsatanija]' das ist, Das mächtige, doch umschränckte Reich des Teufels*, Henrich Wilhelm Meyer

Reynmann, Leonhard, 1523. *Practica vber die grossen vnd manigfeltigen Coniuction der Planeten, die im Jar M.D.Xxiiij*, Hieronymus Höltzel

Richter, Erich, 1938. *Die Welser landen in Venezuela*, W. Goldmann

Ripley, George, 1471. *The Compound of Alchymy*, in Elias Ashmole, ed., 1652. *Theatrum chemicum Britannicum*, J. Grismond

Roberts, Alexander, and James Donaldson, eds, 1867–1872. *The Anti-Nicene Fathers*, 8 vols, T & T Clark

Roberts, Gareth, 1994. *The Mirror of Alchemy*, The British Library

Roos, Keith L., 1972. *The Devil in Sixteenth-Century German Literature: The Teufelsbücher*, Herbert Lang

Rudwin, Maximilian, 1989. *The Devil in Legend and Literature*, Open Court

Ruickbie, Leo, 2004. *Witchcraft Out of the Shadows: A Complete History*, Robert Hale

Rulandus, Martin, 1612. *Lexicon alchemiae sive dictionarium alchemisticum*, Zacharias Palthenius

Rummel, Erika, 2002. *The Case Against Johann Reuchlin*, University of Toronto Press

Russell, Jeffrey Burton, 1986. *Mephistopheles: The Devil in the Modern World.* Cornell University Press

Sabatini, Raphael, 1912. *The Life of Cesare Borgia*, S. Paul

Scheible, Johannes, ed., 1845–49. *Das Kloster*, 12 vols, Scheible/Expedition des Klosters

___, ed., 1851. *Doctor Faust's Büchershatz*, Scheible

Schiebel, Johann Georg, 1685. *M. Joh. Georg Schiebels Neu-erbautes erbauliches historisches Lusthauß*, Rußworm

Schindler, Norbert, 2002. *Rebellion, Community and Custom in Early Modern Germany*, trans. Pamela Selwyn, Cambridge University Press

Schoener, Gustav-Adolf, 2004. 'The Coming of a "Little Prophet": Astrological Pamphlets and the Reformation', *Esoterica*, 6, 59–66

___, 2007. 'The Flood of 1524: The First Mass-media Event in European History', *Esoterica*, 9, 166–78

Schottenloher, Karl, 1907. 'Johann Schöner und seine Hausdruckerei', *Zentralbibliothek für Bibliothekswesen*, 24

___, 1913. *Münchener neuste Nachrichten*, no. 338, 5 July

___, 1913. *Der Rebdorfer Prior, Kilian Leib, und sein Wettertagebuch von 1513 bis 1531*, Friedrich Andreas Perthes A-G

Schreinert, Kurt, 1958. 'Neue Faustsplitter', in Hans Werner Seiffert, ed., *Beiträge zur deutschen und nordischen Literatur*, Akademie-Verlag, 69–95

Schulze, Winfried, 1987. *Deutsche Geschichte im 16. Jahrhundert*, Suhrkamp

Schwab, Gustav, 1836–7. *Das Buch der schönsten Geschichten und Sagen für Alt und Jung*, 2 vols. Leisching

Schwetschke, Gustav, 1855. 'Wer war Faustus senior?' *Deutsches Museum*, 548–551

Scot, Reginald, 1584 [reprint 1972]. *The Discoverie of Witchcraft*, William Brome

Shuh, Willi, 1952. *Goethe-Vertonungen. Ein Verzeichnis*, Artemis

Shumaker, Wayne, 1979. *The Occult Sciences in the Renaissance*, University of California Press

Seward, Desmond, 1974. *Prince of the Renaissance: The Life of François I*, Cardinal

Sillig, Paul Hermann, 1992. *Faust in Leipzig: A Concise Chronicle of Auerbach's Cellar*, Leipziger Verlagsgesellschaft

Smith, Preserved, 1911. *The Life and Letters of Martin Luther*, Houghton Mifflin Company

Spies, Johann, 1587. *Historia von D. Johann Fausten, dem weitbeschreyten Zauberer und Schwarzkünstler*, Spies

Stopar, Ivan, 1992. *Grajske stavbe v vzhodni Sloveniji*, Založba Park

Stoudt, Debra L., 1995. 'Probatum est per me: The Heidelberg Electors as Practitioners and Patrons of the Medical and Magical Arts', *Cauda Pavonis*, 14, 12–18

Strauss, Gerald, 1989. 'How to Read a *Volksbuch*: The *Faust Book* of 1587', in Peter Boerner and Sidney Johnson, eds, *Faust Through Four Centuries*, Niemeyer

Summers, Montague, 1927 [reprint 1973]. *The Geography of Witchcraft*, Kegan Paul

Symonds, John Addington, 1917. *Sketches and Studies in Italy and Greece*, John Murray

Szamatólski, Siegfried, 1895. 'Faust in Erfurt', *Euphorion*, 2, 39–57

___, 1889. 'Der historische Faust', *Vierteljahrschrift für Litteraturgeschichte*, 2, 156–9

Tanner, Norman P., ed., 1990. *Decrees of the Ecumenical Councils*, Sheed & Ward

Taylor, Bayard, 1949. 'Introduction', in *Faust: A Tragedy by Johann Wolfgang von Goethe*, trans. Bayard Taylor, Euphorion

Taylor, F Sherwood, 1953–54. 'Some Metallurgical Processes of the Early Sixteenth Century (1530)', *Transactions of the Newcomen Society*, 29

Telepnef, Basilio de, 1991. *Paracelsus*, Banton Press

Theens, Karl, 1948. *Geschichte der Faustgestalt vom 16. Jahrhundert*, Westkulturverlag

Thomas, Keith, 1971. *Religion and the Decline of Magic*. Oxford University Press

Thorndike, Lynn, 1915. 'Some Medieval Conceptions of Magic', *The Monist*, 25, 123

___, 1923–58. *History of Magic and Experimental Science*, 8 vols, Columbia University Press

___, 1936a. 'Johann Virdung of Hassfurt Again', *Isis*, 25, 363–71

___, 1936b. 'Faust and Johann Virdung of Hassfurt', *Isis*, 26, 321

___, 1942–3. 'Another Virdung Manuscript', *Isis*, 34, 291–2

___, 1947. 'Johann Virdung of Hassfurt: Dates of Birth and Death', *Isis*, 37, 74

___, 1975. *University Records and Life in the Middle Ages*, Columbia University Press

Tille, Alexander, 1900 [reprint 1980]. *Die Faustsplitter in der Literatur des sechzehnten bis achtzehnten Jahrhunderts*, Emil Felber

___, ed., 1899. *Bilderverzeichnis der Bode-Tilleschen Faust-Galerie*, Schmitz

Tlusty, B. Ann, 2001. *Bacchus and Civic Order: The Culture of Civic Drinking in Early Modern Germany*, University Press of Virginia

Todd, John M., 1982. *Luther: A Life*, Crossroad

Toepke, Gustav, 1884. *Die Matrikel der Universität Heidelberg*, Winter

Trithemius, Johannes, 1515. *Liber octo questionum ad Maximilianum Cesarem*, Iohanis Hasselbergen

___, 1518. *Polygraphiae libri sex*, Petri for Haselberger de Aia

___, 1605. *Antipalus malificiorum*, in Johannes Busaeus, ed., *Paralipomena opusculum Petri Blesensis et Joannis Trithemii aliorumque*, Balthassar Lipius

___, 1690. *Annales Hirsaugienses*, 2 vols, J.G. Schlegel

___, 1723. *Nepiachus*, in Johann Georg Eccard, ed., *Corpus historicum medii aevi*, 2 vols, Jo. Frid. Gleditschii B. Fil.

Virdung, Johannes, 1503. *Practica Teütsch Etlich Jar werende*, Mathis Hüpfuff

___, 1506. *Ußlegung und erclerung der wunderbarlichen kunftigen erschrocklichen ding die uns der Stern mit dem schwantz*, Weissenburger

___, 1506. *Practica dudesch*, Dorn

___, 1514. *Interpretatio Magistri Johannis Virdungi Hassfurdensis Mathematici*, Schmidt

___, 1521. *Practica teütsch*, Jakob Köbel

___, 1532. *Nova Medicinae Methodvs*, Iohannem Sinapium

___, 1542. *Tabulae resolutae*, ed. Johannes Curio, Petreius

Vitriaco, Jacobus de, 1894. 'Hist. occid.' in D.C. Munro, ed. 'The Medieval Student', *Translations and Reprints from the Original Sources of European History*, vol. II, University of Pennsylvania Press

Voragine, Jacobus de, 1941. *The Golden Legend*, Longmans, Green & Co.

Waas, Glenn Elwood, 1941. *The Legendary Character of Kaiser Maximilian*, Columbia University Press

Waite, Arthur Edward, 1908. 'The Pictorial Symbols of Alchemy', *Occult Review*, 8.5
___, 1911 [reprint 1995]. *The Book of Ceremonial Magic*, Rider
Waite, Gary K., 2002. 'Between the Devil and the Inquisitor: Anabaptists, Diabolical
   Conspiracies and Magical Beliefs', in Darren Oldridge, ed., *The Witchcraft Reader*,
   Routledge
Walker, Daniel Pickering, 2000. *Spiritual and Demonic Magic*, Sutton
Walz, John A. 1927. 'An English Faustsplitter', *Modern Language Notes*, 42.6, 353–365
Ward, Adolphus W., 1901. 'Introduction', in Adolphus W. Ward, (ed.), *Marlowe: 'Tragical
   History of Dr. Faustus'; Greene: 'Honourable History of Friar Bacon and Friar Bungay'*,
   4th ed., Clarendon
Weber, Thomas, 1990. 'War Goethes "Faust" ein Helmstadter Kind?', *Heimatgeschichte zur
   1200 – Jahr – Feier: Helmstadt 782–1990*, Gemeinde Helmstadt
Widmann, Georg Rudolf, 1599. *D. Johannes Faustus: ein weitberuffener Schwartzkünstler vnd
   Ertzzäuberer*, Hermanni Molleri
Wierus [Wier or Weyer], Johannes, *On Witchcraft*, ed. Benjamin Kohl and Erik Midelfort.
   Pegasus, 1998
Wild, Klaus, 2006. *Franz von Sickingen*, Sutton
Wilson, Stephen, 2000. *The Magical Universe*, Hambledon & London
Witkowski, Georg, 1896/7. 'Der historische Faust', *Deutsche Zeitschrift für Geschicht*, 1, 340
Wollasch, Joachim, 1984. 'Die Benediktinerabtei St. Georgen im Schwarzwald und ihre
   Beziehungen zu Klöstern westlich des Rheins', in *900 Jahre Stadt St. Georgen im
   Schwarzwald 1084–1984*, Stadt St. Georgen, 45–61
Wylie, James A., 1878. *The History of Protestantism*, Cassell and Company
Yates, Frances, 2001. *The Art of Memory*, University of Chicago Press
___, 2003. *The Occult Philosophy in the Elizabethan Age*, Routledge
Ziolkowski, Theodore, 2000. *The Sin of Knowledge*, Princeton University Press

Manuscripts

Dresden, Sächsische Landesbibliothek, Staats- und Universitätsbibliothek, N 110
Göttingen, Niedersächsische Staats- und Universitätsbibliothek, Cod. MS philos. 63
Heidelberg, Heidelberg Universitätsarchiv, H-IV-101-3-S36v
Heidelberg, Heidelberg Universitätsarchiv, *Akten der Artistenfakultät, 1445–1501*, vol. II, I, 3,
   no. 49, fol. 113^v, 114^r, 123^r
Leipzig, Universitäts Bibliothek Leipzig, Stadtbibliothek, 935
Leyden, Rijksmuseum van Oudheden, Papyrus X
London, British Library, Additional MS 10, 764, fol. 109^v
London, British Library, Additional MS 15217, fol. 34^v, 38
London, British Library, Additional MS 36674
London, British Library, Harley 6453
London, British Library, Sloane 1307
London, British Library, Sloane 3826, fol. 1^r–57^r
Malta, National Library of Malta, Valletta, Archives of the Order of St John, 412, fol. 183^r
Manchester, John Rylands University Library of Manchester, Rylands Latin MS 105
Munich, Bayerische Staatsbibliothek MS Cgm 598
Munich, Bayerische Staatsbibliothek, CLM 849
Nuremberg, Germanisches Nationalmuseum, MS 33733, fol. 43–47^v
Nuremberg, Germanisches Nationalmuseum, MS 33740, fol. 8^v–10^v, fol. 13^v–14^v
Nuremberg, Germanisches Nationalmuseum, MS 80061, fol. 156–160^v
Nuremberg, Germanisches Nationalmuseum, MS 198353, fol. 123^v–124^r
Oxford, Bodleian Library MS Ashmole 1487, II:26, fol. 182–196
Oxford, Bodleian Libray, Rawlinson MS D 252

Oxford, Bodleian Library, Rawlinson MS D 893, fol. 103
Paris, Bibliothèque Nationale de Paris, Cod. Lat. Par. 8643 (II), fol. 125^r–125^v
Stuttgart, Hauptstaatsarchiv, A 502 (Kloster Maulbronn), Bü 24
Vatican, Vatic. Palat. Lat. 1375
Vatican, Vatic. Palat. Lat. 1439
Wolfenbüttel, Herzog-August-Bibliothek, MS Extrav. 286.1
Wolfenbüttel, Herzog-August-Bibliothek, MS Helmst. 1169
Wolfenbüttel, Herzog-August-Bibliothek, Cod. Guelf. 92 Extrav.
Würzburg, Stadtarchiv, Biographische Abteilung, cod. o. Sign., s.v. Trithemius
Würzburg, Universitätsbibliothek, M. p. th. F. 64^b

Index